FOR
COMMON
DECENCY

For Common Decency:
The History of Foster Parents Plan, 1937-1983

By Henry D. Molumphy

FOSTER PARENTS PLAN INTERNATIONAL

Warwick, Rhode Island

ISBN 0-918397-00-6

CONTENTS

Introduction: Historical Summary

Foster Parents Plan (PLAN), is a nonprofit, nonpolitical, nonsectarian, international voluntary organization founded in 1937 to provide social services and financial and material assistance to needy children, their families, and their communities. This is accomplished through personal or group sponsorship of a child in a country currently unable to meet its social welfare needs. The Foster Child is a child in a family in great need. The child is never removed from his or her family; rather, the family is strengthened so that the child need never be abandoned. The Foster Parent is a financial sponsor. The Foster Parent sponsor and the child may develop a personal relationship through the exchange of letters, drawings, and photographs and, occasionally, a personal visit by the Foster Parent with the child and family.

PLAN has its International Headquarters in Warwick, Rhode Island, and National Offices in Australia, Belgium, Canada, Japan, the Netherlands, the United Kingdom, and the United States. The National Offices recruit and provide services to Foster Parents and contributors; raise funds for special needs and development projects; facilitate regular contacts between sponsors and children; and carry on a systematic information program about the needs of the poor in developing countries. International Headquarters supervises the programs in developing countries, coordinates systems between those programs and the National Offices, establishes new National Offices, negotiates with governments of proposed program countries, and plans enrollments in program countries based on National Office needs. International Headquarters functions under the International Board of Directors. Each National Office functions under its own National Board of Directors. The International Board of Directors is composed almost entirely of members of the National Boards with voting strength commensurate with the numbers of Foster Parents each National Office brings to the entire organization.

PLAN was established in England as the Foster Parent's Scheme for Children in Spain in April 1937 by John Langdon-Davies, an English journalist. While covering the war in Spain for the London *News Chronicle,* Langdon-Davies conceived the idea of a personal relationship between a refugee or orphaned child and an English sponsor. In England he enlisted the support of the Duchess of Atholl, a prominent Conservative Member of Parliament and former Parliamentary Minister to the Board of Education. As Chairman of both the National Joint Committee for Spanish Relief, to which PLAN became affiliated, and the Basque Children's Committee, the Duchess of Atholl had been responsible for the evacuation, at the urgent request of their parents, of nearly 4,000 Basque children to England. In the spring of 1937 she was trying to establish colonies for orphaned and refugee children in and around Barcelona. Langdon-Davies' scheme provided the means both to finance these colonies and to publicize the plight of the refugee children.

In December 1937, he and Eric Muggeridge came to the United States to raise money for Spanish war relief and to establish the American Committee of Foster Parent's Plan for Children in Spain. Muggeridge, an English social worker, had spent two years in Spain setting up children's hostels and evacuating children from the war zones for the Duchess of Atholl's National Joint Committee.

When the American Committee was established, PLAN worked in concert with the legitimate Spanish government to establish and support children's hostels. The government agreed to provide buildings and staff while PLAN provided administrators and financial support. The first colonies, caring for 300 children, were in châteaux and houses in Puigcerda, a village high in the Pyrenees near the French border, and in Caldetas, on the outskirts of Barcelona, in a safe International Zone. Two representatives of the English committee, J. Barton Carter, an American, and Esme Odgers, an Australian, were responsible for the administration of these colonies.

The first public meeting of the American Committee of Foster Parent's Plan for Children in Spain was held in New York City at the Hotel Algonquin on Sunday, 20 March 1938. Langdon-Davies described PLAN's work and the conditions in northeastern Spain. "Today in Catalonia . . . a province with a normal population of three and a half million . . . almost a million women and children refugees — outsiders — are trying to live." They came from Madrid, Malaga, Asturias, and Bilbao and crowded into Catalonian refugee centers. PLAN alone, with six trucks, brought over 4,000 children from Madrid to Catalonia in the summer of 1937.

The town of Ripoll, a typical refugee center, had a normal population of about 10,000. An estimated 2,000 refugees could be accommodated, 6,000 arrived. "Over-crowded conditions, malnutrition, especially the lack of milk or complete lack of soap and inadequate protection against the bitter cold have created a situation where a whole race of people may be swept away by famine and epidemic . . . already children are dying."

Many of the refugees were evacuated from the Basque country of northeastern Spain and taken by boat to Bordeaux. From Bordeaux they were shipped by train to Puigcerda. Langdon-Davies described one of the newly arrived refugee children in Puigcerda; "one day I was mixing with some refugees . . . who had just come in from France. I came across a little child of about five years. He was a cute little youngster, but I found him shy and hard to draw into conversation . . . Then one of the older refugee women . . . gave me a note she said she had found on him during the journey. It read like this, 'This is Jose. I am his father. When Santander falls I shall be shot. Whoever finds my son I beg him to take care of him for my sake.' "

PLAN was originally affiliated with the North American Committee to Aid Spain (NAC), a politically oriented organization providing support for the Loyalist government of Spain. The conflicts between the political aims of the NAC and the humanitarian aims of PLAN were a problem from the beginning. At the first official meeting of the PLAN Board of Directors, on 24 March 1938 it was resolved that "appeals to the public will be humanitarian, exclusively concerned with refugee children." Fund-raising restrictions prevented total severance from the NAC, but it was resolved that PLAN would open its own office and establish its own bank account. In spite of this, fund raising and organizational friction continued.

The final split came in the summer of 1939. At a Board meeting on 25 June 1939, Ann Landress, Edna Blue,[1] Walter Bluh, Louise Severn, Eric Muggeridge (Executive Secretary), and Josep Gelabert (Chairman) voted unanimously that:

> We would be serving the children of Spain best by being an entirely independent organization. It was felt that we should withdraw from the Spanish Refugee Relief Committee (the NAC) . . . we have dedicated ourselves from the start to

[1]Edna Blue, who was married to Walter Bluh, anglicized her name in April 1939.

preserving the lives of children. Rightly or wrongly the Spanish Refugee Relief Campaign have a political color, which we certainly have not. Our sincere aim and endeavor is to preserve children and this must be continued.

To this end Foster Parents Plan for Spanish Children, Inc., was chartered in the State of New York on 13 July 1939. The lawyer handling the incorporation of this new entity was Julian I. Bergoffen, who joined the Board of Directors in 1947 and served until his death in 1979.

With the fall of Barcelona in January 1939, the children were evacuated once more, this time to southern France. PLAN became Foster Parents Plan for Spanish Children and continued its work. The letters and cables from Esme Odgers and Eric Muggeridge described the appalling circumstances of this evacuation. Hundreds of thousands of refugees walked over the Pyrenees to France. Many of them were lost to the snow, the cold and the Nationalists' bombs.

The conditions in the French concentration centers, holding nearly half a million refugees, were equally appalling. In August 1939 PLAN had eight hostels in and around Biarritz to care for the evacuated children and the children from the French camps. By 1940 there were over 1,200 Foster Children. Esme Odgers described the work in a 15 August 1939 letter to Edna Blue:

> Never have we worked so hard to get a colony organized as with this last lot from the concentration centers . . . All of them are covered with scabies from head to toe . . . For the past six months they have been sleeping on the floor in cafes, barns, stables and deserted factories . . . For the moment organized work of any kind is out of the question. Once the children are well enough to leave their beds, we shall begin taking them on picnics and reading to them.

In addition to the Spanish refugees, France became the haven for Austrian, German, and Polish refugees fleeing from the Nazis. In response to this need, the PLAN Board of Directors voted on 18 September 1939 to change the name to Foster Parent's Plan for War Children, Inc., and to apply at once for a license to continue relief work in France.

As the war spread into Belgium, France, and the Netherlands in May 1940, the position of the children's colonies became increasingly difficult. Spanish and German staff were interned, communications were unreliable, and the German army was steadily advancing. On 17 June 1940 PLAN turned its facilities over to the Red Cross and French public assistance agencies and the foreign children were evacuated. On 22 June Eric Muggeridge and the last of the children escaped to England on one of the last ships to leave St. Jean de Luz before the port was taken over by the Germans.

As a result of the unexpected speed of the German advance there had been no time for detailed plans to be made for the children's reception in England. They were temporarily sheltered at Canterbury Hall, in London, until a permanent home could be found. With the help of the London County Council, the British Women's Volunteer Service, and the International Commission for War Refugees in Britain, space was found for them in the Woodberry Down Estate in suburban London. It was renamed "The Sanctuary" and became the home for Austrian, Channel Island, Czech, German, Hungarian, Maltese, and Spanish children. After the Battle of Britain, in November 1940, and for the rest of the war, homeless British children were taken in. Belgian children, evacuated at Dunkirk by Mamy Bogeart, soon added another nationality.

In 1940 Eric Muggeridge proposed expanding PLAN aid to "outside" children, i.e., children living with their families and not in institutions. This was done and PLAN nurseries were established to provide day care for the children of working mothers.

In December 1940, the PLAN-supported Hampstead Nurseries were opened by Doctors Anna Freud, the daughter of Sigmund Freud, and Dorothy Tiffany Burlingham, an American psychoanalyst. The nurseries were staffed by refugees who had done specialized work in education, medicine, and psychology in Europe. In addition to child care, the nurseries provided lodging, training, and paid work for some of the mothers whose homes had been bombed.

The objectives of the nurseries were:

1. to repair damage already caused by the war to the mental health of the children
2. to prevent further harm
3. to study their reactions to war and early separation from their families
4. to observe the general influence of community life on child development
5. to instruct others in education based on the psychological needs of children
6. to develop a pattern of nursery life to serve as a model for postwar nurseries.

In keeping with these objectives, Drs. Freud and Burlingham wrote a series of monthly reports which were published in 1943 as *War and Children*, the first psychological study of the effects of war on children. J.B. Priestly, the British author, accepted the Chairmanship of PLAN's English Committee in 1939, and in 1941 PLAN began to support the Priestly Nurseries. As each new nursery was added PLAN made substantial grants and the children were enrolled as Foster Children. In addition to children's colonies and nurseries, PLAN established a rest center for wounded and bomb-shocked nurses, a home for the aged whose homes had been bombed, and an overnight station for relief workers. By the end of 1941 PLAN had over 25 hostels and shelters.

PLAN's activities in England were directed by Eric Muggeridge, PLAN's Executive Secretary, until he was mobilized in May 1944. Before he left he appointed Judy (Ivy S.) Mason, a tiny, blue-eyed, former businesswoman, to take over. Not wanting to worry Edna Blue, PLAN's Executive Chairman in New York, they delayed telling her of his mobilization. Muggeridge was to write to Edna Blue explaining the situation and reassuring her that PLAN was in good hands. In the meantime, Judy Mason was to sign his name to the daily cables to New York. Inevitably, this deception failed. After some initial dismay, Edna and Judy became fast friends and PLAN's work continued uninterrupted.

Judy Mason had been with PLAN through the worst of the blitz. The children's hostels were often bombed or damaged by bombs and, although it was nearly impossible to find new lodging, she always did. Miraculously, no Foster Children were killed or seriously injured in the years of bombing in England. On 10 May 1941 a bomb fell in the garden next door to one of the nurseries. It did not explode but there were fears that it would. As a precaution the police insisted that on no account were the children to be allowed in the garden. In spite of the fact that most of the children had experienced bombings, they soon became impatient with the confinement. One nine year-old said in an angry tone: "I wish the bomb would explode so we can use the garden again."

After a long search, safer quarters were found in Essex and the last of the children were evacuated from "The Sanctuary" on 28 July 1944. The next night "The Sanctuary" was destroyed by bombs.

Even before the war ended, plans were made to aid other needy children throughout Europe. Father H.P. Bleach, who had established PLAN in Malta in the spring of 1944, was to enroll children in Italy. Bishop Marshall, PLAN's Honorary Publicity Secretary and Director and an officer in the Free French Navy, was to find housing and staff in France. Mamy Bogeart was to return to Belgium with the children she had evacuated from Dunkirk. Clothes and blankets were stockpiled in anticipation of the children's needs.

In October 1944 Mr. Marshall was in France enrolling children and Father Bleach had received enough money to support 100 Foster Children in Italy. Andre Meyer, head of the Bank Lazare in New York, provided his house in Calvados, Château Bois, to PLAN for use as a hostel. Mr. Marshall turned administration of the hostel over to the Mayor of Calvados and the Abbe Noe and concentrated on getting desperately needed supplies to France.

Father Bleach cabled New York, on 4 December 1944, that he had organized four children's colonies in Rome, two in southern Italy for Yugoslavian children, and one in Catania. In all, Father Bleach had enrolled 125 children in Italy and Malta and was anxious for money to enroll more.

When the war ended, PLAN expanded its programs in France and Italy and moved into Austria, Belgium, Czechoslovakia, China, Greece, the Netherlands, Switzerland, and West Germany. The programs in China, Czechoslovakia, and Poland ended a few years later when government agencies took over child welfare responsibilities.

When Edna Blue died, in 1951, Gloria C. Matthews was named to succeed her. Under Miss Matthews' leadership, PLAN enrollment grew from 6,132 Foster Children in 1951, when she assumed executive responsibilities, to 56,931 in 1975, when she retired. PLAN expanded geographically as well, during her tenure, with the establishment of 12 additional program countries in Africa, Asia, the Caribbean, and Latin America.

By the late 1950s and early 1960s, the European economy had recovered to the point where the countries could provide for their own needy. In response to this, most of the European programs were phased out. In 1956 PLAN's name and charter were once more changed. Foster Parents Plan for War Children, Inc. became Foster Parents Plan, Inc., and PLAN aid was made available to needy children and their families, regardless of the cause of that need.

PLAN's first South American program was established in Bogota, Colombia, in 1962 by Keith R. Turner. Since then, programs have been established throughout Central and South America: Bolivia, Brazil, Ecuador, El Salvador, Guatemala, Haiti, Honduras, Nicaragua, and Peru.

Asian programs, begun in China, expanded to the Republics of

Korea and Vietnam, Hong Kong, India, Indonesia, Nepal, the Philippines, Sri Lanka, and Thailand. In Africa, PLAN established programs in Egypt, Ethiopia, Kenya, Liberia, Mali, Senegal, Sierra Leone, Sudan, and Upper Volta.

The evolution of PLAN's programs and services has kept pace with this geographical growth. From a provider of cash subsidies, gift parcels, and emergency medical aid, PLAN has grown into a professional development agency. Its focus continues to be, as always, children, but it has learned over these many years that children are best helped by strengthening their families and communities so that they may grow up in an atmosphere of greater security and opportunity. Recognizing that development is more than soap, shoes, money, and construction, PLAN uses a comprehensive program approach which incorporates the attainment of development goals with the meeting of basic human needs. This involves the direct participation of the people being helped. Programs may include health guidance and care, vocational training, agricultural cooperatives, credit unions, basic education for children or adults, family planning, and education in nutrition, hygiene, and budgeting. PLAN now has 31 programs in 22 countries providing these services to almost 230,000 Foster Children, their families, and their communities.

PLAN has been honored for its work by the governments of Bolivia, Colombia, Ecuador, the Federal Republic of Germany, Greece, Italy, the Netherlands, the Philippines, the Republic of Korea, and the Republic of Vietnam.

With the growth in programs and services, PLAN has also expanded its base of donors. To better serve the growing number of Canadian Foster Parents, Foster Parents Plan of Canada was incorporated in 1968. In 1970, the Board of Directors approved the organization of Foster Parents Plan of Australia and Miss A. Elizabeth Brown, Director in the Republic of Vietnam from 1961 to 1968, became its Acting National Director.

In 1973 PLAN's International Headquarters was established under the direction of Gloria C. Matthews to better coordinate world-wide program activities. George W. Ross, who established the Hong Kong program in 1959 and had been a member of the headquarters staff since 1964, was named International Executive Director in 1976. Since then, National Offices have been established in the Netherlands (1976), the United Kingdom (1980), Belgium, and Japan (1983).

Throughout its almost 50 years of growth, a basic tenet of PLAN has remained constant. Although PLAN's program methodology has evolved and will continue to evolve as its experience grows, PLAN is still based upon a reaching out to needy children by caring sponsors.

Chronological Outline: 1937-83

1937　300 Foster Children
Foster Parent's Scheme for Children in Spain organized in England by John Langdon-Davies (April)
Evacuation of Spanish Children from Madrid and the Basque Country
First Foster Children's hostels established in Puigcerda and Caldetas

1938　173 American Foster Parents, 500 Foster Children
Foster Parent's Plan for Children in Spain organized in the United States by John Langdon-Davies and Eric Muggeridge
Eric Muggeridge appointed Executive Secretary
First public meeting, Hotel Algonquin, New York City, John Langdon-Davies' speech "Spain Today" (20 March)
First Board of Directors meeting (24 March)
Edna Blue joins PLAN

1939　902 Foster Children
Evacuation from Spain (January)
Biarritz, France, Colonies established by Esme Odgers and Eric Muggeridge
Name changed to Foster Parent's Plan for Spanish Children (3 March)
PLAN chartered in New York (13 July)
PLAN becomes Foster Parent's Plan for War Children, Inc. (18 September)
Receives license to export relief supplies to France
Maria Sola de Sellares, Director of Biarritz colonies
J.B. Priestly and Vernon Bartlett, Jr. named Chairman and Vice-Chairman of English Committee (January)

1940　1,200　Foster Children
PLAN disbanded in France (17 July)
Evacuation to England
Establishment of "Sanctuary"; Woodberry Down, London
Enrollment opened to children living at home
Hampstead Nurseries opened by Anna Freud, Dorothy Tiffany Burlingham and Lilian Bowes Lyon
John Langdon-Davies resigns from PLAN to serve as a war correspondent in Finland.

1941   Priestly Nurseries subsidized by PLAN
      25 PLAN Hostels and Shelters in England
      Gloria C. Matthews joins PLAN staff in New York (August)

1942   English Committee of PLAN disbanded
      Edna Blue named Executive Chairman
      Eric Muggeridge named Executive Secretary of American Committee and Organizing Director in Great Britian

1944   1,228 Foster Children
      Eric Muggeridge enters British Military, replaced by Judy (Ivy S.) Mason
      Bishop Marshall, Honorary Publicity Secretary and Director, enrolling French Foster Children (October)
      Father H.P. Bleach, Director in Malta (April)
      Foster Children's colonies established in Italy by Father H.P. Bleach (December)

1945   Mamy Bogeart, Director in Belgium
      First Dutch Foster Children enrolled

1946   Lucette Fourquard, Director in France
      Rudolf Eldering, Director in the Netherlands
      Frederick W. Mason, European Business Director
      First Foster Children enrolled in Poland and Czechoslovakia

1947   Elma Baccanelli (later Laurenzi), Director in Italy (July)
      Andrew Zoltowski, Director in Poland
      Rev. P. McLoughlin, Director in Malta

1948   Gerald Tannebaum, Director in China

1949   617 Chinese Foster Children
      Separate accounts and procedures established for Canadian Foster Parents
      PLAN assisting children in:
        Austria - Foster Children served through London Office
        Belgium - Mamy Bogaert, Director
        China - Gerald Tannebaum, Director
        Czechoslovakia - Dr. Lawrence D. Alpin, Director
        England - Judy (Ivy S.) Mason, MBE, Director and European Executive Secretary
        France - Lucette Fourquard, Director, Legion d'Honneur recipient
        Greece - Katherine Lee Clark, Director
        Holland - Rudolf Eldering, Director
        Italy - Elma B. Laurenzi, Director

Poland - Andrew Zoltowski, Director, program terminated in December
Switzerland - Trude Singer, Administrator

1950   5,706 Foster Children
       75% of Foster Children have TB
       Chinese and Czechoslovakian programs phased out

1951   6,132 Foster Children
       Edna Blue dies (24 March)
       Gloria C. Matthews given senior responsibility
       PLAN budget over one million dollars for the first time

1952   8,903 Foster Children
       Swiss Foster Children cancelled
       West German program for children in Displaced Persons Camps
       opened, Elizabeth Whitmore, Director

1953   9,796 Foster Children
       PLAN joins American Council of Voluntary Agencies for Foreign
       Service, Inc.
       Republic of Korea, Pusan Office opened, Robert W. Sage, Director

1954   8,653 Foster Children
       Gloria C. Matthews named Executive Director
       Republic of Korea, Seoul Office opens

1955   9,258 Foster Children

1956   10,706 Foster Children
       Name changed to Foster Parents Plan, Inc., enrollment opened
       to any needy child

1957   11,069 Foster Children
       Republic of Vietnam, Saigon Office opens, Harry F.V. Edwards,
       Director
       English and Dutch programs phased out

1958   12,023 Foster Children
       Republic of Vietnam, Jacob J. Burghardt, Director

1959   15,004 Foster Children
       Hong Kong Office opens, George W. Ross, Director

1960   18,725 Foster Children

1961   22,265 Foster Children

Belgian program phased out
Philippines, Manila Office opens, Robert Sage, Director
German program phased out

1962   27,392 Foster Children
Colombia, Bogota Office opens, Keith R. Turner, Director

1963   30,741 Foster Children
Ecuador, Guayaquil Office opens, Frank E. Corwin, Director
Republic of Vietnam, A. Elizabeth Brown, Director
French program phased out

1964   34,946 Foster Children

1965   38,889 Foster Children
Peru, Chimbote Office opens, Robert H.K. Walter, Director
Colombia, Buenaventura Office opens
Greece, Jacob J. Burghardt, Director
George W. Ross, Deputy Executive Director

1966   42,751 Foster Children
Republic of Vietnam, Dalat Office opens
Hong Kong, Frank W. Ryan, Director

1967   45,666 Foster Children
Brazil, Sao Goncalo Office opens, Robert H.K. Walter, Director
Foster Parents Plan (Canada) registered as an unincorporated
charitable organization, Jack M. Mitchell, Information Director

1968   50,063 Foster Children
Italian program phased out
Colombia, E. Glenn Rogers, Director
Republic of Korea, Paeng Yong Island program established
Republic of Vietnam, Tet offensive, 400 PLAN family homes
destroyed, provincial programs suspended
Foster Parents Plan of Canada incorporated (September)

1969   53,069 Foster Children
Bolivia, La Paz Office opens, Don D. Roose, Director
Department of Community Development established, La Paz
Indonesia, Yogyakarta Office opened by Nevin Wiley
Gloria C. Matthews awarded "Order of San Carlos" by the
Government of Colombia

1970   51,611 Foster Children
Foster Parents Plan of Australia established, A. Elizabeth Brown,
Acting National Director

Foster Parents Plan of Canada moves to Toronto, E. Munro Ashkanase, National Director
Republic of Korea, John G. Anderson, Director

1971 48,580 Foster Children
Programs established in:
Tumaco, Colombia
Inchon City and Ko Je City, Republic of Korea
Nha Trang, Republic of Vietnam
Brazil, Niteroi Family Planning Clinic opens
Republic of Vietnam, Saigon Clinic seeing 1,000 patients a month

1972 50,012 Foster Children
Indonesia, Bali Office opened, Frank W. Ryan, Director
Republic of Korea:
Daegu City program established
Sung Nam, Day Care/Community Center organized
E. Glenn Rogers, Director of Field Services

1973 53,451 Foster Children
Hong Kong program phased out
Haiti, Port-au-Prince Office opened, Louis Phillipe Pelletier, Director
PLAN Headquarters moves to Warwick, Rhode Island (1 July)
PLAN International established
Gloria C. Matthews, International Executive Director
George W. Ross, Deputy International Executive Director
E. Glenn Rogers, International Director of Field Services
Robert M. Bergeron, International Controller
John Coller, National Director, Australia
E. Munro Ashkanase, National Director, Canada
Keith R. Turner, National Director, United States

1974 56,520 Foster Children
First International Conference, Whispering Pines, Rhode Island (25-31 August)
Ethiopia, Lalibela Office opened, Lloyd Feinberg, Director
Republic of Vietnam, Frank Campbell, Director
Greek program phased out
U.S. Senator Walter Mondale's Subcommittee on Children and Youth, leading to General Accounting Office audit of PLAN with "most encouraging results."

1975 56,931 Foster Children
Foster Parents Plan of the Netherlands established, Hein Kolk, National Director
Republic of Vietnam program terminated

Ethiopian Revolution, Lalibela Office closed, staff evacuated to Addis Ababa
Haiti, Jacmel Office opens
Philippines, rural programs established in Baguio, Mindoro, and Naga
PLAN receives "Best-in-Class" award from *Philanthropy Monthly*
Reinhart B. Gutmann, National Director, United States
Gloria C. Matthews, retires as International Executive Director, (December)

1976   68,938 Foster Children
George W. Ross, International Executive Director (January)
El Salvador, San Salvador program established, Keith R. Turner, Director
Ethiopia, Arba Minch program established, Leslie Fox, Director
Haiti, Croix-des-Bouquets program established
Mali, Banamba program established, Norman D. Sanders, Jr., Director
Philippines, John G. Anderson, Director
Sudan program established, David McNeely, Director
Upper Volta, Kaya program established, Asbjorn Osland, Director

1977   76,566 Foster Children
Honduras, Comayagua program established, Albrecht Hering, Director
Nicaragua, Managua program established, Vircher Floyd, Director
Sierra Leone, Bombali District program established, Jerry Vink, Director
Ethiopian program terminated

1978   101,629 Foster Children
Nepal, Kathmandu program established, William J. Kieffer, Director
Other programs established in:
     Tambillo, Bolivia
     Chalatenango, El Salvador
     El Progreso, Guatemala
     South Sulawesi, Indonesia
     Boulsa, Upper Volta

1979   127,834 Foster Children
Bolivia, Sucre Office opens
Guatemala, Guatemala City Office opens
Republic of Korea program phased out

1980   158,774 Foster Children
India, Bombay program established (conducted in partnership

with CASP, India's Community Aid and Sponsorship Program),
Norman D. Sanders, Jr., Director

Other programs established in:
Cali, Colombia
Freetown, Sierra Leone
Foster Parents Plan of the United Kingdom established, Elizabeth Liddell, National Director
Philippines, Metro-Manila program phased out
Second International Conference, Bryant College, Rhode Island (August)

1981   186,098 Foster Children
Egypt, Cairo program established, Hubert van Bavel, Director
Kenya program established, Leslie M. Fox, Director
Sri Lanka program established, Anthony English, Director
Thailand program established, James Gershin, Director
Other programs established in:
Bolivar, Ecuador
Cebu and Iloilo, Philippines
Khartoum and Port Sudan, Sudan
Peru, Chimbote program terminated
PLAN recognized by the Economic and Social Council of the United Nations
Paul H. Kraaijvanger, Administrative Director, International Headquarters

1982   206,128 Foster Children
Michael W. Miller, Finance Director, International Headquarters
Kenneth H. Phillips, National Director, United States
H.D. Kote, India, MYRADA/PLAN program established
Brazil program phased out
Liberia program established, Vircher Floyd, Director
Senegal program established, Asbjorn Osland, Director

1983   219,130 Foster Children
Foster Parents Plan of Belgium established
Foster Parents Plan of Japan established, Hiroshi Yamamoto, National Director

1

Organization and Incorporation: 1937-39

PLAN's early structure and organization in the United States were confusing and sometimes ambiguous. Its aims were clear: to provide food, safe shelter, medical care, and education for the starving, homeless, and injured refugee children of the Spanish Civil War. Finding the organizational means to meet these aims most effectively was a difficult process that took more than a year and a half.

PLAN's English Committee, Foster Parents' Scheme for Children in Spain, was in an apparently comfortable and uncomplicated affiliation with the Duchess of Atholl's National Joint Committee for Spanish Relief (the NJC). PLAN's American Committee, Foster Parents' Plan for Children in Spain, was less fortunate. Its affiliation with the North American Committee to Aid Spain (the NAC) and its own internal structure caused difficulties from the beginning.

When John Langdon-Davies and Eric Muggeridge organized PLAN in the United States in December 1937, it was with the hope that PLAN and the NAC would complement each other in their fund-raising efforts for the relief of Loyalist Spain. The NAC was a politically oriented organization providing support for Loyalist Spain and proselytizing its cause. PLAN was to be a humanitarian organization, publicly non-political. At the first official PLAN Board meeting, on 24 March 1938, it was decided to open a PLAN office and establish a PLAN bank account. It was further resolved that "although this Committee is created to aid the Loyalists . . . appeals to the public will be humanitarian, exclusively concerned with refugee children." Theoretically, the NAC's appeals would attract people already interested in Spain or in the cause of liberalism. PLAN's activities would broaden the base of Loyalist support by attracting those whose interest was humanitarian by publicizing the suffering caused by the war in Spain.

Funds from both the English and American PLAN Committees would be partially channeled through the Paris accounts of yet another committee, the International Coordinating Committee (Comité International de Coordination et d'Information pour l'Aide à l'Espagne Republicaine), which was composed of members of various groups, including the NAC and NJC, working for Spanish relief. Funds from PLAN's American Committee would support the Foster Children, while funds from the English Committee were to be used for salaries, rents, and administrative expenses. To further complicate matters, the PLAN administrators in Spain, Esme Odgers and Nick (J. Barton) Carter were to be paid by the NJC.

On 14 April 1938 Eric Muggeridge, PLAN's Executive Secretary, opened the first American office in a two-room suite at the Hotel Bedford, on 40th Street in New York City. One room was used as an office, the other as his living quarters. His weekly salary of US $25 was paid by the NAC. By September 1938, PLAN had 141 Foster Parents and problems with both the NAC and its own internal structure.

John Langdon-Davies, in Spain, remained head of the organization and was responsible for major decisions. Eric Muggeridge was in the United States and worked with the American Committee, but there was confusion over whether the Executive Secretary was answerable to the Committee, or whether it was answerable to him. They wrote to Langdon-Davies for clarification, but he replied that it was a problem for the Committee to resolve.

Muggeridge wanted to return to Spain but the Committee wanted him to stay. Again they wrote to Langdon-Davies for a decision, again he deferred. They did not want Muggeridge to leave until or unless Langdon-Davies appointed his replacement. Muggeridge felt that there was no reason for him to remain in the United States unless PLAN was to continue as an independent organization. He was willing to stay on three conditions: that the non-working members of the Committee be eliminated; that the relationship with the NAC be clarified; and that a new chairman be chosen to replace Tom Cobb.

At a Board meeting on 22 September 1938, attended by Jack Sherman, Organizational Chairman of the NAC, and chaired by Tom Cobb, it was agreed after considerable discussion that PLAN was to be a parallel rather than subsidiary organization to the NAC and was to consult with them to avoid duplication of efforts in mail campaigns, fund-raising drives, and publicity. It was established that PLAN, as a nonpolitical organization, was to enlist the support of people who were not yet contributing to Loyalist Spain or who could not be reached by political organizations.

Tom Cobb stated that fund-raising priorities of the Friends of the Abraham Lincoln Brigade were first, the NAC second, and PLAN third. The priority, he said, was a result of the need to politicize as many people as possible; that people already committed to support for Loyalist Spain could give through the NAC. Committee members protested that they had not been able to extract money from society people and that it was extremely difficult to get money from anyone not already interested in Spain.

Eric Muggeridge insisted that PLAN could not survive with such fund-raising restrictions and wanted to know where PLAN was in conflict with the NAC. Jack Sherman explained that it was determined at the beginning that PLAN, with its avowed humanitarian objective, was to operate in an entirely different field from the NAC and that any attempt by PLAN to interest individuals or organizations who could be reached by NAC propaganda would result in a duplication of efforts and a deviation from PLAN's proper role.

Mr. Sherman went on to point out that personal contacts were really the basis of PLAN's work and suggested that if Mr. Muggeridge spent more time making contacts and less time in the office, he might thereby get the proper results and the NAC would feel PLAN was working in the proper direction. Mr. Sherman reminded the Committee that the NAC agreed to underwrite Mr. Muggeridge's salary and postage because they felt that PLAN could not survive on its own and said that they were willing and prepared to further underwrite PLAN if it concentrated its efforts in the field in which it was supposed to work. However, when the NAC found that PLAN was incurring expenses that arose from a deviation from its proper role it was time for a definite understanding.

After a long discussion, Tom Cobb told the Committee that their primary objective was to get money from otherwise unreachable sources; that this was the original understanding with Langdon-Davies; that the NAC would not otherwise have agreed to help PLAN; and, finally, that it was PLAN's responsibility to raise as much money as possible with as little overhead as possible. Mr. Cobb further suggested that costs could be reduced by cutting down on office staff and reducing duplication of NAC work. He explained that PLAN need not be a large organization if it limited itself to its objective of reaching new people. The meeting ended with the passing of a motion that, until 1 January 1939, PLAN should restrict its work to fields that did not conflict with the NAC.

By the 29 September Board Meeting, permanent office staff had been reduced by one, and two more employees were to continue on a week-to-week basis. Muggeridge had made definite plans to return to Spain in October and the Committee was seriously worried that Chairman Cobb's loyalties lay more with the NAC than with PLAN. The possibility of PLAN getting its own license and becoming an independent organization was discussed but no action was taken.

The problem of PLAN's relationship with the NAC was still unresolved in November. At a Board meeting held on 19 November the advantages and disadvantages of PLAN autonomy were discussed. There was some urgency to the discussion since it was felt that decisions must be made before Eric Muggeridge's 8 December departure for Spain and that, if the Committee wanted him to stay with PLAN, he must be notified of any changes in his role as Executive Secretary. Finally, the full Committee was to meet in eight days to discuss the reorganization of PLAN and to decide whether PLAN should remain as it was, become a completely autonomous organization, or become a subsidiary of the NAC. After Tom Cobb, Jack Sherman, and Eric Muggeridge left the meeting, the remaining members voted that half plus one be considered a quorum and promptly voted to remove the names of David Algase, Vince Callahan, Carol McCormick, and Helen Tenny from the list of active Committee members.

When the Committee met on 28 November, the motion was passed that PLAN become more closely associated with the NAC and work under its direct supervision. The four members dropped from the Committee at the last meeting were reinstated and the decision as to what constituted a quorum was rescinded. A further motion was passed that a sub-committee be appointed to find a replacement for Eric Muggeridge. The replacement was to be a Field Secretary and not an Executive Secretary, and was to be paid by PLAN and not NAC. It was suggested that one of the returning members of the Abraham Lincoln Brigade would be an ideal choice.

Muggeridge finally left for Europe in December 1938 with the issues of PLAN autonomy and his own function in the organization still unresolved. For the moment relations with the NAC were amicable even if they were not very clear. The problem now was with the PLAN Chairman, Tom Cobb. For months there had been concern over the extent of his commitment to an independent PLAN and his occasional tactlessness. In September he had written an angry letter to John Langdon-Davies demanding a detailed financial accounting of the activities of PLAN's English Committee and threatening to break away from them if its performance did not improve. The other members of the American Committee were indignant because of the tone of the letter and the fact that it had been written in their name without their knowledge. They immediately wrote an apology to Langdon-Davies. Many of the major problems seemed briefly to have been solved at the 14 January 1939 meeting. It was decided to bring Muggeridge back from Europe to work as Executive Secretary and Field Secretary. He was to work exclusively for PLAN and PLAN was to pay his salary.

At the same meeting Josep Gelabert, founder of the Catalan Anti-Fascist Society, a long-time PLAN Committee member, and an old friend of Langdon-Davies, was appointed temporary Chairman replacing Tom Cobb. The Committee, in temporary harmony with the NAC, also decided to appoint a sub-committee to work with the NAC to draw up a set of by-laws and procedures for PLAN.

For the first six months of 1939 there was a rare solidarity among the groups working for Spain. Hundreds of thousands of Spaniards had fled to France when Barcelona fell to the Fascists; once in France they were rounded up by the French military and confined in grossly inadequate concentration centers. Their need was so great that relief groups temporarily overcame their ideological differences and worked together.

PLAN, the NAC, and the Medburo (American Medical Bureau to Aid Spanish Democracy) cooperated on booklets, mailings, and public relations. The NAC made PLAN available to all its chapters and both organizations were tied into the Spanish Refugee Relief Committee. The NAC was to handle all of the financial matters directly with Foster Parents enrolled through its chapters and PLAN was to handle only the case histories and Foster Parent/Foster Child correspondence. In view of the close PLAN/NAC cooperation, a PLAN Committee member was to sit in on NAC meetings, as Jack Sherman had frequently sat in on PLAN meetings.

This happy alliance ended with a jolt on 25 June 1939 when the PLAN Board unanimously decided to withdraw from the Spanish Refugee Relief Committee and the NAC immediately. Tom Cobb was unanimously voted off the Committee and plans were made to get a corporate charter as soon as possible. The Committee members voting at the meeting were Edna Blue, Walter Bluh, Josep Gelabert (Chairman), Anne Landress, Eric Muggeridge, and Louise Severn.

The only further explanation of PLAN's sudden declaration of independence is contained in a letter written the next day by Eric Muggeridge to Dorothy Morland, Honorary Secretary of PLAN's English Committee. The letter is informative enough to quote at length.

Dear Dorothy: June 26, 1939

I know you will be pleased to hear that we are already finding benefit from the fact that our finances and general organization were so adequately reorganized and rebuilt when Walter[1] was with you in London. We are going to try to do our very best to keep our machinery working in such a manner that we can fully and properly secure the very best results for the maximum number of children being released from the concentration camps.[2] The entire Committee as I mentioned before listened intently to all that Walter had to say about the London organization and about the various interviews that were carried through in Paris and elsewhere. I hope that you too are feeling less worried and that your normal smiling self remains uppermost once again. It is very nice to feel that the American Committee and the London Committee are more or less married, and will now work in such pleasant relationship. I am saying all this so that you may feel the true personal friendship and sincerity which has been established by Walter's visit to you.

RELATIONSHIP TO THE NORTH AMERICAN COMMITTEE:
We had a special Committee meeting to discuss the above subject. We have all felt for some time dissatisfaction with the method for sending funds through Paris. Recent investigation has only proved that this needed to be changed. We realize that you have had a great many embarrassments and awkwardnesses concerning this. We were very glad, therefore, to receive your cable advising us that you had withdrawn all the money, with the exception of the $180 which we wrote to you about. Now that we are clear of this office financially, the Committee felt that this was an opportune time to withdraw from the North American Committee entirely. It was therefore agreed that we do so at once, and that the Foster Parents' Plan in America be without affiliation of any kind in America. We shall write to the various committees in France of this step. The reason we want this to be so emphatic we feel sure you

[1]Walter Bluh, PLAN Treasurer, had been to England and France in May to improve financial and operational procedures and to inspect the concentration centers for Spanish refugees.
[2]"Concentration camp" was, from 1901 until the Second World War, the accepted term for makeshift facilities in which large numbers of people (refugees, prisoners of war, or political prisoners) were detained or isolated.

will understand. If you think it advisable will you please confirm this announcement to the committees in France. We are worried that the North American Committee may continue to use our name in connection with them. As an illustration, just a day or so ago, they phoned requesting some of our letterheads. Some member of their organization is going to France and he wanted to take them with him. You can see how we could not possibly permit such a thing. You may perhaps hear from him; I have also written to Esme about it. It might be Douglas Jacobs, or some other person.

REGARDING TOM COBB:

You will, of course remember the domestic revolutions we had with Tom Cobb. He is now enroute to Europe. As per our cable, he is no longer a member of our Committee. He has not been informed of this since he was not at the meeting when he was voted out. He has only attended one meeting during the past six months.[3] I have also written to Esme regarding Tom Cobb. I know you will greet him, should he call on you, in your usual charming, tactful manner.

CATHOLIC PRESS:

We thought you would be interested in seeing the enclosed magazine. I have marked page 243 for you to read. You undoubtedly will have seen similar articles in Catholic publications. We have always taken no trouble to reply to things of this nature, but we would like to know your opinion about this. The Spanish Child Welfare Organization mentioned in the article is one of the official Quaker Relief Groups in America.[4]

We thought you would be glad to hear that the National and local newspapers have given a great deal of space to our Treasurer's return and report of the colonies, on society and front pages.

I am sending you copies of recent literature and circular letters. I do not know whether I told you that it is our ambition to have perhaps before mid-year a population of 1000 little citizens in the colonies. With fond personal greetings from myself,

Sincerely,

Eric

[3]The minutes of the meetings indicate that he attended four.
[4]The article apparently charged that children were being kept in hostels against the wishes of their parents. Morland, in a letter to Muggeridge on 4 July 1939, called the charge "infamous" and "untrue." She said they had received only two requests for children to be returned and that they were immediately complied with.

Dorothy Morland replied rather casually on 4 July that "I am interested to hear what you say about the NAC . . . I think it will probably be very much better if you work on your own . . . so far I have heard nothing from Mr. Cobb, but should he call I will treat him in what you term my usual tactful manner."

Anne Landress Rabkin, one of the original PLAN Committee members and an active member of the Board of Directors until 1968, recalled in a 1968 memoir that some of the difficulties were a result of the extreme left wing attitudes of some of the PLAN Committee members who were espousing the NAC cause and "placing obstacles in our way to success if it conflicted with their political ideas."

Arrangements were made to secure PLAN's corporate charter through Walter Bluh, who consulted his attorney Julian I. Bergoffen. In her memoir, Mrs. Rabkin recalled sitting at a corner table in the restaurant of the Hotel Bedford going over the drafts of the charter with Edna Blue and Mr. Bergoffen. The charter was granted by the State of New York on 13 July 1939, and Foster Parents' Plan for Spanish Children, Inc., was finally on its own.

The officers of the new corporation were Eric Muggeridge, Executive Secretary; Josep Gelabert, Chairman; Edna Blue, Vice Chairman; Walter Bluh, Treasurer; and Anne Landress (later Rabkin), Secretary.

There remained only the final step of broadening PLAN's scope to complete the transition from what started as a small-scale, partisan welfare program to a broadly based organization of multi-national concerns. On 18 September 1939, that step was taken when Anne Landress made a motion that PLAN expand its work to include any child in France needing help. The motion was unanimously carried and the decision was made to change PLAN's name to "Foster Parents' Plan for War Children, Inc." and to amend the charter accordingly.

This change opened the way for PLAN aid to reach any children who were, in the words of the amended charter, "orphaned and/or distressed as a result of the wars in Europe."

2
Spain: 1936-39

To understand PLAN's origins it is necessary to review very briefly the Civil War in Spain which gave rise to its birth. The Civil War began in July 1936 when a coalition of monarchists, fascists, and conservatives under the leadership of Generals Mola, Goded, and Franco (variously called the rebels, Nationalists, or Fascists) tried to overthrow the legally elected Popular Front Government (the Republicans, Loyalists, or reds). Hitler and Mussolini immediately came to the aid of the rebels, providing tanks, planes, troops, and materiel; Stalin provided limited aid to the Government.

In an attempt to prevent foreign involvement in Spain and to forestall a direct confrontation with Hitler, British Prime Minister Neville Chamberlain engineered the Non-Intervention Agreement in which England, France, Germany, Italy, and Russia agreed to stay out of the war and to help neither side. When they signed the agreement in August 1936, Germany and Italy were already supplying significant military aid to the rebels and Russia was supplying food to the Republic. Joachim von Ribbentrop, the German representative on the Non-Intervention Committee who was later executed for war crimes, joked that it should have been called the "intervention agreement." The United States was not a party to the agreement because of the already strict isolationist policy aimed at preventing American involvement in foreign wars.

The Germans and Italians supported the rebels to gain strategic influence in the Mediterranean, to gain a future ally in the inevitable world war, and, perhaps most importantly, to provide a training ground for the development of tank and bomber tactics. To this end they provided extensive but carefully controlled aid, just enough to insure an eventual victory in a protracted war.

Russia's motives were equally duplicitous. Stalin apparently wanted to engineer a communist takeover of Spain, but, at the same time, wanted to keep the Germans occupied in Spain long enough for him to develop his own defenses.

It may well have been that Stalin hoped most of all that Chamberlain and French Premier Edouard Daladier would realize the danger fascism presented and give up the policy of non-intervention. Alvarez del Vayho, the chief non-communist supporter of Moscow in Spain, quotes Dr. Juan Negrin, the last Prime Minister of the Spanish Republic, as later saying:

> Moscow tried to do for France and England what they should have done for themselves. The premise of Soviet aid to the Spanish Republic was that ultimately Paris and London would awake to the risks involved to themselves in an Italo-German victory in Spain and join the USSR in supporting us.

If Stalin really was trying to support collective security against Hitler, he failed. The British and French Governments, already deeply suspicious of Stalin, clung steadfastly to the farce of non-intervention, thereby avoiding a direct challenge to Hitler. This, according to PLAN founder John Langdon-Davies, was because they feared a direct confrontation with Hitler would result in the collapse of the National Socialist Government and pave the way for a communist takeover in Germany.

These machinations, which turned the Spanish Civil War into the first act of World War II, resulted in the needlessly prolonged suffering of millions of Spanish men, women, and children. Reichsmarshal Goering's lament over the destruction of Guernica at his trial in Nuremberg sums up the whole bloody tragedy of foreign military involvement in the Spanish Civil War: "It was a pity; but we could not do otherwise as we had nowhere else to test our machines."

By the fall of 1937 the outcome of the war was decided. The rebels controlled western Spain and were advancing through Malaga, Asturias, and the Basque Country. They were well armed, well fed, well supplied, and substantially augmented by German and Italian tanks, troops, and planes. The Republican Government was isolated by non-intervention, American neutrality, and a partial, though illegal, blockade of their coast. The 53,000 foreign volunteers who, at one time or another, fought for the Republic were significantly outnumbered by the 130,000 Germans, Italians, Portuguese, and Moroccans who fought for the rebels.

Conditions in Republican Spain quickly deteriorated. As the rebels, who already controlled much of the prime agricultural lands, advanced, hundreds of thousands of refugees fled before them. Catalonia, hard pressed to support its normal population of three and a half million, had to provide for almost a million refugees from Madrid, Malaga, Asturias, and the Basque Country. Refugees from the Basque Country and Asturias fled in freighters and fishing boats to Bordeaux. Once there, they were locked in trains and shipped to refugee centers in the Catalonian town of Puigcerda.

On 5 April 1938, with Republican Spain nearly cut in half by the advancing rebels, the Government made a last appeal in a note to the Governments of France and England. The note reaffirmed the Republican Government's demand to be allowed "the right to obtain the war material necessary to drive back the foreign invasion" and went on to state:

> The Republican Government feels compelled to address a solemn appeal to the conscience of the Governments of France and the United Kingdom, as initiators of the Non-Intervention Agreement, regarding the appalling and dangerous injustice of maintaining this agreement when its open violation in favor of the rebels—publicly and unashamedly acknowledged by the Governments of Germany and Italy—is so notorious that no man of public affairs with any sense of his responsibilities dares any longer to deny it.[1]

The note had no effect.

The plight of the besieged Republic and the desperate state of the millions of hapless civilians trapped in the Republican zones aroused the bruised idealism, and the thirst for adventure, of people all over the world. George Orwell, one of the thousands who went to Spain, wrote, "If you had asked me why I joined the militia, I should have answered: 'To fight against fascism'; and if you had asked me what I was fighting for, I should have answered: 'Common decency.'"

This fight for common decency in the face of overwhelming injustice took many forms. Thousands of volunteers slipped across the French border to Spain. Some, like George Orwell, to fight; others to relieve the suffering resulting from the war. Many of the latter eventually organized or worked for PLAN. Eric Muggeridge drove a supply truck and evacuated refugees, Nick Carter worked in the refugee camps, Esme Odgers distributed relief supplies, Mildred Rackley was a hospital

---

[1] *Times* (London), 6 April 1938, p. 14.

administrator, John Langdon-Davies publicized the suffering of children and civilians through books and newspaper articles. The refugees were the ordinary people of Spain trying to escape guns, war, and death. Loaded down with their few possessions, they trudged along the roads of Spain under the guns and bombs of the rebel aircraft. They fled Irun in the summer of 1936. They streamed out of Malaga in 1937. In the winter of 1938 they ran ahead of the invaders to the streets of Barcelona.

In Europe, Australia, and the Americas, committees were organized to raise money and collect relief supplies for Spain. In North America the Spanish Child Feeding Mission of the American Friends Service Committee, the Spanish Refugee Relief Committee, the North American Committee to Aid Spain, the Canadian Committee to Aid Spanish Democracy, and the Medburo (American Medical Bureau to Aid Spanish Democracy) sent food, money, and supplies to Spain.

In England the Duchess of Atholl, a prominent Conservative Member of Parliament, organized the National Joint Committee for Spanish Relief to provide food, shelter, clothing, and education for thousands of orphaned and refugee children in Spain. The Basque Children's Committee, also chaired by the Duchess of Atholl, evacuated 4,000 Basque children from Santander to England in May 1937 at the urgent request of their parents. When the children got to England even the appearance of a light civilian plane was enough to send them running for cover, screaming "Bombas, bombas!"—a grim foretaste of the England of 1941, when PLAN children would echo these cries in English, Flemish, Spanish, and Polish.

The Duchess of Atholl made a call for volunteers in September 1936 to deliver a convoy of battered trucks to Spain for the National Joint Committee for Spanish Relief (NJC). Eric Muggeridge, later PLAN Executive Secretary, was one of the volunteers. He had at first planned to stay only six weeks but, in his own words, "was so stunned by the suffering of these youngsters" that he stayed for over a year.

The trucks they were to deliver had once been service coaches on the Isle of Wight but had been discarded as being too far gone for any further transport work. After a trip punctuated by breakdowns, oil leaks, and broken axles, they eventually arrived in Barcelona and from there went on to Valencia. In a 1943 memoir of Mr. J.T. Garret, who led the convoy, Mr. Muggeridge recalled the first of many journeys carrying relief supplies to Madrid and returning to Valencia with refugee children:

On this first journey we went straight to the Evacuation Center which was near the heart of Madrid . . . The name of Mr. Garret in this place meant very much already, and the night of our arrival a big "banquet" had been prepared for our whole party. Food was already short in Spain and this is why I call it a banquet . . . we had plenty of bread . . . we had marmalade and things we had not seen almost since we entered Spain . . . Our friends were a mixed company of Spaniards responsible for the work of arranging the parties of women and children for evacuation. One of our hosts was an anarchist, another a communist, another a democrat, another a socialist, and so on, but all pledged to the flag of the Republic. It was not politics we talked about, but human problems . . .

I can quite confidently say that this partnership of ideas never failed to succeed in the effectiveness of our work or in the happiness with which we all worked together. So our convoy system between Valencia and Madrid was set in motion . . . Always carrying foodstuffs to Madrid and returning with a lorry load of children.

During the first 18 months Muggeridge was in Spain, he covered 35,000 miles in his beat-up old truck. He made 57 of these trips to Madrid from Valencia. He picked up refugees from the road out of Malaga, children injured and dying, children who had left parents and relatives dead on the roadside, victims of the "airplanes of unknown nationality," as they were then discreetly called, which mercilessly machine-gunned the refugees as they fled on the coast road to Almeria.

During these months in Spain, Muggeridge met John Langdon-Davies, an English writer covering the war for the London *News Chronicle*. It was John Langdon-Davies who conceived of the idea of Foster Parents' Plan, the idea of establishing a lasting personal relationship between an orphaned or refugee Spanish child and a foreign sponsor. After the two discussed the idea and sketched out some of the details, Langdon-Davies returned to England in the spring of 1937 to enlist the support of the Duchess of Atholl and her committees to make the plan a reality. The Duchess was at the time trying to establish and support colonies and hostels for children in and around Barcelona and Puigcerda. Langdon-Davies' plan provided the means both to finance these colonies and to publicize the plight of the suffering children of Spain. Therefore, in April 1937, Foster Parents' Scheme for Children in Spain was established in England in affiliation with the National Joint Committee for Spanish Relief with the object that Spanish refugee children be cared for in Spain in colonies supported by English Foster Parents.

The Spanish Government's child welfare agency, Assistencia Infantil, under the direction of future PLAN Administrator in France, Maria Sola de Sellares, provided the houses and the Spanish staff ("responsables") to teach and care for the children. The colonies were first established in Puigcerda, a village in the Pyrenees on the French border, and at Caldetas, a theoretically safe International Zone about 20 miles from Barcelona. The administration of the colonies was carried out by two PLAN representatives—an American, J. Barton Carter, and an Australian, Miss Esme Odgers. Both Mr. Carter and Miss Odgers had for some time been involved in relief work in Spain with the National Joint Committee which continued to pay their salary.

The Foster Parent was to guarantee the sum of a shilling a day for a year to cover the maintenance of one child in a colony. On receipt of the first payment, a child was chosen from among the thousands of homeless children and, in due course, the Foster Parent was sent the name, age, a brief history, and a photograph of the child. The children were told how and by whom they were being provided for, and encouraged to write letters to the Foster Parent. The Foster Parent also received a monthly bulletin from Spain and news, letters, and drawings from the Foster Child. The Foster Parents were asked to send photographs, letters, small personal gifts, and clothing to the Foster Children.

In this way, to quote a 1937 English appeal, "Children who have lost all personal ties are encouraged to feel the existence of a personal friend rather than a vague dispenser of charity. This is the essence of the Foster Parents' Scheme."

A pamphlet based on reports by Dr. Richard Ellis, Assistant Physician for Children's Diseases, Guy's Hospital, and Dr. Audrey Russell, Assistant in the Child Welfare Department, University College Hospital, published in "The Lancet" (15 October 1934), describes the conditions in Catalonia as tens of thousands of refugees from northwestern Spain poured into northern Catalonia through France.

> As the doors are unlocked mothers with their families scramble out of the train that has just arrived . . . dropping from the carriages the mothers collect their children and look around . . . Nearby runs a fresh mountain stream. In a few minutes it is crowded. Mothers are scrubbing their children, the older girls are washing their cotton dresses. In two or three hours the square is bright with newly washed clothes

drying in the sun . . . Lining up to queue for their first meal, two thousand at a time have to be served from one kitchen. Many have to wait as long as five hours . . .

This is how thousands of Basque and Asturian refugees arrived in Puigcerda from Bordeaux. This was the third great wave of refugees to arrive in Catalonia. First had come southerners from Granada and Malaga, then the Madrilenians and, finally, the Aragonese. In the beginning of October, at a conservative estimate, 500,000 refugees in Catalonia were being entirely supported by the government. The new influx of refugees had been so sudden and so great that there had been no chance to arrange facilities for them. They were crowded into any available space, regardless of who was already there or how crowded it already was. The refugee centers were scattered around Barcelona and Northern Catalonia. This overcrowding greatly increased the hardships and dangers resulting not only from the shortage of food and lack of sanitation but also through the spread of communicable diseases.

The refugees from the south were largely from rural areas with a very low standard of living. Many had never slept in beds, some had lived in caves, nearly all of them were plagued by lice or scabies, and their ideas of sanitation were far from hygienic. An added danger was the prevalence of trachoma and tuberculosis among the southerners.

The Basques and the Catalans, in contrast, were generally from more urban, industrialized areas with a comparatively high standard of living.

In the unemotional words of the doctors' report, there were the immediate prospects of:

1. The introduction and spread of new diseases amongst the previously healthy Northern refugees and Catalans.
2. Epidemics due to defective sanitation, lack of soap and overcrowding.
3. Malnutrition affecting particularly infants, young children and pregnant and lactating women.

With the onset of winter, when housing and bedding must necessarily be found increasingly inadequate, there is every prospect of all these dangers being alarmingly increased.

Throughout the refugee districts there were severe shortages of food, blankets, shoes, and soap. Many, if not most, of the refugees were without even a change of clothes. In one refugee center there were only 700 blankets for 1,360 people.

Food was almost as scarce as blankets. One center with 225 refugees, 135 of them children, got only four tins of milk a day. Another, with 147 refugees, 96 of whom were under 14, had only 3½ pints a day. A trachoma hospital with 180 patients had had no milk at all for eight days when the doctors visited.

Bread, too, was scarce. In Barcelona it was not uncommon for people to wait in line for four or five hours only to find that there was none left. The doctors reported that in a typical refugee center children under 13 were given one slice of bread a day. In Barcelona there was widespread anemia, outside Barcelona conditions bordered on famine.

Little unattached children could be overlooked in the crowded centers. Dr. Audrey Russell related the story of one such child who lay asking for water. "Yes, he is very sick," she was told. "The doctor? Well, he may come someday soon, but you understand he is very busy with 12,000 refugees in this part and there is no petrol for his car." Later the same child was found creeping down two flights of stairs to get water from the faucet in the yard. He had simply been overlooked. It was no one's business to look after him.

Another of these children, little Jose, became the archetype for all Spanish refugee children. The story has been repeated so often and with so many variations that the original details have been lost. What remains is the story of a stray child, a doomed city, and a father who is about to die.

John Langdon-Davies told the story at the first public meeting of PLAN in the United States at the Hotel Algonquin in New York City on 20 March 1938. One day in Puigcerda, he said, "I was mixing with some refugees . . . who had just come in from France. I came across a little child of about five years. He was a cute little youngster, but I found him shy and hard to draw into conversation. Then, one of the older refugee women came over to me and gave me a note that she said she had found on him during the journey. It read like this; 'This is Jose. I am his father. When Santander falls I shall be shot. Whoever finds my son, I beg him to take care of him for my sake.' We took the child but at the same time had to turn down 90 orphan children who would be sent to the refugee centers."

These were some of the first Foster Children. Others came directly from the war zones in PLAN or NJC trucks. In the PLAN colonies the children were provided with simple homely care and given a degree of security for, at least, the immediate future; care and attention they could not get in the big, crowded, and under-staffed refugee centers.

The first hostels, collectively called the Children's Republic, were established in grand châteaux and vacation houses in the summer resort area of Puigcerda. According to Langdon-Davies, "palace after palace has been offered if only we can find the funds to care for the children." He described one of them, Colonia Inglaterra, a house for children with English Foster Parents, as a "gloomy great monster of the sort in which rich Catalans love to incarcerate themselves during the summer," but the children had greatly cheered up the place. The Foster Children did much of the work themselves and by January 1938 were printing their own monthly magazine, staging plays they had written on a stage that they had built, and had made a puppet theater.

On New Year's Day, 1938, the children in the Colonia Inglaterra staged a combination Christmas/New Year's musical review for all of the Foster Children. The performance was a smashing success featuring a well decorated stage, skillfully made up performers and excellent singing and dancing. After the program came the Christmas party. The children sang and danced and laughed, not thinking of the tragedies they had been through but acting like any children at a Christmas party. This is what PLAN had been working for with these children, the cultivation of the normal mentality of growing children.

In January 1938 the Puigcerda refugee centers and children's hostels were bombed. Since there were no military targets in Puigcerda, no plans or preparations had been made for air raids. One of the Foster Children, Jaime Gutierrez, described the air raid in the NJC's February bulletin from Puigcerda:

> Last Sunday, after lunch, we were playing at the garden gate . . . and we began to hear the sound of planes. A boy said, "It's the mail plane," and we looked up at the sky and saw lots of aeroplanes. Thinking they were ours, I was quiet. Other children were afraid and went and told the masters, who immediately blew the whistle and shouted to us to run into the fields. When we went out the fascists were already bombing . . . and the little children and girls were crying. The masters and other grown-ups shouted to us to run toward France and we ran hard because the planes were on top of us and many bombs could be heard. When we arrived at the frontier the carabineros would not let us pass. Later the masters arrived and were very angry with a carabinero and then they let us pass. Some French guards spoke to us and sang to us . . . Later we returned to the house.

Air raid drills were begun the next day and work began on shelter trenches and a basement bomb shelter. There was some discussion of moving the children but the difficulty of finding accommodation for 200 children at short notice and the doubt that any other place, no matter how obscure, would be any safer, argued against an immediate evacuation. Moreover, it was felt that if any children were to be relocated there were thousands in far graver danger than the Foster Children.

The air raids which began in February continued with growing frequency and effect. In the summer of 1938, after a raid left four children dead and many more injured, the decision was made to move the children to the relative safety of Torrentbo, on the Catalan coast. Again the children were loaded into trucks and evacuated.

Work continued throughout 1938 with the establishment of more and more colonies, but the refugee situation remained almost over-whelming. The ever increasing numbers of refugees further strained the limited quantities of food, clothing, medical supplies, and transport.

When PLAN was first established arrangements were made to buy food directly from Assistencia Infantil, the government agency which provided the houses for PLAN's use. This system soon broke down and Nick Carter took charge of supplying food for the children. Working with a new truck given to PLAN by the NJC, he arranged to get food in France and Spain. He seems to have been a resourceful fellow with a knack for tracking down food supplies and striking good bargains. His greatest coup was the purchase of 12 tons of unharvested potatoes and the six head of beef cattle he spotted grazing near the potato field. This does not sound like much of an accomplishment, but at the time in Barcelona there was little or no meat to be had, no milk in any restaurant or hotel, no potatoes, and practically no bread. After a week of eating in Barcelona restaurants, John Langdon-Davies lost six pounds. A grim cartoon in a Barcelona weekly showed a hunchback saying, "Everyone looks at me with suspicion nowadays, they think it's potatoes."

Very few records survived to document PLAN's activities in Spain during the latter part of 1938. Esme Odgers stayed on as PLAN Administrator after the departure of Nick Carter in mid-1938. Total enrollment grew to about 500 Foster Children with the number of American Foster Parents growing from 70 in May to 173 in December. As the enrollment grew, additional colonies were established in Figueras, Olot, Sitges, and Torrentbo. The milk fund, later to become the general fund, continued to support milk canteens in the refugee centers and relief supplies continued to be distributed.

PLAN's Children's Republic in Spain ended in the chaos of the fall of Catalonia in January 1939. As the rebels advanced to the north, the air raids became almost incessant. Towns, villages, refugee centers, schools, hospitals, residential neighborhoods, and particularly the refugee clogged roads became the easy targets of unopposed rebel aircraft.

South of Barcelona the roads were full of advancing rebel forces, to the north the roads were full of fleeing refugees. Between the two was the army, exhausted and ill-equipped, no longer able to halt the rebels, able only to buy time for the refugees' escape to France.

3

The Evacuation From Spain:
January-February 1939

By the end of November 1938, the fall of Catalonia was inevitable. In the fighting to hold the Ebro River, near the southern border of Catalonia, 100,000 soldiers of the Republic had been killed, wounded, or captured, and irreplaceable reserves of munitions, artillery, and aircraft had been lost.

The rebels crossed the Ebro on 23 December; by 14 January they were in Tarragona, half way to Barcelona. Barcelona, with more than a million terrified refugees, was bombed every day. As the rebels advanced to Barcelona and the French border, hundreds of thousands of refugees trudged north. No town or village, no matter how remote or obscure, was safe. The colonies of Foster Children along the coast were bombed and the children were moved from one hostel to another as the bombing spread.

In mid-January 1939 Esme Odgers and Maria Sola de Sellares, head of Assistencia Infantil, started to evacuate the children to the north. On 24 January, when most of the children were in Olot and Gerona near the French border, Mrs. Sola de Sellares cabled the PLAN office in London authorizing them to evacuate the children to France.

In May 1939 Miss Odgers wrote to Edna Blue in New York of Mrs. Sola de Sellares' role in the evacuation of the Foster Children.

> Sola was one of the not very many women who remained in Spain up until the last moment helping to evacuate the children . . . doing all she could for them. This is not surprising but she did have a passport stamped by the French consul to pass into France, but she suffered the privations of the last days of Catalonia with only one thought in her mind —what can I do for the children? Up until the moment Eric arrived in Figueras, we were together and many bombardments we went through together, sleeping in the car, her car, on the road with the children from Torrentbo because there was nowhere else to sleep.

Her letter to Eric Muggeridge of 21 March 1939 suggests the conditions as the trapped refugees escaped to France:

> A letter from the Secretary [Mildred Rackley] . . . says the Committee felt very close to me during the horror and danger of the evacuation. Phew . . . remember how many times we could have wished ourselves closer to them. Still I hardly dare think about the scenes on the frontier, Figueras, Gerona . . . with the train appearing from nowhere for you . . . and bombs popping around for me. It is all like a nightmare now, particularly a scene such as the car starting off and dragging the screaming women and guards with it at Le Perthus. The tragedy continues . . . it is not before our eyes en masse, but it is there, real and terrible for the Spaniards. And now the Czechs.

Muggeridge rushed to Spain from London to help in the evacuation. He reached the border on 26 January, the day Barcelona fell to the rebels. Entering Spain with a truck and 150 litres of gasoline, he drove south to Gerona searching for Esme Odgers and the children. The road to France was jammed with refugees, lines of traffic, women, children, old men, and wounded soldiers trudging along, some carrying bundles, a few leading donkeys laden with a few possessions. He described Gerona as a city of the dead, a shambles after the incessant bombardment. Three old men sitting around a candle in the basement of the battered administrative office told him that the offices had moved that day. Esme Odgers might be at the Quaker Relief Organization Headquarters. He found only an empty building. He went as far as the field hospital units just behind the lines but could find no trace or news of Odgers and the 500 Foster Children.

He spent the night at a field hospital and went back through Gerona the next day, joining the masses of refugees slowly moving toward Figueras. At one point the road was chin-deep with water from a flooding river. The refugees struggled through. He reached Figueras just in time for an air raid and searched the government offices for news. There was none. By sheer luck, two trucks drove up and out jumped Miss Odgers.

Between gasps, she told him that the children from Sarria colony, near Barcelona, had been left behind. Trucks had been sent for them but in the confusion the drivers had picked up children from other houses. Bad as that was, some children had been saved and that was what was important. Some of the children from the Sitges colonies were lost. Before they could be evacuated they had run off through the fields to escape the air raids. At least the Torrentbo children were accounted for. They, 50 children and the staff, were with Miss Odgers in the two trucks, packed so tightly under the canvas roofs that they had no room to sit down.

They had tried to get into France before Muggeridge arrived, but the road was blocked, the border closed by the French. Now they were nearly out of gas. The tanks were quickly filled from the 150 litres Muggeridge had brought from France. While Miss Odgers went off to try to find documents to get past the French border guards, Muggeridge stayed with the trucks and children.

In the next 45 minutes there were two more air raids. Merciless raids, with 20 bombers dropping 100-pound bombs, called "civilian bombs" by the Italian pilots. There was no cover or shelter. The streets were so jammed with refugees that there was not even room to lie down. Muggeridge could only stand by the back of a tightly packed truck and pray. Then the planes circled down to machine-gun the crowded streets.

At last they left for the frontier with a new set of papers and documents. The trip from Figueras to the frontier at Le Perthus, less than 30 kilometers, took three days. More than half a million refugees clogged the roads north. On the third day, they reached the border but the guards would not let them pass. That night they slept in a tiny house off the main road, hoping that it would be safe. They slept sitting on the floor, shoulder to shoulder to keep warm. The next day they went back to the frontier. The Spanish guards let them pass and they parked the trucks 500 yards from the chain across the French border crossing.

Muggeridge and Odgers pressed through the thousands of massed refugees, between trucks, cars, carts, wagons, and the wounded lying on the ground until they could look into France. Just beyond the chain were rows of French Senegalese troops with fixed bayonets, ready and, by the look of them, willing to drive back any who tried to cross.

A British reporter recognized Muggeridge and got the two through the lines of bayonets. With the help of a British general, they were able to convince the border guards that the children were and would remain the responsibility of Foster Parents Plan and they finally got permission to walk the children and staff across the border.

They returned to the trucks and lined the children up, two by two along the crowded roadside. As they pushed through the multitudes, crying women tried to put their children in the line, the wounded and dying begged to be taken, women hysterical to the point of madness tried to scream their way in. Muggeridge wrote later (19 February 1939) that he had never before witnessed a scene so gross in its terror or so mountainous in its tragedy. As the children reached the chain they were carefully and individually checked to make sure that no non-PLAN children were being smuggled into France. On 29 January, three days before the border was officially opened, these first 150 Foster Children were put on a train to the new colonies in Biarritz.

Muggeridge and Odgers returned the next day to search for the lost children from Sitges and Sarria. They went first to Beselu, again under the guns and bombs of rebel planes and against the steady crush of nearly a million refugees. There was no news in Beselu, perhaps in Olot. In Olot they heard a vague rumor about some children, perhaps theirs, in a military hospital at Casa la Ribas. When they got there they found some bits of paper wrappers from the chocolate that had been sent with the trucks to Sitges. The children had been there. Yes, they were told, some children had been there but had been taken on to Comprodon.

At Comprodon, again nothing. Someone told them that the children must be at Puigcerda. The trip to Puigcerda was a day's journey over the icy, snow covered roads of the Pyrenees, roads thronged with old men, women, children, and the wounded. No one in Puigcerda knew about the Foster Children. Yes, lots of children had been there, but no one knew where they had gone. On the road out of town they saw two trucks loaded with children. An instant later, Odgers was engulfed in a crowd of hugging and kissing children.

Forty-three of the 112 children they had found were Foster Children. They had been stranded in the snow for two days without food. Some of them were barefoot, others had only light clothing. All of them coughed. The French border guards would not let them pass. The border was still closed. Finally, on February first, with the help of the papers and documents, Muggeridge's best French, and solemn promises that PLAN, and not France, would assume full financial responsibility for the children, the French gendarmes let them pass.

They put the children on the first train to Biarritz and drove back through Le Perthus into Spain to rescue more children. They arrived again in Figueras to be, in Muggeridge's words, "bombed almost out of our skins." Franco was approaching Figueras. The remnants of the Republican army of Catalonia were fighting not to defeat the rebels, for that was impossible, but only to delay their inevitable advance.

In Figueras they found 130 lost, strayed, or orphaned children sitting in the total darkness of an abandoned movie theater. They collected them and drove them to France. The next day Muggeridge wrote to Edna Blue:

> I'm so tired I'm only half alive. I arrived from Figueras yesterday. We brought two lorries full of children across at Perthus. They had been living in a moving picture theater and after the bombardments of Friday afternoon were almost crazy with fear; on top of the fear was the hunger and fatigue of the frightful march, they had been fleeing bombs first at Gerona and then again at Tossa. When these towns were bombed the bombs were so small they could have been hand grenades there were so many. It is not a sight good to have in memory, but one difficult to forget . . .

That day Muggeridge returned to Spain once more. He picked up a little child named Alicia, aged 20 months. Alicia, her mother, and a friend had been trying to escape to France when they were caught in an air raid in Figueras. Alicia was covered with blood, the friend's head was bandaged and her face covered with blood. When they heard the planes come, Alicia's mother had fallen on top of her to protect her. She was killed by the bombs. Her remains were taken away in a truck. The friend, wounded by a grenade dropped from a low flying plane, picked up the child and fled. Muggeridge took Alicia, covered with her mother's blood, and the friend to PLAN's canteen just across the border in France. The child, he said, made no response when he offered her chocolate. "Just two eyes and a little face that looked into mine with utter bewilderment."

On February 9th Franco reached the frontier. PLAN could do no more in Spain.

The urgency of the evacuation from Spain is conveyed in the cables and radiograms exchanged between England, France, and the United States in January and early February 1939.

People and organizations referred to are: Dorothy Morland, Honorary Secretary of PLAN's English Committee; Eric Muggeridge, PLAN Executive Secretary; Esme Odgers, PLAN Administrator in Spain; Committee, PLAN's American Committee. Rhodes, first name unknown, worked with both PLAN's English Committee and the Duchess of Atholl's National Joint Committee for Spanish Relief. Jack Sherman was the Executive Secretary of the North American Committee to Aid Spain (NORCOAID), at the time affiliated with PLAN. The "Spanish authorities" was Maria Sola de Sellares, head of the Spanish children's welfare agency, Assistencia Infantil. "Coordinating" was the Comité International de Coordination et d'Information pour l'Aide à l'Espagne Republicaine in Paris.

```
FOSTER PARENTS          LONDON 19 JANUARY 1939
NEW YORK
     MAY BE NECESSARY EVACUATE CHILDREN FRANCE WILL YOU
     STAND BY OUR DECISION GUARANTEE TRANSFER QUOTA AP-
     PROXIMATELY 15 DOLLARS PER CHILD
                         MORLAND
```

```
MORLAND                 NEW YORK 19 JANUARY 1939
135 HARLEY
LONDON
     AGREE HELP EVACUATE CHILDREN IF NECESSARY AND
     AUTHORIZED BY SPANISH AUTHORITIES
                         COMMITTEE
```

```
SHERMAN                 PARIS 24 JANUARY 1939
NORCOAID
NEW YORK
     ALL FOSTER PARENTS COLONIES MOVED OLOT MOUNTAIN RE-
     GION NORTH CATALONIA NEAR FRONTIER ALL SAFELY INSTALL-
     ED URGENT ALL RELIEF GROUPS RAISE EXTRA FUNDS RUSH
     FOOD FIFTY THOUSAND NEW CHILD REFUGEES CROWDING
     GERONA REGION
                         RHODES
```

```
FOSTER PARENTS          LONDON 25 JAN 1939
NEW YORK
     SPANISH AUTHORITIES REQUEST EVACUATION CHILDREN
     GUARANTEED MONEY NEEDED SEND ALL YOU CAN
                         MORLAND
```

MORLAND   NEW YORK 25 JANUARY 1939
135 HARLEY STREET
LONDON
> CABLING TWENTY FIVE HUNDRED DOLLARS COORDINATING
> PARIS.
> > FOSTER PARENTS

FOSTER PARENTS   PERPIGNAN FRANCE 27 JANUARY 1939
NEW YORK
> FRONTIER WEEPING WITH REFUGEES SOME IN TRANSIT SINCE
> MALAGA[1] PLEASE AMERICA ANSWER THE CHILDRENS PLEA.
> > ERIC

FOSTER PARENTS   LONDON 29 JANUARY 1939
NEW YORK
> SITGES CHILDREN SAFE OLOT TORRENTBO WITH ODGERS
> GERONA ERIC ARRIVES GERONA TODAY TRYING EVACUATE
> CHILDREN STOP MONEY AND CONFIDENCE APPRECIATED
> > MORLAND

FOSTER PARENTS   PERPIGNAN FRANCE 31 JANUARY 1939
NEW YORK
> 150 CHILDREN SAFE IN BIARRITZ ENTERING SPAIN TODAY FOR
> MORE
> > ERIC

MORLAND   PERPIGNAN FRANCE 2 FEBRUARY 1939
135 HARLEY
LONDON
FOSTER PARENTS
NEW YORK
> PERPIGNAN SECOND FEBRUARY HAVE CARRIED TWO HUNDRED
> FOSTER CHILDREN TO SAFETY AT COLONIES BIARRITZ INCES-
> SANT SEARCH FOR REMAINDER BEING CONTINUED STOP BROUGHT
> ONE HUNDRED TINY TOTS FOUND SHIVERING IN THE SNOW
> PUIGCERDA INTO FRANCE STOP IN GENERAL CONFUSION SEPA-
> RATED FROM MOTHERS AND ORGANIZATIONS STOP NEED
> IMMEDIATE SUPPORT FOR THEM STOP THOUSANDS STILL RE-

---

[1]Malaga was taken by the rebels in the first year of the war.

MAIN SCATTERED IN SPAIN STOP RETURNING FOR MORE IM-
MEDIATELY FEAR WHOLESALE DEATHS FROM COLD AND
STARVATION UNLESS BROUGHT INTO FRANCE URGENT APPEAL
NECESSARY FOR INCREASED SUPPORT OUR COLONIES BIARRITZ
IF WE ARE TO SAVE THESE CHILDREN
                          ERIC

FOSTER PARENTS   LONDON 4 FEBRUARY 1939
NEW YORK
   FOLLOWING TELEGRAM RECEIVED TODAY EXTREME EMERGENCY
NOW REQUIRED IMMEDIATE EVACUATION TO FRANCE OF
EVERY CHILD POSSIBLE FIGUERAS UNDER INCESSANT BOM-
BARDMENT COLLECTED 130 CHILDREN FROM CINEMA HAD
BEEN SITTING IN COMPLETE DARKNESS WITH FEAR WAITING
FOR HELP HAVE LOCATED FURTHER FOSTER CHILDREN AND
ARRANGING TRANSFER TO BIARRITZ
                          FOSTER PARENTS SCHEME LONDON

FOSTER PARENTS   PERPIGNON FRANCE (no date)[2]
NEW YORK
   JUST LEFT SPAIN AGAIN TERRIFIC REFUGEE PROBLEM LINES
AND LINES OF PEOPLE STRUGGLING ON WILL LEAVE FOR HOME
IMMEDIATELY I CAN DO NO MORE
                          ERIC

[2]This was most probably sent on February 8 or 9.

4

Biarritz: 1939-40

From the first days of the civil war, Spaniards had sought refuge in France. Many of the same committees and organizations which provided relief in Spain also provided aid for expatriate refugees. In England, for example, the Duchess of Atholl's Basque Children's Committee supported some 4,000 children evacuated from Santander in 1937. Similar committees operated in France and Sweden. Thousands of refugees walked into France from Irun, thousands more arrived in Bordeaux from the Basque coast. Most of the refugees were shipped across France to Catalonia, but a significant number stayed in French refugee centers and children's hostels.

The Swedish Committee, in cooperation with the International Coordinating Committee (ICC, Comité International de Coordination et d'Information pour l'Aide à l'Espagne Republicaine), maintained children's hostels and refugee shelters in and around Biarritz under the direction of a M. Argote. When it became apparent that PLAN's children in Spain might have to be evacuated, arrangements were made with M. Argote to receive them.

By 9 February 1939 the PLAN children were in the Biarritz colonies. The colonies were run along the same lines as they had been in Spain. The extent of M. Argote's control is uncertain. There were troublesome ambiguities in the funding and accounting procedures and confusion over who was responsible for what. These first colonies seem to have been jointly financed by PLAN's American and English Committees, the ICC, the Swedish Committee, and the Republican Government of Spain. The accounts were chaotic. The American Committee Chairman, Tom Cobb, was particularly unhappy about this and wrote to Esme Odgers, John Langdon-Davies and the PLAN Committee in England requesting clarification. Miss Odgers replied:

> We came willy-nilly—the children exhausted and ill, the colonies bare houses, no water in many of them, the children

without clothes or shoes apart from what they arrived in—the personnel distracted and unhappy because they knew not where their families were. These were some of the problems. Under these conditions we could not go forward with high speed American efficiency and I confess that caring for the children came before insisting that the committee have its accounts.

These problems were resolved in July 1939, when PLAN in the United States became an independent organization. After July, PLAN ran its own colonies and was solely responsible for them. Walter Bluh, the treasurer of PLAN's American Committee, went to France in the spring of 1939 to establish sound accounting and organizational procedures. After Mr. Bluh's reorganization, PLAN business went as smoothly as the increasingly difficult and threatening political and economic situation would allow.

Colony life continued in the temporary peace of France. Classes interrupted by the evacuation were resumed. Gardens were planted; letters, drawings, and photographs were exchanged with Foster Parents; and plans were made for the future. Enrollment was expanded by accepting children from the crowded and unhealthy refugee camps as quickly as new Foster Parents could be found.

France was totally unprepared for the massive influx of destitute and terrified refugees who poured in when the border was opened in January. They were temporarily kept in open fields then loaded on trains and sent to hastily prepared refugee camps. Some of these camps were nothing more than empty stretches of sand dunes surrounded by barbed wire, machine guns, and mounted guards. Others were in old factories, former cavalry stables (each family got a stall and some hay for bedding), one was in a disused prison. Food was short, water often scarce, medical supplies almost nonexistent, and sanitation dreadful. Many of the wounded, exhausted by the journey, died. Others suffered from tuberculosis, trachoma, or typhoid. Scabies and lice were almost universal. Even if these camps had been flooded with food and medicine there would have been tragic suffering, but there is some evidence that the French Goverment hoped, by a policy of neglect, to force the unwelcome refugees to voluntarily return to Spain. This lukewarm reception was unfortunate but hardly surprising. Few governments, no matter how liberal, would welcome 125,000 armed foreign soldiers and almost 400,000 destitute civilian refugees. Conditions in the camps later improved but, as in any refugee camps, they were never satisfactory. Eventually about 150,000 of the refugees went to Latin America, some went to England, Belgium, and Russia, 50,000 returned to Spain to face imprisonment and, often, firing squads. Thousands more went to work in France as industrial or agricultural workers, enlisted in the Foreign Legion, or dug trenches and bomb shelters. For this work they received food, clothing, shelter, and one franc a day. When the war began many were expelled from France, some for political reasons, others because they refused to work for one franc a day. Some 70,000 died in France from wounds received in Spain, disease, or hunger. Forty thousand were rounded up by the Vichy Government for forced labor in Germany.

In all there were about 500,000 Spanish refugees in France. The estimated number of children varied between 100,000 and 200,000. Of these, half were estimated to be orphans or semi-orphans.

Reaction to the French reception and treatment of the Spanish refugees was quick. Eric Muggeridge, who had seen the suffering that these people had endured, some of them for as long as three years, was particularly bitter. Seething with ill-contained rage, he described the refugees' welcome in a June 1939 fund-raising speech in New York.

What happened to all the refugees as they marched into France? They crossed over fully convinced that they would be given temporary sanctuary until they could go back to the Republic in the Central Zone of Spain. Those brave men who held the Republican lines up to the last moment limped in too, carrying their wounded. I saw them being marshalled down the road by [the] troops. Tin helmeted Guard Mobile, the most brutal sections of the army that could be found, were used by the French authorities to drive these people like animals into the concentration camps which the French Government had so kindly decided would be their refuge. I saw the French Army at a point on the road fifteen kilometers from the frontier divide the men from their families; more tears and heartbreaking scenes. Some men with tenacity kept to their families and escaped the guards. They passed down the road with the women and children to an open field at Le Boulou. Transport and cattle too came across the frontier, tanks, airplane parts, ambulances, cars, all passed in, later to be commandeered by the French Government. Rifles, machine guns, and all other equipment were stacked at the frontier and also commandeered by the French.

At Le Boulou the refugees tried to make habitation on the grass with old blankets, bits of tin and so on. The French gave them a small piece of bread and sometimes a piece of meat per day. Train loads, five per day, were sent off from this concentration to the interior of France. Women and children packed tightly together and rounded up like cattle by the French cavalry, I saw them ride the people down forcing them to the railway station before they could gather their families and belongings together. We asked the French to let us put up canteens on the camp at Le Boulou. They first told us no, but after 48 hours we at last found a captain of the Gendarmes who gave us permission. We got our condensed milk and field kitchens and started serving — 15,000 women and children per day, with hot drinks and bread. Then suddenly on the fifth day this notice in Spanish was posted up:

WARNING

This field is to be clear by 4 p.m. today. The men who want to remain with the Republic are to take the road on foot to Angeles. The men who want to go to Franco must go to the railway station. *All* women and children are to go to the railway station. If this order is not carried out, the cavalry will be turned on you at noon today.

The cavalry came as promised and the field was cleared. The men who were marched to Angeles-sur-Mer joined their companions from the road to Le Boulou who, along with the wounded and sick, had been marched to the coast and herded into barbed wire enclosures on the sand dunes. The wounded were sheltered under scraps of corrugated iron, the healthy put up makeshift shacks from bushes and scraps of wood. For sanitation there was a hollow in the sand. Water came from four standpipes. After waiting for hours in line they might get a bit of bread and sometimes some meat. Machine guns, manned by the French army, and mounted Morrocan Spahis with drawn sabres kept them from wandering. The 125,000 men, survivors of the Catalan army of the Republic and civilians, had found a new home.

Eric Muggeridge and other representatives of Spanish relief organizations pushed their way into the camps with food, medical supplies, and hospital tents. These provided some immediate temporary relief but did little to solve the problem.

The camps for the women, children, and a few men were not much better. Walter Bluh visited several of these camps in the spring of 1939 and described two in a June 1939 report to PLAN's American Committee.

Oloron—an abandoned beret factory, built in the 18th century, is a barn-like structure. The beds are piles of straw on

the floor . . . I saw one group eating bread and raw chestnuts. They offered me some, so great was my sorrow I had to turn away . . . There is one water tap out in the open which spouts scarcely any water for the entire 650 people. Bathing facilities are nonexistent, for toilets there are five holes dug in the ground . . . France supplies them with bread, some bits of cheese. Now and then salt and some codfish . . .
Polo—The refugee center at Polo (near Bayonne) is an old deserted stable. Uninhabitable for horses. Dark and dank with only the place in the stall for a horse to put his head out serving as windows. Rows of stalls, one after the other. Stalls which once housed one horse in each. Now each stall houses from one to six Spaniards.

Eric Muggeridge visited this camp which, like all the others, was kept under tight security. His special papers from the International Commission got him in. He found many stalls containing a mother, a child or two of her own, and several stray children picked up along the road or found in the camp. A group of about 70 orphans was also there, left to shift for themselves or be cared for by the other refugees. Education, of course, was nonexistent. Esme Odgers wrote that these children:

. . . no longer seem to be a part of society. When we entered they darted away frightened. Their little dark eyes looking almost savage . . . They were very thin and filthy . . . It will take some time to win the confidence of these children and to calm them down. The longer they remain in the concentration centres the more restless and unsocial they become.

The local mayor was responsible for the camp but obviously had no concern for the refugees' welfare. He told Muggeridge that he hoped they would all be driven back very soon to Franco.

The International Commission to Aid Spanish Refugees in France, representing all relief organizations, including PLAN, the American Friends Service Committee, and the Catholic Welfare Departments, received permission to work in the camps and quickly set up canteens to provide milk for the children and brought what medical supplies they could.

PLAN's original difficulties in removing the children from the camps were overcome when the Ministry of the Interior notified the local prefects that PLAN could have as many children as they wanted. After this, the children could be quickly transferred to PLAN colonies as more Foster Parents were enrolled. The assignment of Foster Parents was facilitated by the maintenance of a small group of unassigned children. Public sympathy was aroused by coverage in the world press of the terrible conditions in the camps and enrollment almost doubled in 1939.

In France, as they had been in Spain, PLAN's colonies were more than just asylums for orphans. In recognition of this they were officially registered as private schools. In May 1939, Esme Odgers wrote to Mildred Rackley, then Secretary of the American Committee:

> I do want you to see that we are doing a work not of giving a little food and some beds to children living in wretched barns, prisons and stables, but taking them into healthy surroundings, educating them, giving them a chance to face life with courage and understanding.

After considerable work the colonies around Biarritz had been transformed from empty and often rundown hotels and vacation houses to comfortable and neatly furnished homes for children. There was a rumor that one of the colonies had been the vacation palace of Alfonso, the Spanish king who, at the request of the electorate, left Spain in 1931. When the Committee in New York heard this, they instantly assumed that it was the sort of grand vacation house in which the Spanish colonies were sometimes established and sent a cable to Esme Odgers asking for more details. Miss Odgers quickly disabused them of that happy thought. "Who imagined this Palace?" she wrote. The Swedish Committee had rented a palace of sorts, once owned by a Polish Prince who married a Spanish Duchess. Alfonso was a frequent visitor and, according to local gossip, uncorked many a bottle of champagne there. However, that was years ago and the house had fallen into such disrepair that the Swedes left when it started its slow fall to the sea. "Sorry to disappoint you," she concluded, "can offer you a house with a turret if that is any good."

By August 1939, PLAN had rented seven groups of houses in the neighborhood of Biarritz. The administrative office, staffed by Esme Odgers, Administrator, and Maria Sola de Sellares, General Director, was in Biarritz proper. The colonies were in the surrounding towns of Bayonne, Hastingue, Ustaritz, and Itxassou. Each colony had its own Director and staff of teachers, nurses, and cooks. There was also a visiting staff consisting of a doctor, shoemaker, barbers, dressmakers, and a carpenter. The staff, with the exception of Miss Odgers, were all Spanish refugees, many of whom had worked in children's colonies in

Spain. A farm colony with vegetables, cows, pigs, and chickens provided supplementary food for the other colonies. The hope was that eventually it could supply all of the vegetables and most of the eggs for all the colonies.

The children were usually dressed simply and neatly in tunics and sandals. The tunics were made by the women and older girls from fabric remnants purchased from Biarritz shops. The sandals and shoes were made by refugee shoemakers and apprentices from the leftover odds and ends of a Bayonne shoe factory.

Each colony had one elementary teacher for each 30 children. Children over nine attended the French public schools and had music and art classes in the colonies. In the afternoon there were games, gardening, excursions, and vocational training in carpentry, furniture-making, farming, shoemaking, and dressmaking.

On a normal day the children were up at 8:00 for a breakfast of milk, cocoa, and bread. Classes for the younger children ran from 9:00 to 12:00 and were followed by a lunch of bread and stew. At 5:15 there was a light snack of bread, fruit, or chocolate. Dinner, at 7:30, consisted of stew, pastry, fruit, and milk.

Twelve year-old Lorenzo Murias, a Foster Child of Eleanor Roosevelt, described his life in the colonies in a series of her articles entitled "My Day." Friday, 19 May 1939, was a fairly typical day. It is unclear why he attended classes at the colony and not at the public school.

> Today, after I got up and washed and had breakfast, I went upstairs to play checkers with my friend, Rafael, who sleeps in my room. We had fun for a while, and then we went to class. We studied geography, and as our teacher, who is also our Director, explains everything very well, we were not at all bored, but were very much interested during the class. He also told us that we ought to clean the garden. I think this is a very good idea, as it is not nice to live in a dirty place, but in a clean place, in good order, and for this reason I always keep my room clean and tidy.
>
> As it rained all this morning, and we could not go out to play, we have been in class longer than usual. We were in class with the Director until they told us that we should leave the room because dinner was ready, and as we have lessons in the dining room, the plates and glasses, etc., had to be arranged.
>
> Then I picked up everything, and they got out the football to play with until they told us the table was ready. We were very happy because the sun happened to come out just then,

which was strange because it has rained all the time for several days, and the sun only came out occasionally, but in the other Hastingue, it rains a great deal more than here, and the sun scarcely ever appears from behind the dark clouds.

We were in all the fun of football when they told us dinner was ready. We were really sorry, because the sun was out, but finally we went in, although we were cross, but as soon as we began to eat it did not seem such a bad idea, as the dinner was good.

As soon as we finished dinner we went to the garden until we were called for class. I went to get the copy books and pencils very happily, as I knew we were going to have a good time with the Director. And so we did, and I enjoyed the class very much. The most important thing he told us was all about what the conduct of the citizens of the colony ought to be, especially the solidarity and consideration for others.

We were in class when we saw the Senorita Esme's car arrive. As it was time for our afternoon tea, we all went out to greet her. We rested for a while and as soon as we had our tea, we went to class again; we were all very happy.

When we finished the class, I played with my friend Rafael until they called us for supper.

Lorenzo's idyllic description of life in the colonies is made all the more poignant by the circumstances surrounding it. France, at least, was not at war. The children's almost universal answer to the question "How do you like France?" was that they liked France because there were no air raids. There was no certainty how long that would be so. War with Germany was inevitable, the only questions were how soon it would begin and who would be involved. There were strong fears that when the war broke out Franco would join the Hitler-Mussolini axis and invade France from the south as Hitler moved in from the east. The refugees were afraid that their escape from the Fascists was only temporary and that they would be caught, defenseless, in the refugee camps. The French Government was growing increasingly uneasy about the presence in France of half a million Spanish refugees, many of whom were soldiers. They feared a fifth column in the event of a Spanish invasion and feared, too, that their tolerance of the political ideas of the liberal refugees would serve Franco as a justification for such an invasion. There may have been a basis for at least some of these fears. Eric Muggeridge was told by more than one enraged refugee that it would be worth it to join Franco's army just to invade France and get even for the treatment they had received.

Some of the refugees did, in fact, return to Spain and join Franco's army. There was little else they could do to survive. Most did not return. Under the Law of Political Responsibility, decreed 9 February 1939, the day Franco reached the French border, most of the people in what had been Republican Spain were liable to fines and up to 15 years imprisonment for such crimes as belonging to a Popular Front Party, supporting the Republican Government in any way, or engaging in "grave passivity," that is, not actively supporting the rebels. The law was retroactive to October 1934, two years before the start of the civil war. To have served in the army was to be open to the charge of fighting Franco and a death sentence as an accessory to murder. In July 1939 in Madrid there were between 200 and 250 executions a day; in Barcelona, 150 a day; in Seville, never held by the Republic, 80 a day. The law applied to anyone over 14. Given these circumstances, most of the refugees were understandably reluctant to return.

The refugees who did return found the Spanish economy, never very strong, a shambles after three years of war. There was massive unemployment, particularly among Loyalist supporters or veterans, and shortages of food and transport. There were Spanish children's agencies but, in spite of their efforts, they had neither the personnel nor the resources to adequately care for the thousands of orphans. They had more success reuniting stray children, including those in France, with their families in Spain.

The Governments of France and Spain cooperated in their efforts to reunite these families who were scattered by years of war and evacuations. These efforts continued after the children were taken into PLAN colonies. If their parents were found in other French refugee centers they were usually delighted to leave their children in PLAN's care where they were assured of adequate food, shelter, and education. If the parents were found in Spain, Esme Odgers would notify them and make arrangements to return the children. Some of the children she returned had been separated from their families for as long as three years. In many cases the parents in Spain preferred that PLAN keep the children because of the desperate political and economic circumstances of postwar Spain. The status of the PLAN colonies as private schools forestalled any attempts to pressure the parents or PLAN into repatriating the children.

The saddest cases were the orphaned and stray children, children with no known relatives, and infants. These stray infants often did not even know their names. It was felt that it would be inhuman to return these children to the uncertainties of Spain when PLAN could give them a home, care, and education.

The older children presented different and more serious problems. Many had very strongly formed anti-Fascist feelings, many had had fathers killed or imprisoned by Franco's rebels or had seen their brothers, sisters, mothers, or friends killed in raids by rebel planes. One child, a girl of 13, said that she would rather carry stones from the river than go back to Spain knowing that her father had been killed by Fascist planes and her brother shot in Asturias. Esme Odgers wrote that it would be unthinkable to send these children back to share a similar fate, that they were far too young and emotional to be discreet and would certainly court trouble should they return.

In the light of the terrible uncertainty of the children's future there was a great emphasis on education. The education focused on vocational training to insure that, no matter where the children finally settled, they would have at least the rudimentary skills necessary to support themselves. The boys received training in building trades, furniture-making, farming, and shoemaking. The girls were trained in dressmaking and domestic arts.

With the outbreak of World War II in September 1939 PLAN's work became increasingly difficult. Transport became a problem as more and more vehicles were requisitioned for evacuation work. Some of the PLAN personnel, including Maria Sola de Sellares, General Director, were arrested as security risks and interned as undesirable aliens. Letters had to be censored, foreign language broadcasts and cables were forbidden, and there began to be more serious shortages of supplies.

In addition to the Spanish refugees, there were also refugees fleeing from the Nazis. Austrian, German, and Polish refugees poured into southwestern France along with French refugees from the Mediterranean coast and the Maginot Line districts.

On 18 September 1939, by unanimous vote, Foster Parents' Plan for Spanish Children, Inc., changed its name to Foster Parents' Plan for War Children, Inc., and opened its enrollment to any child suffering as a result of war. Eric Muggeridge returned to France from New York in February 1940 to arrange for the enrollment of war refugees in France and to be on hand should an emergency arise. Arrangements were completed by 20 February for the enrollment of Polish, German, and French refugees.

The Polish children, first enrolled in March 1940, were largely from the families of Warsaw army officers and civil servants. During the first week of the war, the Polish Government ordered the evacuation of all civil service and military personnel and their families from Warsaw. As the Germans advanced, the evacuees marched to the east with the government and the army. When the Russians advanced, the refugees sought shelter in Hungary and Rumania. They were soon joined by members of the Polish landed nobility who were prepared to face a German occupation but not a Bolshevik one.

Thousands of these refugees eventually made their way to France and many of their children were enrolled in PLAN colonies. One of the children, a boy of 11, had walked from Warsaw to Paris by himself. The stories told by the refugees were almost beyond belief—aristocrats disguised as peasants, stealthy midnight border crossings, horses hitched to cars when gasoline was unavailable, cold nights hiding in the woods, and bombing and strafing by the German pilots who had so recently learned their trade in Spain.

The German and Austrian children were almost entirely Jewish refugees. It is not clear whether they had just escaped from the Nazis or had fled to France before the war began. Very little information survives about these children. A cable to Edna Blue from London indicates that Muggeridge had made arrangements with Baron Rothschild on 21 February 1940 to enroll some German Jewish refugees. The numbers and locations of these children are vague.

In May, Muggeridge was again transporting refugees, this time they were Belgians fleeing the Germans. On 16 May he cabled Edna Blue that it was Figueras all over again, with thousands of benumbed refugees streaming in.

The first French Foster Children enrolled were the children evacuated from the Maginot Line district. These children, like the Belgian, German, Austrian, and Polish Foster Children, were established in PLAN colonies similar to the colonies for Spanish children. They were arranged by nationality and staffed by refugees.

PLAN kept the Spanish Foster Children for as long as possible after the outbreak of the war but time was short. In June 1940, the difficult and bitter decision was made to return them to Spain. In the confusion following the occupation of Paris, no one knew what to expect. Anything could happen. Anticipating a Spanish invasion, Odgers and Muggeridge had looked for houses farther from the Spanish border but none were available. The flood of refugees from Paris and the Mediterranean coast meant that all available housing was taken—rented by the wealthy or requisitioned for the poor.

In the second week of June there was an unconfirmed report that the entire coast was occupied by the Germans. Odgers and Muggeridge decided that they could no longer base the safety of PLAN children and personnel on the dubious authority of two British subjects in occupied France.

The future of the Spanish children was to be either in Franco's Spain or Hitler's France and there was nothing that they could do about it. Evacuation to England was impossible, there were neither boats nor visas available for the Spanish children. In spite of the fact that many, if not most, of the surviving fathers of the Spanish children were in Franco's prisons, the decision was made to return the children. Neutral Spain at least was their own country and now, while there was no fighting in the area, they could be well provisioned and returned in an orderly fashion. Muggeridge and Odgers were afraid that if they waited too long they would be forced to repeat the desperate evacuation from Spain to France, only this time it would be back to Spain.

Arrangements were made through the Spanish consulate in Bayonne for representatives of Auxilio Social, the Spanish welfare agency, to meet the children at the border and on 17 June 1940 the children with parents in Spain left France. Names and addresses were carefully pinned to clothing and the children were off. With them they took supplies of shoes, jerseys, socks, blankets, sandals, dried fruits, chocolate, and enough food to last three days, the expected length of the journey.

Esme Odgers described the scene at the station in a report from England:

> In the dirty, dreary railway station of Bayonne whilst we waited for a train three hours late, the children—except for the little ones and for them it was a grand and exciting adventure—spoke affectionately of their Foster Parents and wanted to know if they could continue to write to them. I said yes, but to write direct saying that it would save time, but knowing that we could not stay in Biarritz much longer. The children were almost all excited about the train journey, their new clothes, the extra chocolate, figs and big loaves of bread with large omelettes inside. So peaceful had they been in their colony world that they didn't realize how close the war was to them . . .

Next came the Spanish children with parents in France. In spite of the fact that the military had taken over the railway and had suspended passenger service, they managed to get the children onto a midnight train to Montauban.

The following days were spent getting Polish and Belgian children and staff onto military boats for England from St. Jean de Luz. On Saturday, 22 June 1940, another group of Spanish children left for Spain with their mothers, space was found on a Polish troop ship for more Polish children, and Marguerite Falconet was engaged to look after the last of the Spanish, French, and Belgian Foster Children in France until they, and PLAN's material resources in France, could be turned over to the Red Cross and local French public assistance organizations.

The English consulate officials left Bayonne for St. Jean de Luz on 22 June and Miss Odgers was told that Sunday's boat would probably be the last. The last of the Polish children and their mothers were left at the dock in the morning while arrangements were made for a final group of Spanish children to leave on Monday for Spain.

They returned to the dock in the late afternoon to see if the Polish children had left. They had not, naval authorities told them there was only room on the ship for British citizens and Belgian, French, and Polish soldiers. Polish military officials told them that the Germans were on the way from Bordeaux and that the Polish children and their mothers must leave immediately. The children were loaded onto trucks, given money and orders for food, and sent to the supposed safety of Lourdes.

Eric Muggeridge and Esme Odgers were hustled aboard the boat at midnight and PLAN's work in France was ended.

5

England: 1940-57

When Eric Muggeridge and Esme Odgers arrived in England on 27 June 1940, their first concern was, as always, the children. Muggeridge cabled Edna Blue in New York for permission and funds to evacuate children from England and to establish PLAN's first English colony for 80 foreign refugee children. A plan had been drawn up, under the auspices of the Children's Overseas Reception Board, to provide for the mass evacuation of children to Canada, Australia, other Dominions of the Empire, and to the United States for the duration of the war. On 13 July the plan was suspended because there were not enough available naval vessels to insure the safety of a convoy of children.

The suspension of the evacuation scheme and the poor state of the English economy left the future direction of PLAN aid in question. The unavailability of suitable housing for children's colonies in safe rural areas of England added to this uncertainty.

Letters from English supporters showed warm sympathy and a desire to help but very little cash was sent. Because of the uncertainty of continuing support from individual Foster Parents for specific Foster Children, the English Committee, on the recommendation of Committee Member Dr. Audrey Russell, favored using English funds for the support of children needing short-term care. Esme Odgers saw such a move as directly contrary to the personal long-term relationship between a child and a sponsor upon which PLAN had been based. She saw a greatly expanded group sponsorship program as the most effective way to preserve this relationship. Eric Muggeridge favored the establishment of an exclusively American colony, equipped and supported by funds from the American Committee and housing the Foster Children of American sponsors.

These questions were resolved in July when suitable accommodations were found with the help of the London County Council, the

British Women's Volunteer Service, and the International Commission for War Refugees in Britain. The building was a large old estate called the Woodberry Down Estate in the London suburb of Stoke Newington. On 23 July 1940 Esme Odgers wrote to Edna Blue describing the search for housing and the new quarters:

> . . . And now we are in business all over again. Tomorrow we start with our new colony and hope to have children in it at the end of the week. It has really been difficult to obtain a house . . . The majority of very big houses outside London are in areas "prohibited" to foreigners and they are empty because of the very fact that they are in either prohibited or restricted areas. The tremendous advantage of the place we have taken is its excellent state of repair, and the fact that there are three houses along side—just waiting to be occupied as we grow again.

The size of the Woodberry Down Estate allowed an easy flexibility in the range of the services PLAN could offer and the accommodating buildings were quickly put to a variety of uses. Children were soon taken in and colony life began again, following the familiar patterns established in France and Spain but also creating new patterns uniquely suited to the circumstances of wartime London.

In August the Central Committee for War Refugees from the Netherlands, Belgium, and France transmitted PLAN's offer to shelter refugee children at the Woodberry Down Estate to the various refugee committees. PLAN was prepared to offer limited term accommodation for children from five to 15 years of age whose mothers required hospitalization for disease or childbirth. The children were at the time being billeted with their mothers but the conditions in the billeting household did not always allow the children to stay while the mother was hospitalized. PLAN's hostel was to provide shelter during the last weeks of pregnancy and to provide transportation to the hospital. The shelter was specifically intended for short-term care and represented a major change in the nature and scope of PLAN aid.

PLAN also offered a home for the duration of the war to children from five to 15 who were orphans or whose parents or guardians were unable to care for them. The first such colony, at Woodberry Down Estate, was to be entirely American, equipped and maintained by American funds and housing the Foster Children of American sponsors. Polish and Basque children were among the first to be assigned to these American sponsors.

"The Sanctuary," also in the Woodberry Down Estate, provided temporary shelter to children of all nationalities until they could be housed elsewhere or taken into permanent PLAN colonies.

By the end of 1940, PLAN was working in concert with the London County Council, the various refugee committees, governments-in-exile, and local officials to provide a variety of services geared to the specific needs of the time. PLAN's work was in urban London and was caught up in the conditions of the city during the blitz—blackouts, Anderson shelters, boarded-up windows, and nights spent in shelters and tube stations. A list of PLAN projects shows the diversity of needs to which PLAN responded in its first winter in England.

Residential Colony for Children, Woodberry Down Estate:
Provided long-term residence to Foster Children. Resident staff: cook, assistant cook, teachers, doctor, nurse, house mother, and administrator.

Nurses' Rest Home, Woodberry Down Estate:
Provided accommodations for wounded and shocked nurses whose Nurses' Home at Hampstead was destroyed in an air raid. Resident staff: cook and domestic staff, doctor, nurse, and administrator, same as children's colonies.

Home for Aged People, Woodberry Down Estate:
Provided accommodations for old people whose homes had been destroyed by bombs. These were people who had no friends or relatives in safe areas to give them shelter. There was one cook, a doctor, and a nurse. As the great majority of the residents were able to look after themselves there was no need for a domestic staff.

Overnight Station, Woodberry Down Estate:
Provided temporary accommodations for relief workers who found it necessary to remain in London for any length of time. Same staff as children's colonies.

Day Nursery School, Stoke Newington:
Accommodated neighborhood children whose schools had been demolished by bombs. Provided afternoon tea. The school was staffed by the British Women's Volunteer Service.

Residential Colony for Children, Melton Mowbray,
Leicestershire:
A suburban residential colony for children evacuated from

London with special cottages where shocked and injured children could stay with their mothers until they recuperated and could be billeted elsewhere. Resident staff: cook, domestic staff, teachers, doctor, nurse, house mother, and administrator.

Hampstead Child Therapy Clinic, Hampstead:
Residence for mothers and children whose homes had been bombed. Resident staff: cook, domestic staff, doctors, and nurses. Supervised by Anna Freud, Dorothy Tiffany Burlingham, and Lilian Bowes Lyon.

Farm Colony:
In the planning stage. It was to house children too old to remain at the regular children's colonies. This colony would accommodate children between the ages of 14 and 17 who would operate the farm.

A December 1940 article in the London *Daily Herald* announcing the opening of the Melton Mowbray Colony provides a glimpse of the daily life of the children in the Woodberry Down Sanctuary. The headline reads "Five Language Republic for Children."

A children's Republic is to be formed next month near Melton Mowbray, Leicestershire, where refugee children from European countries at war will find a sanctuary.

I met some of the children yesterday in the London Headquarters of the Foster Parents Plan for War Children, Woodberry Down, N. "Previously we have taken Polish, Spanish, Dutch, Belgian and French children," the American secretary, Mr. Muggeridge, told me.

"Now our gates are open to English children as well. We have five little Londoners here who have been orphaned by the blitz."

COCKNEY ORPHANS
Because most of the 25 children at The Sanctuary are Spanish—their mothers and fathers killed in the raids on Bilbao—the five small Cockneys are learning to speak Spanish too!

Little Barbara White, aged 4, thoroughly enjoyed her Spanish dinner of niños en vuelitos and fritura de Manzana—cooked by a chef whose nationality is Austrian.

Nationalities don't count at The Sanctuary. Neither will they count at Colony House, the children's new home at Melton Mowbray.

The Foster Parents Plan does not lack funds, but it needs more staff.

ANY OFFERS?

For instance, an extra teacher must be found who can speak Spanish, French, and, of course, English.

An assistant housekeeper is wanted as well—someone who doesn't mind children laughing all day long. "And who can play pong-ping," added Paquita and Chiqui, two little Basque children.

Thirdly, the organization wants a matron who must be able, I suggested to Mr. Muggeridge, to sing lullabies in at least five languages.

He smiled and shook his head. "Not necessarily, but she must be fond of children."

This air of optimism was sometimes difficult to maintain in the face of the almost daily air raids. A telegram received in New York on 5 October 1940 conveys the precariousness of wartime life in London.

TIME BOMB FELL IN GARDEN 12 YARDS FROM COLONY HOUSE SHATTERING PLASTER IN MANY PLACES STOP ALL CHILDREN AND PERSONNEL WITH BAGGAGE SAFE IN CHURCH STREET SCHOOL HALL IMPOSSIBLE TO SAY WHEN BOMB WILL EXPLODE OR WHAT DAMAGE WILL BE CAUSED TO THE HOUSE.

The bomb was safely disarmed and removed but the air raid alarms, sometimes almost hourly, continued. On a wet November afternoon, the children's dancing rehearsal was interrupted when a plane dived to almost rooftop level and machine-gunned the house. Children and staff took what shelter they could and, as the older children shielded the younger ones, the plane made two more passes before disappearing into the mist and the rain. When the danger had passed the rehearsal continued without a tear or complaint.

Eric Muggeridge summarized PLAN life and work during the blitz in a November 1940 letter to Edna Blue:

As you probably know from my cables this district has been heavily bombed. We can no longer consider this a safety zone. There is not very much we can do about shelters until we have the funds to build them. The basements could be used but actually they are not safe. It happens all too often that people are buried in the basement or cellar they are sheltered in . . .

We have found it best to keep the children indoors during the raids, especially because of the falling shrapnel. Each night the children go to bed normally in their dormitories and we just pray for their safety. They are all courageous and calm . . . They keep cheerful and take it all in stride. There seems to be no end of bombardments. Each night as the children say goodnight with their smiles and their confidence— I wish I could feel certian that they were safe. There is no true safety in total war, but the shelters would be a great help. During the raids now and again tremendous crashes seem to lift the house right into the air. We just look at each other.

I feel it is unsafe to undress and lie in bed in my clothes or just sit in a chair and nod. I feel I must have one eye open all the time. In the morning the children rush out into the gardens to pick up shrapnel and commence another day with other bombardments.

These constant bombardments have thrown everything pretty much out of gear. We have been without water and gas for some time. For awhile the gas burned weakly and then gave out. We are now using a coal stove. Our cook has a great deal to contend with and so does Mrs. Sanders, the house mother. Shopping is very difficult because during the alarms all the shops are shut. Sometimes there are only two hours out of the entire day for shopping. No shops will deliver food. During the lulls I drive Mrs. Sanders to the stores in the truck so that we can get the food back in time for the children's dinner. . . "

In spite of these difficulties, PLAN continued to expand. By 1941 PLAN projects were providing aid and shelter for Austrian, Belgian, British, Czech, Dutch, French, German, and Spanish children. In September of that year, PLAN was operating or helping to support 25 children's colonies where more than 4,000 children of all nationalities found shelter. Wherever possible the children attended local English schools. Young foreign children were given special English instruction to help them overcome the language difficulty. Brothers and sisters were kept together as much as possible and the mothers of colony children were hired to try to maintain at least some semblance of a normal family life to insure the healthy development of the Foster Children.

This interest and concern for the future well-being of the child had been of paramount importance to the PLAN committees in England and the United States since PLAN was founded. The intention from the start was for PLAN colonies to provide an environment which would promote and foster the development of children who could grow up to be useful and contributing members of their society. It was this guiding principle that drew the first volunteers to Spain and gave direction to the colonies in France. With these commitments, the Hampstead Child Therapy Clinic, established by Anna Freud, Dorothy Tiffany Burlingham, and Lilian Bowes Lyon, was a natural choice for PLAN support.

Anna Freud and her associates founded the clinic in 1939, after the death of Dr. Freud, for the study of children and the training of analysts. The clinic was in a house at 20 Marsefield Gardens where the Freuds had settled when they came to England from Austria in 1938.

Anna Freud, the youngest of Dr. Freud's six children, had been both pyschoanalyzed and trained in psychoanalytic therapy for children and adults by her father. She had maintained a private practice in Vienna as a psychoanalyst, had been the Director of the Vienna Institute of Psychoanalysis, and, with Dorothy Tiffany Burlingham, had established and co-directed an experimental nursery for children between the ages of one and two.

Dorothy Tiffany Burlingham, co-founder of the Hampstead Clinic, was the daughter of Louis C. Tiffany, artist and head of Tiffany and Company jewelers, and Louise Wakeman Knox, one of the founders of the New York Infirmary for Women and Children, the first hospital to employ solely women doctors. Mrs. Burlingham had spent 13 years in Vienna working and studying with the Freuds and had had a private practice as a psychoanalyst in Vienna, in addition to the experimental nursery she ran with Anna Freud.

Lilian Bowes Lyon, the third co-founder and a supervisor of the clinic in 1939 and 1940, devoted much of her life to the care and well-being of the young, the old, and the sick. After 1940 she lived and worked in London's East End providing relief aid to victims of the blitz.

On 16 March 1940 Anna Freud stated that "entry into Foster Parents Plan has made it possible now also to continue our work with children and to utilize the experiences previously gained in our Vienna institutions. I have the good fortune also to employ many of my former co-workers who are now living in England." PLAN continued its aid to Miss Freud's clinic until 1957 when PLAN concluded its work in England.

Drs. Freud and Burlingham and Miss Bowes Lyon had four overall objectives for their three nurseries:

> *To repair* damage already caused by war conditions to the physical and mental health of children.
> *To prevent* further harm being done to the children.
> *To do research* on the essential psychological needs of children; to study their reactions to destruction and early sepa-

ration from their families.

To instruct people interested in the well-being of their children and generally to work out a pattern of child life which could serve as a model for peace-time education.

In keeping with these objectives, Anna Freud and Dorothy Burlingham wrote monthly reports summarizing their findings, published books, and conducted formal and informal educational programs, including university-accredited course work.

Anna Freud, for all practical purposes, invented the systematic study of the mental and emotional life of the child in her work at the Hampstead Clinic. She was one of the earliest researchers to realize the significance of the fears, phobias, wishes, obsessions, and dreams of young children. She also provided clinical documentation for the stages of emotional development described by her father.

One of her more important books, *War and Children*, written in collaboration with Dorothy Burlingham, was based upon case studies of the Foster Children in her care during the war. The most significant finding of her research was that war, air raids, and bombing, per se, were not nearly as destructive to the emotional health of children as had been thought. "General sympathy has been aroused by the idea that little children, all innocence, should come into close contact with the horrors of war," the authors wrote, and went on to demonstrate by example that children were not at all saddened by the sights and experiences of war's destruction.

"Love for the parents is so great that it is a far greater shock for a child to be suddenly separated from its mother than to have a house collapse on top of it . . . It is surprising how little interest children show in sirens, bombs, guns and all clears." What did affect the children, and affect them deeply, was the reaction of their parents to the sirens, bombs and all clears. The children relied so much upon the attitudes of the adults around them that, if the adults panicked, so, too, would the children, if the adults remained calm, the children also would remain calm. This observation became one of the guiding principles of the Hampstead staff in dealing with the children's reaction to the effects of the war. They found no substitute for calm influence in providing and promoting the normal behavior and development of the Foster Children.

One easy example of this was provided by two young sisters who had spent a disagreeably long time buried in the debris of what had once been their home. After they were taken into the clinic, they very quickly settled down to colony life playing happily, eating well, and sleeping soundly, apparently unfazed by their experience. The staff found that the girls had come from a calm and stable family and concluded that the calm and confident surroundings of their youth had enabled them to endure the bombing of their home with an almost inbred equanimity.

Russell Landstrom, a reporter for the *London Mailer*, was told in a 28 October 1943 interview that the air raid games and commando games so popular with the children were really nothing to be concerned about, that they were nothing more than the 1943 equivalents of cops and robbers or cowboys and Indians. The Hampstead staff explained that the children were primarily attracted to these games by the adventure and heroism of the air attacks and military operations and that the children were too young to understand the tragedies of war. "Instead of turning away from them in instinctive horror, as people seem to expect, the child may turn toward war-like expressions with primitive excitement. The real danger is not that the child, caught up all innocently in the whirlpool of war, will be shocked into illness. The danger lies in the fact that the destruction raging in the outer world may meet the very real aggressiveness which rages inside the child. At the age when education should start to deal with these impulses, confirmation should not be given from the outside world that these same impulses are uppermost in other people."

The unnamed staff member, very likely Anna Freud, further explained that children had to be safeguarded against the "primitive horrors of war, not because horrors and atrocities are so strange to them but because we want them, at this decisive stage of their development, to overcome and estrange themselves from the primitive and atrocious wishes of their own infantile natures."

Drs. Freud and Burlingham stressed the importance of protective, supportive, and educative attitudes toward the children in their care. Their staff echoed the often repeated PLAN statement that incoming Foster Children were, in effect, joining a family, the best and only family available to them under the circumstances, and not simply coming to a refuge for stray children. Children taken into the Hampstead Nurseries ranged in age from newborn to six years old.

After the massive air attacks of 1941 ended, the nurseries PLAN supported received progressively fewer blitz victims and a growing number of children suffering the effects of the nonviolent break-up of their families. Families came to be divided more often by evacuation plans, the mobilization of the fathers, and the mothers going to work to support the war effort than by the bombings.

In spite of the growth in the number of PLAN colonies and children's projects and the evacuation of hundreds of thousands of children to rural areas of England, PLAN was still unable to meet the need for shelter and child care. Between five and ten applicants a day had to be turned away for lack of space. To insure that PLAN aid would reach those who most needed it, PLAN staff tried to limit enrollment to those children and families recommended by the British Women's Volunteer Service, the government-in-exile or refugee committee of the child's home country, recognized welfare agencies, or the local Lord Mayor.

J.B. Priestly accepted the chairmanship of PLAN's English Committee in 1939, and in 1941 PLAN began to subsidize the Priestly Nurseries. These nurseries had been established early in the war by Mr. Priestly and his wife to provide day care and shelter for young blitz victims and the children of working mothers. As each new nursery was added, PLAN made substantial grants and the children were enrolled as Foster Children.

In addition to providing residential and day care for children and their mothers in PLAN and PLAN-supported facilities, aid was also provided for "outside" children (children living at home or billeted in private homes) and, in emergencies, to aged, incapacitated, or destitute victims of the blitz. This relief consisted of clothing, food, coal, or an occasional cash grant.

As a result of the demands of the war, administrative problems, and the loss of English Foster Parents, the English Committee withdrew from PLAN on 27 January 1942. Eric Muggeridge was named Organizing Director in Great Britian and an Advisory Committee, consisting of Stephen Spender (Chairman), Dorothy Burlingham, and Anna Freud, was established.

Eric Muggeridge had the responsibility for PLAN's activities in England until he was mobilized by the British Army in May 1944.[1] He appointed his assistant Judy (Ivy S.) Mason, a tiny, blue-eyed, former businesswoman married to a Royal Air Force bomber pilot, to take his place. Not wanting to worry Edna Blue, PLAN's Executive Chairman in New York, they delayed telling her of these changes. Muggeridge was to write to her of his mobilization and assure her that PLAN was in good hands. In the meantime, Mrs. Mason was to sign his name to the

[1]Miss Odgers left PLAN for personal reasons in January 1941.

daily cables to New York. Inevitably, this deception failed but Edna Blue and Judy Mason soon became fast friends and PLAN's work continued without interruption.

In spite of the Allied invasion of France on 6 June 1944, the bombings once again increased in frequency and intensity. This time they were flying bombs and rockets. When the flying bombs started their systematic destruction of London, Mrs. Mason realized that safer quarters must be found. The search was difficult since practically every large house in the country had already been taken by other evacuees. By the first of July 1944, most of the Woodberry Down Foster Children had been transferred to "The Grange," PLAN's farm colony at Market Rasen, and the search for office space and quarters for the children remaining in London went on.

A house was finally found in Eastwick, Essex, 25 miles from London. On 27 July 1944, Mrs. Mason signed the agreement for the house, called "Eastwick Manor," and wrote to Edna Blue describing it:

> I have today signed the agreement for the New House. I really do feel the responsibility of having made this change, but had such a strong urge to do it. I do hope that everything turns out for the best. It has of course involved all sorts of complications and difficulties. We shall keep our clothing store here, also a typewriter, and shall come backwards and forwards to look after the house and the gardens, etc.
>
> The house in Eastwick has a lovely garden attached to it, also a number of acres of ground, so I am hoping that we shall be able to grow most of our own vegetables. This house had been rented by the R. A. F. as a convalescent home, but it was found to be too small. We shall be cooking by an Aga Cooker; it is worked by anthracite. As, however, it is rather small, we are getting a small electric cooker as well. Margaret has been down here for more than a week now, getting people in to clean the floors, etc. Also, the agents have managed to get some workmen to clean and distemper some of the walls that were very dirty indeed.
>
> There will be plenty of grassland there for the children to play in and I think that once they get used to the country life, they will really love it. Fortunately, it is not very far really from London and as we have the ambulance, we shall be able to get to and fro quite easily.

Three days later she wrote again.

> I hope my cable arrives safely telling you that we really have been bombed out at headquarters. All my hopes have

been dashed to the ground, as now it will be impossible for us to keep either the Sanctuary or the storehouse. The doodle bug actually fell in the garden and the place is a shambles. The best thing of all is that nobody was hurt. Fritz had just come out of the bath and Charles who has been helping us was up on the first landing with Fritz—otherwise everybody else was in the shelter. There is nothing for us to do now of course, but to salvage as much of the furniture as possible and get down to Eastwick . . .

I have today been there walking over rubble and ceilings —it is impossible to describe the mess to you. Unfortunately lots of our furniture and beds were in the ground floor—beds lying flat on the floor, waiting for Monday for the removal men to come and take it to Eastwick—it is of course covered in ceilings and everything else possible. I got a heavy rescue squad to come and move parts of ceilings to get into the storehouse to enable me to rescue some of the large amount of clothing buried there. They did a wonderful job and were able to get most of it out, which although very dirty has now been wrapped in blankets and ready for transport to Eastwick. Most of the toys were broken, of course.

We got some of the stuff out into the front to wait for transport and, of course, as it usually does on an occasion like that, it simply poured with rain . . . You don't know how thankful I am that I took this other house—otherwise we should have been absolutely stranded.

Please do not worry Edna—we are all well and cheerful and feel that everybody and everything has had a lucky escape. I have just told you these details, because I know you would want to know just what has happened and to know that headquarters and storehouse will no longer be at Woodberry Down. Both houses are completely lost.

By August third PLAN had moved into Eastwick Manor with everything that could be salvaged from the London office and work went on without serious interruption. There were two major drawbacks to the new house, one practical and the other psychological. When they moved in the plumbing did not work and when it was repaired the water needed to be boiled before it was safe to drink. A nearby military installation supplied them with water until their own was made safe. The other problem concerned the location of the house. Eastwick Manor was on the direct route between the launch sites of the flying bombs and London, their primary target. Worse yet, the house was on a hilltop and, as the bombs flew at a very low altitude, they roared by uncomfortably close to the roof. The PLAN staff and Foster Children were fairly certain that the bombs would fly on for another 25 miles but were still less than comfortable when they passed low enough for their flames to light up the rooms in the house.

The beneficial effects of life in the country were obvious in spite of the drawbacks. Judy Mason wrote in May that "they have chickens and rabbits, and everybody, including the staff are extremely happy . . . it is amazing what the country has done for the children—really Edna, they look quite different."

Throughout the war, children evacuated from London and other English cities to houses and camp schools in rural areas of England were enrolled as Foster Children. Many of these children and their mothers started to return to London during the spring and summer of 1944. As the scattered families were reunited, many of the Foster Children no longer required PLAN assistance and were dropped from PLAN's rolls. With the war in Europe drawing to a close, PLAN hoped to gradually reduce the numbers of Foster Children in England and to replace them with children on the continent. Plans were made for expansion into liberated Europe as soon as possible—supplies were collected, financial arrangements made, and correspondence begun with various agencies and governments. By October 1944 the frequent trips back and forth to London to arrange for this expansion became enough of a bother to justify the search for a new office with attached warehouse facilities in London. The search intensified with the recognition that, with the end of the war in sight, many firms would be rushing back to London and, with so many bombed buildings, space would be at a premium.

Throughout October Mrs. Mason considered renting a house rather than an office in London so that when Eastwick Manor had to be given up there would be a place for the children to stay. She realized that such a house would be almost impossible to find in London because of the great number of homeless families and the scarcity of undamaged houses.

She wrote of her dilemma to Edna Blue on 20 October 1944.

I do hate to think that we shall have an office without children. It does sometimes have its disadvantages, but the advantages are greater . . . You might think that to have an office without children is quite alright, but when one has been used to working with them, they will be missed.

New office space was found in December and PLAN moved into

the Wool Exchange Building in central London which would become the European Headquarters until the English program was phased out in 1957.

When Germany surrendered on 8 May 1945, the storerooms were piled high with crates of supplies destined for Europe, case histories were arriving from Belgium, France, and Italy, and the enrollment of Dutch children was expected to begin any day. PLAN had over a thousand Foster Children. In the four years PLAN had been in England, not one Foster Child had been killed or injured by the air raids and bombings.

The diminishing number of English Foster Children created doubts about the future of "The Grange," PLAN's farm colony, and Eastwick Manor, which were the only hostels leased and operated exclusively by PLAN. The lease for "The Grange" was to expire six months after the cessation of hostilities; the Eastwick Manor lease ended in October 1945. The problem was that, although children were now leaving these colonies and not being replaced, there was the strong possibility that European children would be sent to England for recuperation.

In September Mrs. Mason decided to consolidate the children in one house. She chose "The Lea," a large hospitable old house in Denham. Describing the house and her plans for it in a letter to Edna Blue she said:

> The more I see of the house the more I like it. It really is lovely and when the children are settled I will get Bish [Bishop Marshall, Honorary Publicity Secretary and Director] to take pictures of the house and children. It is a lovely very old rambling house and I can just imagine what it will look like when it is furnished and filled with children. We hope to have between 20 and 25 children there, so it will really be a lovely family . . . There is also a little cottage attached . . . Our gardner is hoping to get married so that he can live in it. His wife (to be) is a cook so it may be that we shall be able to take her into the staff.

The Lea was kept until 1957 and, with the other PLAN supported hostels, received children from Belgium, Czechoslovakia, France, and other liberated countries. Some of these children required surgery, others, psychological treatment. Many children who had grown up in German concentration camps received special help. The surgery that removed the tattooed numbers from their scrawny arms was a first step in the rehabilitation of these children. When the European children returned to their home countries, they returned as Foster Children and formed a nucleus for future PLAN growth.

Later came displaced persons and refugees. The last Foster Children in England were refugees from Poland and the Ukraine. Before they came to England they had suffered war and occupation first by the Germans, who took over western Poland, then by the Russians in eastern Poland. There were mass arrests and deportations. In western Poland young men and women were sent as forced labor to the factories and farms of Nazi Germany. The life expectancy of a slave laborer in Germany was about three months. The survivors were freed by the advancing allies.

In the east, they were sent by the Russians to the forests and mines of Northern Siberia and the Urals. The cold was brutal and shelter was primitive, often improvised by the deportees on arrival. Thousands died. Those who managed to survive were released in 1941 when Germany attacked Russia. A treaty between Poland and Russia allowed the deportees to travel southwards. Before the war ended they had drifted into Iran, the Middle East, India, Africa, and Italy.

International relief organizations arranged for new homes for these displaced persons. Many went to Great Britain where they were housed in camps established in disused army bases and air fields. The houses were mostly Nissen huts, partitioned to accommodate several families. If a member of the family could find work a nominal rent was charged. Those unable to work were supplied with food from communal kitchens and public assistance. A mother with three children received about US$2 a week, from this she had to purchase clothing, shoes, extra food, and personal necessities. These were the families helped by PLAN.

Stefania was a typical Polish Foster Child from the displaced persons camps. Her parents had lived in eastern Poland and had two children. When the Russian Army arrived they were sent to the mines of Siberia. Her mother was pregnant, the child was stillborn. Her seven year-old brother died. They were freed in the general amnesty of 1941 and walked south. They were evacuated through Iran to Uganda, where Stefania was born. When the war ended, the family was sent to England. Stefania's father's health, physical and mental, declined and he was admitted to a mental hospital shortly after their arrival.

From 1948 on, over 250,000 of these people arrived in England and many of the neediest of the children, like Stefania, were enrolled as Foster Children.

Frederick W. Mason, Judy Mason's husband and PLAN's Director of European Business until 1957, recalled some of the children as they had come to PLAN during and immediately following the war and as they appeared in 1957. The occasion was the closing of "The Lea" and everyone—former Foster Children, former staff from "The Lea," and the London Office—was invited to a reunion and farewell party.

All the Foster Children who ever lived at "The Lea" truly regarded it as their home, and returned to visit frequently after they had gone out into the world. Peter, once a child in a Nazi Concentration Camp, regarded "The Lea" as "home" to the extent that when he found a girl friend, he brought her to meet Leslie and Elsa Sharp, the wardens, and when he became engaged, he said that as "The Lea" was still his old home, he wanted to have his engagement party there.

It was almost something of a shock to see all the bright cheerful young people who congregated. The metamorphosis was so complete. How could these gay, healthy, well cared for, well poised young men and girls be even remotely connected with the sad, thin, mistrustful children who came to us when the concentration camps spewed forth their survivors in 1945.

There was Max, the half-Jewish German child who arrived at "The Lea," fresh from a concentration camp, and had somehow managed to secure two murderous sheath knives which he carried hidden under his jacket.

He refused to part with them; stood defiant and suspicious, staring up at us, a thin, undersized figure with vivid blue eyes. Max obviously believed that those knives were his only protection in a hostile world, for he had witnessed nothing but brutality during his short life.

Max was at the party, dancing the Rock and Roll with a pretty girl, once a Foster Child and now a nursing trainee. Max has not grown particularly tall, but he's sturdy and simply glowing with health. He looks like a sailor, but has in fact settled down to a steady job in the tailoring trade.

He is gay and jolly; is going to be a good man and a good citizen. Thinking of him as he was when snatched from the Nazis, and as he is now—well, that's PLAN progress. Perhaps the nicest thing of all, at that reunion of the pitiful, pathetic little bereaved war children we once knew, was to see Harry, standing there proud and beaming, with his wife and small chubby child. We felt that we had become grandparents, or in any case, that the PLAN had.

Harry was another half-Jewish child from a Nazi camp. He still has something of an accent. Although not yet 22, he is a good self-reliant, law-abiding member of the British community, supporting his young wife and a positively beautiful young son. Something has just cropped up in connection with Harry that we feel is too interesting to omit. He called us on the phone last Friday; he had heard from his brother, the brother he thought had been done to death in a camp in Germany. All these years he had thought of himself to be utterly without kith and kin and now, the wonder of it, he has a brother.

But the brother's letter comes from Jerusalem and is in German, the language Harry has forgotten. So we shall translate the letter for him.

The miracle comes about thus: Harry, in common with all the refugees who suffered loss in Germany, had filed his application in London for a share of the reparation now made available by the German Government. The lawyer dealing with Harry's case remembered his name when he saw a circulated tracer for relatives, in which the name was listed.

A few days ago, one of our oldest Foster Children came to see us. Although now approaching her 20th year, and safely ensconced in her chosen career of nursing, she has continued to receive support from a particularly devoted Foster Parent. We had to tell her that the time had come for her Foster Parent to transfer her material help to a young and needy child.

Of course she understood, and of course she knew that she and her Foster Parent would continue to correspond. Nevertheless, she felt the break—she had ceased to be a Foster Child.

She wept and said "I feel I am losing everything that I ever had." Indeed, since early in the war, she has in fact had no one but her Foster Parent.

In June 1957, after 17 years of service to children and their families from England and all over Europe, PLAN's program in Great Britain ended. Funds released by the closing of the program in England were to be used to establish programs in the Far East.

6

Europe: 1944-75[1]

By 1944 it was clear that the Allies would eventually win the war. PLAN staff in England and the United States realized that there would be a tremendous need for PLAN aid in Europe not only for the refugee Foster Children in England, who would be returning to their native countries, but also for children who had remained in their own countries throughout the war. These European children had not only suffered the neglect, persecution, and oppression of the Nazi occupation of their countries, but they were often helpless victims caught in the war's cross-fire. There were thousands of these young orphaned, destitute, maimed, or mutilated war victims who would find little support or comfort in the economic disarray of postwar Europe. Accordingly, plans were begun in the spring of 1944 to establish children's hostels in the liberated countries of Europe as soon as possible.

The first of these new hostels was established in a Catholic school in Malta. This was soon followed by the establishment of PLAN in Belgium, France, the Netherlands, and Italy. By 1949 PLAN was providing services to approximately 5,000 Foster Children and, in some cases, their families as well in Belgium, China, Czechoslovakia, England, France, Greece, Italy, Malta, the Netherlands, Poland, and Switzerland.

Malta and Italy: 1944-47

Father H.P. Bleach established a colony for Foster Children at St. Patrick's School in Sliema, Malta, in the spring of 1944. For more than

[1]The records pertaining to PLAN's work in Europe after World War II are extremely uneven. There are complete files for only Greece and Italy. There are fairly comprehensive publicity files, a few reports, and some correspondence but very little else for the other program countries. The London files, containing letters from Ivy Mason to PLAN Headquarters in New York through October 1945, refer to the establishment of PLAN in Belgium, the Netherlands, Italy, and Malta but are primarily concerned with PLAN matters in England.

two years the people of Malta had suffered almost daily bombardment. They had taken refuge in the island's natural rock shelters and caves. As more and more houses were destroyed, these caves became semi-permanent homes. The first 50 photographs and case histories of Maltese children arrived in London on 22 April 1944. Four days later more arrived. By September Father Bleach had enrolled 80 Maltese Foster Children, all of whose homes had been destroyed by bombs. Of these 80 children, only two had both parents living.

In October Father Bleach received authorization to enroll Italian and Yugoslavian children living in southern Italy. On 4 December 1944 he cabled Mrs. Mason that he had established four PLAN colonies in Rome, one in Catania, two for Yugoslavian children in southern Italy, and one in Naples.

Very little information exists relating to either these colonies or to Father Bleach's activities in Malta. What little documentation there is is secondary, contained in occasional references in letters from Ivy Mason to Edna Blue. He remained in Malta as PLAN Director for both Malta and Italy until 1947, when a Rev. P. McLoughlin took charge of the Maltese Foster Children. The program appears to have ended in 1947.

Italy: 1947-69

In May 1947, Fred Mason went to Italy to engage a PLAN Director, find office space, negotiate with the Italian authorities, and find Foster Children. After several weeks of frustration, Mr. Mason was able to obtain agreements from the government for a favorable U.S. dollar exchange rate and the promise of free office space from the Commissariat Maternita y Infanzia.

Mr. Mason hired Elma Baccanelli, an American of Italian extraction, to direct the new program. She was a tall, attractive, well-groomed young woman who had at one time served on the staff of New York's Mayor Fiorello LaGuardia. She was working as an Assistant Cultural Attache in the American Embassy in Rome when Fred Mason met her and convinced her to direct PLAN's Italian program. Miss Baccanelli moved into PLAN's palatial new office, located in what had been the headquarters of a Fascist youth organization, and went to work establishing a viable and long-lasting PLAN program in Italy. She married a well-known Italian journalist, Carlo Laurenzi, and continued to direct PLAN in Italy until March 1969, when operations in Italy were phased out. She died of cancer four months later on 11 July.

In June 1947, Mr. Mason visited the Orfanatrofio di San Michele, a home for mutilated children on the outskirts of Rome, and immediately started to enroll them. PLAN's early enrollment focused on these and other institutionalized children. The institution PLAN supported for mutilated children in Milan received considerable publicity when PLAN built a specially equipped operating room with a donation from Arturo Toscanini.

Edna Blue recounted her visit with these children in a 1949 report to Foster Parents.

> ROME: Today we visited some war blinded children, many of whom were also maimed . . . this colony has good relief maps for geography lessons . . . We called off the names of Italian cities, and like a flash the little arms (sometimes the little stumps) moved around the map until they found the city . . .
>
> We next visited the youngest blind. They gathered around us and nestled their heads close to our bodies . . . they were so quiet . . . There is one little boy, totally blind, with both arms missing above the elbows. The child has developed his stumps to almost the same sensitivity as his fingers would have had. And he uses his lips to read braille . . . He found his own desk, remember he has only stumps . . . so he goes very carefully . . . And so it is with most of the children, which is why it is so quiet . . . We asked him to read us a story, and as I stood over him and watched him reading with his lips I had to turn away.
>
> The blind children love to have their photos taken because several can distinguish the bright gleam of the flash bulbs . . . They love music . . . and we promised them harmonicas, drums, etc. Their faces lit up with joy . . . after all, to sing you don't need arms or legs, or sight . . .
>
> It seems that during the war many bad amputations were made . . . Some doctors were so rushed they just guillotined the limbs without leaving decent fleshy flaps . . . and the child must be operated on again to saw the bone . . .
>
> The zig-zag lines of children marching, the thumps of the wooden legs, the flying stumps of arms, and the fumblings of the blind ones . . . it is too grotesque a world to live in, and man has made it so . . .

There were thousands and thousands of mutilated, blind, and psychologically disturbed children in postwar Europe. In 1949 Edna Blue estimated that 37 percent of the 12,000 children under PLAN care needed artificial limbs, plastic surgery, or glass eyes.[2] This number did not include the children suffering from malnutrition or the 75 percent who had, or were suspected of having, tuberculosis. There were 15,000 mutilated children in Italy alone, and 7,000 in Belgium. Other governments had not yet released their national figures. With the continued fighting in Greece the number was increasing daily.

To better serve these children, the International Doctors' Committee for Foster Parents Plan for War Children was formed in February 1949. Members of the Committee included Dr. T. Twistington Higgins, OBE, FRCS, Senior Surgeon at the Hospital for Sick Children, London; Drs. Jean Benot and Paul Martin, plastic surgeons, both of Brussels; Dr. G.F.M. Bar, Director and Orthopedic Surgeon-in-Chief of St. Maartens Clinic, the Netherlands; Dr. Joseph May, Director of the Shanghai General Hospital, China; Dr. Egon Lewit from the Czechoslovakian Ministry of Social Welfare; Dr. Teresita Sandesky-Scelba from the Anti-tubercular Clinic in Rome; and Dr. Henry Kessler, Director of the Newark Home for Crippled Children, Newark, New Jersey.

In recognition of PLAN's work for the rehabilitation of Italy's mutilated children, Edna Blue, PLAN's International Chairman, received two awards in 1950. The first was the "Croce al Merito de Prima Classe del Sovrano Militare Ordine di Malta," presented by Prince Luigi Rangoni-Machiavelli. The second was the "Stella della Solidarieta," presented by the Italian Government.

PLAN continued to work with injured children until 1952. By then, crippled, maimed, and blind children were receiving regular pension payments from the Italian Government and PLAN aid was no longer necessary.

PLAN enrollment quickly spread from Rome to impoverished areas throughout Italy. The poverty was most severe in southern Italy, particularly in areas which had been the scenes of heavy fighting during the war. Fred Mason traveled through southern Italy in 1951 investigating new areas for PLAN expansion:

> The mere fact that PLAN help, extensive as it is, can take care of only a tiny fraction of so much really sickening misery, makes it imperative that we assist only the worst cases, which means that we have to be selective to a degree that would seem positively inhuman, to an untrained observer. In spite of my supposed conditioning to this sort of thing, my trip into

[2]This figure represents both Foster Children and nonsponsored children living in institutions receiving PLAN aid.

southern Italy brought back all too actively, the old familiar gnawing heartaches which leave me miserable and depressed at the end of a long day, during which I have had to bid adieu to so many people who are so obviously in every conceivable kind of want, . . . the doubly unfortunate children for whom, utterly destitute relatives are striving, scheming and stealing —yes—stealing, some of them—to keep the children alive, and when I say "keep them alive," I mean just that and no more.

The phrase "poor beyond belief" kept running through his head. He met a woman in Naples who had lost her husband, her house, and all her possessions in an air raid years before. After the bombing she had no place to go. There were no relatives to take her in and the few still habitable houses in the neighborhood were full to overflowing. A cave in the rocks at the edge of town offered the only available shelter. She and her fatherless children were still there in 1951. The children were dressed in rags; old cartons and cardboard kept some of the wind and rain out of the cave and provided a bit of privacy. She cooked her meals on a fire outside of the mouth of the cave. Often the only meal she could offer her children was a thin soup made from boiled dandelion greens and grass. Boulders stuck up from the uneven floor of the cave. The family's furniture, a bed and a table, were made from broken packing crates. She shared the cave with 64 other families.

When Mr. Mason said that he wanted to go to Cerignola, about 25 miles south of Foggia, he was told "you don't want to go there—they are all Communists." He went anyway, of course, and found a town of some 50,000 people. The only nonagricultural industry in town was a salami company employing six people. Although the land was rich enough, there was simply not enough work to go around. The streets were full of unemployed agricultural workers. There was unemployment compensation but in order to qualify for it a man had to have worked for six months. Few were so fortunate. Demobilized veterans did not qualify for unemployment benefits.

The story, told by Fred Mason, of one of many sick children, gives a graphic and poignant illustration of the region's poverty. A collection list was hung in the local Christian Democrat Center to raise money for the child's medicine. The need was for streptomycin and penicillin, both readily available and fairly inexpensive. The average donation was the equivalent of about three cents. There were already many names and many donations listed but the total was still far below the purchase price of the drugs. The drugs cost Lira 2,400—about US $3.80.

Mr. Mason went immediately to the drugstore, bought the medicine and gave it to the family. "This was not a case we could continue to help," he wrote, "the baby was not a war baby and had both parents to fend for it."

Conditions in Foggia were just as bad. Two devastating air raids had killed nearly a quarter of the population and destroyed whole sections of the city. With the wholesale destruction of the city, thousands of families had to find shelter wherever they could. The bomb-wrecked church of Santa Chiara became a home for many families who found shelter in the nooks and crannies of the ruin. Others moved into a battered convent—one family in each of the tiny dark cells. There was no water in the convent and no sanitation. A sewage cart stopped outside the convent every morning. The building had been condemned as unsafe for human habitation but the people stayed on. There was no place else to go.

PLAN was working all over Italy by 1960, helping needy children and their families regardless of the cause of their need. There were 3,450 Italian Foster Children receiving monthly cash grants and parcels of food and clothing from Foster Parents in the United States and Canada. PLAN cooperated with the various local branches of Italian governmental and private welfare organizations, such as the Italian Red Cross, the Italian National Organization for Child Welfare, the Pontifical Relief Agency, and ENAOLI (L'Ente Nazionale per l'Assistenzia agli Orfani dei Lavorati).

Generally, children under 12 were enrolled as Foster Children and remained eligible for PLAN aid until the age of 16. Exceptions were made if the 16 year-olds were attending high school or a vocational training school, in which case they continued as Foster Children until they finished their studies.

By the mid-1960s the Italian economy had improved considerably and more and more PLAN families were able to provide for themselves. As the families became self-supporting the children were dropped from PLAN rolls. Paralleling this economic improvement was the expansion of the Italian social welfare system. By 1966 nearly all of the Foster Children who were orphans and semi-orphans had begun to receive support from ENAOLI and no longer needed PLAN aid.

The combined effects of the improving economy and the growth of governmental social welfare programs allowed PLAN to gradually reduce the numbers of Italian Foster Children through attrition and, in March 1969, the program was ended.

France: 1944-64

In August 1944, details were formulated for the establishment of
PLAN in France by Bishop Marshall, PLAN's Honorary Publicity Secretary
and Director and an officer in the Free French Navy. Ivy Mason wrote of
these plans to Edna Blue on 4 August.

> The thing is, Edna, we are hoping that we really will be first in
> France. Bish's chief is more than interested and will work
> with us right through until we really attain something . . . The
> best thing for the moment is that immediately it is possible,
> Bish gets into France. The Medical Unit will of course have to
> be in at an early date and if we can get in at the same time it
> will be wonderful. Bish would have plenty of lady helpers,
> too, and then we could get our own staff . . . Bish has
> promised his chief something definite by Monday if at all
> possible . . .
>
> This is the thing we have been waiting for and I feel that it
> is going to be something good. We thought it best to start
> with 50 children and then increase the number . . . it, of
> course, depends upon the size of the house we are able to
> obtain.

The plan called for Mr. Marshall to get a three-month leave from
the Free French Navy and go into France with the Medical Unit. Once
there, he would take photographs, collect case histories, and look for
suitable quarters for a PLAN hostel.

In the first week of September 1944, Judy Mason started to
stockpile supplies and to make arrangements for the transfer of funds
from England to France. That same month the American Red Cross
agreed to provide and deliver in France all the clothing PLAN would
need to establish its first colony. This solved at least some of the supply
problems. There remained the difficulty of obtaining a license to
purchase large quantities of such "couponed" goods as towels and
linen.

By mid-September PLAN had stockpiled supplies of blankets,
pillows, and dishes for the French colony, had met several times with
the Council of British Societies for Relief Abroad to get rationed items,
and had opened a section of the PLAN accounts for "Liberation Colony,"
the proposed name of the first French colony.

Bishop Marshall left for France with a camera and a supply of case
history forms on 10 October 1944. He planned to stay for only a week
to collect histories. His one-week trip stretched out to three and on

28 October he wrote that he had enrolled 25 children he found living in one house. The location of the house is unknown but it was apparently in a poor rural district of northern France. The house had neither electricity nor sanitation. For warmth there was one blanket to share among the sick and undernourished children. Mr. Marshall left blankets and money to the Abbe Noe, who had been looking after the children, and wrote to Mrs. Mason asking for candles, lamps, a stove for heating, and food supplies. Early in November he was back in England packing a PLAN ambulance with scrub brushes, toys, clothes, kitchen supplies, and chamber pots for the children in France.

The children he had enrolled were moved to the Château Bois, renamed the "Liberation Colony," in Calvados. The château was a large country house on a hilltop six miles from Deauville with a view of the sea. The woods behind the house would provide ample firewood for the approaching winter. The electricity, they were assured, would soon be turned on and the plumbing for the six bathrooms soon repaired. Abbe Noe and the local mayor were responsible for looking after the house and children. The first French case histories were sent from England to New York on 22 November 1944, and PLAN was established in France. Other colonies were quickly established in Brittany and elsewhere in France.

A number of problems arose in connection with the Liberation Colony which had far-reaching effects on the future direction of PLAN services throughout Europe and Asia. The first problems had to do with the building itself. There were major differences of opinion with the wife of the owner over the extent, cost, and responsibility for the repair and maintenance of the building. Transportation of supplies to Calvados was difficult, and there was a lack of trained personnel.

On 29 May 1945, Judy Mason detailed these problems and suggested a solution in a letter to Edna Blue:

> I have come to the conclusion that it will be best to do away with Liberation Colony altogether. For one thing if we did get the staff here and send them over—by the time we got the people over, all their visas and exit permits ready—passports, etc., and then get the children into the colony practically six months of our one year [lease] will have passed . . . it just isn't worth it . . . I feel Edna that there are so many mix-ups there and so many things which I don't understand . . . that it will never be any different. The transport difficulties too are being tightened very considerably and I think for a few months at least it will be better for us to get as many children

as we can living in orphanages and homes—until the country and everything else is settled.

. It has taken me a long time, Edna, to come to this decision and I have been terribly worried about it.

The decision to emphasize the enrollment of children living in independent institutions enabled PLAN to quickly increase the number of children receiving aid and at the same time forestall a parallel rise in staffing and administrative costs. This general policy of enrolling institutionalized children rather than establishing PLAN institutions continued throughout the postwar period.

Although institutionalized children rarely totalled more than 50 percent of the enrollment at any one time, these children had a great effect on the type of aid provided by PLAN. Children in institutions for the blind, maimed, crippled, or orphaned had very different needs than children living at home. PLAN supplied prosthetic devices for otherwise almost immobile children, cosmetic surgery for children so horribly maimed they were ashamed to go outside, and glass eyes for the blind. Braille instruction, rehabilitation, and vocational training prepared these children for productive employment.

Clearly, it would have been unconscionable to single out particular children in an orphanage to receive the benefits of adoption by a Foster Parent. To give one child clothes, food, and the emotional benefits of sponsorship while ignoring another equally needy child was unthinkable, so all the children benefited in PLAN-supported institutions.[3]

The major drawback to the subsidization of these institutions was the unevenness of care. Some institutions were very good and provided excellent care while others were only slightly better than nothing. Administrative and accounting competence varied widely from one institution to another as did the ability and integrity of the supervisors. There were numerous cases of minor mismanagement and occasional instances of outright fraud by the directors of the institutions. Others had the best of intentions but lacked the necessary skills, facilities, or money to provide adequate care. Much of the work of PLAN staff with institutionalized children consisted of the distribution of gift parcels and monitoring the performance of administrators.

[3]Years later PLAN would apply this same principle to children and their siblings living with their families and to all families within some communities. This practice eliminated the resentment and dissension that a have/have not situation can create within a small community.

This style of social work, or, more accurately, personalized welfare work, was an element of PLAN care for the duration of PLAN's stay in Europe. Throughout the early and mid-1950s, PLAN's institutional enrollment declined. By 1956 less than 20 percent of the Foster Children were institutionalized. The few remaining hostels in Belgium and England were geared more to short-term stays for rehabilitation and recuperation than for long-term residential care. The Hampstead Nurseries, under the direction of Anna Freud, served only a limited number of Foster Children needing psychiatric care. With these exceptions, by 1956, PLAN's European programs were geared to the development of the child in the family.

Lucette F. Fourquard succeeded Bishop Marshall, in 1946, as the Director of PLAN in France and led the program until her death in 1963. Miss Fourquard had been a teacher, army nurse, active member of the resistance, and a social worker for UNRRA in Germany. During the war she was decorated for bravery and, after the war, inducted into the Legion of Honor. Under her direction PLAN aid helped, first, war victims and then children from displaced persons camps.

By 1963 France was well able to provide social services to the needy and the PLAN program was phased out shortly after the death of Miss Fourquard.

Belgium: 1945-61

Preliminary planning for work in Belgium began with meetings between Judy Mason and Madeline Bogaert in the spring of 1944 and continued through that summer and fall. Madeline Bogaert, known to PLAN staff and children alike as "Mamy," was a Belgian nurse who had rescued a group of Belgian children and escaped with them to England during the evacuation from Dunkirk in 1940. Throughout the war she directed and supervised PLAN's Westfield Colony for these and other Belgian and Dutch children.

Initial plans called for Mamy to go to Belgium as soon as possible to establish a colony for 50 Foster Children. At the time they thought Belgium would quickly be liberated and plans were made for the speedy return of Belgian Foster Children living in England.

On 14 September 1944, Ivy Mason wrote to Edna Blue that Maurice, one of Mamy's Belgian children, was excited at the prospect of going home and, like the other Belgian Foster Children, was busily making plans and preparations for the trip. Mamy was to make a two-week trip to find quarters for the proposed hostel, collect case histories and photographs, then return to England for the children.

Meetings were held with various Belgian officials, letters were exchanged with the Belgian Government, the weeks and months dragged on, and still Mamy could not get to Belgium. By February 1945, it seemed definite that Mamy would soon be in Belgium. Her husband, who had been in Belgium throughout the war, was to find suitable children for her to enroll when she arrived.

Mamy finally left in April and found Belgium in a terrible state. There were thousands of stray and fatherless children and shortages of food, clothing, soap, medical supplies, and housing. She was back in England on 20 April with completed case histories and promptly received authorization for the enrollment of 100 Belgian Foster Children. The plan called for the establishment of a first hostel for 50 children and the enrollment of 50 children living with parents or relatives.

As was the case in France, supplies of all kinds were so scarce that they would have to be shipped from England and the United States. To overcome some of the inherent difficulties in shipping, Mamy was to take as many supplies with her when she returned as she could and to concentrate on the enrollment of children living at home.

The Belgian Minister of Health had promised in May to do all he could to help PLAN get established but still there were delays. Finally, in July 1945, Mamy and the children were in Brussels and PLAN was firmly established in Belgium.

In December PLAN outgrew the house in Brussels and established the West Heath Colony in a large, dark, dreary-looking château outside Brussels in Tourneppe. The lease described the building as an "old property occupied throughout the war by the armies and bearing evidence of their stay." In addition to the armies, the property had held 1,800 Russian prisoners of war and, after liberation, had housed SS and German military prisoners.

The château was soon filled with destitute and orphaned children. As time went on and the Belgian economy improved, there was less need for PLAN to help Belgian children but an increasing need to provide for the children of stateless and displaced persons. This need, too, was mitigated as these people emigrated, returned to their home countries, or were absorbed by the improving Belgian economy.

Through the years the condition of the building, never very good, had deteriorated and the number of resident Foster Children had fallen to 96. Newer and smaller quarters were found and in 1955 the West

Heath Colony was closed. The new house was known as "La Pommeraie" and became one of the most publicized of the PLAN institutions. It was a wonderful house with adjoining cottages, surrounded by beautiful old apple trees, large gardens, and land enough for the children and a flock of sheep. The building itself was modern, well appointed, and overlooked the lake at Genval.

A school was established in the colony with the Ministry of Education meeting the cost of converting some of the out-buildings for use as classrooms. The Belgian Government also subsidized teachers' salaries and the cost of school supplies.

The colony soon became the site of a health program for Foster Children from all over Europe. Among the European Foster Children were some whose health was especially precarious, some suffered from malnutrition, others from severe anemia. Many were suspected of being predisposed to tuberculosis. After much discussion it was decided that La Pommeraie was the ideal place for the special care of these children. At first it was a small scale experiment with five children from each PLAN country staying at La Pommeraie for periods of up to three months and, if necessary, longer. The experiment was a success and La Pommeraie was renamed the "International Colony."

The children were in the care of Mamy Bogaert, who lived in the house with her mother and husband. Many of the children who came to the International Colony had never before slept in a real bed or had an adequate meal. One child, from a Displaced Persons Camp in Germany, wrote ecstatically that they ate four times a day. Francois, a six year-old from a camp in France, doubled his weight. Savas, a rundown 14 year-old Greek child predisposed to TB, gained 22 pounds before he returned to his home in a Salonica barracks for war refugees.

Elma Laurenzi, PLAN Director in Italy, wrote to Mamy,

> How can we ever thank you for the miracles you are performing with our children? They were almost unrecognizable on their return. Physically, they are so well developed, but more than that they seem so much more 'civil.' The girls all love you and want to go back to 'Mamy' . . . you may be interested in knowing that the Carchitti children who returned from Belgium plan to build themselves a 'shower' in Carchitti. They have told us they will get some cans, make holes in them, throw pails of water in . . . so they can have their 'douche' in Carchitti, too. I hope you will take time out when you come to Rome to visit Carchitti . . . so you can see the girls. They simply adore you.

Under Mamy Bogaert's care, thousands of the children who came to La Pommeraie were restored to health. She remained PLAN's Director in Belgium until the economy of Belgium had improved to the degree that PLAN aid was no longer needed. In September 1961, La Pommeraie was closed and PLAN's Belgian program ended.

The Netherlands: 1945-57

PLAN's first Dutch Foster Children were enrolled in England in the summer and fall of 1945. During the last months of the war the Dutch Government-in-exile made plans for undernourished Dutch children to spend from three to six months in Belgium, Denmark, England, and Sweden recuperating from the deprivations of war. The Reception Committee for Young People from Occupied Countries was to coordinate the program in England. Mr. Rudolf Eldering, who was to become PLAN's Director in the Netherlands, was the liaison between the Ministry of Social Affairs and the Reception Committee.

The first children arrived from the southern areas of the Netherlands in April 1945 and from the rest of the country after the 8 May 1945 surrender of Germany. For the first three months the children stayed in the camps in the Midlands formerly occupied by children evacuated from London. After this period of adjustment and English lessons they were placed with English families.

Judy Mason contacted the Reception Committee and through them enrolled 700 children from Amsterdam. After their six months of recuperation in England, the children returned, as Foster Children, to Amsterdam where Mr. Eldering took charge of them as PLAN's Director in the Netherlands.

PLAN was established in Amsterdam in 1946 when PLAN moved into a rent-free office in the government-owned Red Cross Headquarters building. The city of Amsterdam provided warehouse space for PLAN until 1957.

Because so many war relief agencies were working in Amsterdam, the Dutch government asked PLAN to enroll children from the countryside where the fighting had been heaviest. This was done and the original Dutch Foster Children were gradually replaced by children referred to PLAN by the District Officers for War Victims and, in Arnhem and Nijmegen, the Union of Women Volunteers.

In the Netherlands, as in Italy, the most dramatic work done by PLAN was with children who had been maimed or mutilated during the war. Hein, a Dutch Foster Child, had been so burned by phosphorus that he could not close his eyes. One hand was so disfigured by burns that he was ashamed of it and kept it hidden.

Europe was full of such disfigured children. Edna Blue described a visit to one of the many maimed Dutch children in a 1948 report.

> We met Eldering and Dickey, the young lady who is our own social service worker . . . in Roermond . . . the little boy who lost both legs, for whom we were carrying crutches, lives in Roermond. It was just a short drive to Franz' father's farm. They were expecting us. Always when you are going to visit these children, you try to steel yourself and hope you will say the very right thing. We pulled up in front of the little house and saw . . . it was partly boarded due to damage.
>
> Franz came out to meet us. He is quite a small boy for 11 years of age, blond with twinkling blue eyes. No wonder his eyes twinkled, he was wearing his new artificial limbs and managing without crutches!
>
> We were invited inside. This family once owned a nice little farm and did quite well. Now there were land mines buried in the ground. That is how Franz lost his legs . . . Franz came out to the car with us. He steadied himself for a moment, and waved with both his cane and his hand . . .

PLAN support and the generous cash gifts from American and Canadian Foster Parents enabled many of these maimed children to receive orthopedic and cosmetic surgery in Amsterdam and at the St. Maarten's Clinic in Nijmegen. The Director of St. Maarten's Clinic, Dr. G.F.M. Bar, was appointed to PLAN's International Doctor's Committee and was invited to America by Edna Blue to visit the Mayo Clinic in Rochester, Minnesota, and to address American and Canadian Foster Parents.

Under the direction of Mr. Eldering, PLAN provided cash gifts, goods in kind, and educational support for victims of the war until 1953. After the disastrous floods of 1 February 1953, children whose parents had drowned were enrolled and placed in Dutch families.

Mr. Eldering remained Director in the Netherlands until 1957 when the recovering economy allowed PLAN to phase out its program and Mr. Eldering to return to academe. When Foster Parents Plan of the Netherlands was established in 1975, Mr. Eldering became one of the first members of its Board of Directors and served until his death in November 1983.

Greece: 1949-75

One of the first cables Frederick Mason sent from Greece in 1949 described the conditions he found there:

CHILDREN ARE DYING HERE IN HUNDREDS FROM EXPO-SURE AND PRIVATION STOP BEG YOU MAKE PEOPLE UNDER-STAND AND HELP STOP THOUSANDS WITHOUT SHELTER TRAGICALLY ORPHANED WITHOUT FOOD OR CLOTHING STOP PLEASE SHIP WARM CLOTHING IMMEDIATELY DELAY MEANS DEATH

When Mr. Mason arrived, Greece was suffering the double sorrow of the effects of World War II and an ongoing civil war. PLAN was officially established in Greece in March 1949, when Mr. Mason signed an agreement with the Greek Ministers of Coordination, Finance, and Social Welfare. The agreement called for PLAN to "provide aid and succour to indigent victims of war." The aid was to be "directed to children orphaned or severely disabled or deprived partly or entirely of family care or crippled by reason of the war or as a result of the continuing guerilla warfare in Greece." The selection of Foster Children was to be "at the free and absolute judgement of the Foster Parents Plan without political, religious, or racial discrimination."

Katherine Clark, an American journalist working for the London *News Chronicle* in Athens, was appointed PLAN's first Director in Greece and enrollment began.

Eleven year-old Barbara Nikoli, an orphan from Piraeus, was the first child enrolled. Her father died of starvation in 1941, her mother, of tuberculosis in 1948. Barbara lost her right eye and some use of her left eye, and had facial scars as the result of the blast from a mortar shell. The child had been taken into the already overcrowded one-room hut of a neighbor. All of them were on the verge of starvation. The publicity resulting from her sponsorship by Tallulah Bankhead brought a quick response and Greek enrollment grew.

In 1950 there was peace in Greece for the first time since 1939. The civil war was officially over and fighting was limited to occasional skirmishes with the disorganized remnants of the rebel forces in the north. Food was plentiful in the restaurants of Athens and there was the appearance, at least, of relative prosperity. But the appearance was deceptive. The worst of the poverty was in the isolated villages in northern Greece and on Greek Islands.

There were enormous numbers of orphans and semi-orphans, particularly in northern Greece where the fighting in the civil war had been most severe. The numbers reflected the need: 270,000 children had lost one parent; 36,000 had lost both. There were also large numbers of abandoned and mutilated children. In 1950 PLAN was often the only source of aid available to these children for there were no state institutions for the handicapped.

An estimated 750,000 refugees lived under terrible conditions in northern Greece. One refugee center in Salonica was little more than the skeleton of a building. The walls and stairs were unfinished red brick. There was garbage on every landing. Each of the four floors had three makeshift toilets. Twelve toilets for 12,000 people. There was no running water.

As Edna Blue walked through the room in 1950 a crying woman thrust her baby forward, begging for something to be done. The baby suffered from trachoma, its eyes were covered with large sores. Nothing could be done, the child was already blind. Kathy Clark said to Edna Blue as they were leaving,"I hate to say this, but the tobacco warehouse is a nightmare compared to this."

And so it was. The warehouse was a big two-story building with cracked wooden floors and rickety wooden stairs. The almost over-whelming smell of tobacco mingled with the combined stench of overcrowded people, excrement, garbage, filth, and disease. The floors had been divided into makeshift rooms with pieces of rag, burlap sacks, flour bags, old rugs, and scraps of canvas tied together with bits of cord and strung on ropes to give some illusion of privacy. These "curtains" were about six feet high. All had gaping holes in them. Some of the refugees had been living there for as long as four years.

Each "room" accommodated a family—old men, children, women, all together. There were few young men, most had been killed in fighting. The families cooked, ate, slept, and sat around on the floor in their compartments. Some had old boxes and packing crates for furniture. A few boxes put together made a bed. Others had no furniture at all. Each compartment had some sort of a makeshift stove, often nothing more than an open tin for burning kerosene.

These people had once lived in villages. Now that the civil war was over plans were being made for their return. One woman cried when she heard that she might be sent back to her village. "Return to what?" she cried, "The house is gone and here at least I have a roof over my head. I can't dig a hole in the ground in which to live, I have not the strength . . . "

Conditions in some of the villages were sometimes slightly better, but the poverty was as severe. The village of Bogiati, just outside Athens, was picturesque but nearly destitute. The 26 families of Bogiati lived in thatched huts. The women, dressed in traditional costumes, walked around spinning yarn or sat in front of their grass houses spinning. The whole village looked like the setting for an operetta. The families consisted of women, children, and old men. The husbands and fathers had all been killed in the civil war. The grass huts were tiny, their walls and roofs infested with rats, mice, and insects. At night what little furniture they had was pushed against the walls and bedding unrolled on the floor. Meals were cooked outside over wood fires. Little piles of bricks or stones served as fireplaces.

Most of the children went to school and appeared to be in relatively good health. Although there was no running water, electicity, or any sort of sanitation facilities, the villagers seemed to manage fairly well. Compared to the people in the tobacco warehouse these people were enjoying a relatively high standard of living, but it was essentially a high medieval standard of living.

Eight years later, in 1958, conditions had improved slightly. Enrollment still emphasized war children, though PLAN's charter allowed the enrollment of any needy child. It was felt that it would not be practical to extend aid to all needy children. There were simply too many of them. Almost 40 percent of the population was indigent by Greek standards. The 1958 standard was a daily income of less than US $0.24—enough to buy bread for three children for one day. In the light of such overwhelming need, PLAN limited enrollment to fatherless children or the children of incapacitated fathers. Even in these narrow categories there were more children than PLAN could possibly assist.

From its establishment in 1949, PLAN helped destitute children and their families scattered throughout the Greek mainland and in isolated villages on remote islands. The Athens headquarters consisted of an administrative staff of about 30 people and a large warehouse for the storage of gift parcels, clothing, and household items. Under the terms of its agreement with the Greek Government, PLAN carried out its programs through 63 government-run social welfare centers scattered throughout the mainland and the islands. Greek civil servants who worked in these centers did PLAN work in addition to their regular duties. The preparation of case histories, cash grant payments, distribution of gift parcels of food and clothing, and all Foster Child-Donor related activities were carried out by these civil servants. Since most of the Greek Foster Children lived in remote villages, often accessible only by foot or donkey, PLAN's services were largely limited to cash payments, educational support, and gift parcels. The Greek civil servants rarely had either the skills or the time to implement comprehensive social work and development programs.

Every month the accounting staff in the Athens headquarters had to prepare 63 separate bank transfers to fund the cash grant and cash gift payments made by the social welfare centers. The warehouse staff prepared 63 separate shipments of clothing, gift parcels, and other items for distribution. The procedures for operating and controlling PLAN's program in Greece were elaborate and complicated but functioned well because of the dedication of the staff, many of whom had worked for PLAN since 1949.

PLAN in Greece became more and more of an anachronism as increasingly sophisticated programs were implemented in other countries served by PLAN. In 1967 Keith R. Turner, who had established PLAN's program in Colombia, was appointed Director in Greece with the specific charge of investigating the possibility of concentrating PLAN services in one or two areas so that more effective programs could be initiated. Because of the nature of poverty in Greece, this proved to be impossible. There were simply not enough needy children in any single area for such programming to be effective.

By the early 1970s the Greek economy and social welfare systems had improved to the point where PLAN could consider phasing out. Poverty still existed, as it always had, in scattered isolated areas but the overall national conditions had improved significantly. The average yearly per capita income was equivalent to US $1,000 a year, there was no longer chronic severe unemployment, and the population growth had stabilized. By 1973 both PLAN and the Ministry of Social Welfare felt that the Greek Government could provide sufficient welfare and social services to those in need. PLAN program termination was scheduled for 1975.

Mr. Turner described the phaseout process in a 1981 recollection of his career with PLAN:

> This was done by a process of attrition. As Foster Children were cancelled, for whatever reasons, they were not replaced . . . Later on in the phaseout program a fixed monthly quota of cancellations was begun and it is assuredly one of the unhappiest tasks a PLAN Field Director can have, both because

of its effects on our client-families and because PLAN's staff know that the end of their service is not in the distant future . . . During those years of phaseout PLAN's program in Greece was not in the mainstream of new developments. The purchase program of clothing and household items for PLAN Families was eliminated first and the warehouse closed . . . There remained in the end only cash grant and cash gift payments with additional sums of money given to each Foster Child in lieu of the goods received under the old purchase program. We did not participate in the new ideas of preventive rather than curative medical programs. We could only read with interest the exciting reports about the developing projects in Material Aid and Service in the areas of health, education and community development which were taking place in other PLAN program countries.

The sensitivity of the Popodopolus regime to Greece's image abroad provided a further impetus to PLAN's phaseout. The government did not want pictures of needy Greek children used in PLAN publicity and in 1969 banned any mention of Greece in PLAN promotional material.

The phaseout was completed in 1975 and the Greek program ended. In its more than 25 years in Greece PLAN helped over 17,000 children. PLAN support was instrumental in the rehabilitation and education of 14,529 children and 82.9 percent of the children left PLAN rolls because of improved living conditions. Approximately 7 percent of the children were enrolled for between 10 and 17 years; 44 percent between five and 10 years; and 49 percent between one and five years.

Austria: 1956-59

When PLAN first started in Europe after the war, enrollment was restricted to children suffering directly as a result of the war. They were destitute orphans or semi-orphans; children whose fathers or mothers had been killed or incapacitated in the war; children of deportees or concentration camp survivors; maimed, crippled, or sick children; and children in displaced persons camps. As time passed, the number of these "war children" decreased but poverty remained. It became increasingly difficult to enroll "war children" while ignoring other children who were equally destitute.

This conflict was resolved on 3 January 1956 when the PLAN Board of Directors voted unanimously to drop "War Children" from

PLAN's name and to amend the corporate charter to allow for the enrollment of any needy or suffering child anywhere outside of the United States. On 4 April 1956 the amended Certificate of Incorporation was filed in New York and Foster Parents Plan for War Children, Inc. became Foster Parents Plan, Inc. Enrollment was now open to "children orphaned and/or distressed as the result of war, disaster, economic poverty, or any other condition which inflicts upon or causes suffering, misery, or distress to children."

Among the first groups of children to benefit from the expanded enrollment criteria were the Hungarian refugees fleeing to Austria to escape the violence of the Hungarian Revolt of 1956. Frederick Mason, PLAN's European Business Director, received instructions on 5 November 1956 to go to Vienna and arrange for 100 unaccompanied Hungarian refugee children to be sent to PLAN's International Colony in Belgium. The following Sunday (11 November) at 10 a.m. he cabled that there were not 100 unaccompanied children to be found and suggested instead that he enroll all of the children—about 100—in a refugee camp for Hungarians in Austria near the Hungarian border. At 2:15 p.m. that same Sunday, after a quick poll of the Board, PLAN Secretary Tom O'Hagen cabled PLAN's approval for the enrollment.

A *New York Times* article (15 November 1956) gives a cheerful sidelight to the otherwise unhappy story of these refugees:

HUNGARIAN BABIES GET DIAPERS AND PINS IN SWIFT REPLY HERE TO EMERGENCY APPEAL

All kinds of vital supplies have been rushed in volume by a number of American agencies to Hungarian refugees, Foster Parents Plan, Inc., disclosed here yesterday, but a curious oversight brought a cablegram to the organization's headquarters last Saturday.

It said: "Please airship 1,000 diapers sorely needed Hungarian refugee babies. Need towels, sheets, but diaper situation critical."

By the time the cable was in the hands of Mrs. Lenore Sorin, associate director, it was too late in the day to reach department stores. She searched the classified telephone directory, got a diaper service, and the man at the other end said he would send 1,000 breechcloths over immediately, and did.

Pan American Airways does not ordinarily pack freight in passenger ships, but because of the emergency it yielded free space for the diapers. It promised the cargo would be on its way from New York International Airport at Idlewild, Queens, at 3:30 P.M. Monday.

The Foster Parents Plan women, pleased at such cooperation, were congratulating themselves on the speed with which
they were meeting an emergency when one of them sat
suddenly bolt upright. She said: "My Heavens, what good will
that shipment do without safety pins?"

Mrs. Sorin grabbed the classified directory again. Under
"Pins – Common, Safety," she chose a dealer at random. She
swiftly outlined the Plan's dilemma. The dealer said: "I'll rush
thirty-five hundred baby pins right over to the airport." He
did, and they were aboard just before trans-Atlantic take-off.

Yesterday a comforting cable came from Vienna. It said:
"PLAN has undertaken complete support all Hungarian children in refugee camp Feffernitz nearest sizable town Villach
in Province of Kaernten. Presently eight children but more
expected. Refugees there only four days so still unrecorded.
Will be several days before possible start taking histories in
camp which nine hours from Vienna. Miserable wooden huts
at mountain foot. Already snowing. Refugees lost everything.
Women seem saddest."

The lines at the end of the message warmed the women
most. It said: "Hungarian baby refugees comfy tomorrow.
Diapers arrived this afternoon. Thanks remembering safety
pins and gratitude prompt gift."

A 16 November 1956 report from Mr. Mason gives additional
information on the choice of Camp Feffernitz:

... I finally became convinced that I was chasing a myth as far
as the unaccompanied children were concerned, and it was
obvious that if the Plan was going to be able to make any
claim at all to participating in the help to Hungarian Children,
something had to be done quickly. . .

In the circumstances, I had to think of something that
would not only take the place of our hundred-children
project, but also lift us with some distinction out of the crowd
of agencies rushing about distributing much needed but at
random relief.

The idea the Plan might . . . adopt an entire camp seemed
attractive, but likely to be difficult, if not impossible, to
achieve . . . The problem was to find a Hungarian refugee
camp which had not been penetrated by other organizations,
and the obvious thing was to look for one far distant from
Vienna. The one at Feffernitz, sixty kilometers beyond Klagen-
furt, seemed likely, but I knew I had to get there quickly.

At the camp I had the usual meeting with the Commandant,
made quite sure that he knew precisely what I was about, and
particularly that PLAN exclusively would be sponsoring the
children, and then went on a partial tour of the somewhat

extensive camp with the photographer and camp officials . . .

There is a central kitchen on the camp, and the families go to collect their food in a wide variety of pots and utensils issued to them. This was at midday, and they were eating what seemed to be some kind of shredded cabbage soup. In the Commandant's office, I saw the menu for the week, and it was good enough to make one realize that as one stands there inquiring how many blankets these people have, what sort of clothes they have been given, what kind of food is being dished out to them, and for which they must necessarily be grateful, the awful thought is that just three or four days before, all these families had been sturdy, self supporting, individual groups, with their own home and hearth, and now, because they preferred freedom to tyranny, they were utterly without possessions, were herded together with nothing to do but stand and wait until someone gave them another meal, or another pair of cast-off pants . . .

At this point, I think I should mention the unstable conditions which obtain, and discuss how far that instability affects any potential PLAN program in Austria. The preceding paragraphs appear to assume that PLAN is already committed to embark on an extension of its work to Austria . . . I just had to assume . . . that such an extension was a distinct possibility . . .

Owing to the fluid quality of the situation, I realize how difficult it will be for the Committee to reach any decision on whether or not we are now going to extend our work to Austria as a permanent factor.

As I see it, confining ourselves to this one camp could produce a very streamlined kind of arrangement, resulting in practically no additional overhead territorial expenses; just a few social service expenses in the camp, and the addition of one extra clerk in the Munich office, plus, of course, the additional translation costs . . .

There is a good deal more to be told; of my trip to the border, and of the refugees that I saw there; of how I proposed to tackle the job of making out the case histories at the camp, and my arrangements with Elizabeth[4] for her and a member of her staff to come out here.

However, what I have already written completes one phase of my trip, and I feel that this report is already long enough.

PLAN worked with these Hungarian refugees until 1959. Programs included the establishment of a sewing room, a nursery school, and the subsidy of a day care center, in addition to the provision of relief aid to children and adults living in Camp Feffernitz.

[4]Elizabeth Whitmore, PLAN Director in the Federal Republic of Germany.

The Federal Republic of Germany: 1952-61

In 1952 the Bavarian Government accepted the offer from PLAN to assist children living in displaced persons camps. Elizabeth Whitmore, Director of the program, and her staff were provided with office space in the Rathaus of Munich. Within a few years the West German program was providing aid and services to children and their families in over 90 camps scattered through Germany from Lubeck in the north, to the Black Forest in the south. Thousands of children of 18 different nationalities were enrolled as Foster Children of American and Canadian sponsors.

The program was phased out as the children and families emigrated or were absorbed into the expanding West German economy.

Poland: 1947-49

The documentation for PLAN's program of aid for needy children in Poland is almost totally lacking. The first Field Director of PLAN in Poland was a woman known now only as Sophie. By 1948 she had been replaced by Andrew Zoltowski, a former Polish count who, in Edna Blue's words, was "madly in love with Sophie."

PLAN remained in Poland until December 1949. Edna Blue's December 1949 letter to Foster Parents for Polish Children gives the few details known about the termination:

> It is with regret that we must inform you that because of recent actions on the part of the Polish Government, the Foster Parents' Plan for War Children will no longer be permitted to operate in Poland. When I visited Poland in 1947 I was informed that the Government in that country did not wholly approve of our kind of relief work. The Ministry of Social Welfare told me that they would much prefer having us send large quantities of goods to Poland to be distributed by them. The same thing took place in 1948, but the words were fewer and stronger. I explained many times by word of mouth and also by letter that friendship with the Polish children was part and parcel of our work and that Foster Parents' Plan for War Children had been built and organized, and could function only around the principle of a personal relationship between Foster Parent and Child.
>
> There is no question about it . . . every single child we have been helping in Poland needs help . . . most of them need it desperately. When I was in Poland, I spoke not only with the children, but with mothers, grandmothers and

teachers. The loss of this American link, I can tell you, will be heartbreaking to them. I cannot permit myself to think of the armless and legless children to whom we promised limbs. Many have already received them, but hundreds are still waiting. It is not easy for us to close the door on the Polish children . . . the choice was not ours. We gave them love and friendship with no thought of politics . . . we feel sure they must know that we have not failed them.

Czechoslovakia: 1947-50

PLAN began enrolling Czechoslovakian children in late 1947. In Czechoslovakia, as in the other PLAN countries of Europe, the Foster Children were the orphans, semi-orphans, and strays of war. Very few records survive to document PLAN's activities in Czechoslovakia. The Director was an American social worker named Lawrence G. Aplin. His assistant, Miss Aplinova, was a Czech citizen.

The Ministry of Social Welfare provided for many of the neediest children and PLAN concentrated on the children who were outside of the Ministry's aid categories. These were primarily children who had lost one or both parents in the underground. Conditions were generally better in Czechoslovakia than in Poland but there were still serious shortages of food (particularly milk) and clothing.

Edna Blue visited Prague in February 1948. While she was there the Ministry of Social Welfare convened a special meeting to familiarize her with the problems and needs of the Czech children. Attending the meeting were Dr. K. Slapak, Chief of the Tracing Department for Lost Children; Maria Uurplova, Superintendent of the Department of Handicapped Children; and Dr. L. Pivec, Cabinet Chief of the Ministry of Social Welfare.

Through Dr. Slapak, a tall, thin, sharp-eyed man, she learned of the Lebesborn program, perhaps the most squalid and cynical of the Nazi enterprises. Dr. Slapak's Department was trying to locate the Lebesborn children who had been kidnapped from Czechoslovakia and sent to Germany. Once in Germany they were to be raised by approved adoptive parents. Apparently these children would acquire the "racial purity" of their adoptive parents and grow up to be proper Aryans. About 10,000 children were known to have been kidnapped. Others had been sent to Germany from concentration camps. The most famous of these children were from Lidice, the town destroyed by the Nazis in 1942 in retaliation for the killing of the German administrator, Reinhard Heydrich.

Dr. Slapak was excited and pleased that these children were still being found. If there was any thought that a child might be Czechoslovakian and not German, someone would spend a few days with the child and speak to him or her in Czech hoping that even one word might evoke a long buried memory. If the child was old enough this sometimes worked, then the child could be gently probed for other memories which might lead eventually to his or her name or home town. Of the 10,000 stolen children, only 1,679 had been found. At least one of these children, Benig Bedrich, a survivor of the destruction of Lidice, was a Foster Child.

In spite of the warm reception Edna Blue received in Prague in 1948, two years later PLAN was asked to leave Czechoslovakia. PLAN received the request in a barely civil note from the reorganized Ministry of Labor and Social Welfare in the fall of 1950:

> The Ministry of Labor and Social Welfare is thanking you for the help which you have rendered to some Czechoslovak children who were orphans and needy especially in the time when in Czechoslovakia was temporary shortage or basic food and textile because of the occupation and war.
>
> Thanks to the economical and political undertakings of our government, thanks to the altruistic help of the USSR and thanks to the endeavour of our working people our food situation has improved considerably and we have possibilities to take care of our orphans and half-orphans from our own means, and do not see any reason for further existence and activity of your organization on Czechoslovak territory.
>
> The Ministry of Labor and Social Welfare will be grateful to you if you stop your activity in Czechoslovakia not later than till the 1st October 1950. Send us kindly the report about the undertaken liquidation.

In September 1950 Edna Blue wrote to the Foster Parents sponsoring children in Czechoslovakia notifying them that PLAN would soon end its program.

> Dear Friends:
>
> It is with regret that we must inform you that the Ministry of Labor and Social Welfare in Czechoslovakia has requested the withdrawal from that country of the Foster Parents' Plan for War Children. They have extended their thanks for the help which we have rendered to the children and ask that we stop our activities by 1st October 1950.

7

Asia: Introduction

With the exception of the years 1951 and 1952 PLAN has been providing aid to needy children and their families in Asia since its establishment in China in 1948. PLAN has extended its services to the Republic of Korea (1953), the Republic of Vietnam (1957), the British Crown Colony of Hong Kong (1959), the Republic of the Philippines (1961), the Republic of Indonesia (1969), the Kingdom of Nepal (1978), the Republic of India (1980), the Democratic Socialist Republic of Sri Lanka (1981), and the Kingdom of Thailand (1981). Six of these programs continue to provide development assistance to needy children, their families, and their communities; programs ended in China (1950), Hong Kong (1973), Vietnam (1975) and the Republic of Korea (1979).

The first tentative plans to work in China were interrupted by the Second World War. These plans were revived in October 1946 and PLAN's General Committee, then functioning as a Board of Directors, began the search for a Field Director.

In 1947 Gerald Tannebaum was named Director in China. Mr. Tannebaum was at the time working with Madame Sun Yat Sen's China Welfare Institute and took on the additional responsibility of directing PLAN's program. Termination of the program in China followed closely upon the termination of PLAN's program in Czechoslovakia and Poland and lent impetus to the General Committee's determination to begin work in the Republic of Korea as soon as possible. The war in Korea delayed these plans until January 1953, when Robert W. Sage opened the PLAN office in Pusan. PLAN has been alleviating the plight of needy children in Asia ever since.

The programs in the Republics of Korea, Vietnam, and the Philippines are particularly interesting. Their histories illustrate the evolution and cultural adaptability of PLAN's philosophy of assistance as development ideas changed and as these countries themselves changed.

The difference between the PLAN of 1950 and the PLAN of the 1980s is graphically illustrated by the relations between PLAN and the Government of the People's Republic of China in 1950 and its present relations with other host country governments in Asia. The program in China was terminated shortly after the founding of the People's Republic, on the grounds of government interference in the allocation of funds and supplies.

On 11 October 1950 Gerald Tannebaum wrote to Edna Blue presenting the situation:

> Last week the Vice Secretary of the People's Relief Administration of China was in Shanghai and I had an opportunity to discuss . . . the relation of PLAN to his organization. I think I should first explain that the People's Relief Administration of China is an organization formed (in April 1950) . . . in a conference held in Peking which I attended. This organization, according to its charter, is to guide and lead all relief and welfare work in the country . . . All relief supplies and funds which come into China must first receive the approval of PRAC. The reason for this . . . is that a national plan on relief and welfare is being developed and it is their intention to muster all possible aid to effecting this plan.

Mr. Tannebaum was enthusiastic about this integrated approach to the solution of China's considerable social and economic problems. He wrote that the Vice Secretary fully understood and agreed with PLAN's goals and operation and foresaw no difficulties.

The General Committee considered Mr. Tannebaum's letter and all other aspects of PLAN's work in China at a meeting on 2 November 1950. Not the least of these considerations was the steadily diminishing number of Foster Parents of Chinese children, whose total had declined from 350 in January to 134 in November. An August letter to the sponsors of Chinese children attempted to allay the criticism of PLAN's apparent support of the new Communist regime and to explain why PLAN should remain in China:

> . . . Many of our Foster Parents feel that the Plan should not continue to work or support a child in such a country. We know that it will be increasingly difficult for us to obtain support of our work for these Chinese children.
>
> It may help you to understand more fully at this time why we are continuing our work in China if we quote from our charter the purpose of the PLAN . . . "To provide an organization purely humanitarian in character which should be free

from any connection with, or allegiance to any group having any political or propagandistic interest of any kind . . . To provide for the care, maintenance, education, training and well-being of children orphaned and distressed as a result of the ravages of war."

At their 2 November meeting, the General Committee concluded that the conditions outlined by the People's Relief Administration of China for the clearance of funds and goods would compromise PLAN's purely humanitarian character and were therefore inconsistent with PLAN's charter. Ann Landress, one of the founding members of PLAN, made a motion for the immediate termination of the Chinese program. Mr. Bergoffen, who drew up the charter in 1939, seconded the motion and it was carried unanimously.

While PLAN still does not channel its funds through host governments, integration with the host government's overall development plan has become a basic part of PLAN's program philosophy. John Anderson clearly expressed this in the 1970 Statement of Purpose for PLAN/ROK:

Foster Parents Plan in the Republic of Korea will function in relation to the stated purposes and objectives of PLAN, perform its activities in a manner consistent with government direction and guidelines, [and] integrate itself with existing local agency effort, believing that by working closely with local resources that PLAN's overall contribution towards the Foster Child, the family, and community will be of greater positive impact . . .

8

Republic of Korea
1953-79

The 26 year history of PLAN in the Republic of Korea reflects the overall postwar evolution of PLAN's philosophy, programs, and services. In those years PLAN evolved from a child relief and welfare agency offering direct cash and material aid to the neediest children to a multidimensional human development agency involving needy children, their families, and their communities in their own development process.

In addition to PLAN's educational programs, medical care, cash assistance, and specific family and community development projects, PLAN established the only nonprofit hospital in the city of Sung Nam, a cattle raising cooperative in Daegu, credit unions, a cooperative medical clinic, day care centers, night schools, mobile clinics, recreational facilities, and a broad range of family and community income-producing projects.

The underlying constant in all these projects was the basic concern for the well-being of the child. PLAN learned through the years that this concern could be expressed most effectively through programs which involved not only the child but also the family and community.

In October 1950 Frederick Mason, the European Business Director, wrote to Walter Bluh, PLAN Treasurer, about plans for establishment in Korea:

> At the beginning of the year, we were planning to start work in India . . . Now, it is certain that there will be much work to do in Korea, and from every aspect I can visualize, it seems that we should choose Korea rather than India. Heaven help us—it will be some headache.
>
> From what one reads, it is too chaotic at present to attempt anything like the organization we require, but we certainly ought to be thinking about it.

In November 1950 large-scale relief began in the Republic of Korea (ROK) when American Relief for Korea (ARK) was organized by a consortium of voluntary agencies. The organization would channel goods and food supplies to a port on the west coast of Korea and the military authorities would then distribute them to the needy.

Fred Mason discussed the difference between PLAN's work and ARK's in a 4 December 1950 letter to Gloria Matthews:

> . . . Naturally, if the agencies are going to combine to work on a mass relief basis, we will have to stand aside. It is an unfortunate feature of our work that we cannot commence until conditions in a country have at least some form of stability. The distribution of general relief presents no such problems. CARE, for instance, can go in with a truckload of packages . . . throw the packages over the tailboard to the assembled populace, and drive back to the base—they have done their job. We . . . have to have all our elaborate set up of Director . . . translators, bank balances, and children who will stay put . . . for us to do anything in Korea at present would be a waste of time.

Three years later, in May 1953, Robert Sage, PLAN Director in the Republic of Korea, wrote of the hit-or-miss style of relief work then current in Korea:

> Most of the relief is mass relief—a "hop" (handful) of rice today, nothing tomorrow . . . a piece of clothing for the body, nothing for the bare feet in the snow. This is where PLAN is so important . . . help is consecutive and individual, personal.

In September 1952 Gloria Matthews met with Helen Wilson, Voluntary Agency Liaison with the United Nations Korean Reconstruction Agency (UNKRA), and Joseph Lehman, former Executive Director of ARK. It was made clear at the meeting that UNKRA would "prefer that PLAN be the first to make a survey and set up in Korea since the record of PLAN in the past, continuing as such in Korea, would set a fine example for other agencies to follow."

The decision was quickly made to establish a program. The idea at first was to organize PLAN in Asia along the same lines as PLAN in Europe. The central office and overall Director in the Republic of Korea would coordinate a number of Field Offices spread throughout Asia. It is unclear why this administrative design was abandoned.

Gerald Tannebaum, who had directed PLAN's program in China,

was the first person to be considered as a possible Director of the program in the Republic of Korea, but it was soon realized that he would be inappropriate. His continuing work in China for a Chinese agency made it very unlikely that either the Republic of Korea would grant him a visa or that he would be acceptable to the American military authorities.

Robert Sage was appointed PLAN/ROK Director on 1 December 1952. Mr. Sage had been Chief of Welfare Field Services for UNKRA and had worked with the United Nations Civil Assistance Command Korea (UNCACK). He arrived in Tokyo on 3 January 1953 to make preliminary arrangements with UNKRA, establish a dollar account for PLAN with the Chase Manhattan Bank in Tokyo, and engage the accounting firm of Loew, Bingham and Thompson. He left for Tokyo on Sunday, 18 January, and was in Pusan with an office, an assistant and membership in the Joint ROK/UNCACK/UNKRA Committee for Child Welfare by the following Sunday.

The office consisted of two rooms in a Korean-style house and doubled as the Director's living quarters. Ha Sang Nak, Mr. Sage's assistant and PLAN's first Korean employee, had been the top ranking Korean official in the Social Affairs section of UNCACK.

Close working relationships were established with the Korean Ministry of Social Affairs, the officials dealing with child welfare within UNCACK, and the Voluntary Agencies Officer of UNKRA. Liaison with all other voluntary agencies in Korea was maintained through membership in the Joint ROK/UNCACK/UNKRA Committee for Child Welfare and the Korean Association of Voluntary Agencies (KAVA).

The shaky Korean economy of 1953 added to the uncertainty of work in the war-torn republic. Accordingly, Mr. Sage was careful with PLAN funds. His cautious approach to finances was reflected in the rather complex arrangements he made for PLAN/ROK funds. PLAN had a U.S. dollar account with the Tokyo Branch of the Chase Manhattan Bank and both dollar and won accounts with the Government-run Bank of Korea in Pusan. Because Korea was at war and Korean finances were somewhat precarious, Mr. Sage recommended leaving the funds sent from New York in the Tokyo dollar account and transferring only small amounts to Korea as needed.

Mr. Sage's caution was justified by the 15 February 1953 currency reform which converted the old won to the new hwan at the rate of 100 won to one hwan. Despite several weeks of confusion, PLAN did not book any losses as a result of this conversion.

To compensate for the unrealistically low official exchange rate, the Korean Government had a policy of granting a much higher exchange rate, the so-called "Missionary Dollar," to missionary societies dealing through approved import-export firms and recognized nonprofit agencies, including PLAN.

The first case histories from Korea were sent to New York in mid-February 1953. Choi Ok Bong, a nine year-old boy, became the first Korean Foster Child. He was sponsored by the ship's company of the USS Missouri, the first battleship to be called into action with the United Nations forces in Korea. The sponsorship was the idea of the Commanding Officer, Capt. W.R. Edsall, who was killed in action before the child could be assigned. In a letter to PLAN Headquarters Capt. Edsall wrote:

> I am glad that the ship will be able to participate in your nobie undertaking. The Missouri has done many things, from bombarding the enemy in two wars, to furnishing a berth for a precedent-making surrender ceremony. And now it is looking forward to this "adoption."

Choi Ok Bong was born in what became North Korea and fled to the south with his family when war broke out. Wandering from town to town with thousands of other refugees, the family was soon cold, ragged, and starving. His father was separated from the family during the flight from an advancing army in 1952 and was never seen again.

The family consisted of the mother, Choi Ok Bong, two sisters aged 11 and 2½, and a sick 71 year-old grandfather. Like thousands of other refugees, they had neither food, shelter, nor employment. The nine year-old boy supported the family by begging in the streets of Pusan. He was a bright child whose teacher had offered to pay his tuition but he could not go to school and support his family at the same time. The boy was looking after his grandfather and little sister when Mr. Sage met him. His mother had been gone for two days searching for his older sister who had disappeared.

Mr. Sage was thinking about children like this when he wrote of the ironic situation of destitute children in Korean families in a May 1953 report:

> The picture of the children without anything, roaming the streets in their silent suffering cannot be described . . . The lucky are in orphanages . . . some good and some bad. But, even the bad ones offer protection of some kind and so, a full

orphan, ironically, is fortunate. But the child who is a half orphan or has destitute sick parents is indeed a lost one . . . no food, shelter, clothing, schooling . . . what queer circumstances that make a comparatively happy child of one who is a complete orphan living in an institution!

PLAN's early enrollment emphasized these children who were not in institutions. Most were the children of widowed mothers; all were destitute. Mr. Sage and the New York staff felt that the entire family, and not just the Foster Child, should benefit from PLAN's program and services.

PLAN also sponsored children in nationally and privately owned institutions. Three better than average orphanages were chosen to start—Nam Kwang Hak Won (South Light Learning Home), So Hwa Bo Yuk Won (Little Flower Protection Feeding Home), and Kun Ro Hak Won (Diligent Work Learning Home). Additional institutions were supported only upon the recommendation of the Korean Ministry of Social Affairs. Preference was given to those recommended institutions scheduled for improvement under an UNKRA project to upgrade orphanages.

There was a possibility that there would be some duplication of relief efforts in PLAN-supported institutions because all that were officially registered with the Ministry of Social Affairs were eligible for UNCACK relief supplies. This duplication never became a problem since the UNCACK ration provided only the barest necessities; PLAN aid was never superfluous. With the basic necessities of food and shelter provided, the cash grants could be used for educational and medical services. Cash grants to Foster Children living in institutions were given to the orphanage to be used for the common good rather than to the individual Foster Child. In the Republic of Korea, as in Europe, all children in a PLAN-supported institution received the benefits of PLAN aid. In effect, all such children were Foster Children, some were enrolled and had Foster Parents, some were not, but all benefited from PLAN's presence.

Providing cash grants to children living with their families was a more time consuming and complicated process. The principle was the same as in PLAN's European programs. Children accepted by PLAN up to the fifteenth of the month received their first cash grant on enrollment; children enrolled after the fifteenth received theirs the following month. The complication came in the delivery.

The cash grants could not be mailed to the parents or guardians for the simple reason that most of the families lived in shacks without any street address. Even permanent buildings, like the PLAN office, had no street address. (PLAN got its mail only because Mr. Sage carefully cultivated a friendship with each new postman.) Two PLAN employees, Mr. Ha and Miss Chang, climbed up and down the Pusan hills visiting each PLAN family to ask the parent or guardian to come to the PLAN office with the child, identification, and a letter to the Foster Parent on a given day. They could not pay the cash grants on the visits because it would attract too much attention and cause envy among neighbors. There was also the added danger of robbery and the practical problem of hauling around heavy sacks of bank notes.

Mr. Sage described the cash grant payment process in a memo to Gloria Matthews on 23 April 1953:

> On Monday morning I sent Mr. Moon to the Bank of Korea to cash a check for hwan 180,000—on Tuesday one of hwan 100,000—and on Wednesday, one of hwan 150,000 . . . on all three days the bank was out of bank notes in any denomination higher than hwan 10.[1] Therefore, we had to take 18,000 bills the first day, 10,000 the next and 15,000 on the third. Each 100 bills are . . . bundled together, and each 10 such bundles are again packaged together with a string. Hwan 180,000 are therefore 18 fairly heavy packages . . . Moon could hardly carry them. Then we had to count off 264 bills for each child and put this into an envelope.

On the appointed day the children and their parents or guardians arrived at the PLAN Office and were finally lined up by payroll number. Once this degree of order had been established, Mr. Ha made an appropriately ceremonial speech explaining PLAN's program, asking them to come back on the same day next month, and asking them to keep PLAN informed of any change in the address or general circumstances in their or the Foster Children's lives. Then the payment process began.

The children were identified by their case history photographs and payment was made to the parents or guardians. If a child had come alone or with a substitute parent or guardian, payment was withheld

---

[1]Mr. Sage later found out that the Bank of Korea was following the government's strange anti-inflation policy of paying out bank notes of no larger denomination than hwan 10, worth less than five cents. PLAN soon opened an account with the Commercial Bank of Korea which was authorized to issue hwan 100 and 1,000 notes.

pending further investigation. The parents or guardians acknowledged the payment by stamping the receipt with their chop mark (Tochang) after a PLAN employee had written his or her name. The chop marks were used in lieu of a signature and served the same purpose of making a document, contract, or receipt legal and binding.

PLAN had enrolled 946 Korean Foster Children by October 1953. Since the scheduled enrollment for PLAN/ROK's first year was 1,000, enrollment was slowed and plans were made to determine the form the Korean program would take and future areas of enrollment.

Although children who lived with their families had a greater need for PLAN than did institutionalized children, there were logistical problems with their enrollment. The enrollment process, the interviews and investigations, the taking of photographs, the filling out of forms, and the delivery of gift parcels and cash payments all took much longer with "outside" children. An orphanage director could do much of this and what he could not do could be done quickly by PLAN staff because the children were all in one place. "Outside" children required PLAN staff. The families had to be visited regularly and they lived all over Pusan, often in areas inaccessible by car. These problems were alleviated somewhat by conducting most PLAN business at the office when the families came to pick up their monthly cash payments and to drop off letters to Foster Parents. Because of the limited number of staff, the enrollment of children living with their families had to be confined to the Pusan area. PLAN was forced to limit its enrollment in other areas of Korea to institutionalized children until sub-offices could be opened and more staff hired.

The PLAN program—the services and aid provided to Foster Children, consisted primarily of cash grants, gift parcels of food, clothing, household supplies, educational support, and medical care. Many of the children living with their families had never been able to afford to see a doctor or go to school. The monthly cash grants, supplemented by gifts from the Education Fund, enabled many of these children to pay the entrance fees and attend school for the first time. The Children's Charity Hospital and the German Red Cross Hospital in Pusan, through an arrangement made by Mr. Sage, provided free medical care to any PLAN referred child. Arrangements were made for PLAN to pay the salaries of institutional teachers if the institutions would provide their room and board.

PLAN's first major setback in Pusan came on the night of 28 January 1954, when the PLAN office burned down. The fire destroyed the whole neighborhood, leaving three people dead and nearly 3,000 homeless. The next day Mr. Sage wrote:

> What I have dreaded for a year has finally happened: we have completely burned down. The fire started early this morning . . . and spread so quickly to our office building and the whole Yong Ju Dong district that it was impossible to save anything, except our lives. I was awakened by cries of "mul" (water) which, of course, wasn't there, put quickly some pants on, packed my children into the station wagon and whoever of the staff slept there and drove off, just about 30 seconds before it would have been too late. I put the kids into the Nam Kwang Hak Won (a PLAN supported orphanage) . . . and immediately established our temporary headquarters there.

The morning after the fire Mr. Sage made an appointment with a General Whitcomb to try to get temporary use of a United States Army quonset hut in downtown Pusan. The visit was not a happy one:

> Used to everyone saying "Yes, Sir" to him, he was rude and discourteous. Now, since my discharge from the Army, I am no longer very impressed by discourteous high brass, so I thought, "the hell with you," and returned in kind every one of his discourtesies. This, as I found out through the grapevine yesterday, had the astonishing result that he scared the dickens out of all the lesser brass threatening them that, if the Foster Parents' Plan would not get a quonset hut at once, there would be fireworks, because he had enjoyed it enormously that for once someone had dared talk back to him.

PLAN was given the quonset hut and Mr. Sage began the search for suitable permanent office space. The search continued until November, when PLAN moved into the second floor of a building owned by the city. There was a day nursery on the first floor which had been established by PLAN to provide child care for the children of working war widows and was jointly funded by PLAN and the municipal government. Mr. Sage, as chairman of the Joint ROK/KAVA Committee on Widows with Dependent Children, had urged the establishment and maintenance of such nurseries to give widows who could get work a viable alternative to institutionalizing their children or leaving them unattended.

Throughout 1953 and early 1954, Mr. Sage had been developing plans to open a sub-office in Seoul. After the 1953 Armistice, government offices and businesses gradually returned to Seoul. As the city regained its former importance it became a magnet for the homeless and destitute.

On 30 March 1954 Mr. Sage was authorized by PLAN's General Committee to use a US $5,000 grant from UNKRA to establish a sub-office in Seoul. This office was opened in May with a skeleton staff of five Pusan employees under the able direction of Ha Sang Nak. The UNKRA grant was to be held in reserve for use in the construction or purchase of a PLAN building.

Plans were made to gradually transfer responsibilities and personnel from Pusan to Seoul, with the Seoul office eventually becoming PLAN/ROK Headquarters. Mr. Sage divided his time between the two offices. The transfer to Seoul was delayed by the long search for suitable office space. Construction costs were prohibitively high and available office space unsatisfactory.

Suitable accommodations were finally found in April 1955. The new office was an old Korean-style house lacking all modern conveniences, except electricity.[2] Its location in central Seoul near the capital allowed easy access to PLAN children and their families from all districts of the city. The rent was US $120 a month and plans were made to rent the extra rooms to PLAN employees for a total of US $20 a month.

On 1 November 1955 the Pusan to Seoul transition was completed and the Seoul office became PLAN's Headquarters in the Republic of Korea. The Seoul facility would serve the children living with their families in Seoul and all institutional children of the provinces of Kyongsang Pukdo and Cholla Namdo. The Pusan office would continue to serve the children in and south of these provinces and continue its subsidy of the Pusan day nursery. When headquarters was transferred to Seoul, the Korean program was PLAN's largest. There were 1,894 Korean Foster Children: 1,043 served by the Seoul Headquarters and 851 served by the Pusan sub-office. Over half of these children lived with their families or guardians. At this time, PLAN was the only foreign voluntary agency providing services to children living with their families in the Republic of Korea. All of the other agencies confined their aid to institutionalized children.

Although it was the care of these "outside" children that earned

[2]Few other agency directors would have found the house suitable. Mr. Sage aroused a certain amount of resentment among the staffs of other agencies who would not, or could not, get along without plumbing and heating.

PLAN such high regard in Korea, the care of institutionalized children was continued, and even expanded. The reason for this was that Korea Civil Assistance Command (KCAC), which had been formed shortly after the outbreak of the Korean War as United Nations Civil Assistance Command Korea (UNCACK), was withdrawing more and more of its institutional support and would, perhaps, dissolve as the United States Army reduced its presence in Korea. KCAC had given rice and relief supplies to all accredited orphanages in Korea. Without these supplies most of the institutions would be forced to close and there were no viable theories from any quarter as to what would happen to the children when the orphanages closed.

The contributions by KCAC, temporary agencies, and U.S. Army units steadily decreased. By 1957 institutions caring for Foster Children had come to depend more and more on PLAN for financial and material support. In some cases they relied almost exclusively upon PLAN for their survival. The economy of the Republic of Korea was still too weak to provide either adequate support for the institutions or alternative solutions to the problem.

The plight of the orphans was made worse by the unwritten rule of voluntary agencies in Korea—an institution could only receive support from one such agency. Since PLAN did not generally enroll all of the children in an institution and therefore provided only partial support, PLAN aid had the effect of disqualifying the institution from any other support.

This conflict was resolved in two ways. The first was the obvious one of increasing the enrollment of children in institutions supported by PLAN. Although the value of PLAN services to children living with their families was recognized by all, the increase in institutional enrollment was vital for the continued well-being of those institutionalized children already enrolled. The second and much better solution was to find alternatives to the institutional care of destitute children.

Under the direction of Frank Ryan, who became PLAN/ROK Director when Mr. Sage was transferred to the Philippines in 1961, a program was started to get orphans and semi-orphans out of institutions and into the homes of Korean families. Along with this placement program, Mr. Ryan made scheduled and unscheduled inspection visits to PLAN-supported institutions. He made it clear to the directors of these institutions that continued PLAN support was contingent upon the proper care of the children. As a result of these inspections, 156 children were transferred to better orphanages in October 1961. An inspection in April 1962 showed a dramatic improvement in institutional child care.

The program to return institutionalized children to their families and to place orphans with Korean Foster Families was the best solution and had far-reaching effects. It started in 1961 with 20 children. The idea was for PLAN to return the children to their families or the families of their relatives without effecting their status as Foster Children. The Korean Government was so impressed with this program that, when the Ministry of Health and Social Welfare was re-established in 1961 with a more adequate budget, it planned a similar program.

In 1962 PLAN and the Ministry of Health and Social Welfare cooperated in a pilot project to place institutionalized children with Korean Foster Families. The Minister of Health and Social Welfare stated that the PLAN/ROK pilot project was the pattern he wanted other voluntary agencies to follow.

Except for PLAN, all other voluntary agencies in Korea were increasing their support of institutions and institutionalized children. The enormous and ever growing number of orphanages and orphans so long after the war ended had finally become a source of embarrassment to the government and especially to the Ministry of Health and Social Welfare. The reason for the growth in the number of orphans and orphanages was clear: that's where the money was. Government social welfare programs were totally inadequate to meet the needs of destitute families with young children, child day care was minimal, and the economy was weak. The orphanage directors, not surprisingly, knew that if they had more children they would get more support for their institutions from voluntary agencies. They obligingly provided as many orphans as the traffic would bear. It is interesting to note that, although PLAN cut back on the number of Foster Children in institutions by placing them in families, the ratio of enrolled to unenrolled children remained about the same in PLAN-supported institutions.

The first joint PLAN/ROK child placement project involved the placement of children from Seoul and Kyungii Province orphanages in the homes of relatives or suitable Foster Families. It was to be a one-year pilot project to test the effectiveness of such a program. The project was so successful that before the year was out a second PLAN/ROK project was started for children in Pusan and Kyongsang Province orphanages.

In 1962 Frank Ryan reached an agreement with the directors of the 20 orphanages PLAN supported concerning the future of their institutions. The orphanage directors agreed to reduce the number of children in their care from 2,550 to 1,300 over a two-year period. During this period they were to begin family and community related activities such as day nurseries for the children of working mothers, primary, middle, and high school education, and vocational training. These activities were eventually to be self-supporting. To provide support for the institutions during this transitional period, Mr. Ryan agreed to enroll up to 90 percent of the remaining institutionalized children. This program was strongly supported and highly praised by both the Ministry of Health and Social Welfare and local government officials who used it as an example of what other voluntary agencies should be doing.

The short-term goals of this plan were to get as many Foster Children as possible out of institutions and, at the same time, to convert the orphanages into family and community related service centers.

The long-range goal was to insure the establishment of self-supporting child, family, and community resource centers operating independently at the local level and responsive to the needs of the community. In effect, the orphanages were treated in the same way as PLAN families, and with the same intention—to make them independent of PLAN support.

As the months went by, the orphanages PLAN supported defined their new roles: ten would establish day nurseries; five would begin or expand vocational training schools; three would open primary, middle, or high schools; and two would establish pilot projects in farming and animal husbandry.

Paralleling this reduction in the institutional enrollment was an increase in the number of caseworkers on the PLAN social work staff and a broadening of the focus of their casework. This broadened focus was to have profound effects on the program and enrollment policies throughout the PLAN world by stressing the potential for self-sufficiency of individual PLAN families. This led, inevitably, to the inclusion of this potential in the enrollment criteria and an increased emphasis on education and job placement.

Education for the Foster Child had long been a major program focus in the Republic of Korea. A report prepared by Robert Sage, Anne Davison[3], Edward Francel, and Kenric Marshall for the Joint ROK/KAVA Committee on Widows with Dependent Children summed up the reason for this emphasis:

[3]Miss Davison was later to direct PLAN's program in the Republic of Vietnam.

With the almost universal Korean passion for education, a mother will go to any length to keep her children in school. It is not unknown for a mother to literally die of starvation to meet the high cost of education.

PLAN enabled Foster Children to attend school by providing funds through monthly cash grants, Special Services Funds, and the Korean Education Fund.

The increase in family caseworkers led to a much greater emphasis on vocational education, specifically for the parent or guardian of the child. The idea was to provide quick, low cost job training and placement for the parent to make the family independent in as short a time as possible. Clearly, such training would be wasted on those with neither the ambition nor the potential for such independence; therefore, this potential became a requirement for entrance into a training program and was later to become a criterion for enrollment.

The 1957 ROK/KAVA report already mentioned described some of the obstacles to financial independence faced by Korean widows:

> Cut off from the power, the industry, and the mines of the North, the rehabilitation and industrialization of the South have been necessarily difficult. There are but few work opportunities for women and Korean culture further imposes limits on occupations acceptable in the community. It takes a great deal of courage for a woman to branch out to do something new and different. The woman is traditionally dependent and finds it easy to rely on even small amounts of relief goods that come her way.
>
> Tying in with [the above] point . . . is the tendency of the aid agency to institutionalize "projects." Instead of working to rehabilitate the individual widow, to make her independent and self-supporting, we frequently perpetuate her dependence.

The report contained practical guidelines for effective job training projects. It stressed the need for projects teaching specific, clearly defined skills which were closely tied to the present and probable needs of the Korean economy. Close and continuing liaison with industry would assure the relevance of the training. The courses should follow sound vocational guidelines, enroll carefully selected trainees, and provide a placement service.

The basic working thesis of this report was the necessity and desirability of considering vocational education as economic assimilation and rehabilitation projects for individuals.

By increasing the number of caseworkers, Frank Ryan was able to apply this emphasis to the individual parent and his or, more often, her family. His vocational education and job placement program trained specific people for specific jobs. He summarized the program and its results in his Quarterly Report (July-September 1963):

> Sixty-six young men and women of families in which we support children were started in vocational training this quarter. Their training was determined beforehand with specific employers. This means that their jobs were obtained beforehand with actual placement when training is completed.
>
> This program . . . promises to be one of our best efforts in Korea in promoting a higher degree of family rehabilitation in a shorter period of time. It is also developing a new standard of casework in Korea in vocational training requiring careful selection of family members most capable of providing economic support. Also, we have learned that vocational training schools in Korea do not meet the needs of most employers, particularly in manufacturing.
>
> As a consequence, we have undergone a most interesting experience in finding out, on the one hand, what a potential employer required . . . and, on the other hand, finding a suitable training school that was able and willing to change its curriculum to meet the standards of training set forth by the employer . . . After the job placement we are concerned with his progress and subsequent effect upon family rehabilitation to the point where cancellation can result.

The average cost per trainee was about US $20. The courses lasted a maximum of six months and prepared trainees for employment in such fields as radio assembly and repair, tailoring, machine tool operation, barbering, typing, watch repairing, sewing, knitting, accounting, and jewelry making. When the trainees had completed their training and were working, their supervisors were interviewed. The supervisors were well pleased with their new employees and said that the program had provided the trainees with a clear edge over other employees and that they would soon be promoted.

Three hundred seventy-three (373) people from the families of Foster Children benefited from these training programs in Fiscal Year 1964. Of the 224 people who had completed their training during the fiscal year, there were only five dropouts and two failures in job placement. The remaining 142 had not as yet completed their training. These figures clearly show the success of the caseworker's selection processes.

Throughout 1965 Mr. Ryan and the PLAN/ROK staff became increasingly concerned with the potential of the family, typically a widow with three children, for achieving financial independence. It was this potential that determined which of the many needy families would be enrolled. In general, the mother's ambition for her children's education and her initiative were decisive factors in enrollment. The caseworkers also looked at the potential for older children to contribute to family support. The vocational training programs were usually geared to the oldest child in the family, particularly a Foster Child approaching cancellation age. Job placement efforts had the goal of providing or supplementing family income by finding employment for the mothers in such quickly learned occupations as sewing machine operation or fishnet making.

Ideally, the mother would soon be able to contribute to the family income while an older child learned a more profitable skill through a PLAN vocational education program. With the two incomes a family could keep the youngest children in school and could soon be entirely self-supporting.

Mr. Ryan felt that the enrollment of Foster Children and the PLAN program should be based upon the potential and the motivation for improvement shown by a family and not based solely on need. This was a major change in the PLAN development philosophy and heralded a broadening of focus from the development of individual children to the strengthening of the family for the benefit of the children. Mr. Ryan saw in this expanded focus a change from relief to rehabilitation for Foster Children and their families. He made the distinction clear in an 8 December 1965 letter to Gloria Matthews:

> In the case of families when a Foster Child reaches cancellation age and his family is as needy as the day our support began, this is relief. It is rehabilitation when, with Foster Parent support, we can help a family become economically self-supporting.

Mr. Ryan used the harsh but apt analogy of a hospital to illustrate his concern for the rehabilitation of PLAN families and the integration of the Foster Child and his or her family into the Korean economy:

> The practice in Korean hospitals that treat patients with tuberculosis is not to admit any terminal patients. They will provide beds only for patients with a reasonable chance for

recovery. This, of course, is explained by the limited number of beds available in the face of a much larger number of cases of tuberculosis . . . Our PLAN enrollment is 7,500 in Korea. We have 7,500 "beds" to offer a larger number of needy cases, and we want "patients" who possess a reasonable chance for recovery.

By August 1970, when John Anderson became Director, PLAN/ROK was firmly committed to the idea that children could be most effectively helped through a program geared to motivated families.

During Mr. Anderson's tenure, this emphasis on motivated families soon grew to include an emphasis on motivated communities. PLAN programs spread to rural areas and involved communities through close integration and cooperation with local authorities, agencies, and service organizations.

A number of projects started by Mr. Anderson were designed to be taken over by the participating families and communities and continued after PLAN phaseout in 1979. Such ongoing projects as the hospital PLAN initiated in Sung Nam, the credit unions in Daegu and Sang Ju, and the Sang Ju cattle raising cooperative are examples of the kind of successful, self-sustaining projects which PLAN hoped to leave behind after phaseout.

One of Anderson's first priorities when he took over as PLAN/ROK Director was to review and evaluate all aspects of PLAN's operations in the Republic of Korea. His first step was to appoint Kim Kyong Mo, a longtime staff member, to the newly created position of Deputy Director. September and October 1970 were set aside for a program review. Committees and discussion groups provided a formal structure for PLAN/ROK staff participation in the review process.

The Director of the Social Work Department at Seoul National University, Professor Ha Sang Nak, Mr. Sage's former assistant and PLAN's first Korean employee, offered his assistance in this review and arranged for the participation of social work students.

The evaluation revealed that, in spite of the movement toward social work methods, revised enrollment criteria, credit unions, and cooperative ventures, PLAN/ROK was still functioning primarily as a charity-relief agency. There had been real and significant progress toward professional social work in some areas but, overall, PLAN/ROK was still doing relief work.

On the basis of the evaluation and discussion with representatives of various governmental and private agencies, Mr. Anderson and the

PLAN/ROK staff drew up new goals:

> Foster Parents Plan in the Republic of Korea will function in relation to the stated purposes and objectives of PLAN, perform its activities in a manner consistent with governmental direction and guidelines, integrate itself with existing local agency efforts, believing that by working closely with local resources, that PLAN's overall contribution toward the Foster Child, Family and community will be of greater positive impact, and finally Foster Parents Plan and the PLAN/ROK staff will attempt to relate to Foster Children and their family members in a manner that can be categorized as professional social work.

In keeping with these goals, Anderson reorganized the social work staff. The Chief Social Worker, responsible for the supervision of 21 social workers, was replaced by three Senior Social Workers, each responsible for the supervision of seven social workers.

The evaluation and review resulted in Program Development Seventy-One, which was to provide the new direction for PLAN/ROK. It called for close cooperation with local agencies in a number of projects and pilot projects geared to the material and psychological development of PLAN children and their families. The hope was that PLAN's overall contribution to the community in which Foster Families lived would be enhanced by working with existing local resources and agencies.

Examples of Program Development Seventy-One projects are:

YWCA/CRS/PLAN — A cooperative pilot project for the mothers of Foster Children. The mothers were to meet bi-monthly for group activities including embroidery, knitting, and group discussion. The YWCA provided a group worker and Catholic Relief Services provided the space.

YMCA/PLAN — *Indoor Program* — A pilot project for 60 teenage boys at the Seoul YMCA.

Taiwha Social Center/PLAN — A pilot project to provide recreational group activities.

Sam Yook Children's Rehabilitation Center/PLAN — A cooperative project for the provision of corrective surgery, prosthetic devices, and appropriate therapy for Seoul Foster Children with physical disabilities.

Pusan City Child Guidance Center/PLAN — A cooperative

project to provide a series of three-day educational programs for the mothers of Foster Children. The project provided for education in health and sanitation, domestic welfare, home education, and economic rehabilitation. One hundred mothers participated in the first program.

Pusan City Child Guidance Center/PLAN — A program to provide library services to Pusan Foster Children and their families.

SCI/YMCA/PLAN — A series of camping programs for Foster Children organized in close cooperation with Service Corps International and using YMCA camps.

Mother's Credit Union — Pusan, Seoul, Paeng Yang Island, and Koje Do. Inchon C.U. being organized. The Pusan Mother's C.U. was the largest in the Republic of Korea. PLAN staff worked very closely with the mothers.

Annual Children's Drawing Contest and Exhibition — Held in Pusan and Seoul in the summer. All Foster Children were invited to participate. Drawings were exhibited at various locations and prizes were awarded. All drawings were eventually sent to Foster Parents.

Other projects initiated by Mr. Anderson in Fiscal Year 1971 included the establishment of a medical clinic in the Pusan office, the expansion of the educational program of the Mother's Credit Union, and the upgrading of the social work students' training program.

The projects of Program Development Seventy-One were, for the most part, successful. The next year Program Development Seventy-Two called for a total of 61 educational, recreational, medical, and rehabilitative projects, the majority of which were performed jointly with local agencies and organizations.

To provide better services and create a more systematic approach to child and family development, newly enrolled children and their families were required to participate in at least one project in their first six months in PLAN. All newly assigned children and their families were also required to have general physical exams, x-rays, and blood tests. Foster Children and their school-age brothers and sisters received eye and dental examinations.

The obligatory participation in PLAN activities insured quick contact between the Foster Children, their families, and PLAN staff. As children were enrolled, they were organized into groups of 100. In a visit to the zoo for preschool children, for example, a group of 100 children and their families would spend a day at the zoo with PLAN social workers, social work students, and members of the PLAN Community Service Volunteer Corps. The purpose was to provide a relaxed setting for the families and PLAN staff to get to know each other. While the children played, the parents, volunteers, students, and social workers could discuss the needs of the families and the services PLAN could provide.

By 1971 PLAN was committed to these family-oriented projects and was supporting fewer and fewer institutionalized children. In February 1971, Mr. Anderson and Mr. Kim, PLAN/ROK Deputy Director, met with Miss Kim Yung Ju, Director of the Women's and Children Welfare Section of the Ministry of Health and Social Welfare, to report the results of a joint PLAN/Ministry of Health and Social Welfare study of children's institutions. The study confirmed the appropriateness of PLAN's institutional phaseout schedule. At the time, PLAN/ROK was the only PLAN program involved with institutionalized children.

They also discussed the integration of PLAN's program with the efforts of local agencies and organizations. Miss Kim was obviously impressed and said that this was exactly what the government wanted the voluntary agencies to be doing.

"Out of the blue," to quote Mr. Anderson, Miss Kim presented the government position that agencies such as PLAN might be able to do significant work in rural areas of the Republic. The Ministry, reflecting the government view, felt that there were too many foreign agencies in Seoul and Pusan and not enough in the impoverished rural areas. She went on to say that the government would lend its full support if PLAN was interested in expanding its rural programs.

At the time PLAN had already established a rural project on the island of Paeng Yong Do (1968) and was planning programs for Koje Do Island and the rural areas around Daegu City. The basic reason for the move to rural areas was the conviction that PLAN's limited resources could be more effectively used in rural areas. Mr. Anderson and Mr. Kim had come to question PLAN's relevance to many of the children and families in the rapidly developing cities of Pusan and Seoul. Many of the families who were dropped from PLAN's rolls because of their improved living conditions had, Mr. Anderson thought, the ambition and talents necessary to escape from poverty even without PLAN aid. They also felt that the inordinate amount of time the social workers spent during pre-enrollment investigations in search of unde-clared sources of income among urban families was both a waste of energy and an indication of the generally improving economic environment in cities. These increased urban opportunities were largely a result of the continuing emphasis on industrialization by the Government of the Republic of Korea. An unfortunate result of the push for industrial growth was the relative neglect of agricultural development. There had been great progress in the cities, but only minimal change in the rural agricultural areas.

There was a clear need for PLAN to develop community level programs. The question was whether PLAN/ROK was flexible enough to adapt its programs to a rural environment. The success of a rural program involving children and their families in isolated areas would depend upon how far the PLAN/ROK program could be modified to suit the particular needs of individual communities. Related to this was the degree to which cash grant funds could be channeled to meet family and community needs defined by the people in the villages and PLAN social workers. The most basic question was whether PLAN/ROK could change its program orientation from material aid to projects promoting the efforts and ability of whole communities to identify and solve their own problems; whether PLAN could act as a catalyst to promote significant and lasting change in children, their families, and their communities.

The anticipated problems of staffing, transportation, and communications in rural areas were avoided by the careful selection of sites. Paeng Yong Do and Koje Do islands could both be reached by relatively short boat trips from Seoul. In the Daegu area, the program was to begin in the city. Once PLAN was firmly established in urban Daegu, work could spread to the rural area of Sang Ju. Trained social workers with experience in rural areas were found to staff the rural offices. In addition to the new rural community programs, urban offices were opened in Sung Nam and Inchon.

In Seoul, PLAN gradually shifted its enrollment to "PLAN areas," areas of the city with concentrations of needy children and enough motivated parents to make successful neighborhood rehabilitation and development possible. This concentration allowed Foster Families to work together to achieve common goals.

One of the most successful of the PLAN/ROK programs was in the new City of Sung Nam. Sung Nam, first called Kwangju, had been established by the government to relieve the overcrowding in Seoul. Its people were the relocated shack-dwellers of Seoul.

PLAN's interest in Sung Nam began in 1971 when a number of

Foster Children and their families moved to the new city. As more families moved from Seoul to Sung Nam the need for child and family service programs increased significantly. PLAN, in cooperation with the Sung Nam authorities, developed plans for a combination day care center and community center. The day care center would provide care for the three to six year-old children of working mothers. The community center would offer a wide range of family and community educational and rehabilitative programs, including vocational training, family planning, youth club activities, a credit union, and child care classes. The day care/community center was so successful that it became the model for similar centers planned by other agencies and by the Ministry of Health and Social Affairs.

The building, which also housed the PLAN offices, was built with a US $15,000 grant from a Miles for Millions fund-raising walk held in Toronto.[4] The land was provided rent free by the city of Sung Nam under the agreement that the building would be turned over to the city when PLAN left.

To publicize the new center and to raise funds for its operating expenses, John Anderson organized the first fund-raising walk ever held in the Republic of Korea. The tremendously successful walk took place on 18 March 1973 with nearly 3,500 people walking 15 miles from Seoul to Sung Nam to raise over US $16,000. The walk was a cooperative effort with PLAN, local high schools, the United States Eighth Army, Korean universities, officials of the Ministry of Health and Social Affairs, the International Lions Club, and the Seoul business community all taking part. The walkers were sponsored for a minimum of US $0.25 a mile by American, Australian, and Canadian Foster Parents, PLAN staff members, world-wide Lions Club members, and thousands of Koreans.

A memo from John Anderson to Glenn Rogers, International Director of Field Services, mailed on 28 February 1973, lists 17 ministers, vice ministers, chairmen, and directors from 12 different agencies whose approval was needed for the walk to take place. The success of

[4]Miles for Millions was first organized in 1967 as a project of the Canadian Government to focus attention on the needs of people in developing countries. Government involvement ended the following year and the organizational responsibility was assumed by local community committees who also chose the projects to be funded. The Ottawa based National Walk Committee, composed of representatives of voluntary agencies, was responsible for national planning and provided information and organizational assistance to the local committees.

the walk for Sung Nam development proved that the lugubrious bureaucracy could be overcome. During the next six years, ten more walks were held for the Sung Nam center.

In January 1975, PLAN opened a medical clinic for Foster Children and their families in Sung Nam. The clinic grew into the Yang Chin Hae Hospital, the only nonprofit hospital in Sung Nam. A number of public and private organizations gave PLAN generous assistance in its transformation of the clinic. The U.S. Agency for International Development donated over US $80,000 for equipment, supplies, and an ambulance. The Sung Nam City authorities built a bridge and paved the road to make access easier. Foster Parents from Australia, Canada, the Netherlands, and the United States supplied funds for construction, equipment, and pharmaceuticals. Other major contributors included the Canadian International Development Agency (CIDA), the Chase Manhattan Bank, the Direct Relief Foundation, and the Korea Oil Corporation. The Ministry of Health and Social Affairs gave legal and administrative aid. American doctors from the Eighth Army regularly volunteered their services to supplement the medical staff. Further support came from the credit union organized by PLAN.

The hospital received its license in March 1977 and became a secondary referral hospital, which meant that all government classified "poor" and "incomeless" people in the city who needed secondary health care were referred to the hospital. To provide a legal basis for the continued existence of the hospital after PLAN phaseout, it was established as a distinct legal entity. Though the hospital was a nonprofit institution, the decision was made to provide services to a limited number of patients who could afford to pay for treatment to help offset the costs of those who could not. By 1979, the hospital was in full operation and had a nurse's aide training program, a day care center, a kindergarten, and a nursery school. Mr. Kim Kyong Mo, the last Director of PLAN/ROK, became the Director of the combined hospital and social service center after PLAN's June 1979 phaseout.

By 1974 it was apparent that the economy of the Republic of Korea was recovering and that, in the foreseeable future, PLAN services would no longer be needed. Planning for the phaseout, begun in 1974, concentrated on leaving viable, self-sustaining community resources behind when PLAN left and on implementing projects to meet specific developmental goals in predetermined time periods.

Ideas for limited "Term of Service" projects had been discussed as early as March 1971, when Kim Kyong Mo made the first preliminary study for the opening of a PLAN office in Daegu (at that time called Taegu). When George W. Ross, then Deputy Executive Director, read the report, he wrote back to John Anderson (10 March 1971):

> Do they really need us? These people sound great. They have initiative and the desire to succeed. What is PLAN going to provide? Money? We should be more meaningful than that. Well, it's up to you to make a recommendation. Maybe it is with exactly such people as these that our little bit can reap the greatest rewards . . . for them, not us. Maybe, instead of digging ourselves in . . . we should wait to set up the kind of development scheme that would have us in and ousted by the end of a ten year period. Maybe we should plan to reach goals that include developing local resources that would take over from us . . . I can't help feeling that these people really have what it takes . . . and that our role should be guide for a while, and then go elsewhere.

In December 1971 John Anderson recommended and received approval to establish PLAN in Daegu and phase out of Pusan. The following contrasts influenced that decision:

DAEGU	*PUSAN*
1. Strong interest by government and local people (agencies and private citizens).	1. Little interest by government in PLAN.
2. Definite needy population to serve.	2. Definite needy population to serve.
3. Facilities for establishment of PLAN program to be provided by the city or jointly by PLAN and city. Very inexpensive.	3. PLAN's rent and insurance charge is raised every year. City refused on two occasions (during 1971) to provide PLAN with free or 'token' cost space. Costs will be increased every year we remain in Pusan.
4. Daegu presents an opportunity for PLAN to work both in urban and rural setting.	4. Pusan would continue to be an urban program similar to one we have had for 18 years.
5. No foreign voluntary agencies are working in Daegu.	5. Numerous foreign voluntary agencies are in Pusan and will continue until at least 1980.

6. PLAN will have an opportunity to assist in the development of local leadership and local social welfare program development.

6. Much leadership exists in the social welfare field—both from foreign voluntary agencies and local agencies.

7. Costs—at first in setting up office might be additional cost —but will be a most worthwhile investment.

7. Costs continue to increase with little chance for making such an investment work for the benefit of PLAN or its families.

The Daegu office was opened in the Daegu City Welfare Center in March 1972 and moved to the larger Puk Ku District Office in August 1973. The new office had space for a playground and room for PLAN to provide day care for the children of working mothers. Medical, dental, and educational projects were soon begun and a credit union was organized.

The most effective projects were the credit union, cooperatives, night school, and the fund-raising walks. The fund-raising walks served two purposes: the first, of course, was to raise money for PLAN projects; the second, and more important, was to stimulate the direct participation of the community in its own development by showing how effective such participation could be. The interest of the Daegu Community was clearly shown by the 19,000 walkers who participated in the 1976 Daegu walk.

The Daegu Credit Union soon became the third largest credit union in the Republic of Korea. Its membership grew to include every PLAN family in Daegu. As in other PLAN program areas, the Daegu Credit Union gave its members alternatives to borrowing from "loan sharks" and had the added benefits of providing interest on savings and funds for cooperative incoming-producing projects.

The PLAN clinic in Daegu was opened in 1973 and staffed by a volunteer doctor from Kyungpuk National University, a nurse, and a medical social worker. It provided medical care to an average of 1,000 patients a month. In April 1975, psychiatric counseling was introduced.

The Night Middle School began in March 1974 and was expanded in October 1974 when students from Kyungpuk National University and other colleges took over as volunteer teachers. The first graduation ceremony was held in February 1976.

In March 1975, the "Term of Service" approach was initiated in Daegu. The basic idea of "Term of Service" was to establish a realistic schedule of short and long-term family development objectives that could be reached in a predetermined time period. In Daegu the maximum time period was five years. The families, together with their PLAN social workers, defined their development objectives and worked out a practical program for their achievement. Since financial independence was one of the primary objectives, the development plans were closely integrated with the credit union and income-producing projects for both individual families and groups of families working together.

By the time PLAN phased out of Daegu, the credit union had been established as a separate legal entity, registered with the Ministry of Finance, and associated with the National Credit Union Federation of Korea. Members received yearly interest of 18 percent on regular accounts and 25 percent on term accounts. Members borrowed at the relatively low rate of two percent a month. (Loan sharks, the traditional source of loans for the needy, charged as much as 6 percent a month.)

In September 1979 the credit union had 2,500 members. Two thousand of the members were former PLAN affiliates. The other 500 had been accepted, based on set criteria, in the three months since PLAN's June phaseout. The credit union was obviously becoming a useful and accepted community resource.

As of July 1979, the credit union had assets of US $500,000 and was growing steadily. Proper fiscal controls were assured through association with the National Credit Union Federation of Korea, which performed regular audits, and an informal arrangement with the Sung Nam Legal Entity, established by PLAN, which provided monthly audits of both the Daegu and Sang Ju Credit Unions. There had been no evidence of wrongdoing in the seven-year history of the credit union.

The credit union established in 1974 in Sang Ju, a rural area north of Daegu, was in many ways similar to the Daegu Credit Union and enjoyed similar success. It, too, was made a distinct legal entity before PLAN phased out. The major difference was that the Sang Ju Credit Union incorporated an income generating production cooperative.

The members of the Sang Ju Credit Union felt that an ongoing profit making cooperative project would not only supply funds but also provide the cohesion and incentive necessary to further strengthen their credit union. They decided that a cattle and swine raising project would best meet their objectives.

Following approval by the Federation of Credit Unions, the cooperative project was begun. Initial funding was provided by a 1977 Canadian International Development Agency (CIDA) grant of US$24,000. The money was used to purchase animals for 200 families.

In 1978 the cooperative received an additional US $50,000 grant from CIDA. The members provided the labor and construction materials to build barns for 90 cows and sties for 100 swine purchased with the CIDA funds.

The former PLAN Sang Ju Regional Representative served as a paid advisor for the credit union and as manager of the animal raising cooperative. His rural background and four years with PLAN in Sang Ju provided the basis for his effectiveness.

The survival of the Sang Ju projects after PLAN phaseout resulted from the carefully planned interaction of a variety of factors.

1. The rural background of the Sang Ju PLAN staff was a major factor in their acceptance by, and understanding of, the families in the rural communities.
2. Foster Families were from the same communities and knew each other.
3. Funded projects met the needs of the people involved as expressed by their family development goals.
4. Clients participated directly in the planning and implementation of the projects.

These factors illustrate the kind of thinking and planning that went into the selection and operation of PLAN programs and projects in the Republic of Korea. By July 1976, when John Anderson moved to Manila to become PLAN's Director in the Philippines, PLAN/ROK was serving about 6,900 Foster Children and families, a total of about 30,000 people, in seven locations.

John Anderson's six years of service in the Republic of Korea were marked by initiative and creativity in bringing basic services to PLAN families through group and community programs. These programs were a logical extension of the work of his predecessors Frank Ryan and Robert Sage. Mr. Sage first brought direct financial and material assistance to thousands of destitute Korean children and established PLAN's long and fruitful relationships with other public and private social welfare agencies. Mr. Ryan established family motivation as a factor in PLAN enrollment and focused on child development in the context of family development. Mr. Anderson took the process one step further by involving the community in programs which were of direct benefit to the children but which were beyond the reach of individual PLAN families. Throughout PLAN's 26 years in the Republic of Korea, its program was held in the highest regard by officials at all levels of the government and by the people PLAN served.

The number of former PLAN families continuing their association with PLAN-initiated projects is a good indication of the relevance of the projects. By the third quarter of 1978, well along in the phaseout process, 83 percent of the cancelled families were continuing their credit union membership. In Sung Nam, 65 percent of the cancelled families stayed in the Credit Union, in Daegu, 85 percent, and in Sang Ju, 100 percent.

From 1976 to June 1979 John Anderson's successors, Dorn Leslie Winter and Kim Kyong Mo, were responsible for phasing out PLAN and insuring that PLAN-initiated projects would continue as Korean projects. In June 1979 the process was completed and PLAN's 26-year program of service to needy children, their families, and their communities in the Republic of Korea came to an end.

9

Republic of Vietnam: 1956-75

Throughout the spring and summer of 1956 the PLAN General Committee, then functioning as a Board of Directors, considered new countries into which PLAN might expand. Austria, India, Israel, Pakistan, the Philippines, Puerto Rico, the Republic of Vietnam, and the countries of Islamic Africa were investigated. On 8 August 1956, Director Gloria Matthews, Committee Secretary Thomas O'Hagen, and Treasurer Ludwig Prosnitz submitted their recommendation for establishing PLAN in the Republic of Vietnam.

They were sympathetic to Vietnam because of the long period of fighting in that country and its acute refugee problem. They felt that Southeast Asia was an appropriate choice for PLAN because the need there was more in keeping with PLAN's purpose and past actions— helping victims of war. Further considerations were the great need for aid and the apparent American sympathy for the Vietnamese. Its many similarities to the Republic of Korea suggested that in terms of both relieving the suffering of children and engaging the sympathy and support of American and Canadian Foster Parents, PLAN could be as successful in Vietnam as in Korea. They recognized the risk of an invasion from the north and the overthrow of the Republic, but saw no alternative to taking that risk. At the New York meeting of PLAN's General Committee on 23 August 1956, the motion was made and unanimously carried that PLAN proceed with its activities relating to the establishment of a program in the Republic of Vietnam as soon as possible. The decision was made at the same meeting to close the European Headquarters in London and to phase out of England and the Netherlands by 30 June 1957.

On 2 January 1957 Harry Edward was unanimously approved as a new Field Director and on 18 January the General Committee appointed him PLAN's first Director in the Republic of Vietnam. He arrived in Saigon one month later to find a new country in the process of organizing itself to make the transition from a rural, war-torn colony to a modern state. The need for such reorganization was apparent everywhere. The Republic, established less than three years before, had to deal with the effects of colonialism, partition, civil war, and nearly a million refugees from North Vietnam. Illiteracy was widespread, as was poverty, disease, drug abuse, and crime.

Compulsory primary and secondary education had been legislated only two years before and had had, as yet, little effect. As a result of the limited funds available for public education many private schools had opened. In both public and private schools, students were required to buy their books and school supplies. Tuition fees for the private schools ranged from US $0.50 to US $2 a month for students at the elementary level and US $3.00 to US $25 a month for students at the secondary level. These fees were well beyond the reach of many Vietnamese.

Medical care was equally out of reach. There were 370 qualified doctors to care for the Republic's estimated population of 13 million. The children's case histories revealed TB, cholera, smallpox, typhus, yaws, hepatitis, and congenital venereal disease.

When Mr. Edward arrived in Saigon, there was not even a uniform civil code. The legal system was a pastiche of leftover laws from the French Colonial Administration of Annam, the French Protectorate, and the former colony of Cochinchina. The laws concerning polygamy were an indication of the disorder: in some areas of the Republic it was legal, in other areas it was not.

Mr. Edward spent his first months in Saigon establishing and staffing the PLAN office and negotiating an agreement with the government. On 31 March 1957 the PLAN office opened in space provided by the government. The Administrative Services of the United States Operations Mission (USOM) supplied desks, chairs, filing cabinets, and typewriters. On 3 May 1957 the agreement defining the terms under which PLAN was to operate was signed and enrollment began.

The first children were enrolled from the poor districts of Saigon and Cholon. As had been the case in Pusan and Seoul, Korea, these districts were labyrinthine slums of unnamed streets and unnumbered shacks. The people who lived there were refugees from the north, refugees from the civil war, and the rural poor in search of a better life in the city.

Few of these people found the better life they sought. Six year-old Thi Tu, sponsored by Foster Parents in the United States, wanted to go to school but could not. Her family had barely enough money for food. Her blind father had been a part-time policeman for the colonial regime but lost his job when he lost his vision. Because of his part-time status he was not eligible for a pension and there was no Social Security. Thi Tu's mother supported the family by carrying water for the neighbors in two five-gallon cans hung from a bamboo yoke—80 pounds of water. The French Red Cross had given her the cans as "capital" so she could earn a living. She usually earned about US $0.40 a day to support her family of six. Enrollment in PLAN allowed the younger children to go to school and provided clothing and supplemental food for the whole family.

Van and Nam, two brothers aged 12 and 17, had been living on the street. Nam had sold a pint of blood to pay his school fees. Their father had been a colonial administrator with the French Colonial Government in what became the Democratic Republic of Vietnam (North Vietnam). When North Vietnam became independent their father was taken away and never seen again. Their fields were nationalized and their mother, suspected of knowing the location of gold allegedly stolen by her husband, was questioned several times a week. The children were mistreated in attempts to make the mother talk. Eventually the mother was driven to suicide. The two boys fled to the south in 1954. An older brother stayed behind to cover their escape.

They arrived in Saigon in October 1954. They washed dishes, worked as servants and went to school at night. Eventually they were taken in by a family of refugees from their own village. The family of ten lived on an income of US $55 a month. In his first letter to his Foster Parents, Van wrote:

Dear Foster Mother:
This is the first time I write to you, a stranger, and call you mother. It seems very funny, daring, bashful, but I rely on your understanding, even now I feel something sacred I lacked for a long time . . .

PLAN grew slowly in its first months in Vietnam. Total enrollment at the end of six months was only 140. This slow growth was largely a result of a series of misunderstandings between Mr. Edward and Nguyen Luong, Director General of the Ministry of Social Action. The misunderstandings soon led to mutual distrust and a general breakdown of communications between the two men.

The 1957 shoe drive illustrates the effects of this breakdown.

Barefoot children in Vietnam were subject to infection from cuts, insect and snake bites, a variety of parasites, and leprosy. Mr. Edward saw the clear need for shoes and decided that simple, thick soled wooden clogs would answer that need. The shoe drive was launched in the United States and Canada on 5 February 1957 when Richard Nixon, then Vice President of the United States, presented a US $5,000 check to Gloria Matthews in Washington.

At the end of the campaign Mr. Edward presented 40,000 pairs of shoes to the startled Director General with the expectation that they would be immediately and gratefully distributed by the teachers in the public schools. He was disappointed. The shoes were eventually distributed to any children who wanted them, but the wooden clogs were not at all comfortable for children who usually wore rubber sandals if they wore any shoes at all.

By August 1958 Mr. Edward and Mr. Luong were in constant disagreement about all things relating to PLAN. Their relationship deteriorated until October when Mr. Edward left Vietnam. When Gloria Matthews, Ludwig Prosnitz, and Robert Sage arrived in October 1958 to try to salvage the program, they found Nguyen Luong to be pleasant, cordial, and cooperative.

Mr. Sage remained in Saigon as Acting Director until January 1959 when Jacob J. (Jack) Burghardt took over. Jack Burghardt and his wife, Ann, became close friends with the Director General and were soon seeing him almost every day for English lessons. The lessons were more free ranging discussions than classes and provided Mr. Burghardt with useful information about the welfare and rehabilitation needs of Vietnam and, more importantly, about the culture and character of the Vietnamese.

Mr. Burghardt's growing knowledge of Vietnam and his close contact with other agencies and Vietnamese ministries facilitated PLAN's steady growth in the Saigon/Cholon area and in refugee camps between Saigon and Da Lot, 300 kilometers to the north. Within a year the number of Vietnamese Foster Children more than doubled.

In June 1960 there were nearly 1,500 Foster Children. In addition to monthly direct financial assistance, cash gifts, and gift parcels from their Foster Parents, the children and their families regularly received a wide variety of material from PLAN. The following material, distributed during the six-month period from April to September 1960 is typical of the supplies then provided by PLAN to its families:

2,901	meters of poplin cloth
2,052	meters white batiste
1,622	meters blue drill (fabric)
2,840	tubes of toothpaste
1,638	toothbrushes
3,058	bottles of multivitamins
1,360	plastic raincoats
1,418	pairs of rubber sandals
1,529	hats
4,016	towels
31,774	copy books
1,622	tins of insect spray
420	spray guns
2,714	book covers
1,766	no-spill ink bottles
4,021	mosquito nets
4,507	rulers
1,437	boxes of colored pencils
2,997	ball point pens
9,440	kilograms of laundry soap
36,240	bars of face soap
3,123	pens
15,588	pen points
4,989	erasers
1,766	compasses
8,830	sheets of blotting paper

Before Mr. Burghardt arrived most of the supplies distributed in Vietnam were sent from New York. Because of the differences in the two cultures, the supplies were not always useful. Vietnamese children, unlike Korean children, were not accustomed to western style clothes and shoes. When these were distributed, the families, or the children themselves, generally sold them and bought the clothes and shoes they were accustomed to. Realizing this, Mr. Burghardt convinced the New York staff that more appropriate supplies could be purchased locally.

As PLAN grew it was able to provide more and better services. In April 1960, with the help of a Dr. Brooks and the Saigon Seventh-Day Adventist Hospital, PLAN children began to receive regular physical examinations and x-rays. Ninety-eight percent of the children examined had intestinal worms. The program provided treatment for this and for the many other diseases that were diagnosed.

PLAN expanded geographically as well. Local officials from Nha Trang Province and from the newly established Social Welfare Office in the Central Highlands had expressed an interest in PLAN's work and programs were established there in 1960.

Nha Trang Province consisted mainly of fishing villages, actually refugee camps, along the coast north of Saigon. The villages were settled by groups of refugees from North Vietnam. There had been some attempts at farming but the sandy and acidic soil barely support-ed agriculture. The fishing, too, was poor. To support themselves, the refugees augmented the poor catch with meager crops of sweet potatoes and corn. The poverty was severe enough to appall even PLAN's Vietnamese social workers.

The Central Highlands, the area around Ban Me Thuot, was pioneer country. The government was clearing the forest and settling families, mostly refugees, to farm their allotted land. Their prospects for the future were good, but, in the meantime, PLAN help was needed.

PLAN also hoped to enroll the children of the mountain tribes in the area. The Vietnamese government was making a concerted effort to integrate these tribes into Vietnamese society by encouraging them to settle into permanent houses, take up farming, and educate their children. The tribes, called by the French term "Montagnards," in preference to the Vietnamese term "Moi" (savages), lived in the forests and mountains of the highlands. They wore little or no clothing (loin cloths for the men, sarongs or skirts for the women), had little regard for work, thinking of it as, at best, an unfortunate and occasional necessity, and did not live in permanent villages.

The government had attempted to educate Montagnard children but met with little success. PLAN hoped that it could encourage the parents to keep their children in school by paying school fees and providing monthly funds for food and housing. The program for these children, and the children of other aboriginal tribes, was delayed until 1962 and limited by security considerations.

From 1960 on, there was a marked increase in the activities of the Viet Minh (Viet Nam Doc-Lap Dong-Minh—the League for the Independence of Vietnam) throughout the country. There had not yet been any incidents of terrorism in Saigon, but Americans had been warned to be careful in public places at night. Mr. Burghardt had taken the precaution of consulting the Ministry of Social Action before he or PLAN staff took any trips beyond the Saigon/Cholon area.

Security became one of the prime factors in the consideration of program sites. PLAN worked where it could, where there was a reason-able chance of safety for the staff and the Foster Children. A second consideration was cooperation and help from the local official and unofficial community leaders. The limited number of trained social workers and the concern for their safety made it impossible for the provincial program sites to have full-time PLAN staff. The resulting program was similar to PLAN's Greek program which was implemented largely through rural government welfare centers. PLAN social workers from Saigon would enroll the children and return as often as time and safety would allow. Between their visits, the local government welfare staff or PLAN liaison would handle the monthly payments, collect and distribute letters and supplies, and handle the program details. In general, PLAN's work and expansion in the provinces was determined by the varying levels of security. Under such conditions, the program was limited. Potentially, it could have had a much greater impact in the villages and provided far more opportunity for long-term planning.

Provincial towns generally consisted of a cluster of villages surrounding one or more developed centers. The villages were distinct, with separate names and small markets. Families usually had space around their homes for a garden with a few fruit trees, manioc, bananas, vegetables, or tea. Some had a few chickens, ducks, or pigs. Villagers were poor, but seldom starving. They augmented what they could grow with income from whatever work was available: tea picking, fishing, rice harvesting, or charcoal making. When employment was seasonal, scarce, or unavailable, there was no money for clothing, education, home repairs, or medical needs. For these people PLAN aid meant the beginning of independence, the possibility of planning the future.

PLAN assigned Saigon caseworkers to each provincial center and they tried to visit the families every other month. By 1966 road travel was so risky that they had to fly. PLAN depended on Air Vietnam and, in emergencies, USAID planes, army aircraft, or Air America. The caseworkers usually felt much safer in civilian planes, planes which were not made targets by their military markings.

The local liaison in the centers was usually with the provincial welfare bureau. PLAN's program was often the only social service program available to the provincial social workers and, since it gave them a caseload, the local staff was glad to cooperate with PLAN. Where the liaison was a local religious leader, every effort was made to insure the impartiality of the program. This impartiality became increasingly important as the political and religious differences deepened.

A 6 December 1960 memo from Jack Burghardt to Gloria Matthews describes some of the hazards of provincial travel:

I returned last week from a trip to Ban Me Thuot and Nha Trang. From what we could learn, the area in and immediately near Ban Me Thuot is, for the present, fairly safe. There has been considerable trouble further north at Kontum, however, and I recently learned that the Viet Minh have been posting notices in the "Montagnard" villages reading "kill all Americans."

In Nha Trang itself things seem fairly calm but outside the city they are having considerable trouble. When we went to the refugee camps 50 kilometers to the south, we had an armed jeep escort leading the way and found additional security forces posted in the camps during the time we were there to make the payment. The government officials were most anxious to have us leave as quickly as possible, traveling at break-neck speed to get back to the city before dusk. We were told that there had been shooting just behind the one camp the night before our visit.

In Saigon itself, it begins to appear that the commies are moving closer. On Sunday morning at 10 a.m. a time bomb went off at the Golf Clubhouse located about 1½ kilometers from our house. One person was killed and several injured. There is much speculation as to whether this is a prelude to a terrorist campaign within the city itself. Meanwhile life goes on pretty much as usual but one can sense a bit of uneasiness. Rest assured we will take no unnecessary risks but it is making it difficult for us to maintain close contact with some of our children.

On 9 December he wrote a sequel:

It seems that while visiting the two refugee camps about 50 kilometers from Nha Trang, we happened to change our schedule at the last minute, visiting Xuan Ninh camp first instead of last. From the reports they received, the communist Viet Minh arrived in Xuan Ninh about 15 minutes after we had left—they apparently were operating on the original schedule. That's a bit close for comfort.

During Mrs. An's and Miss My's[1] visit there, they had an escort of eight armed men who followed them about all the time. With conditions such as this, I feel we had best not take on any more new work in that area for the time being—I'm sure you will agree.

Mr. Burghardt's schedule could have reached the rebels in any

---

[1] Mrs. An and Miss My were PLAN caseworkers who had just come back from a week in Nha Trang enrolling new Foster Children.

number of ways. The Ministry knew his plans, as did the local officials, the social workers, and some of the families; they had to know in order to make arrangements for the visit. The rebels got their information through sympathizers in the government or through the local villagers. In the villages the people had to talk to both sides. During the day, the government was in control, at night, the rebels. The villagers were caught in the middle.

In response to the memo from Mr. Burghardt about security, Tom O'Hagen, PLAN Secretary, ordered him to stay in Saigon:

> Julian Bergoffen and I have seen your letters of December 6th and 9th about the Communist terrorism in Vietnam. We are, of course, worried about your safety, and after having discussed it with Gloria, have come to this conclusion and issue the following order to you:
>
> You are not to leave the city of Saigon on Foster Parents' Plan business.
>
> This is not a suggestion or request, it is an order; nothing is left to your discretion. And this order will stand until further notice.
>
> You can keep us informed on conditions and increasing or decreasing safety in the country and if we see fit to revise our present instruction you will be notified. You can tell Gloria as fully as you can what effect this is going to have on our operations.

Mr. Burghardt replied that, while he appreciated and shared their concern for his safety, he certainly could not ask his staff to go where he could not. The travel restriction was lifted and explained on 19 January 1961:

> Julian Bergoffen and I both thought you'd bridle against the instruction. It was written as emphatically as it was because we are deeply concerned about your safety. We decided to leave nothing to your discretion for fear that you'd not exercise it wisely. You and your staff have had at least two close escapes as reported by you in your letters of December 6th and December 9th. We presume that you exercised what you thought were proper precautions on those trips, but nonetheless they were both near things and fraught with danger that apparently could not be anticipated. We made our instructions peremptory for another reason; we know that the average American or other Westerner in your position is sensitive to the possible charge of timidity, and hence will sometimes exercise his judgment as to personal safety with

that in view, and consequently will not always make a proper judgment.

We were also conscious that in our letter of December 20th we made one rule for you and another for the staff. We thought you might quickly pick this up and object, which you have done. We wrote as we did because we decided that you, as an American, are more vulnerable than natives working for us—you are the prime target and therefore stricter measures for your safety were necessary.

The security situation deteriorated as the Viet Minh intensified its efforts to embarrass and discredit the government of President Diem. Ambushes increased and the first American civilian was killed. In January 1961 American civilians were asked to remain in Saigon until the elections were over. A coup attempt added to the already tense atmosphere.

At the end of 1960 there were 2,092 Foster Children receiving benefits. The medical program continued with the Adventist Hospital. In addition to the US $8 monthly financial assistance that families received, Special Services Funds were available for artificial limbs, surgery, funerals, home repairs, and other emergency needs. In one case, a child was "bought" out of bondage by paying her parents' debt.

During 1961 and 1962 the fighting intensified and the conflict with the Viet Minh, now reorganized as the National Liberation Front (NLF), was openly called a war. Travel in the provinces became even more difficult. Civilians were regularly kidnapped. Rice shipments had to be limited to daylight hours. A dusk-to-dawn curfew was imposed on truck and bus traffic north of Saigon. Grenade attacks began against United States Army billets and places where Americans congregated. The increasing number of visiting American officials and senior officers suggested a major American presence in the near future.

The problem of trying to defend the many rural villages and, at the same time, control the growth and activities of the NLF was alleviated briefly by the Strategic Hamlet Program. Under this plan the villages were fortified with moats, barbed wire fences, foot traps, sharpened bamboo stakes, and gun towers. The villagers, as much prisoners as defenders, were given training in small arms and defense tactics. Schools and basic medical facilities were provided as well as adult "civic education" classes. PLAN worked in the relative safety of these camps and the number of Foster Children steadily increased.

Mr. Burghardt directed PLAN/RVN until February 1963 when he left Saigon to become the Director of PLAN's program in Greece. In an interview at his New Hampshire home in 1982, he recalled rehabilitation work as one of the most successful and personally satisfying of PLAN's efforts in Vietnam. The Vietnamese, he said, were generally fatalistic about their handicapped children. Since they could not have afforded treatment, even if it had been available, there was little they could do but shrug their shoulders and accept the handicap as inevitable. PLAN was able to provide treatment and rehabilitation for many of these children through the close personal and professional relationships Mr. Burghardt had established with the doctors of the Seventh-Day Adventist Hospital, the government hospital, and the visiting doctors from the hospital ship HOPE.

When the HOPE volunteers arrived in the Republic of Vietnam, PLAN asked for their aid and they responded with a team of orthopedic surgeons. Some of the doctors became close friends of Mr. Burghardt and he was able to call them up and say, "I've got this case . . . could you try to do something about it?" Usually they could and did. The doctors were glad to help, many of them had never seen such cases before and worked almost continuously, often spending eight or ten hours a day in surgery.

One child of 11, a polio victim, had never walked. He had been crawling on his hands and knees all his life. PLAN got the boy into a surgical program which eventually enabled him to straighten his legs and walk with the help of braces. When he was older, he became a social worker involved with the relocation of refugee families in Saigon. When the Republic of Vietnam collapsed in 1975, he and his family joined the thousands of "boat people" and eventually settled in the United States.

Miss A. Elizabeth Brown, a Canadian, became PLAN's Director in Vietnam on 18 January 1963. One of her first concerns was the unevenness of medical care available to Foster Children and their families. PLAN families in the Saigon/Cholon area had a variety of medical services available to them. PLAN staff could provide the education necessary for them to know what was beyond the scope of traditional medicine and funds or referrals for treatment. The relationships Mr. Burghardt had established with the Saigon medical community continued to develop and children were regularly brought in from the provinces for treatment, but there was no uniform medical program. The escalating war frustrated all attempts to provide regular examinations, inoculations, and x-rays to all Foster Children.

There were 41 public health centers scattered throughout the country, but the inadequacies of equipment, trained personnel, and supplies made them less than ideal. Arrangements were made in three villages for PLAN to use these centers. In Binh-Tuy the Foster Children used the clinic in the local hospital; in Da-lat a Seventh-Day Adventist Hospital doctor made periodic visits; in Kontum the Catholic Hospital was available.

A Mennonite Clinic on the outskirts of Nha Trang agreed to provide examinations and treatment to a dozen PLAN families a week. The clinic served PLAN families within a 60 mile radius of Nha Trang. The families accepted the long trip to the doctor because no other facilities existed. The distance made comprehensive medical care almost impossible. If people were only mildly ill, they might not choose to make the inconvenient trip to the doctor; if they were very sick, they could not.

An itinerant medical team and an interpreter from the Seventh-Day Adventist Hospital in Saigon examined PLAN families in the hilly tea-growing country around Bao-loc, 125 miles from Saigon. Luckily for these PLAN families, the team enjoyed themselves on their first venture into the provinces and were eager to return regularly. They were put up in a hostel for visiting government officials and the local Vietnamese Catholic priests catered to their vegetarian diet with bantering good will. In Honai, where PLAN had its largest provincial program, the Canadian Brothers of St. John gave the Adventist team the use of their clinic one day a week for PLAN families from the Honai/Bien Hoa region.

These medical programs, made possible by PLAN's Special Services Funds, resulted in a noticeable improvement in the health of Foster Children which was reflected in letters to their Foster Parents. Many letters praised the "PLAN doctors" who examined the whole family and provided medicine as needed. This was not the uniform, preventive medical program Miss Brown wanted to provide, but it was, in the circumstances, the best available. Many of the children could not even get chest x-rays; though there were government owned mobile x-ray units available, their use was limited by a combination of bad roads and poor security conditions.

The problems of providing adequate medical care to Foster Children were typical of the overall problems of providing services to children in Vietnam. Successive governments concentrated their energy and resources on fighting the NLF and staying in power. The social welfare needs of the Vietnamese were recognized but few resources were appropriated for them. The Ministry of Social Action was renamed the Ministry of Social Welfare in 1964. The Ministers did what they could, but, with limited funds and personnel, they could do little.

In 1964 there were no government authorized social work education programs in Vietnam. The only social work education in the country was the "Ecole d'Infirmières et d'Assistantes Sociales," established by Caritas, which provided high school graduates with a three-year program of class and field instruction. Sister Francoise, who organized the program in 1948 and directed it until her death, was highly respected and generally considered to be the embodiment of everything a social worker should be. She was killed in 1973 by a careless terrorist who blew up the wrong plane. Miss Brown recruited as many of Sister Francoise's graduates as she could. In spite of the competition from the government and other agencies, a large percentage of each graduating class usually went to work for PLAN.

The shortage of social workers led to very large caseloads and limitations on the services PLAN was able to provide. Relief work remained a major part of PLAN's program in Vietnam. The large caseloads obviated the more comprehensive rehabilitation and developmental programs PLAN implemented in other countries. Work in the provinces was even more difficult than work in the urban areas because of transportation and communication problems. Many of the villages where Foster Children lived were surrounded by areas considered "insecure," that is, more or less in the control of or influenced by the NLF. This "insecurity" severely limited the movements of the caseworkers. Sometimes it was possible for the caseworkers to use government vehicles to visit the villages; sometimes it was safer to go by taxi or motor bike. Some areas could not be visited at all.

Elizabeth Brown described the caseworkers' travels in her Quarterly Report (January-March 1965):

Caseworker's visit to Binh Tuy in December was marked by the appearance of five Viet Cong from the roadside to stop the car. Travelling with our liaison officer, a French priest, in his little Renault station wagon, she sat out the twenty minutes while they took Father into the forest. A hundred odd case records reposed under the seat, and in her pocket book a few thousand piastres to be used as Special Service Funds (for in all but one center, our grants go by money order as a security precaution), but the Viet Cong let them off "easy" with a fine of 50 piastres (less than a dollar) and they went on their way. No one can blame the caseworker, a married woman with her own family, for declining to take such a journey again. No one would ask her to, though the buoyant Norman priest says "The Viet Cong control and will demand a tax of the driver on any road in the country, but for passengers, pooh! There's no risk." Maybe so. For the time being we have no staff contact with the caseload in Binh Tuy.

Our worker in Da-lat makes her trips back and forth to Saigon by seat in a taxi. On such occasions she takes with her no evidence of PLAN's work, no evidence that she is even associated with an American organization, as she knows this would make her vulnerable to Viet Cong reaction were they to be stopped. This is her practice also in travelling the roads from Da-lat to Lao Lam and Dran. The road to Blao is still open, and travel on this road with case records and PLAN papers offers no difficulty. All four of these centers, as mentioned above, receive their payment monies by money order.

One may ask official clearance perhaps from USOM, to travel the roads. In some areas one will get "no permission" simply because there are no intelligence reports on the area. This is so up-country in the less populated areas. In the area surrounding Bien Hoa-Honai, a fairly populous region, the lines of definite insecurity are fairly well defined, the roads intermittently declared closed or open and as incidents increase the possibilities of keeping appointments lessen.

The conditions described by Miss Brown in 1965 prevailed for the next ten years. Sometimes one area was safe; sometimes another. Sometimes Saigon was subject to street fighting and rocket attacks; sometimes only the occasional grenade or murder. The basic circumstances and problems of work in Vietnam did not change. The shortage of qualified staff continued, as did the shortage of doctors and the disheartening corruption that pervaded every level of government. The difference was that all of Vietnam's difficulties were enormously magnified by the massive United States military presence.

The build-up of the American presence in the Republic of Vietnam, which started in 1965, brought hundreds of thousands of American soldiers and civilians, a massive influx of money and material, and opportunities for corruption almost beyond the dreams of avarice. It created new social problems and exacerbated old ones. With the American presence came dozens of voluntary agencies, a much greater emphasis by the government on providing relief and social welfare services, and the material and logistical support of social welfare programs by the United States. The often repeated goal of the American and South Vietnamese governments was to "win the hearts and minds of the Vietnamese." One obvious way to do this was to provide for their basic human needs, to define and implement adequate standards of education, medical care, nutrition, and housing. Both governments soon lost sight of the fact that there were two distinct sets of problems. The first were the problems shared by all underdeveloped countries: the effects of poverty, disease, illiteracy, and malnutrition. The second were directly related to the war: massive displacement of populations, the disruption of social institutions, the breakdown of the infrastructure, inflation, the growing number of widows with young children, the destruction of crops and farmland, and the ever increasing numbers of civilian and military casualties. The actions of both governments suggested the naive belief that a military victory would provide the solution to all the ills of the Republic. Miss Brown did everything she could to convince the authorities that solutions to war-related problems should be planned with a view to meeting the long-term development needs of Vietnam.

For PLAN, the uncertainty continued. In February 1965 American dependents were evacuated and the PLAN executive staff in New York discussed closing the office. Miss Brown wrote that PLAN's work was going along as normally as ever and suggested holding on until the British ordered their dependents to leave. This was agreed to, and the work went on.

NLF activity in the provinces increased dramatically. On 6 April 1966 Miss Brown wrote:

> Things are sufficiently uncertain there [Danang] that we are not at all sure what future planning we can make. Indeed, at the moment it is difficult to plan for any provincial center.

At that time the government held only the larger cities and towns. Until these enclaves were expanded and linked, the countryside was inaccessible. The highways and railroads were effectively closed, side roads could only be travelled by, at the very least, paying tolls to the NLF forces or bandits manning the roadblocks. Consequently, little food came in from the countryside to feed the refugee-swollen populations of the cities. Although Vietnam had long been a rice exporting nation, the government was forced to import rice and other food supplies from Thailand and the United States. Prices skyrocketed. During the month of January 1966 the cost of living in Saigon rose by 48 percent. In spite of the growing chaos, PLAN continued its efforts to provide much needed services to children and their families in Saigon and the provinces. The Rev. Verent J. Mills, Director of Operations of the Christian Children's Fund,[2] singled out the work of PLAN and Elizabeth Brown in a 10 March 1966 report to his Board of Directors on child welfare in South Vietnam:

> As to agencies in South Vietnam concerned with child welfare, mention must be made of the contribution Foster Parents Plan has made and is making through the capable efforts of Miss Elizabeth Brown. Her work has been fraught with difficulties during the past five years, but her dogged perseverance and organizing ability have brought to fruition a very effective program through which some 5,000 children are being assisted.
>
> We had several conferences with Miss Brown and, due to the similarity of our programs, we benefited much from her experience and her counsel.

With the restrictions on PLAN's activities, the chance for creative and innovative work came through cooperation with the various community groups, other voluntary agencies, governmental ministries, and the Council of Voluntary Agencies and its associated committees.

The Council was established in 1966 to coordinate the relief and social welfare efforts of the foreign voluntary agencies, Vietnamese agencies, USAID programs, embassies, and Vietnamese ministries. The purpose of the Council, as stated in its constitution, was to learn and better understand Vietnamese needs as interpreted by Vietnamese. The Council would pool the members' experience, coordinate their efforts, and seek to foster cooperation on as wide a level as possible with local, governmental, and intergovernmental organizations in Vietnam.

Miss Brown was active in the organization of the Council and her long experience working with Vietnamese children and families made her a logical choice for Chairman of the Children's Welfare Committee, whose goal was to enhance the effectiveness of the member agencies' child welfare programs. The task of the Committee was to study the problems of child welfare and the developments which affected it, plan and research programs, coordinate child welfare programs of the member agencies, and be available for consultation. Members of the Committee included representatives from the American Friend's Service

---

[2]Christian Children's Fund had at that time been in Vietnam for 14 years, working, for the most part, with children in Nha Trang, Danang, and Ban Me Thuot.

Committee, Catholic Relief Services, Community Development Fund/ Save the Children Federation, International Social Service, ORC/USAID, Oxfam, the Salvation Army, UNICEF, Vietnam Christian Service, and the United Nations consultant on child welfare at the Ministry of Social Welfare. Specific areas of investigation included the institutional care of children, the problems of illegitimate children of American personnel, and medical care for wounded children, particularly for amputees and children burned by napalm or phosphorous bombs.

The Korean example lent urgency to the investigation of the institutional care of children. When the Korean War began there were 70 orphanages in Korea, when it was over there were 595. The Committee was afraid this could be repeated in Vietnam through spontaneous and unregulated generosity to orphanages which would, inevitably, reduce aid to families and communities. In Vietnam, as in Korea, most of the institutionalized children had at least one parent alive. The children were institutionalized as a last resort because the parents or, more often, the widowed mother, could no longer provide for their care.

The extremely high death rate of children in their first year in Vietnamese orphanages graphically and grimly illustrates not so much the poor quality of the institution, but the desperate efforts the Vietnamese families made to stay together. A child in Vietnam was traditionally the responsibility of the whole family and institutional care was directly counter to this. Most children orphaned by the war were taken in by relatives. Vietnamese mothers often came into the PLAN office trailed by a line of children to say that a relative's home had been hit and the parents killed. She would happily accept responsibility for the children of her sister, brother, or cousin if only she could get financial assistance. PLAN, by enrolling one of the school age children, could help to keep the whole family together.

A survey of 1,000 families in 20 refugee camps showed 25 teen-agers listed as heads of families, but every young child was attached to a family unit. A survey conducted by Lawson Mooney of the Catholic Relief Services for the Children's Welfare Committee corroborated these figures.

If the extended family was broken up by relocation, death, or poverty, a widow with children was on her own. She would keep the children as long as possible and only as a last resort take them to an orphanage. By then it was too late: the children were more dead than alive. The Children's Welfare Committee reported that only 20 percent of the children survived the first year in an institution.

The success of the Committee and the concern by the Council for family aid, rather than institutional aid, is shown by the slow growth in the number of orphanages in Vietnam. In 1965, when the American escalation seriously began, there were 72 orphanages; in October 1969, 18 months after the devastating 1968 Tet offensive, there were only 98.

As the war dragged on there was an increasing concern in the United States for the children of American servicemen and the young victims of napalm and phosphorous bombs. With the concern came a growing feeling that something should be done for these children.

There had been Eurasian and Afro-Asian children in Vietnam for years. These were the children of the French and the Senegalese Legionnaires. When the French were forced to leave Indochina they recognized the children as French citizens and many went to France. Many people in the United States felt that the Amerasian children of Vietnam should be brought to the United States for adoption to spare them the stigma and discrimination that would result from their mixed background. Others felt that special institutions and aid programs should be established. There was little concrete information about these American fathered children. Their numbers, location, and circumstances were unknown.

The Children's Welfare Committee found that there were really not very many Amerasian children in orphanages. Ann Forder of Catholic Relief Services had seen very few. Dani Adjemovitch of International Social Services had encountered a few Amerasian problems on a counseling level but had seen only a few such children in institutions. Johanna Korlu of the World Health Organization had visited a great many orphanages and had never seen any Amerasian children at all.

The group had serious doubts about the advisability or necessity of either foreign adoption or the establishment of special institutions or programs for American and foreign fathered children. The consensus was that placing the few available children with Vietnamese families would be the best way to integrate them into Vietnamese society. While there was concern that the children of Afro-American or Korean soldiers might face more discrimination than the children of Caucasian Americans, there was, as yet, no reliable information about their number or location.

The Committee felt that there was a great need for social services for all children and that to single out one particular group at the expense of all the others would not only be unjust, but would add substantially to any discrimination to which they might be subject.

After 1970 there were a disproportionate number of American fathered children in Vietnamese institutions, but they were there for economic reasons and not because of discrimination. One of the unanticipated side effects of the American phaseout on the sordid economics of war was the collapse of the thriving prostitution business. Many women, who had earned up to US $1,000 a month, were suddenly unemployed and could no longer support their children. Children who could not be raised by relatives were placed in orphanages. In spite of this, no large scale inter-country adoption scheme was carried out.

The confusion over the numbers of American fathered children continued for years. The problem was discussed in a hearing before the Committee on Foreign Relations of the United States Senate on 5 April 1972:

> Senator Percy: The estimates vary a great deal as to how many Vietnamese children have been fathered by American soldiers, ranging from 10,000 to 200,000. That is a pretty wide estimate. Can you narrow this down any? . . .
>
> Mr. Nooter[3]: The only estimate we have is the Government estimate that there might be 10,000 or 15,000. But, I must say I am sure that is an approximation and I do not know any way to—
>
> Senator Percy: What is your own private guess as to whether it is a very conservative figure or a realistic figure?
>
> Mr. Nooter: I have no particular basis to question it. I would think that with the large American presence through so many years the number would be substantial, but I really do not have any basis for thinking that that number is either high or low.

The Vietnamese Government was opposed to any large scale inter-country adoption program. In a letter dated July 1971, quoted at the same hearing by Wells Klein, Director General of the American Branch of International Social Service, the Vietnamese Minister of Social Welfare stated:

> My Ministry's policy is not to distinguish racially mixed orphans from the others, for the former, although they are racially mixed, are Vietnamese-born citizens. Therefore, my

[3]Robert H. Nooter, Deputy Coordinator, Bureau for Supporting Assistance, Agency for International Development.

Ministry has no intention of establishing separate orphanages for racially mixed children for this would have a traumatic effect on them.

The Ministry's position not only applied to children in institutions, but to all racially mixed children. Most of the American fathered children lived in Vietnamese families and had full Vietnamese brothers and sisters who would not benefit from special assistance. If special assistance programs were established, they would identify and isolate these children who would, for the most part, grow up and live in Vietnam.

Thus, because of the views expressed by the Vietnamese Government and the voluntary agencies, special programs for American fathered children did not become an acceptable approach to child welfare in Vietnam and were not implemented. Whatever was done for American fathered children was done as part of larger programs for the broader and much larger population of needy children and their families in Vietnam.

The "problem" of children burned by napalm and phosphorous bombs was, in some ways, similar to the "problem" of American fathered children. These children aroused considerable feelings of guilt and responsibility in growing segments of the American public opposed to their government's involvement in Vietnam. Photographs of horribly burned children appeared with grim regularity as the war became more and more a media event for the American and European press. Miss Brown's committee investigated children in hospitals and clinics in 1967. They found the publicity given to the burned children, like the publicity given to the American fathered children, drew attention away from the larger more serious problems of medical care for children. There were children burned by phosphorus and napalm, as there were children burned by kerosene stoves, house fires, and brush fires. Burned children were treated as burned children and not classified by the causes of those burns.

There was no way to know how many young victims of firebombs had died before they could receive treatment. Because of the difficulty of putting out burning napalm and the impossibility of putting out burning phosphorus, most of the victims died. If they survived the bombs, if there was a hospital or clinic nearby, if they survived the journey, they received the same treatment as other burned children.

The consensus among the voluntary agencies, based largely on information provided by the Child Welfare Committee, was that the most practical approach, by far, for wounded and burned children was to treat them in Vietnam in facilities aided and developed by foreign agencies working in cooperation with official and unofficial Vietnamese agencies. An agency planning to evacuate children for treatment estimated that it would cost between US $20,000 and US $30,000 for each child—money that could be much more effectively used for medical care in Vietnam. Aside from the great expense, foreign treatment would separate children from their families and might cause the child to suffer unnecessary psychological harm.

The Committee of Responsibility, organized at Howard Medical School in 1966, planned to bring children who were victims of the war, particularly burned children, to the United States for treatment. The Committee received wide support from doctors and hospitals throughout the United States who volunteered their services and facilities.

An investigating team sent by the Committee of Responsibility reported the results of their nationwide survey to the Child Welfare Committee. They had found far fewer children who would benefit from treatment in the United States than they had anticipated. They found that the publicity given to the burn victims had drawn attention away from the other, more numerous, injuries. Ninety percent of the war injuries to children were multiple fractures, many of which led to amputation. Though the amputations had been skillfully performed and needed no further surgery, the team questioned whether all of them would have been performed if there had been more skilled medical personnel available.[4]

There were serious shortages of hospital space and trained personnel in Saigon and in the provinces. Vietnamese doctors, it was reported, were more than willing to let foreign doctors bear the burden of the work. The foreign doctors were usually lacking the time or interest to teach new skills and methods to the indigenous staff. Army of the Republic of Vietnam (ARVN) doctors often devoted most of their energy to private practice to supplement their monthly income of US $60 and spent only the minimum time required in provincial hospitals.

There was a strong role for the voluntary agencies in several areas of health care and treatment. They could provide and support trained technicians, administrative staff for existing hospitals and clinics, and

---

[4]The Rehabilitation Center in Saigon could handle 300 amputees a month. Other proposed centers in Danang, Quang Ngai, and Can Tho would be able to handle an additional 200 a month. There were far more than 500 amputations a month.

provide funding to establish and develop more medical facilities. Children and their parents needed education in basic health, nutrition, and sanitation. They also needed education about weapons. Vietnam was littered with guns, unexploded mines, grenades, booby traps, and ordnance which often killed or maimed the children who found them. The United States and ARVN forces added to the problems by rewarding children for turning in weapons or leading them to weapon caches.

Thus, though PLAN's programming activities were often restricted by the war, the influence it and other similar agencies were able to exert had broad effects on medical and social welfare programs throughout the Republic of Vietnam which strengthened, rather than further undermined, the Vietnamese family. The ability and experience of Miss Brown in Vietnam made her a valuable and frequently called upon resource for other voluntary agencies, USAID, and Vietnamese officials.

Still the war continued. One of the most difficult periods for PLAN, its children, and its staff came during and after the Tet offensive of 1968. Tet, the Vietnamese Lunar New Year, is the most important holiday in Vietnam. It is a time when families gather for religious services, visit with neighbors, and celebrate. In Saigon the roads were crowded with vehicles of every sort bringing flowers and vegetables from Da-lat and fruit from the Mekong Delta. In the countryside, Tet comes at the end of the second harvest and after the planting of the next season's rice crop.

In 1968 Tet lasted from 29 January until 1 February. It was the Spring of the Year of the Monkey and a shattering exception to the traditional joy of the season. Fred Chaffee, Assistant Director in Vietnam, was combining a going-away party for a USAID friend with the traditional Tet celebrations on 29 January.

> Thus, it was that on the first day of the Year of the Monkey we found ourselves going from Vietnamese home to Vietnamese home drinking Pernod, cognac, and beer, while munching shrimp popovers and salted nuts. It was an experience that left us dizzy by noon but the conversation was light and lively. Invariably talk would turn to the war and the mood was hopeful. Hadn't the NLF and the North Vietnamese suffered serious reversals at Loc Ninh and Dakto? Weren't they on the run everywhere, effectively operating only out of sanctuaries in Laos and Cambodia? The bombing in the North and the constant harassment in the South has had its effect. They're tired and want to talk. Of course, of course, and my astrologer, whose record of true predictions you all are well aware of,

has said that this is to be the year peace comes to Vietnam. And then the 6 o'clock news with the report that the "secure" cities of Nha Trang and Qui Nhon were under attack and the sudden intuition that Saigon was going to be hit that night. Saigon was strangely quiet for a time when the curfew had been lifted to allow the visiting with friends and neighbors that is so typical of this season. The hours dragged on marked by seemingly endless cups of coffee until shortly after 1 a.m. the thump of incoming mortars signalled the eruption of explosions throughout the city. This lasted for several minutes and was followed by an eerie silence broken only by the sporadic clatter of small arms and automatic weapon fire.

Wide awake now we sat on our beds smoking cigarettes and conjecturing as to what had been attacked and the extent of the damage that had been done. Some forty minutes passed until the calm was again interrupted by the roar of helicopter after helicopter passing over the house and then silence. Sleep came easily now. The attacks were over, and at 10 that morning I was to serve as interpreter for a Canadian Foster Parent when he met his Foster Family.

Morning brought a rude awakening as news reached us of the extent of the attack both in Saigon and throughout the rest of the country, and the announcement that all Americans were under a 24-hour curfew. Discussing this news with Elizabeth at the office we decided that the Foster Parent, even if he had arrived in country, would not be able to come to PLAN. As we prepared to leave for home we were brought to the window by the clanking of tanks rumbling up Yen Do onto Cong Ly and out towards the airport. "Not since the time of Diem" was Elizabeth's parting comment.

The next three days were as an instant, filled with apprehension, frustration, and tragedy. As the seriousness of the situation became evident, more and more allied troops poured in, and the rage of battle filled the air. Sniper fire was everywhere. A hasty barricade of oil drums and furniture cut Yen Do off from Cong Ly just across from the office. Topless jeeps with sandbagged windshields screamed down Cong Ly packed with men and guns at the ready. And the estimated total of Viet Cong fighting units within the city kept on rising.

Refugees fled down the street, pausing only to stare incredulously at the tanks, armoured personnel carriers, and flame throwers that roared past. Cooks and maids away for their Tet holidays came rushing back to the compound with their families, telling of the horrors and devastation, pleading to be allowed to stay. Outside the gates were the not so fortunate struggling along with whatever they could carry seeking the nearest church, school, or pagoda.

A new sound came to Saigon as gunships emptied their lethal loads into heavily populated areas. As if in a dream, we stood on the roof of a four storied apartment building in the back of the compound and watched the strafing and bombing taking place two, three, and four blocks away.

Thursday morning the battles of Cholon and the An Quang Pagoda were enjoined and the war came a little bit closer. Corsairs dove shrieking over the house to slam their rockets in half a mile up the street. At 11 a.m. a 2½ ton army truck drove by with 18 dead GIs neatly laid out in the back. The afternoon and the following day were to see many more such vehicles.

Thursday afternoon police control became tighter as all males over the age of 12 were stopped and abruptly thrown into trucks and carted away to jails or military camps if their identification papers were questionable. Those who hesitated to stop were shot as we witnessed in front of the house that afternoon. The man approached the check point on his Honda and began to make a U turn some ten yards away. A whistle was blown, a warning shot fired, and the Honda rider continued to make his turn but never finished it as six police jumped up from behind sandbags and cut him down.

Early Friday evening another flurry of shots rang out near the house but this was different. Three VC were running up Cong Ly, rifles in hand, two on one side and one on the other. They had reached a point some eighty or ninety yards from the compound when two jeeploads of police descended upon them at great speed just spraying both sides of the street and knocking the three Viet Cong down on the first pass.

The weekend was much of the same thing. More bombing, rocketing, and fire fights, until one wondered if you could ever go to sleep without the thumps, the whine of the mini-guns, and the booms of 750 pounders. The weekend also saw the end of a two day graham cracker and Roka cheese diet as we were able to get out and buy bread and a few canned goods in the local markets which had begun to reopen. Tet was over but it would be a long time before things approached the pre-holiday normality.

Monday, the 5th of February, PLAN's office reopened at 8 a.m. and prepared for the inundation of families who had suffered seriously during the attacks. As families and staff came in over the next two weeks, what we had guessed at before was all too tragically verified.

Mr. Hung, a driver living in Cholon, told of spending eight sleepless nights in the street with his family. Twenty-four of the surrounding houses had burned to the ground and he had feared that he would fall asleep and his would also go up in flames. Bodies were everywhere with no one and no place to bury them. The stench of decay was overwhelming and there was no water. People were carrying in water from a few miles away and selling it for 17¢ a gallon. He had no food and needed an advance to buy some rice for his wife and four children.

Mr. Phiet, the warehouse man, was trapped in his home near the 4th military camp on the outskirts of Saigon. The VC had occupied parts of the camp and it took three days of heavy fighting before they were dislodged. Dead and wounded were on every street. The fourth day the wounded were evacuated to hospitals and the dead trucked away. The Viet Cong casualties were thrown in a pile on the street and burned.

Miss Tuyet Nuong, a caseworker, went to her village in Long An, a province just south of Saigon, to celebrate Tet with her family. Heavy fighting broke out on the first day of the New Year and continued for a week and a half. Torn between staying with her family and coming to Saigon to help, she finally left home on 11 February, travelling by Lambretta, horsecart, and walking more than 15 miles before she reached Saigon. Part of the journey was through VC held areas, part through ARVN. Villages on the way could be distinguished only by their charred remains and again everywhere there was the smell of death. Her first words upon walking into the office were, "I never thought I would see you again."

Miss Xuong, a caseworker, had wanted to visit her home in Long Xuyen, far to the south of Saigon in the Delta. The journey was too dangerous, however, and she went to spend the New Year with an uncle in Baria, a small town some 25 miles east of Saigon. Casualties were heavy in Baria as the VC activity was intense. Many people died on both sides of her uncle's home, caught in the crossfire of the VC and ARVN who were fighting at such close quarters that an air attack hit them all. Coming back to Saigon on a rented Lambretta, she had to walk almost more than she rode because of destruction to the road. On the way, dead VC snipers dangled like twisted baubles from the ropes that had secured them to the palm trees.

Miss Vo Thi Nhung, a caseworker, was able to reach Saigon on 26 February. She had returned to her family home in Kien Phong, 120 miles south of Saigon in the Delta, and spent two weeks living on the floor of her home as fighting raged throughout the area. She tried three times to return to Saigon but was unsuccessful until she was able to get on a fishing junk headed for the large Delta town of My Tho. They sailed three days up the rivers and waterways and were hailed many times by the VC but refused to stop. From My Tho she was able to get a bus into Saigon. Her remark: "I was afraid."

There are other stories about other staff, but miraculously no one suffered great damage or injury. PLAN's families, however, were not so fortunate.

Le Thi Ngoc Suong (V.2867) and her family lived in Hoc Mon, a pleasant town six miles outside of Saigon. Last December mother and father repaired the house at a cost of US $555.00. They still had a debt of US $324.79 when their home was bombed as the government forces followed the Viet Cong who were retreating.

Dang Quang Hi's family (V.2218) have been on PLAN's rolls for seven years. Three years ago they went into debt to buy a house for US $174.00. With help from Special Services Funds, they cleared the debt and in January of this year they put a new roof on it at a cost of US $42.74. They lost everything when the An Quang Pagoda came under a bombing attack on February first.

Nguyen Thi Nhuan (V.5156) and her family lived in Thi Nghe, a sprawling suburb that once contained the shacks so typical of this city's slums. In May 1967 mother gathered together her savings of three years and combining it with money borrowed, put the total of US $128.21 into house repairs. On January 31st the house was burned to the ground, the fire being caused by rockets detonating in the area. Nhuan's nine year-old brother was shot and killed while the family was fleeing their burning home.

The stories are the same everywhere and our list of families whose homes were destroyed and whose members were injured or killed grows daily. One thinks of Hue and the more than one hundred families who had been living on the West wall of the Citadel, of Ban Me Thuot where 25 percent of the city is destroyed, of My Tho and Vinh Long where there was heavy and protracted fighting, and waits apprehensively for particulars on PLAN families in the provinces.

One has the awful impression that there is nothing left over here. Four, five, and seven years of PLAN's help has been wiped out overnight. And it is disheartening to have to begin a third and fourth time also. How much can these people stand? Hundreds of thousands of acres of their forests defoliated, their rice paddies pock-marked by bomb craters, and now even their last refuge, their homes, existing no longer.

While writing this report, I came across a December letter written by Tran Thi Ngoc Hien (V.5590) a 13 year-old Foster Child, to her Foster Parent. An excerpt from the translation goes:

"As I write these lines a heavy rain is falling outside.

Still, I can hear the sound of the guns from somewhere afar. Night after night I have prayed so hard for peace to come soon to Vietnam. Sometimes I just wonder why God permits such a horrible war to take place in my beloved country. I dream and long for the day when the Vietnamese people can live in peace and prosperity."

One wonders what she thinks now.

Twenty-six thousand homes were destroyed in Saigon during the Tet offensive. In the provinces 136,500 homes were destroyed. The May offensive added to the carnage. Travel in Saigon was restricted; travel in the provinces impossible.

The bitter decision to cancel 1,025 provincial Foster Children was made in July. There had been no contact with these children in six months. PLAN staff had been unable to reach them either in person or by mail and there was no way to know whether the children were still living in their villages or even if they were still alive.

The offensives of 1968 brought new streams of refugees to Saigon and added to the city's already severe housing shortage. Refugees were housed in schools, churches, pagodas, and any other place that could provide shelter. A huge temporary refugee center was set up at Petrus Ky.

Within a few months most of the temporary shelters closed as refugees found or built shelter. The Petrus Ky shelter remained open and showed signs of becoming permanent. Large apartment complexes modeled on the resettlement blocks in Hong Kong were planned for the homeless, but even if they had been built, many of the refugee families could not have afforded them. PLAN enrolled the poorest of these families.

The schools gradually reopened as the refugees who had been living in them found places to live, but hundreds of students dropped out because of the disrupted school year. The opportunities for making money in Saigon were often more attractive, and more immediately necessary, to the children and their parents than education. With the deteriorating economy many children had no alternative to dropping out of school. In the six months after the Tet offensive, food prices went up 40 percent. The textile industry, one of Vietnam's largest, was wiped out and thousands of small businesses closed. Beggars proliferated, as did shoeshine boys, black marketeers, pimps, prostitutes, bar girls, and temporary wives. PLAN social workers often found themselves in the difficult position of counseling a desperately needy young mother who was torn between working as a seamstress for US $30 a month and working as a bar girl for US $800 a month.

The refugees were in an almost hopeless position. Many were homeless; more were jobless. Most had to depend heavily upon the government for subsistence, but the government had been overwhelmed for years. Inadequate funds, poorly trained personnel, ineffective distribution, and corruption combined to thwart all relief efforts.

Resettlement, always a poorly planned and badly implemented process in Vietnam, was a total failure after 1968. Plans for government housing never materialized. Government rehousing allotments of cement, tin roofing, and money were not consistently distributed and, when they were, were grossly inadequate. The material provided by the government was never enough to rebuild a house and was usually sold by the refugees for much needed cash. The few families who could rebuild often did not because they had seen their first and second homes destroyed, others had been relocated three times in as many years. One man who had rebuilt twice killed himself when his third house was destroyed.

The lack of security and its accompanying fear affected everyone. With increasing numbers of roadblocks and security checks, PLAN staff did not know when they left for work whether they would get there. Once there they did not know if they could get home again or even if their home would be there. Home visits to Foster Children were equally precarious. The long curfew meant staff arrived late and left early. PLAN's strategically located office was occupied once by ARVN troops and, if fighting broke out again in the neighborhood, would probably be occupied again by whichever side got there first. The house of the PLAN Director was in an equally unsafe area near the strategically important airport in a compound where Vietnamese civil servants and military officials lived. Between the house and the office was a bridge that would be blown up by the ARVN if an attack came from that direction.

All of these factors affected PLAN's program. PLAN continued to help keep the poorest families together, fed, and sheltered. The Special Services Fund continued to provide for home repairs and medical care, Foster Children tried to attend school, and life went on as well as it could, but only the most tentative of plans could be made.

At the end of August 1969, there were 5,635 Vietnamese Foster Children; 3,457 were in the Saigon area, the rest were in the towns and villages east of Saigon. The exception was Hue, near the North Vietnamese border, where there were 225 children enrolled.

Elizabeth Brown directed PLAN's program in the Republic of Vietnam until January 1970, when she left to establish the PLAN National Office in Australia and become its first Acting National Director. Marian Guild, the new Director, was an experienced social worker and, like her predecessor, a Canadian. She hoped to realize the long thwarted goals of establishing a PLAN clinic and of upgrading and reorganizing the social work staff.

On 11 February 1970 Marian Guild wrote to George W. Ross of the difficulties she was encountering in her new environment:

> We talked of delegating responsibility and until this can be done I will not be able to begin to think of expanding into new programs or assess the possibility of a provincial office. Unfortunately, the way things are I do not see anyone I could delegate supervisory responsibility to. As I read progress reports coming over my desk, I wonder if anyone has any judgment at all. Many caseworkers are advising their clients to buy gold jewelry with the monthly grant and cash gifts they receive and when I discussed this with Mrs. Tri (Senior Caseworker) she thought this was reasonable since anybody's home might be destroyed tomorrow and if they escaped with their lives they would have the jewelry for a start. When I tried to interpret the fact that I thought most Foster Parents would rather see their Foster Children have a more comfortable life now, she said to me: "We have been at war for thirty years and we have no future—for many people the greatest gift anyone can give is the little security represented in a gold bracelet. It means more to many than food or medicine." Is there any reasonable answer to such logic?

Mr. Ross replied on the 16th:

> I liked your conversation with Mrs. Tri about gold jewelry!! Winnipeg was never like that, was it??! And, of course, Mrs. Tri is right. Anyone who has lived in the Far East for any length of time (just about any part of that world except Japan) has to learn that gold jewelry is the only real material security. And if we have to teach our Foster Parents that good common sense in Asia may not result in quite the same thing as good common sense in America, then we just have to accept that teaching role.

The expansion of the war into Cambodia and Laos in 1971 provided a period of tenuous, relative, and short-lived peace. The

"Vietnamization" of the war continued and the United States forces were gradually withdrawn. As the United States presence decreased, so, too, did the supporting services provided to the voluntary agencies. The agencies had had free transport of supplies and personnel on Air America, the use of military post office mail service, and commissary privileges.

As support for the voluntary agencies declined, the need for their services increased. Inflation was out of control; crime, violence, and social unrest grew; robberies and vandalism became so rampant that all theft insurance policies were cancelled. Even the poorest families, the families of the Foster Children, did not dare to leave their houses unattended. In May 1971, the PLAN driver was robbed and a Foster Child injured slightly by gunfire in the PLAN office compound. In October 1971 the Assistant Director and his wife were robbed and terrorized in their apartment.

After 25 years of occupation, corruption, and war, the social fabric of Vietnam was disintegrating. Survival had become the overriding concern and only value for many Vietnamese. PLAN's most experienced social workers estimated that eight out of every ten people who applied for PLAN enrollment misrepresented their circumstances.

In spite of all this PLAN went on. Marian Guild's main goal during her two and a half years in Vietnam was to upgrade the skills of the social workers and give them more responsibility. To this end she organized the social work department into Supervisors, Senior Social Workers, and Social Workers. Her in-service training program covered all aspects of counseling and resulted in a marked improvement in the social workers' performance. The major drawback continued to be the shortage of staff. With their large caseloads, PLAN social workers simply did not have time for the in-depth counseling most of the families needed.

The most dramatic successes were with the "special caseloads." The best caseworkers were given the "special cases." These were the children and families about to be dropped from PLAN's rolls because they were uncooperative—families where children did not go to school, where the children were neglected, where drug addiction, alcohol abuse, or juvenile delinquency were ignored or accepted. Three quarters of these families were rehabilitated to the point where they could be transferred back to the regular caseworkers.

PLAN's clinic opened in January 1971 with a half-time doctor and a full-time nurse and soon 1,000 patients a month were receiving examinations or treatment. The clinic was supplemented by a dispensary staffed by foreign volunteers. PLAN's family planning and birth control program, using birth control pills provided by Church World Service through Vietnam Christian Services, was an important part of the medical services to PLAN children and their families. Miss Guild frankly described the medical care available at the clinic as poor by western standards, but about average for Vietnam and far better than nothing.

Work in the provinces continued and in late 1971 the sub-office in Da-lat was reopened and another established in Nha Trang. In January 1972 PLAN was working in over 500 towns, villages, and hamlets in Vietnam in areas around provincial offices of the Bureau of Social Welfare.

In the provinces PLAN had become known as the organization that helped the children of the poorest families in the villages. Usually no more than 15 or 20 children were enrolled in any single village. PLAN was respected for the fairness of its enrollment and for the fact that enrolled families really did receive regular aid.

There was a consensus of feeling among the provincial social welfare staff, provincial officials, and liaison people that this was the best way PLAN could help the neediest provincial children. Other agencies were attempting community organization and development programs but were meeting with very little success. The experiences of the people in the villages, many of whom had been relocated two or three times already, left them little faith in either each other or in the permanence of their villages. All lived with the possibility of relocation at a day's notice.

PLAN was so highly regarded that most of the people who helped PLAN in the provinces felt honored to be associated with the agency. PLAN was a standing topic on the agenda of the Second Corps Social Welfare Chiefs and each knew exactly how many families were being helped and were anxious for PLAN to expand its caseload.

Administratively, PLAN's work in the provinces was difficult, to say the very least. In terms of program, it was an anachronism, little different than the programs carried out years before in the isolated villages of Greece and Italy. It was continued because it met the needs of the most desperately poor. It was the most needed and most effective work PLAN could do in the particular circumstances of rural Vietnam. It was made possible by the universal respect for PLAN in the provinces and by the help and cooperation of a great many committed local officials and volunteers without whose aid the provincial program would have ended years before.

In 1972 there were new offensives and greater social unrest. Hue was under seige and contact with the children was once again impossible. Once more plans were considered for evacuation and program termination. In the meantime work went on in the hope, if not the faith, that PLAN did have a future in Vietnam. Marian Guild planned to return to Canada in June 1972, unless she and the Chaffee family were forced to evacuate before then. It was clear that if the Director and Assistant Director were forced to leave, PLAN would leave with them.

Anne Davison, who had worked with Robert Sage in Korea in the 1950s, was appointed to be Marion Guild's successor. On 19 April 1972 George W. Ross wrote to Marian Guild:

> On the assumption that you and PLAN are still in Vietnam on May 17, 1972, Anne Davison will arrive at 2:00 p.m. . . .

In April and May of 1972 that was a large assumption to make. On 17 May Miss Davison was in Manila wondering whether she would be able to go to Saigon at all. Miss Guild cabled that the situation was better and so, on 22 May Anne Davison arrived in Saigon.

Miss Davison directed PLAN's program in Vietnam until January 1974 when she resigned to get married. The withdrawal of American combat forces in August 1972 and the official cease fire on 28 January 1973 brought not peace, but less war. Two months later, on 29 March 1973, the last American combat personnel were withdrawn. Large scale offensives ended for the time being, but incessant low level assaults continued. The relative peace only added to the uncertainty of life and work for the staff and families of PLAN. According to the Government of Vietnam's questionable figures nearly 140,000 people were killed or wounded in the first year of the cease-fire. Life and work went on as normally as possible.

PLAN's program in the Saigon area expanded and developed. Provincial sub-offices were opened in Phan Thiet and Bien Hoa. Group work increased. Rural community projects in rat control and hygiene were started in cooperation with Caritas. Psychological testing of Foster Children began. A nutritional supplement program, partially funded by a USAID grant, was started. A loan fund was set up.

Joseph Siwy, PLAN Assistant Director, took charge of the office from the time Miss Davison left until Frank Campbell arrived at the end of May 1974 to become PLAN's last Director in Vietnam. For the next year, the two concentrated on increasing the enrollment of needy children in the Saigon area and planning for expansion in the provinces. Conditions for the ever growing numbers of poor families in Saigon were as bad, or worse, than they had ever been. Between 1973 and 1974 prices steadily rose as the value of the piaster steadily fell. The price of kerosene, for example, rose nearly 300 percent, firewood prices rose almost as much. The poor stripped bark from trees that lined the streets of Saigon to fuel their stoves.

Conditions in the rural areas were sometimes a little better because of the possibility of growing some food or raising an occasional pig or chicken. Messrs. Campbell and Siwy hoped to expand rural group pilot projects in chicken and duck raising, banana and mushroom cultivation, and other income-producing projects but travel restrictions made this very difficult.

By the middle of March 1975, the Republic was in its death throes. Ban Me Thuot was unreachable, as were Hue, Nha Trang and Phan Thiet. In Da-lat and Bao-loc, where PLAN hoped to expand, people were starting to leave their villages to stream toward the coast. The Government of Vietnam was withdrawing from Hue; Quang Tri, Kontum, and Da-lat would soon be abandoned. Two weeks later Saigon was near collapse.

On Wednesday, 2 April 1975, Frank Campbell received a letter couched in diplomatic terms from the Canadian charge d'affaires telling him that he and his wife should make arrangements to leave Vietnam. On Friday the charge d'affaires telephoned to say that a Canadian military aircraft would land in Saigon the next day to evacuate Canadians and ordered the Campbells to be on it. Mr. Campbell did everything he could to get Joe Siwy and his Vietnamese wife and child on it as well, but could not. Even if he had been able to, the Vietnamese authorities would not have allowed Mrs. Siwy and their child to board the plane. When Mr. Campbell arrived at the airport, the Vietnamese authorities were allowing Canadian citizens permission to leave without proper exit visas but were turning away their Vietnamese husbands and wives. When the cargo plane left it carried only 15 adults and 63 Vietnamese orphans.[5]

Joe Siwy, his wife, and their eight month-old daughter had a much harder time amid the chaos of the mass evacuation. They were evacu-

[5]The children had been among the 243 orphans who had left the day before on the first flight of an airlift intended to take 2,000 orphans to North America for adoption. One hundred of the children and 25 of the adults escorting them were killed when the plane crashed a few minutes after take off.

ated from Saigon by the U.S. Air Force on 24 April and, after spending two days in a Guam refugee camp, arrived in Mr. Siwy's native Rhode Island on 28 April. Two days later President Duong Van Minh announced the unconditional surrender of South Vietnam. Mr. Siwy left Mr. Tuoc in charge of the PLAN office and hoped to return as soon as possible.

George W. Ross met with Madame Phan Thi Minh of the Provincial Revolutionary Government of South Vietnam's Mission in Paris on 2 May 1975 to discuss the future of PLAN's program. Speaking quietly in French and often smiling, Mme. Phan told Mr. Ross that PLAN's direct work with the children and families was exactly the right thing to do under the old regime. "But," she said, "now there is a new government, and you may feel confident in providing your assistance to us. We will see that the needy children receive it." She expressed gratitude and thanks for Mr. Ross' desire to continue PLAN's program but said that everyone must now be helped equally, that individual families could no longer be singled out for special help.

The last direct news of PLAN in Saigon came from Joe Siwy, who said that the staff was intact and the office functioning when he left. The next news came on 9 July 1975 in response to the cabled message "Hope office is still helping children and their families cable reply." Western Union called to say that the addressee had gone and left no forwarding address.

> In a land where changes in government can happen over-
> night, where newcomers in power struggle with the practical
> role they are cast to play, where pressures of political maneu-
> verings, insecurity, and inherent uncertainties distract atten-
> tion from anything that's simple and good one turns with
> relief and delight to the realistic relationships in PLAN's work:
> caseworkers' conversations with our mothers, and the chil-
> dren talking to their Foster Parents through their letters. You
> can hear the strength of these bonds whether you are on
> hand in one of five casework rooms, or whether you scan the
> myriads of children's letters that pass through our office every
> month. The child may struggle to express himself, sometimes
> his letters are flat, frozen, uninteresting. Sometimes they are
> full of oriental floweriness. But in the main the child captures
> bits and pieces of his every day life, expresses as best he can
> his love for his Foster Parent and what it means to him to
> have the supporting affection and concern in his well being,
> his schooling, his family and his play.

With Christmas and the year end at hand, we decided to let the children write the quarterly report. The following excerpts

. . . undoubtedly could be repeated by PLAN children any-where . . .

I pick up my pen for it to speak to you in place of me. I take your letter in both my hands and read it.

When eating the fruit I should remember the person who planted the tree. I am very grateful to you.

We children go to school regularly. After school I row the boat so mother may pick up firewood on the river.

My family is keeping a couple of pigs thanks to savings made from two months allowance, because we did not go to school those vacation months. With these savings Mother bought two pigs costing 1350 piastres (about $18.50). The whole family concentrate on those pigs. Every afternoon after school we children, go to gather vegetables to feed them. We pray that they grow fast so we may sell them for a profit to cover our school expenses.

Every month when I go to PLAN office with Mother I see other children getting letters from their Foster Parents. I do not know why you are quiet for two years.

I am very sorrowful to know that my foster uncle was killed in an aircraft here which was shot down by Communist guerilla gunfire! You told me that you flew with my foster uncle's wife to Washington to take care of the funeral for him. Grandmother and all of us send you our sympathy.

We have a white hen and a rooster. When I come home from school the rooster goes up on my shoulder and moves its tail from left to right. Though small, the rooster is very helpful to us. Its crowing tells us the time. At the second crowing of the rooster, which is five in the morning, my mother gets up and makes preparation to go out peddling in order to provide for us. I value my rooster very much.

Mother has sold our pigs and has bought tin sheets to have a new roof put up instead of the battered one we had. She has bought a table for us to do our homework on, a book for me to study English. Moreover she has bought a tub for us to take our baths in.

Time went by so fast and the main fishing season is over. Fishermen are now catching fish with poles and lines, and also with trap baskets. Of course they work hard, but they really enjoy their work thanks to the fresh air, the ocean and the nice scenery. My father was a fisherman and is now lying at the bottom of the immense ocean. But that is just bad luck.

When it rains at night we children sleep under the bed because the roof leaks.

Father has built new mud walls in our house. He also built a hollow behind the house with mud walls three feet thick for us to hide in when the shells come.

At night we all gather together in our house. In the oil lamp's light my brother Han studies, my elder sister Bay practices a foreign language and does her homework while my mother does needle work. When father feels well enough he teaches us about our country.

Last night before I went to sleep I listened to the night bird in the bamboo outside our house, and I thought of you.

I am coming to the bottom of the page and I still miss you.[6]

---

[6]Elizabeth Brown, Quarterly Report (October-December 1965).

10

Hong Kong: 1959-73

The British Crown Colony of Hong Kong, which includes the island of Hong Kong, Kowloon on the mainland, and the leased New Territories, is slightly larger than New York City, but the extremely mountainous nature of the land and the use of the New Territories for agriculture significantly reduce the space available for residential use. In 1959 the vast majority of the population lived in the ten square miles of urban Hong Kong and Kowloon. The result was a population density ten times that of New York City. In some parts of the city, a population density of 3,000 people per acre was not uncommon.

A 1958 study, cited by George W. Ross, then PLAN/Hong Kong Director, in a December 1959 report to Gloria Matthews, revealed the appalling results of the overcrowding. Two hundred sixty-five thousand (265,000) "households" in central Hong Kong were studied: 95,000 of these families lived in cubicles of less than 10 by 12 feet; 43,000 of the families rented bedspace, a 7 by 4 foot bunk. These bunks were built in tenements, alleys, and back streets, tucked into nooks and crannies wherever they would fit. The tenements were large two and three story buildings intended for industrial use. The open floors were filled with long rows of wooden bunks, each with a shelf above it. Light came from windows at either end of the rooms. Electricity, running water, and sanitary facilities were usually absent or nonfunctioning. Families of up to seven or eight people would rent these bunks. The father and older sons usually slept under the bunks, leaving the infants, women, and grandparents to sleep on the bunk. Four thousand (4,000) families lived on verandas. Other families lived on rooftops, on or under staircases, or simply on the street.

Uncounted thousands of refugee families on the jagged mountain sides of Kowloon lived in shacks made of discarded wood and canvas as crowded as the warrens of Hong Kong. These shack cities, hanging on the edges of cliffs, had no water, electricity, or sanitation. Cooking and, at night, light came from burning wood or kerosene.

The government had no overall housing policy and, for the most part, counted on the expanding economy to absorb Hong Kong's poor until December 1953 when a fire in a shanty town left 50,000 people homeless. The government responded with a massive housing program which had placed 300,000 people in huge resettlement blocks by 1959. Adults were allotted 24 square feet; children under 12 counted as half an adult and got 12 square feet. The living conditions were far from ideal, but, with windows, running water, toilets, and electricity on each floor, the families were delighted with them.

Mr. Ross opened the PLAN office in Hong Kong on 18 November 1959 and by the end of the year the first 58 Chinese Foster Children had been enrolled. PLAN received the enthusiastic help of both public and private agencies who recognized the importance of PLAN's emphasis on keeping families together. The program had at first been intended to provide for the housing, vocational training, and education of refugee children and families from the People's Republic of China, but the terrible conditions under which all of Hong Kong's needy families were living quickly changed the original plan and enrollment was opened to any needy family not receiving aid from another agency.

In spite of and, in part, because of the booming economy, Hong Kong was unable to provide for the needs of its people. In a June 1962 address to the Hong Kong Legislative Council, the Colonial Secretary summed up the problems of Hong Kong and the solution:

> Not from choice, but from necessity, we are a manufacturing and commercial community. Our only real asset is the industriousness, and efficiency and the strong instinct for survival of our people. Hong Kong's rapid industrialization is the key solution of its problem of people. Indeed, the prosperity of Hong Kong's industry provides the reason why the world does not have an additional million refugees on its conscience at this moment; and its continuing prosperity provides the best hope, perhaps the only hope, that the needs of our expanding population can be met in a constructive and efficient way . . . The Government can see no better way in which effective help, in the form in which it is most needed, can be given to people about whose future the outside world has shown so much concern. These people's welfare depends upon our trade . . .

Employers knew that shipping and industry were the mainstays of Hong Kong's development and, through fear or greed, were reluctant to raise workers' wages or lower their own. They argued, perhaps justly, that any increase in wages would hurt business. Mr. Ross described the result in a 30 June 1962 report to Gloria Matthews:

> This is a city of great wealth and massive poverty. It is a place of incredible profits and frequent bankruptcies. It does not offer great hope for the average young man; the limitations are too narrow, the restrictions of space here and markets abroad too obvious. And yet, it is the only hope for those millions who are here and for those thousands who will inevitably come each year that conditions in communist China continue as they are.

The Social Welfare Department's limited funds could do little and the burden of Hong Kong's social welfare services fell on voluntary agencies. In 1964 the Social Welfare Department had a budget of under two million Hong Kong dollars; the total voluntary agencies' budget was ten times that and still not enough.

Refugees, legal and illegal, continued to pour into Hong Kong, overwhelming all attempts by public and private agencies to provide for their needs. In the first six months of 1962 they arrived at the rate of 1,000 a day.

In the previously cited report, Mr. Ross praised the government's housing effort but pointed out its inadequacy:

> Commendable as the work of the local government is, the fact remains that conditions for hundreds of thousands of people here are deplorable. Government housing now consists of 7-story blocks, divided into cubicles that usually measure ten feet by twelve feet. One block will house more than 2,000 people. At the present time, they are going up at the rate of one such block every nine days. This is phenomenal, and means housing for over 80,000 people this one year. But in the same time that it takes to provide this housing, the population will increase, through natural growth and immigration, at least 160,000. Since there are several hundred thousand people in squatter shacks, and tens of thousands still sleeping on the street, the fact that the housing situation, in spite of remarkable feats by the local government, becomes worse each year, is truly frightening.

Housing was only one of the problems facing the people of Hong Kong. Most of the immigrants were from rural areas, agricultural people escaping famine and crop failure. They were as ill-prepared for urban life as Hong Kong was to receive them. Their culture, skills, and orientation were those of traditional farmers and were unsuited to the necessities of an urban industrial economy.

Once they were in Hong Kong, the familiar institutions, values, and mores of a rural society no longer served them. The large, interdependent, extended family necessary for agriculture was a drawback in a city of daily wages. The farming skills, learned over a lifetime of work, were utterly useless. Untrained in any other area, most of the men could only get occasional work as coolies, work which they found humiliating. Coolie work involved hanging around in the street waiting for someone to come along who needed a manual laborer for a day or two.

For the women, it was worse. Traditionally, the woman had maintained the home and raised the children. If her husband died, she was expected to move in with his family and remain single to honor his memory. There were statues of such faithful wives in China and they were pointed out as examples of a life lived in the highest virtue. In Hong Kong, there were many widows, and many more women whose husbands, unable to bear the humiliation of their total inability to support their families, had disappeared. Without the traditional village structures, these women were on their own. Even if the husband's family was in Hong Kong, they would be unable to provide for the women and children. The women could work, if work could be found, and leave their children to grow up on the street unattended, or they could remarry and bear the personal shame and public scorn of being unfaithful wives.

PLAN's role in the integration of these destitute and often demoralized families into the Hong Kong economy was primarily to see that the children got enough education to get and keep a decent job. PLAN support enabled children to go to school. Gift parcels and budget purchases provided material for clothes, school supplies, school uniforms, and textbooks in addition to blankets, folding cots, and much needed household supplies. Monthly cash payments supplemented meager incomes and Special Services Funds provided for medical emergencies and home repair.

A typical PLAN/Hong Kong family consisted of the parents (slightly less than half of the mothers were widowed) and four or five children. Of the family's US $34.53 monthly income, US $21.96 went for food and US $4.65 went for rent. The remaining US $7.92 had to cover all other expenses: clothing, school fees, school books, school uniforms, bus fare, medical and dental expenses—everything.

The family of Foster Child Leung Woon Kam is representative of the families enrolled in PLAN. Woon Kam, her grandmother, sick mother, twin brothers, and sister lived together in an open six by ten foot row boat. Her father was in a mental hospital.

They lost their boat-home in a typhoon. Then her mother's health got worse. Once homeless, they were housed by the city in a temporary shelter where all of the children caught the measles. Woon Kam's grandmother took charge of providing for the family until her mother's health improved. When they received notice that they must leave the temporary shelter they had nothing and no place to go. Direct appeals from Mr.Ross to the Director of Social Welfare finally secured them a cubicle in a government resettlement block.

For US $2.45 a month the family of six was able to rent a cubicle. A gift from Woon Kam's Foster Parent provided funds to buy a metal bunk bed and the family put up a partition to divide the cubicle into eating and sleeping areas. In some ways Woon Kam's family was luckier than most. Through PLAN aid the children could go to school, the grandmother could baby-sit for the young children when their mother's health recovered enough for her to work, and PLAN's Special Services Fund provided for medical costs. Best of all, they were living in the relative safety and comfort of a resettlement block.

During the summer vacation from school, camping programs gave the children a chance to get away for a week from the dreary cubicles, piecework jobs, and life on the streets, stairways, and rooftops. In the summer of 1963, 1,200 children participated in the camping program. This was the first opportunity many of these children had ever had to be in a clean, quiet place. The camps were in scenic wooded areas on an outer island of the Colony and offered organized activities, swimming, hiking, handicrafts, and a great deal of food. The children usually gained two pounds in their week at camp.

Day camps, organized in cooperation with the YMCA, met in schools, YMCAs, churches, and playgrounds. Like the residential camps, they offered handicrafts, games, sports, and plenty of food. The two hot meals a day came from PLAN, Church World Service, and Caritas. The average cost of US $2 per child was covered by PLAN.

Mr. Ross made arrangements with the local government respiratory clinics and private doctors to provide for the medical needs of Foster Children and their families. The children and all members of their families were referred to government clinics for examinations and any necessary treatment for lung problems. The pressure on the clinics by

the enormous population forced other arrangements for general curative and preventive health care.

To meet the need for general medical care, Mr. Ross arranged for
eight private doctors to give a fixed period of time every day to PLAN
families. The hours were generally from 11:00 a.m. to 1:00 p.m. and
3:00 p.m. to 5:00 p.m. In emergencies the families could, of course, call
at any time. Each doctor was assigned specific families and was paid a
set monthly fee. About 35 percent of the approximately 4,000 PLAN
families visited their assigned doctor each month. Monthly reports were
sent by the doctors to the families' social workers for any necessary
follow-up. The need for medical care increased in the hot, humid
summer months and decreased in winter. The complaints were usually
for anemia, bronchitis, intestinal disorders, and eye problems.

PLAN's monthly payments to the doctors covered the families'
visits and less expensive medication. The doctors agreed to charge
PLAN separately for any expensive medications, but there was considerable variation in these charges. The more affluent doctors donated
the medications, while the others charged anything from a token fee to
the full price.

Further care was provided by three dentists and an eye specialist.
An agreement with an optometry firm provided eye examinations and
glasses to Foster Children and members of their immediate family for
US $1.49.

If a member of a PLAN family needed hospitalization, efforts were
made to place them in the inexpensive government hospitals. When
the overcrowded hospitals, often with two patients in each bed, could
not take them, they were referred to private hospitals. The Special
Services Fund was used, if necessary, to cover the costs.

The basic idea of the medical program was for members of PLAN
families to feel that they could call upon a doctor whenever they
wished. Thus, a minor cough could be treated before it became
pneumonia; anemia could be caught and treated at an early stage. The
hope was that serious, disabling, and expensive diseases could be
prevented by early and adequate medical care and regular examinations. For PLAN families, a day of work missed because of illness meant
a day without enough to eat. If children missed school and had to drop
out, they could expect little more than the exhausting life and early
death of a coolie.

In addition to their medical, economic, and housing needs, PLAN
families often had emotional problems; problems the PLAN social

workers of 1964 were poorly equipped to deal with. Staff development, therefore, was an ongoing process with the social work staff regularly attending conferences, courses, in-service training sessions, and pursuing independent studies of the literature in the field. A mark of PLAN's reputation was the fact that of the more than 100 voluntary agencies in Hong Kong, PLAN was one of only three accredited for practical training of social work students from Hong Kong colleges and universities. Still, the emotional upheaval of the families were their own and the staff's most intractable problem.

While the father worked all day, if he was lucky enough to find work, earning an inadequate income, the mother did the best she could in her crowded cubicle, tenement, or rooftop shack to see that the children were clothed, fed, and educated and then tried to supplement her husband's income. At the end of a long day the parents, hungry themselves, saw their children ill-fed, ill-housed, ill-clothed, and ill-educated.

Family life naturally suffered in this environment. Marriages broke up, arguments and domestic violence increased, alcoholism and drug abuse spread, ulcers proliferated, and children, husbands, and wives ran away. The native villages of these refugees had offered little material or economic sustenance but had provided recognizable, familiar, and supportive cultural institutions. Long-standing and accepted rules of conduct had meaning and effect in the village. In Hong Kong none of the old rules applied. PLAN caseworkers in 1964 had little training in psychiatric social work and could only listen and try to create an atmosphere in which the mothers could talk freely and thereby reduce at least some of their anxiety.

There were many such families who needed intensive casework, but there was no place to refer them except mental hospitals. Rather, PLAN was one of the agencies to which these families were referred by others. The caseload of 225 families for each social worker limited the amount of time they could spend with any single family. To remedy this, Mr. Ross hoped that the caseload could be reduced to 200 within a year and that two or three caseworkers could be assigned specifically to working with problem families. Other priorities included streamlining the medical program, finding new office space, and modifying or eliminating the troublesome and increasingly anachronistic purchase program.

The purchase program had been an aspect of PLAN aid since the Spanish Civil War when food, clothes, and even toys were sent to the children in Catalonia. During and after the Second World War, material unavailable in England and Europe was shipped from the PLAN warehouse in New York. By the time PLAN reached Asia, circumstances had changed and many of the goods were readily available locally and no longer needed to be imported.

The purchase of such general material as blankets, notebooks, toothbrushes, and kitchen utensils was a fairly simple matter of placing an order and distributing the goods, but problems arose when individually sized items were needed. Properly fitting nearly 6,000 children with shirts, blouses, and shoes presented massive logistical problems. If large scale purchases led to significant savings in unit costs, the trouble would have been justified, but in Hong Kong this was not always the case.

Mrs. Lucile Chamberlin took charge of PLAN/Hong Kong in January 1965 when Mr. Ross was transferred to PLAN Headquarters in New York to become the Deputy Executive Director. When she assumed the directorship, PLAN was serving 5,650 Foster Children and their families in Hong Kong.

In her two years as PLAN/Hong Kong Director, Mrs. Chamberlin concentrated on upgrading the skills of the social work staff, improving the quality of casework, and continuing the emphasis on vocational training and education for PLAN families. In keeping with Mr. Ross' suggestion, the purchase program was reduced, but not entirely done away with until 1970.

When the PLAN/Hong Kong staff learned that Mrs. Chamberlin had chosen to leave at the end of her two-year assignment in Hong Kong, they wrote to Gloria Matthews (30 November 1966) praising the work she had done:

> The loss of Mrs. Chamberlin's services will be a loss to Foster Parents Plan and, indeed, to the social work field in Hong Kong. With her broad experience and knowledge she has contributed a very great deal to the community and the professional respect she has earned as a leader in the social work area is immeasurable. PLAN's image as a casework service agency has been greatly enhanced by her leadership.

Frank Ryan followed Mrs. Chamberlin as Director and shared her concern for the development of an emotional support structure to promote the families' development. Writing of the program in July 1965, he said:

> Our casework in Hong Kong is coming to an important crossroad. Our material help in Hong Kong is probably not as significant as in other less-developed economies in countries where PLAN operates. There is an increasing need for non-material help in Hong Kong in the form of casework services . . . In its nuclear form, the Hong Kong family is fragile. It requires more in the way of casework services than our present program provides.

Group programs provided a means to allay not only the fragility of the families but also their educational, emotional, vocational, and, to a degree, health problems without incurring the prohibitive expense of a greatly enlarged staff.

Many of these problems were directly related to the cultural dislocation of the families and the changes they had had to make in their world view to adapt to life in Hong Kong. The basic reason PLAN had gone to Hong Kong was to provide material and financial assistance to destitute families and this continued. It was generally agreed that an average family living on a monthly income of US $90 was close to the poverty level. PLAN families usually earned between US $30 and US $50 a month and were dropped from PLAN's rolls when their income reached US $90 a month. By the late 1960s an equally important goal was to provide the families with the social services they needed to make the material and financial assistance worthwhile.

Had Hong Kong not been so crowded or so heavily industrialized, the traditional patterns of culture might have served and PLAN could have continued its traditional social welfare program. However, the traditional habits of PLAN families were inadequate. PLAN's social services were necessary to help them deal with the social and economic differences between a traditional rural life and a modern urbanized one.

Economic changes centered on the family. The extended family had been the basic economic unit for generations of rural Chinese. They worked the land, harvested the crops, and provided emotional support. The family patriarchs gave direction and children gave assurance of continuity. In Hong Kong, the nuclear family was the viable economic unit. On the mainland, the family's economic life had been the responsibility of the matriarch or patriarch. PLAN's young families in Hong Kong had little knowledge of savings, budgeting, and economic planning. PLAN credit unions and economic groups provided a means for them to learn these skills. For families who found that large numbers of children were no longer an asset but a liability, PLAN provided birth control information, referrals to birth control clinics, and, most importantly, organized educational groups.

Social changes were inextricably connected with economic changes and called as much for case, group, educational, and medical work as it did for material and financial aid. Education for the Foster Children continued to be the best hope for the families' success and was the focus of the material and financial aid, but 60 percent of the children repeated at least one year of school. They failed because they had no place to study, no one to supervise them, and no one to help them.

PLAN made significant efforts to improve this dismal statistic through the establishment of after-school study centers. Little homework could be done at home, usually a huge building full of crowded and noisy cubicles. The study centers provided a quiet place for study and homework, while volunteer tutors provided the advice and help the children's often uneducated parents could not give. PLAN's educational counseling guided children into accounting, typing, vocational, and industrial training programs unavailable in Hong Kong's traditional school system.

Hong Kong provided the ideal environment for delinquency, parent/child difficulties, and family problems. In 800 families surveyed, 150 children had behavior problems. Discipline broke down and parents complained that they did not know how to handle their children. Children of remarried or divorced parents had adjustment difficulties as did children who had lost a parent through death or desertion. Many children were left with neighbors or relatives while their parents worked; many others were left with no supervision for at least half of every week day. PLAN study centers, special interest groups, and recreational programs lured many of these children away from the attractions of the street. Remarried mothers, exhausted from trying to cope with the fierce discrimination of their neighbors, met in small groups to share their common problems and support each other's efforts to deal with them. Additional groups provided support for deserted, widowed, or unhappily married women. Still other groups met for budgeting, health, and nutrition education. Groups of fathers helped each other cope with the humiliation of being unable to provide for their families and of being reduced to coolie labor. PLAN could not find jobs for all of these fathers but could, through support groups, motivate them to keep working as coolies until they could get steadier, better paying, and more prestigious work as tradesmen or builders.

Many of the educational and recreational activities and groups depended upon the willing volunteers from PLAN families, PLAN staff, and the community at large. Volunteers were first used in 1969 to staff the after-school study centers. The success of these volunteers led to a special summer program for Foster Children staffed largely by 57 of their older brothers and sisters. In July 1969 a three-day training camp was held for the volunteers who then received additional training at the PLAN office. At the end of the summer they formed their own social service club to participate in community activities, the after-school study program, and PLAN's club groups.

In a 1980 memoir, Mr. Ryan recalled the role of volunteers in the establishment of PLAN/Hong Kong's first credit union:

> In Hong Kong, PLAN's staff were not interested in forming their own credit union, but were enthusiastic in helping to have our clients form credit unions of their own. The remarkable fact . . . was that we had PLAN staff working after hours, on their own time, to help people from lower economic and lower social classes on a voluntary basis.

Even though there were groups concerned with health and nutrition education, the medical program continued to be largely curative rather than preventive. The PLAN clinic, emphasizing prenatal and postnatal care for infants and their mothers when it opened, had expanded to provide care for all PLAN family members. From January to March 1969, when PLAN/Hong Kong reached its peak enrollment of 7,505 Foster Children, 45,814 members of PLAN families availed themselves of the medical and dental care, hospitalization, optical examinations, supplemental food, and vitamins offered by PLAN.

The families had the choice of receiving either traditional Chinese or Western medical treatment from the 75 Western-trained and ten traditionally trained doctors available through PLAN. They nearly always chose to see the Western-trained doctors, but there were benefits to the few members of PLAN families who were attended by the traditional herbalists. Patients were referred to their choice of doctors by a PLAN nurse. In cases of repeated visits to an herbalist the patient was referred to a Western-trained doctor. Many of the patient's complaints were treated equally well by either type of medicine. In spite of the strong criticism of traditional medical practices, the program continued because this ancient form of treatment had a strong hold on a small number of PLAN families. PLAN began to use traditional doctors after a 1966 survey revealed that about 7 percent of the families were consulting herbalists at their own expense.

After 1969, a combination of an overall improvement in the standard of living and the long overdue assumption of greater responsibility for the welfare of its people by the Hong Kong authorities led to a gradual reduction in the numbers of Foster Children in Hong Kong. Until this time Hong Kong had had no social welfare policy, rather it responded to particular problems or emergencies. The massive resettlement project illustrates the successes and shortcomings of the process. The building program began and continued with commendable speed but little forethought or long-range planning. As temporary emergency shelter the resettlement cubicles were dreadfully overcrowded, but at least they were safe; as permanent housing they were clearly inadequate.

Hong Kong, like most countries in the 1960s, had a purely phenomenological approach to social welfare. There were programs directed to identify and meet specific areas of need, but there was no overall development of social policy. In the late 1960s the emphasis changed and more integrated and coordinated policies were planned and implemented.

Governor Sir David Trench, in his October 1971 farewell speech to the Legislative Council, clearly stated the government's new orientation:

> I believe that we can now turn our attention increasingly to rather specialized and personal problems, and pay more attention to individual rather than mass needs. In short, we are coming out of an era of emergency action to ameliorate massive and immediate problems, and into an era in which we can hope to think in terms of refining and sophisticating over a wide field the quality of the various services we try to make available to the public.

PLAN's gradual phaseout process continued for four years. During its 14 years in Hong Kong, major steps were taken in the development of more professional attitudes and programs of assistance. In 1959 the emphasis was on providing long-term financial and material assistance and the emotional support of a continuing relationship with a Foster Parent. By 1973, PLAN social workers had developed group approaches that enabled PLAN mothers, fathers, children, and their neighbors to share their problems and learn from each other. PLAN's first medical clinic was established by Mr. Ryan in Hong Kong in 1967; six years later there were clinics in every PLAN Field program.

Frederick Chafee and Henry Tsang directed the last year of the Hong Kong phaseout. By then the government's public assistance program was providing food, clothing, school fees, and medical care to Hong Kong's needy. A single person who was eligible for assistance received US $19 a month from the government, family assistance was higher and varied with the family's size and circumstances.

In January 1973, Mr. Chaffee wrote: "Hong Kong now truly is able to take care of its poor, and . . . there is no further need for a PLAN program here."

Six months later PLAN's Hong Kong office was closed.

11

Republic of the Philippines: 1961-83

Dr. Carlos P. Romulo, the Philippine Ambassador to the United States and former President of the United Nations General Assembly, invited PLAN in the summer of 1960 to establish a social welfare program in the Philippines. The PLAN Board of Directors appointed Robert W. Sage, who had established, and for eight years directed, PLAN's program in the Republic of Korea, to undertake the new program.

The program in the Philippines would have some immediate advantages over the programs in the Republics of Korea and Vietnam. The Philippines was not suffering the effects of either a recent or on-going war. It did have a long history of foreign domination but it had been an independent state since 1946 and, with neither belligerent neighbors nor a major civil war to contend with, had achieved a degree of stability lacking in some other PLAN countries of Asia. There were sporadic instances of political unrest based on religious, ethnic, and economic differences between the various groups in the Philippines, but Manila was generally peaceful.

The problems of the Philippines were the problems of all developing countries: high unemployment and underemployment, high rates of illiteracy, high infant mortality rates, short life expectancy, inadequate medical care, and an economy more oriented to subsistence agriculture than to industry or technology.

Mr. Sage arrived in Manila on 18 February 1961 and wrote in his first Quarterly Report (February-March 1961):

> PLAN is "in" in the Philippines and a going concern. It has been officially accepted by the Philippine Government as a voluntary relief agency qualified to participate in the relief program in the Philippines under the terms and conditions embodied in pertinent notes exchanged between the United

States Embassy in Manila and the Department of Foreign Affairs of the Philippines.

The need for professionally trained social workers had been recognized in the Philippines for a number of years and, in response to this need, a School of Social Work had been established at the Philippine Women's University. By a happy coincidence, the first class of professionally qualified social workers graduated in 1961, just in time to staff the social work section of PLAN's fledgling program.

PLAN's social work was based on individual casework and the belief that the needs of children could not be met in isolation from the family, that child development was inseparable from family development. In keeping with this philosophy, only children living with their families or guardians were enrolled.

The first case histories were sent to New York in March 1961. The first Foster Child from Manila was a shy, reclusive, and ragged orphan named Norma who lived with the destitute family of an older sister. Norma was sponsored by the 440th Oxford Wing of the Royal Canadian Air Force Association of Woodstock, Ontario, and was soon attending her first elementary school classes in a new yellow dress.

The typical Filipino Foster Child lived in a large, single-parent family on the brink of starvation. The head of the family was usually a widow or deserted wife. With little or no education these women could earn only a peso (then valued at US $0.25) or less a day by selling snacks or small items in the market or doing laundry. If the father was present, the early enrollment criteria stipulated that he be unable to support the family because of a disability, handicap, or chronic ill health.

Foster Families received monthly cash grants of US $8 and PLAN allocated US $35 a year for monthly budget purchases of clothes, school supplies, bedding, toilet articles, and other supplies. In a typical month a child might receive a dress or pair of pants, a shirt or skirt, pillow cases, soap, toothbrush and toothpaste, mosquito netting, and kitchen utensils. One dollar a month was set aside for a Christmas package. The Special Services Fund, a useful and adaptable PLAN service, provided for such unusual circumstances or emergency expenses as hospital costs and medicine, overdue rent, emergency home repairs, supplemental food, and, sometimes, funerals. Individual Foster Parents provided occasional supplemental gifts of money or parcels of clothes and toys.

Foster Children and their families lived in the slums and squatters districts of Metropolitan Manila and its suburbs. The poor living conditions constantly exposed the children and their families to disease and infection. Mr. Sage wrote that it was safe to assume that at least two members of each newly enrolled family would need medical attention. The families usually showed clinical symptoms of vitamin deficiency caused by malnutrition and poor dietary habits.

Inadequate shelter was one of the foremost contributors to the general ill health of Foster Children and their families. The majority lived in makeshift shanties built of woven palm leaves or junk salvaged from the dumps and streets of Manila. The shanties were far from weatherproof and during the rainy season led to a marked increase in upper respiratory tract diseases. Gastrointestinal diseases and parasites were always prevalent but increased with the water pollution resulting from seasonal flooding. Poor housing, the absence of sanitary facilities, shallow wells, and a general ignorance of the causes of diseases and infection combined to make Manila's poor both the victims and transmitters of a host of preventable illnesses. More serious afflictions included blindness, post-polio paralysis, heart disease, Hansen's disease, organic brain syndromes, and acquired or congenital mental retardation.

PLAN's health program was established in September 1963. Under the terms of an agreement with PLAN, a group of doctors in Manila, Medical Specialists Associates (MSA), agreed to establish, equip, maintain, and staff a clinic near the PLAN office to serve Foster Children and their families, whose members now comprised nearly 20,000 people. Patients requiring hospitalization were referred by the clinic to St. Jude's Hospital, also near PLAN's office. PLAN families in some of the more rural areas received treatment through arrangements made by MSA with local doctors, hospitals, and clinics. In emergencies, or when the office and clinic were closed, patients could go to the nearest medical facility for treatment.

Newly enrolled Foster Children and the members of their immediate families received complete physical examinations. Previously enrolled children and their families were scheduled for examinations when their yearly progress reports were due. By the end of the clinic's first 18 months, all PLAN affiliates had been examined.

There were two immediate problems when the program began. The first, the overcrowding of the clinic, was resolved by more efficient scheduling. The second, involving confidentiality, was not so easily resolved. The difficulty arose at one of the first meetings of doctors and

PLAN social workers. One of the doctors brought up the subject of privileged communications between the doctor and the patient. He used the example of a hypothetical Foster Child's mother suffering the aftereffects of an illegal abortion requesting to have this information withheld from her social worker for fear that it would result in her child's cancellation from PLAN. The social workers were in unanimous and vigorous agreement that, in the interest of the team approach of the doctor and social worker, the doctors should share all of the information available to them. The doctors, as unanimously and as vigorously, disagreed. To the dismay of the social workers, Mr. Sage sided with Hippocrates. The meeting ended with no sign of a compromise.

The head of the Social Services Center of the Philippine Association of Social Workers, a Father Mitchell, was invited to the next meeting to discuss the ethics of the relatively new science of social work and the long established ethics of the medical profession. Within an hour the conflict between the two disciplines was resolved. The doctors agreed to try to convince their patients to share all privileged communications with their social workers. The social workers conceded that the doctors must be guided by their consciences and their professional ethics.

By June 1966, dental care was also available and the clinic became one of the most needed and appreciated of PLAN's services. At the end of the year, PLAN had enrolled 5,380 Foster Children. During the year children and their families visited the clinic a total of 50,469 times for examinations and treatment. PLAN staff and their dependents, who were also eligible for clinical services, received medical and dental consultation and care 493 times. The new dental program added US $0.25 per month to PLAN's cost per Foster Child.

The arrangement with MSA to operate the PLAN clinic worked so well that Mr. Sage planned to establish a similarly structured vocational training center. On 1 July 1965, after nearly a year of planning and background study, the center was opened. Preparations included a survey of the unemployment and underemployment in Manila, the skills or lack of skills of PLAN family members, and of the opportunities for training available in Manila.

The available training courses usually ran for six months at a cost of from US $25 to US $50 and were primarily geared to high school students. The cost and entry requirements were beyond the means of PLAN's budget and the educational level of the potential students. Mr. Sage and his staff decided that the best way to bring vocational training to PLAN families was to establish PLAN's own training center. The Filipino Technical Group was contracted to operate the new center, called the Foster Parents Plan Opportunity Vocational Training Project.

Trainees were chosen by PLAN's social workers from the parents and older brothers and sisters of Foster Children so they could contribute to the family income while the Foster Child continued his or her education. The first three-month training period was to provide introductory skills in general automotive and diesel mechanics, practical electricity, carpentry and cabinet making, dressmaking, cosmetology, and hairdressing. During each quarter, 150 trainees were admitted to the three-month courses. They met three hours a day, six days a week. During the third month the students did outside contractual work under the supervision of the center's staff. At the end of the training period the trainees were awarded certificates of proficiency in their newly acquired trades. Since training without placement would be a frustrating and futile endeavor, a Job Placement Bureau was established as an integral part of the training center.

The first graduation ceremony for the trainees was scheduled for Sunday, 3 October 1965, but had to be postponed for a week because of the eruption of the island volcano in Taal Lake, 45 miles south of Manila.[1] The success of the training program became obvious when nearly all of the trainees were either successfully placed or able to earn their living at home.

PLAN paid the Filipino Technical Group 3,000 pesos (US $771) per month to run the center. At the rate of 150 trainees per quarter or 600 per year, the US $15.42 cost per trainee was a very inexpensive investment in the families' future, and, in long-range terms, perhaps an even greater contribution than the medical services of PLAN's clinic. Still, the decision to use Special Services Funds for the vocational training program was a difficult one. The choice was between establishing the training center and funding other projects including a day nursery, stores, and community cooperatives. Funding of the training center took nearly half of the available Special Services Funds and forced the postponement of other projects.

In November 1967, with nearly 7,000 Foster Children, PLAN moved into an imposing old white-columned mansion with expansive lawns

[1]This disrupted life in Manila for a week, though it involved no PLAN families and caused no damage in Manila. PLAN provided relief aid to many of the people evacuated from the island.

and an annex building. The two buildings provided ample space to centralize and expand the services available to PLAN's families in Metropolitan Manila. The annex provided space for the PLAN clinic and newly established day care center; the lawns and main building would provide room for group programs, a cooperative store, and the counseling, guidance, and aftercare program. The PLAN compound soon became a "family center," offering recreational, social, economic, and medical services.

With the clinic housed in the PLAN compound, communications and opportunities for close cooperation between the medical and social work staff were greatly improved. The establishment of a day care center, supervised by the clinic's staff, added another dimension to PLAN's services and enabled mothers with young children to work outside of their homes. The mothers' initial hesitance to leave their infants and young children in the care of PLAN staff was overcome by inviting them to come with their children for a day to observe the center's activities. These visits also provided an opportunity for the mothers, their children, the clinic staff, and the social workers to get to know each other better and to discuss how PLAN's programs and services could best meet the family's particular needs.

The newly organized counseling, guidance, and aftercare program focused on preparing older Foster Children for adult life. Guidance and counseling were a normal part of PLAN's regular casework service, but this program focused particularly on the problems of career choice and personal adjustment to the group and community.

In cases of severe mental deficiency, group educational therapy was provided by psychologist Dr. Josefina Estalas and her associates from the National Coordinating Center for the Study and Development of Filipino Children and Youth in coordination with the PLAN social work staff. Continuity of treatment was assured by referral to existing community resources when the children left PLAN.

The aftercare program established by Mr. Sage involved particularly promising Foster Children whose continuing education would be impossible without further PLAN aid. These Foster Children, cancelled from PLAN rolls when they reached the age of 18, continued to receive assistance from their Foster Parents until they finished their courses of study.

The PLAN compound also housed a cooperative store operated by a group of PLAN mothers. The independently operated store was established with a grant of US $1,300 and was soon registered with the

Cooperative's Administration Office of the Philippine Department of Commerce and Industry. The nonprofit store, offering rice, canned goods, and household supplies, undersold the much overpriced local stores and, not surprisingly, did very well. PLAN provided budgeting advice to enable more PLAN families to join the cooperative, but the store was open to all PLAN affiliates and staff whether they were members or not. The store provided PLAN families with cooperative training and clearly showed the benefits which could result from group efforts.

Group activities became a distinctive feature of the program in Metropolitan Manila. Within a few years there were recreational, social, educational, and economic affinity groups with interests ranging from basketball to poultry raising and from family planning to ping pong. The groups were organized in cooperation with the Manila YWCA which provided volunteer group workers. Even former Foster Children organized groups for community projects. The various groups presented lectures, demonstrations, performances, and concerts for each other, for the general public, and for PLAN's annual mini-bazaars. The bazaars provided an ideal opportunity for the marketing of group made articles, demonstrations of nutritious low-cost cooking, performances by musical and dance groups, and readings by literary groups. Beyond the obvious benefit of sharing a common interest, the group members gained experience in working closely with others, developed leadership skills, and had the experience of planning, organizing, and completing cooperative projects. Group activity was particularly effective with children living in PLAN's rural areas in the satellite communities around Manila.

The first of these rural projects was started in the province of Bulacan on the island of Luzon using the already established administrative services of the government's Social Welfare Administration. The project started with 48 Foster Children as an experiment to see whether or not PLAN could extend its services to needy rural children and their families through the preexisting channels of other Philippine agencies. Mr. Sage hoped that, by cooperating with rural agencies, PLAN could expand without incurring the otherwise prohibitive expenses of a large social work staff. The cooperative effort was as successful in the Philippines as it had been in Vietnam, Italy, and Greece. By July 1963 PLAN had brought its services to children and their families in the Luzon provinces of Cavite, Laguna, Pampanga, and Rizal.

The agencies cooperating with PLAN in the rural villages—the

Philippine Red Cross and the Social Welfare Administration, were generally very effective. However, problems arose in disaster situations when these agencies had to concentrate their human and financial resources on their own priority affairs.

In such emergencies PLAN families necessarily took second place. In view of this, Mr. Sage limited the number of Foster Children in the provinces to five percent of the total enrollment. To alleviate the problems of the Social Welfare Administration and the Red Cross in such matters as home visits, data collection for progress reports, Special Services applications, overdue letters, and special inquiries from PLAN's New York Headquarters, PLAN social worker Dr. Amauri G. Martinez was assigned to cover Foster Children in the provincial areas. Dr. Martinez was also responsible for the supervision of PLAN's community development project in Sapang Palay.

The Sapang Palay project, like the program in Sung Nam, Korea, resulted from a government slum clearance project. The residents of Sapang Palay were relocated squatters from the Intramuros district of Manila. Intramuros, one of the oldest districts of Central Manila, was once a picturesque area of stately buildings, monuments, and historic landmarks. The area was devastated during the war and soon became a refuge for squatters who found shelter in its ruined buildings or built makeshift shanties of their own.

In December 1963 the Mayor of Manila resolved to rid Intramuros of its shanties. The residents had the choice of relocating in Manila or moving to small plots of land in Sapang Palay, 25 miles from central Manila. About half of PLAN's Intramuros families moved to Sapang Palay. The other half, saying it was too far away and lacked schools, markets, electricity, and water, moved in with relatives or, with the help of PLAN's Special Services Fund, rented new quarters in Manila. PLAN social workers made every effort to find adequate housing for families remaining in Manila because of the inherent unhealthiness of the shanties and because of the Mayor's announced plan to clear all remaining squatter's areas by the end of 1964.

Mr. Sage and his staff planned and, in January 1964, implemented a "poverty plan" based on group work rather than individual casework for PLAN families in Sapang Palay. The new town was lacking in all the facilities and opportunities that make a community attractive. Settlers from the city were faced with new economic and social difficulties and would probably return to the shanties of Manila unless viable and comprehensive community development projects were quickly initiated.

Well aware of this possibility, public and private agencies in Manila quickly went to work to extend their services to Sapang Palay. Unfortunately, government coordination was lacking and each agency went off in its own direction. With no clear plans these agencies could do little more than react to each event or crisis as it occurred.

PLAN hoped to set an example of what could be accomplished by following a comprehensive program for child, family, and community development. The overall purpose was to establish a program which addressed the housing, educational, occupational, health, and recreational needs of Foster Children and their families in Sapang Palay. The hope was that PLAN's program could be imitated by other agencies and families in the community. There were five specific goals:

1. To help build homes for Foster Families.
2. To enhance the economic potential of Foster Children and their parents.
3. To provide educational and occupational training for Foster Children and their families.
4. To provide medical care for Foster Children and their families.

   To help to establish recreational facilities for children and adults which would provide group experiences and leadership training.

PLAN social workers were organized into committees on housing, cottage industries, education, health, and recreation to implement projects designed to reach these goals.

The Committee on Housing worked with the People's Homesite Housing Corporation, the government agency responsible for land allocation, to obtain land for PLAN families. Eligible families were entitled to a 350-square-meter parcel, enough to grow ample supplies of vegetables. The families would live on the land rent-free for the first year and pay a nominal monthly rent thereafter. If the families stayed on the land for 20 years they would receive title to it. The minimal rent could be paid with a portion of their monthly cash grant from PLAN.

Houses were to be built with salvaged material or woven bamboo and with galvanized iron supplied by the government. The maximum construction cost was US $50, some or all of which could be met from PLAN's Special Services Funds. Foster Families' homes made up a neighborhood that would serve as a model for other residents of Sapang Palay. Through their proximity and cooperation a sense of community developed.

The Committee on Cottage Industries worked in concert with the National Cottage Industry Development Association, the Philippine College of Arts and Trade, and the Office of Vocational Rehabilitation of the Social Welfare Administration. PLAN group workers initially selected 12 trainees who learned basketry from a skilled craftsman. The first products were too rough to be sold but, with practice, quality soon improved.

The Committee on Education surveyed families for illiterate adults and children not attending school. The Department of Education gratefully provided teaching materials and permission to teach classes in basic literacy to children and adults in a classroom provided by UNICEF. The Committee hoped to turn the educational program over to the local educational authorities once it was firmly established.

The Committee on Health lent assistance to the overworked and understaffed Rural Health Unit in Sapang Palay. A Manila-based PLAN team, consisting of a doctor, nurse, and social worker, made weekly visits in the PLAN station wagon. Loaded with a supply of medicines, basic implements, and health education materials, the "mobile clinic" brought medical services to PLAN families and others in the outlying districts where the most prevalent health problems were tuberculosis, scabies, and intestinal parasites. Ambulatory patients visited the PLAN clinic in Manila. The medical team also ran health education classes in nutrition, disease prevention, and personal and environmental hygiene.

The Committee on Recreation grouped Foster Children and their siblings by age for recreational activities including supervised games, singing lessons, and art classes. Activities for preschool children were also available. The Committee on Recreation worked with the Philippine Youth Welfare Coordinating Council and used space provided by UNICEF.

The Sapang Palay program began as an experiment involving 29 families and a small office. The program grew slowly. In September 1964, when a typhoon struck, there were only 46 PLAN families in Sapang Palay. Quick relief action after the typhoon provided funds for the families to rebuild their storm damaged houses and made it possible for them to stay in their new community and not be forced back to the shanties of Manila.

By June 1966 Robert Sage was able to write that in the past two and a half years PLAN had achieved its goals in Sapang Palay, that it had helped build a viable community. Very few of the resettled families returned to the city slums and almost all the families were firmly settled and felt they belonged to the community.

On the basis of the success of the Sapang Palay program, similar programs were begun in Taguig (1968) and Cavite (1969). These were designed around health and sanitation, leadership development, civic consciousness, social integration, and the meeting of specific community needs through the participation of the people most affected. PLAN's initial task was to help the people in the villages define their most urgent needs and to encourage families to work in groups to meet their individual and community needs.

Group work soon became as normal a part of PLAN's programming as educational or health services. Group work, casework, and community organization were all useful approaches to resolving the problems of needy children and their families and all were used to enhance the lives of Foster Children.

Until 1973 PLAN's Philippine program had enrolled primarily Roman Catholic children on the island of Luzon in the greater Manila area. The much less developed island of Mindanao had a minority Muslim population never successfully integrated into the Filipino culture. The government's vigorous attempts to foster this integration, and the equally vigorous attempts on the part of certain elements in the Muslim population to resist it, resulted in disturbances and dislocations of large groups of Muslim villagers.

In 1973 the Council for the Rehabilitation of Evacuees and Assistance to Mindanao (CREAM) was organized by the First Lady, Madam Imelda Marcos, to provide a coordinated program of assistance for the displaced villagers of Mindanao. Mrs. Marcos described the project as one of the highest social priorities and, at a meeting of representatives of the voluntary agencies working in the Philippines on 21 August 1973, called for "all the help everyone of us can give to this project."[2] PLAN responded with a project for 169 families (a total of 1,150 people) living in the Rio Hondo Evacuation Center in Zamboanga City, in western Mindanao.

When the program started the families were living in precarious shanties built on stilts above the beach or in bunk houses. There were neither toilets nor electricity. Water came from one unreliable faucet. High tide flooded much of the village.

The naked and near naked children and adults were close to starvation. Most of the children and a third of the adults were totally

[2]*Philippine Daily Express.* Vol. II, No. 108 (22 August 1973).

illiterate. The evacuees had come from fishing villages and had the skills necessary for self-sufficiency, but without boats, nets, or money, were dependent upon the scant emergency relief assistance provided by the understaffed and poorly funded Department of Social Welfare. There was a clear potential for development. The community was surrounded by a productive sea and the nearby Zamboanga markets would provide a ready source of income from the sale of fish and handicrafts.

The Rio Hondo program was to be a two-year experiment in group rehabilitation and development, serving as a model for possible future projects with dislocated persons and evacuees. Monthly cash grants for the 169 families were to be pooled in a common fund. Half of the fund was to be used for the palliative efforts necessary to keep the people alive. These efforts included an emergency feeding program, nutritional supplements for children suffering from malnutrition, and the provision of clothes and basic household goods. The other half of the fund was to be used for income-producing ventures, skills training, literacy classes, day care, and community improvements.

PLAN provided comprehensive health services through Medical Specialists Associates, who ran PLAN's Manila clinic. During the first year of the project there were 7,353 visits to the Rio Hondo clinic, an average of six visits by each person in the community. Nearly 3,000 of the visits were for the treatment of malnutrition and parasites, the rest were generally for upper respiratory tract infections, gastrointestinal conditions, and skin diseases.

The first phase of the project was completed in 1974. In 1975 PLAN's efforts focused on enabling families to earn a living and to acquire skills and experience which would be of use to them when they returned to their permanent homes. Guidance and psychological counseling were arranged with the local Bureau of Public Schools. Mothers received health and nutrition education. Community toilets were built by the evacuees in cooperation with PLAN and the Zamboanga Health and Engineering Offices. A day care center was established and evening literacy classes were initiated. Since most of the evacuees had come from fishing villages and planned to return to them, income-producing projects, planned in cooperation with the Fisheries Commission, focused on fishing. PLAN organized boat building teams which built three fishing boats and one excursion boat to be used for Zamboanga tourists. Fishnets were produced by teams of netweavers and apprentices organized by PLAN. The catches were sold through a marketing cooperative and the profits equally divided among participating families.

By the time the Rio Hondo project ended in 1975, Mr. Sage had made plans to gradually reduce by half the number of Foster Children in Metropolitan Manila and replace them with children from the rural areas where PLAN could have a greater impact. PLAN simply did not have the funds to meet the needs of urban communities. It could not install the sewer systems or water systems or provide the housing necessary for a healthy urban environment. However, PLAN did have sufficient funds, and could usually get the necessary cooperation of local authorities, to dig wells in rural areas or provide building materials for schools, community service centers, and home improvements. These projects, small though they were, could have a tremendous impact on a rural village and make a fundamental difference in the quality of life for children and families in these areas.

In January 1975 PLAN was working in 20 rural communities. Group cottage industry projects produced mats, hats, bags, candy, candles, and rugs. Individual projects included piggeries, poultry raising, sewing, embroidery, and mushroom growing. Educational training and seminars focused on land reform, improved farming methods, child and family relations, family planning, home improvement, and gardening. A Live-in Leadership Training project identified known and potential community leaders and brought them to Manila for community organization seminars.

Though these programs and services were primarily geared to PLAN families, many projects benefited all the people in a village. The rationale for designing projects to meet perceived needs and the mobilization of the people to work cooperatively to implement them, naturally involved the whole community. As, years before, it would have been unconscionable for PLAN to single out only the sponsored children in an institution for supplemental food, clothing, or education so, too, did common sense and decency demand, for instance, that water from a PLAN-financed well in Taguig be accessible to all residents.

Robert Sage described the changing program in the 1975 Annual Report:

Traditionally, PLAN in the Philippines has brought our Foster Parents' assistance to distressed children and families living in crowded urban centers as well as in provincial areas. Now, more than ever, we are bringing solace and the prospect of advancement to people in remote villages.

An unproductive environment, lack of skilled manpower, ignorance of ways and means to exact optimum yield from dormant natural resources, inadequate facilities and welfare programs, all these impede the development of many rural communities in this country. PLAN's increasing work with such village populations has as its goal accelerated growth and viable communities. We strive to enable each individual residing in PLAN-assisted villages—members of our Foster Children's families as well as of families who are not recipients of direct support—to contribute to circumstances that result in self-contained or self-sufficient communities.

Through the personal concern of our sponsors we are able to evolve approaches, schemes and programs that eventually fill voids. It is not our aim to assume obligations and functions of local and national government authorities. Instead, we evaluate and stress the need for concerted effort toward total community involvement in attaining socio-economic upliftment. This exertion not only benefits a barrio's needy families but whole communities.

Plans were made in early 1975 to establish five more community development programs in northern Luzon. Five teams of PLAN social workers and support personnel surveyed impoverished villages with the cooperation of the Department of Social Welfare. The original plan called for the enrollment of about 120 Foster Children in each of the villages.

Village and family selection was based on specific criteria. A village needed to have enough families with sub-marginal incomes to affect the overall socio-economic life of the community. More importantly, it had to be a community in which PLAN could significantly contribute not only to the development of Foster Children and their families, but to the community as a whole.

Mr. Sage did not intend for PLAN to be in competition, either in the quantity or the quality of its projects, with any existing public or private agencies working in a village. Rather, PLAN would work in cooperation with existing agencies to provide a comprehensive and integrated program to enable people to improve their standard of living and make informed choices concerning their lives and their future.

By May 1975 the plans had expanded to include the islands of Mindoro and Marinduque. The Philippine Government was in full agreement with PLAN's shift toward rural community development and promised the full cooperation of the regional social welfare offices.

The projects were to be five-year development programs enabling marginal communities to become economically and socially viable. The first phase was to alleviate the more pressing needs of the villagers and prepared them for the second (economic) phase. Services included health care, guidance and counseling, day care, nutritional education, supplemental feeding, and the organization of social and economic groups.

The economic programs offered in the second phase would vary with individual communities. Specific projects would be undertaken only if the need had been established by the PLAN social worker to be relevant to the community, and if other agencies could be involved.

The final criterion involved the people in the local community. They must agree that the project was needed, that it would contribute to their lives, and they must be willing to contribute their time, effort, and money to achieve it. The interplay of a community development program with the cultural institutions and traditional values of village society was the hardest factor to predict or plan for; if a program did not "fit," it would fail. Since a fundamental purpose of PLAN is to promote positive change in people's lives, its programs must be in accord with the values of the community. The success of these programs depends largely upon the direct participation of the community and the skill and sensitivity of individual staff members.

Although individual self-help projects were not altogether ruled out, the emphasis was to be on group projects which would both strengthen the community and enable PLAN's limited funds to affect the largest number of people. In addition to the economic groups PLAN would organize, Mr. Sage hoped that secondary groups, such as clubs and special interest groups, would create and develop additional projects on their own initiative. The goals and objectives of the programs were to be clearly and realistically established during the planning stages to provide a measure for evaluation.

The collapse of the Republic of Vietnam and the subsequent mass cancellation of over 6,000 Vietnamese Foster Children led to a rapid increase in the number of requests for Foster Children from the Philippines. In response to this, the rural family and community development programs planned for 1976 were begun a year earlier. By 30 June 1976 there were 10,020 Filipino Foster Children and PLAN/ Philippines was the second largest of PLAN's programs.[3]

The following list of specific group projects completed between

[3]The Indonesian program, with 14,986 Foster Children, was the largest.

January and June 1976, reflects PLAN's growing commitment to improving the quality of life in the Foster Child's community.

	NUMBER OF PEOPLE SERVED
Construction of community centers in:	
Cavite	110
Nueva Vizcaya	121
Pangasinan	130
Batangas	111
Playground equipment for Taguig community	50
Electrification project in Benguet	120
Toilet construction in Cavite	10
Deep-well construction in Cavite	110
Community drug store in Nueva Ecija	137
2 artesian wells in Benguet	165
1 artesian well in Cavite	104
10 sewing machines each for:	
Pampanga	125
Nueva Ecija	196
Nueva Vizcaya	180
La Union	173
Cagayan	175
Water-sealed toilets in:	
Cavite	60
Pampanga	52
Sapang Palay	51
Laguna	21
Retail store in Pangasinan	175
Retail store in Cavite	104
Capital for retail store in La Union	173
Capital for retail store in Marinduque	172
Capital for broom making in Ilocus Sur	166
Capital for fish vending in Ilocus Sur	166
Capital for bamboo furniture making in Abra	178
Medicines for community drug store in Cagayan	175

In spite of the importance of group and community projects, they remained only one aspect of the total PLAN program. Other projects for individual families and family members included guidance and counseling, day care centers, nursery schools, health projects, vocational training, and agricultural cooperatives.

In July 1976 Robert Sage sent his last Quarterly Report (April-June 1976) to International Headquarters before retiring after almost 25 years of PLAN service. In it he wrote of the development of PLAN's program in the Philippines in the 15 years since its establishment in Manila:

I have seen PLAN worldwide develop into a professional and comprehensive welfare organization of which I am sure there is no equal. I know (trying to avoid false modesty) that my co-workers and I have made our contribution in this process. While in early 1961 PLAN in the Philippines began its work mainly as a cash assistance agency operating in urban slums —gradually my colleagues and I evolved programs and services which would accelerate the rehabilitation process of the Filipino Foster Children and their families and, later, their communities. It was not only the families' economic improvement we concentrated on, but every aspect of their life and problems was viewed and identified with the goal to work for upliftment.

. . . .

Particularly dear to my heart was to see the children develop socially . . . PLAN's group work programs give the Foster Children and their siblings the opportunity to . . . explore, discover and enhance cultural values and their innate capacities. Annual camping programs . . . make for the children's mental, social and moral growth and development through organized group living and contribute to leadership and citizenship training through democratic participation.

John Anderson succeeded Robert Sage as PLAN/Philippines' Field Director on 15 September 1976. In Manila, as in Korea, his first priority was to review and evaluate all aspects of the program and its administration. During the month of September he established nine staff committees to review the program and to make recommendations for improvement or to develop alternatives to existing practices.

On the basis of the committees' recommendations, Mr. Anderson made two major changes in the Metropolitan Manila program with the goal of more fully integrating PLAN with existing resources in Manila. First, the position of Vocational Educational/Job Placement Coordinator was established. This staff member would work closely with the social work staff to identify all available training facilities in Manila and assist in referring PLAN family members to them.

The second change was organizational. The Metropolitan Manila area was divided into 35 geographic zones with individual social workers assigned to approximately 225 Foster Children in each one. Under the guidance of their social workers, PLAN families in each zone organized Family Associations to plan and participate in programs and activities. The central Guidance, Counseling, and Day Care Center in the PLAN compound was closed and replaced by local resources which the social workers identified in each zone. The idea was that the convenience of neighborhood services would enable and encourage more PLAN family members to use them. At the same time, it would strengthen local resources and decrease dependency on PLAN.

In the rural areas where both PLAN and non-PLAN families were benefiting from community development programs, a minimal fee was charged for PLAN day care, medical and dental, vocational training, and nutrition projects. The rationale was that user fees would increase the families' active participation and responsibility in such activities, thereby making them more a development, less a relief, effort.

The budget for Fiscal Year 1978 reflected the growing emphasis on direct family participation in program planning. In the beginning of February 1977, budgetary forms and instructions were distributed to PLAN social workers. In discussions with the elected representatives of PLAN Family Associations in each of the 35 zones of Manila and the rural community development areas, they reviewed the funds provided in Fiscal Year 1977 and developed recommendations for the coming year. These discussions covered cash grants, health and dental services, educational and recreational programs, revolving loan funds, Special Services Funds and self-help projects. By the end of February each social worker presented a mini-budget to Mr. Anderson. He and the accounting staff then reviewed the mini-budgets and developed an overall PLAN/Philippines budget for approval by International Headquarters. Once approved, the budget was shared with the social workers who, in turn, discussed any adjustments with the Family Associations. Ideally, the families' direct participation in the planning process would ensure that PLAN reached its goal of implementing the most relevant and effective programs possible.

Mr. Anderson discussed this method of budgeting and program planning at a meeting with his counterpart at the Department of Social Services and Development in Manila. The government was very much in favor of such a process and was planning to use a similar method in its own rural programs. On the recommendation of the government, PLAN budgets for the various zones and rural areas were shared with local mayors and staffs of local Departments of Social Services and Development. The sharing of information would reduce duplication of efforts and lead to a greater coordination in local development plans.

The program for Fiscal Year 1978 had to be drastically revised as a result of the tremendous success of PLAN/Netherlands. The sudden growth in the number of Dutch Foster Parents by mid-July forced

International Headquarters to request that PLAN/Philippines submit 6,500 new case histories by the end of October.

Staff was organized, case history forms and supplies were ordered, and intake teams traveled to dozens of rural villages to interview needy families. They traveled on overnight trains, conducted interviews in the midst of typhoons, and overcame countless obstacles, but by the last day of October more than 8,000 families had been interviewed and the quota had been met.

In September 1977 PLAN families in 18 locations were involved in various family and community development activities—an effort that would soon evolve into the more integrated and structured Family and Community Development Program (FCDP). Each program location had an average of 250 Foster Children and was served by a professionally trained social worker and a community social work aide. By the end of 1977, 32 more such programs had been established.

With the growth in the rural areas, PLAN had, in effect, two separate programs in the Philippines: the Metropolitan Manila program and its Family and Community Development Program (FCDP) in rural areas. The Metropolitan Manila program, scheduled for phaseout in 1979, served 5,531 Foster Children in September 1977 and the rural program 6,093. Two new offices were opened in 1977 to provide better service and supervision for the greatly changed and much larger rural program. The Benguet (Baguio) office opened in July to serve the Northern Luzon region and, in August, the Naga City office opened to serve the Southern Luzon region. Both offices were provided rent free by the Philippine Government for as long as PLAN needed them.

In the fall of 1977, Mr. Anderson explained the new FCDP approach to Foster Parents in an Informal Report:

> The Family and Community Development Program (FCDP) has recently been implemented in all rural areas served by PLAN/Philippines. Upon identifying a rural community for PLAN's work, we meet with the local Mayor and sign an agreement. The agreement states that the community accepts the responsibility of providing . . . office and program space. PLAN, on the other hand, agrees to provide its package of programs and services for the enrolled families. The municipality provides building materials (for a new community center) and PLAN families actually construct the building on a volunteer basis. We have also seen families repair and repaint unused buildings for the social workers to use as a base for implementation of the FCDP.

To accomplish the overall goal of independent and self-reliant families, we make use of what we have termed the Family Development Plan (FDP). The FDP mobilizes all available resources of the family, community and PLAN and directs them towards the attainment of specific objectives for the family's eventual independence and self-reliance.

During November and December 1977, the social workers in FCDP locations met with their assigned families to review the new program approach, prepare the budget for the coming year, and introduce the family aspect of the program. The Family Development Plan (FDP) involved a comprehensive and coordinated use of PLAN resources, the resources of the individual family, and community resources directed toward the attainment of specific goals for each family's independence and self-reliance. It incorporated the physical, economic, and psycho-social development of the family.

There were a number of difficulties to be overcome and a number of common reactions. The majority of the families seemed convinced that the plans were necessary for their self-reliance, others were skeptical, viewing such planning as inconsistent with the fatalistic outlook produced by a lifetime of poverty and hopelessness. A few families were apprehensive, feeling that they would be dropped from PLAN's roles—punished, in their view—if they met their goals.

By December 1977, with over 12,500 FDPs completed, the staff began to marshall the resources to implement the plans. The social workers naturally considered PLAN's established programs as means to achieve FDP goals. They also channeled PLAN's revolving loan fund, cash gifts from Foster Parents (unless they were specifically designated for other purposes by the Foster Parents), and self-help project funds to the written FDP goals agreed upon by the social worker and the family. Special Services Funds were, of course, still available for the emergency needs of PLAN families.

Family resources included such intangibles as motivation, skills, initiative, knowledge, and the willingness and potential to cooperate with their neighbors and the tangible assets of their crops, land, animals, tools, equipment, materials, and, in some cases, modest savings. The community could provide leadership experience, materials, funds, labor, equipment, volunteers, the resources of other public and private agencies or groups, and the collective resources of the PLAN Family Associations.

The actual implementation of the FDP approach was to be a

process leading to the Foster Child's cancellation from PLAN's rolls in a fixed number of years because of the Foster Family's improved living conditions.

In the first months of enrollment the Foster Family and its social worker discussed specific short and long-term ambitions and objectives and the resources available to meet them. On the basis of these discussions, they would draw up a list of objectives for the first year. For the remainder of the first year the family and their social worker worked to reach the stated goals. During the tenth month the family's progress was evaluated and incorporated in the Annual Progress Report sent to the Foster Child's sponsor. This was also the time to formulate the FDP for the coming year.

Any objective not met in a given year was considered for inclusion in the following year's FDP. During the term of the FDP, the family and its social worker continued to set specific objectives, mobilize resources to meet them, and evaluate their progress. As the families developed, their goals would also develop. The FDP was therefore a structured guideline, amenable to revision, and not a rigidly adhered to series of unchanging obligations and commitments. Early objectives usually focused on such basic needs as adequate food, shelter, medical care, and education. As these needs were met, the emphasis shifted to group endeavors and income-producing projects necessary for greater family and community self-sufficiency.

In April 1978, Mr. Anderson was transferred to PLAN's International Headquarters to become an Assistant Director for Field Services. He was succeeded by Mr. Frank Campbell, who had directed PLAN's programs in the Republic of Vietnam and Yogyakarta, Indonesia. When Mr. Campbell arrived to take over as the third Director of PLAN/Philippines the expatriate staff had grown from one to four—a Director and three Assistant Directors. James Byrne, Assistant Director for Administration, worked with the Director in Manila; Assistant Director William Fallon managed the Northern Luzon Regional Office; and Assistant Director James Gershin was responsible for the Southern Luzon Regional Office.

The elections for the National Parliament, the first elections since the imposition of martial law in 1972, and Mr. Campbell's arrival coincided with the Parliament's promulgation of a five-year development plan. The government's plan would focus on the improvement of individual and family welfare through the meeting of basic needs, expansion of social services, economic development, better resource management, and development of depressed rural areas.

In recognition of PLAN's contributions and continuing cooperation with the government's development efforts, the Department of Social Services and Development presented a commemorative plaque to Mr. Campbell inscribed:

TO

FOSTER PARENTS PLAN, INC.

Whose sustained partnership with the Department of Social Services and Development, as well as its dedication and commitment to uplift the living conditions of the most disadvantaged Filipino people, has contributed meaningfully and helped facilitate the government's social development-oriented programs.

Mr. Campbell's main tasks were to complete the Metropolitan Manila phaseout and further develop the rural programs on the islands of Luzon, Mindoro, and Marinduque. The phaseout was completed, as scheduled, by the end of June 1979 and the programs in the rural areas grew and developed as health, educational, family and community development, and recreational projects were implemented. The Council for International Assistance of the Canadian Province of Alberta provided funds for a corn mill, an irrigation project, a building block factory, an animal raising project, and 387 sewing machines for PLAN families in rural areas.

In the Philippines, as had been the case in Korea, there were difficulties in staffing the rural program areas. Nearly all of the social workers were young women recently graduated from college and assigned to small, relatively isolated communities. Between January and September 1978, for example, there was a 30 percent turnover. Social workers left because of pressure from their families to work closer to home, or because of work pressures, health problems, continuing education, incompetence, loneliness, or matrimony. To counter this high turnover, social workers from rural areas and rural colleges were recruited. Urban applicants were more carefully screened and new employees given more orientation, training, and support. These steps effectively reduced the turnover and resulted in a staff that was better trained and more qualified to bear the considerable responsibility of implementing the Family and Community Programs.

A report by social worker Lydia B. Ortile indicates the range of a PLAN social workers' activities. Miss Ortile was a 21 year-old graduate social worker on the island of Luzon. She had worked with PLAN families in Magarao since November 1977, when the PLAN program began. A year later, at the community Christmas party, she summarized the year's PLAN related activities. Among the year's accomplishments were leadership training, school and library projects, home repairs, economic cooperatives, recreational activities, and projects for individual family, group, and community development.

Miss Ortile ended her report with PLAN's philosophy of development:

> The projects . . . relate to the realization of family and community needs but are tempered by PLAN goals. All the available resources of the family, community, and the agency have been mobilized, and we hope to achieve our goal of . . . independence and self reliance within the specified time.

The range of projects illustrate the changes not in PLAN's goals, but in PLAN's methods. A child who has access to clean water, medical care, a school, and a library, who lives in a community of people cooperating to improve their lives, their homes, their health, and their environment, has a much greater chance of becoming a useful and contributing member of society than the PLAN child of 30 years before who could be instantly identified by his barefoot friends because of his new shoes.

Once the phaseout of the Metropolitan Manila program was completed, the regional programs in Baguio, Mindoro, and Naga were made fully independent Field Offices. Additional Field Offices were soon established in Iloilo (1981) and Cebu (1982). With an average of 25,000 Foster Children receiving benefits in Fiscal Year 1983, PLAN continues to deliver and develop its program of aid and services to needy children, their families, and communities in the Philippines.

The most recent developments in the Philippine programs emphasize even greater participation of families in the development process and are still being evaluated.

In 1981, Dr. William J. Kieffer was named Director of PLAN/Baguio and, with Assistant Director Myrna Setunga, began a review of the program. After discussions with staff, families, and community leaders, they decided that they could take a new approach to development using the knowledge gained from the Family and Community Development program. This approach called for the organization and motivation of PLAN families and their neighbors to take direct responsibility for the planning, implementation, and evaluation of family and community projects.

This change was reflected in organizational as well as philosophical changes. The social workers, who usually worked alone in their assigned villages, were replaced by two-member community service teams. The team consisted of a health worker and someone, not necessarily a social worker, with experience or training in human services work. These teams visited their assigned villages and, over the course of 18 months, nurtured the new program and the community groups who would carry it to fruition.

The program was organized around a four-tenet doctrine of participatory development. The first tenet called for an awareness by the individuals and families of their community identity, that they, as members of a community, shared a great many common concerns and were not isolated units unique in their needs. The second tenet of the approach was mutual responsibility. This followed from the first and brought the sense of group responsibility for community conditions, behavior, and decisions. With the realization of community identity and responsibility came community organization groups, formed to discuss common concerns and consider the ways and means to remedy them. The final step was community action. This action involved the community as a whole, PLAN families and their neighbors, participating in groups addressing such common concerns as health, education, finance, and home or community improvement. There were even groups concerned with letters to Foster Parents.

These groups, and not the PLAN staff, took the responsibility for their areas of concern. The elected group representatives met regularly with the PLAN team to share information. The representative of the educational group, for example, would report on the progress of the school children, the state of the schools, the activity of the tutors, and any other school related concerns. It was the educational representative, and not a PLAN social worker, who saw to it that children went to school. If a child needed special attention or if a family needed money for school fees or uniforms, it was the responsibility of the group representative to see that the need was met.

PLAN funds, formerly disbursed by PLAN staff for the goals defined in Family and Community Development Plans, were deposited into a Family Project Proposal Fund where they accrued for 18 months as the responsibility of a finance committee. If, for example, a family wanted a pig, they would fill out a Family Project Form and submit it to the finance committee. The committee would release the funds if the family had taken an extension course and knew how to care for a pig, if they had built a sty, and if they knew someone who had successfully raised pigs.

Similarly innovative programs are being implemented in the other program areas of the Philippines. In the PLAN/Cebu "Binhi" (seedling) approach, under the direction of William P. Fallon, family and community groups determine their needs, plan and carry out projects to meet them, and evaluate their results. The families themselves, not the PLAN staff, make the decisions. PLAN:

> . . . merely provides the impetus (constant motivation . . .), the opportunity (through . . . awareness, leadership, and responsibility training), and an added resource (. . . project funding).[4]

Charles A. Gray, Director of PLAN/Iloilo, works with families and communities accustomed to being the passive recipients of other peoples' charity and welfare programs. To combat the debilitating effects of charity, PLAN/Iloilo is providing motivation, training, and funding but groups of families must plan and implement their own development programs. In Fiscal Year 1983, 176 family groups were organized. Through regularly held meetings, with or without the presence of PLAN community workers, these groups were able to present 168 viable proposals for group development projects to be funded by PLAN. These projects were primarily related to health and income generating projects.

Director Brenda Cupper in Mindoro and Assistant Director Peter Hawkins in Marinduque are working to transfer the responsibility and resources for development to groups of PLAN families with similar interests or needs. Fiscal Year 1983 saw a 90 percent increase in group project participation. More than half of the 6,000 PLAN families of Mindoro and Marinduque had planned and carried out income generating and cooperative projects. The most encouraging result was that nearly half of these groups seem to have become permanent, with the members continuing to meet and work together after their original goal had been met.

[4]Annual Program Report, FY 1983, William P. Fallon, Director in Cebu. 18 August 1983, p. 2

Under the direction of Meredith Richardson and Assistant Director Kadarusamsi, the PLAN/Naga staff is providing basic management training necessary for groups of families and communities to organize themselves, identify their problems and plan solutions. When the planning stages are complete, the groups mobilize all their available skills and resources to meet their shared needs.

These new approaches to development in the Philippines are not the result of any particular love of group meetings and committees on the part of PLAN staff. Rather, they are the result of the conviction that there is an intrinsic value in people working together to do things for themselves instead of being dependent upon a PLAN social worker, or any other outside agent, to do things for them. If this approach is successful, the PLAN program staff will succeed in making themselves unnecessary. They hope that when they leave they will neither be noticed nor missed.

12

Expansion In Asia: 1969-83

From 1969 to 1982 PLAN's Asian programs spread from Hong Kong, the Philippines, and Vietnam, to India, Indonesia, Nepal, Sri Lanka, and Thailand. These programs are bringing desperately needed services to children and families and, with the programs in Africa and Latin America, are the groundwork for the anticipated growth in the number of Foster Parents recruited by PLAN's National Offices. The average enrollment figures for the 1983 Fiscal Year suggest this potential. The by now well established program in Indonesia had an average of nearly 40,000 Foster Children, while the four new Asian programs had only 7,833. These figures will grow as the new offices in Belgium, Japan, and the United Kingdom establish themselves and the older offices in Australia, Canada, the Netherlands, and the United States continue their enrollment of new Foster Parents.

Indonesia: 1968-83

George W. Ross, at the time PLAN Deputy Executive Director, arrived in Jakarta, Indonesia, on 29 October 1968 to investigate the possibility of establishing a PLAN program in Indonesia. In his two-week stay, he toured possible program locations and met with businessmen, government officials, staff of other voluntary agencies, and United Nations' and United States' officials.

In his first report to Gloria Matthews, on 3 November 1968, he wrote:

> There is a great deal more to do in the approximately ten days that I have left here, but one thing is very clear: conditions in Indonesia are *MUCH* worse than I had expected.
>
> Mr. Dradjat, a competent man and a senior civil servant, earns $9.00 per month plus a rice ration for his family equal to another $3.00 per month. This is enough for them to survive on for one week. Mr. Dradjat, with a social work

degree from the Netherlands and further training in Chicago, supplements his income by teaching in four institutions. By so doing, his family stays alive, but he is killing himself. This story is repeated everywhere I turn except for the few who are very rich. One old friend, graduated from a government Teachers Training School in the field of Physical Education, teaches in a town far from the capital. His salary is $3.60 per month, so he teaches in two other schools where he is not allowed a salary but is paid by the hour. In this way he earns another $2.00 per month. Since his wife and two children can not survive on this grand income from three jobs, he drives a horse-drawn cart after hours and earns another $3.00 per month. This happens to be a fine, bright, hard-working fellow. His family is barely surviving. What is happening to those much farther down on the scale?

It soon became apparent that Indonesian social welfare programs were centered in Jakarta and that little was being done in the rest of the country. Both the Minister and the Secretary General of the Department of Social Affairs were highly receptive to Mr. Ross' suggestion that PLAN locate its programs in some other city. They enthusiastically suggested Yogyakarta (then spelled "Jogjakarta").

On 9 November 1968 Mr. Ross reported from Yogyakarta that there was a vastly greater need for PLAN there than in the capital and described his two-day visit:

> The Secretary General of the Department of Social Affairs went to Jogjakarta on the same express train I took . . . We had good opportunity to talk during the trip . . . a journey of 11 hours to cover the 400 miles. I also carried letters of introduction to the head of the provincial Social Affairs office and to His Highness, the Prince Pakualam, who governs the Jogjakarta district.
> The district of Jogjakarta had about two-million people, while its capital city (also called Jogjakarta) had a population of about 300,000. The good land in the district boasts a population density of 700 per square kilometer which means that although it produces two good crops of rice per year it can not feed the number of people who depend on it. Some sections of the district have poor soil and a disastrous lack of water, leading to recurrent periods of starvation. However, as I have previously written, this region is the heart of Javanese culture. There are beautiful temples dating back a thousand years, and even today in this poor, poor area with its shabby homes, ill-clad people, and general economic backwardness, it is a major education center and an artistic mecca.

I was received by the Prince Pakualam . . . a charming man [who] welcomed PLAN with open arms, and said he would have his staff look around to see what office space and housing would be available for us to rent.

At 5:30 p.m., I met Agung Juwono,[1] and as earlier agreed, we went to see the living conditions of families at the bottom of the scale. We went to see a village headman, though his "village" was right in town. He led us to a cottage of woven bamboo strips, dirt floor, and thatched roof . . . Here was the beginning of knowledge, and is, of course, the sort of thing that PLAN's Director in Indonesia will have to do at great length . . . should we develop a program here. Of the village of 249 families, I learned that the majority live mostly outside a money economy. Neighbors help neighbors to get jobs done such as house-building and repair. Occasionally a meal is given in exchange for work. Occasionally the wife hawks fruit in town, and occasionally the husband gets money for work done. Husband has no skill, but sometimes gets laboring jobs in rice fields, on the roads, etc. They had a hard time trying to figure out just how much cash they received in an average *month* but finally came up with about 300 rupiah. . . US $0.60. The children are not in school because they can not afford the monthly fee of 10 rupiah (US $0.02), nor the price of paper and pencil and books, nor the clothes to wear. There are families worse off than this one, especially where there is a widowed mother and several children. Because of the mass slayings after the abortive communist coup two years ago, there are *many* such widows. There are families better off, too. The best families in a village such as this have a cash income of about US $3.50 per month. Such families are able to send perhaps two of their children to school but not more because they can not afford the necessary paper, pencils, books, and clothes. Gloria, these people are *so poor!*

After nearly a year of negotiations, agreements were signed by Mr. Nevin Wiley, PLAN/Yogyakarta's first Director, and Dr. A.M. Tambunan, then Minister of Social Affairs. Under the terms of these agreements, PLAN was to carry out its program in concert with the activities of the Department of Social Affairs (DEPSOS). DEPSOS, for its part, agreed to recommend PLAN to local, regional, and national offices and officials; to give non-binding recommendations and advice for program areas and activities; and, finally, to spread the word that PLAN was a recognized agency operating with the consent and approval of the government.

[1]Agung Juwono was at the time with the BPPS (see next page).

In October, at the request of Mr. Wiley, the Government's Institute of Social Research and Observation (BPPS-the Balai Penelitian dan Penindjauan Social) conducted a survey of the social and economic conditions in three subdistricts of the city. The data was used in the selection of both the first program site and the first Foster Children. Since the program was to include a community development component, existing or potential community resources were carefully considered.

The first Indonesian Foster Children were enrolled in the Mantridjeron subdistrict in December 1969 and, in January 1970, 62 Foster Children received their first cash grants. In the next four years PLAN/Indonesia decentralized itself with four local offices in Yogyakarta serving nearly 5,000 children and a second independent program on the island of Bali which Frank W. Ryan established in November 1972.

Nineteen seventy four brought a broad range of changes to PLAN in Indonesia: steadily increasing rural enrollment; greater coordination and cooperation with Indonesian agencies; an increase in outside funding, particularly from the Canadian Province of Alberta; and a growing recognition of the importance of preventive as well as curative medical care.

In 1974 the first five-year economic and social development program of the Government of Yogyakarta ended and, not surprisingly, another one began. The second emphasized social welfare and community development. A community development agency was established to coordinate public and private development efforts in rural areas and an interagency group was organized for urban projects.

These were to be small-scale, grass roots efforts to stimulate neighborhood and village development, just the sort of activities with which PLAN could cooperate. PLAN would supplement government projects. Government expertise in, for example, crop improvement or animal husbandry, would be available to PLAN as would technical advice for the establishment of cooperatives.

The possibility of collaboration in health related projects made a change in emphasis from curative to preventive care more feasible and increasingly attractive. The basic aim of the preventive care was to provide the simplest health services to the maximum number of people through locally available and, ideally, locally trained personnel. This aim at once eliminated the need for large and expensive centralized hospitals. It also required that the thrust be on health maintenance. Frank Ryan, who succeeded Mr. Wiley and served as PLAN/ Yogyakarta Director from 1973-75, wrote that the medical units operating out of

PLAN's four Yogyakarta offices did little coordinated preventive health care, concentrating instead on efforts to cure the direct consequence of an unhealthy environment. PLAN was, he wrote, "wasting [its] money and doing nothing for the community on an effective and sustained basis for good health care."

As he was writing his report, he had already begun to implement such community health related projects as the digging of public wells and drainage systems and the construction of public toilets and bathhouses. These efforts were augmented by agricultural development and insect control which would clearly have an impact on the general health level of the community though they were not specifically designed as health projects. Nonetheless, there was more than an element of truth in Mr. Ryan's assessment. Curative measures certainly do not have the long-range impact of preventive measures but, until a preventive program could be implemented, there would be a need for curative treatment. PLAN could not close its clinics until there were other available services for PLAN children and their families.

By July 1974 the program was shifting more and more to rural areas and there was a necessarily greater reliance placed on nurses, midwives, and medical paraprofessionals. Economy, effectiveness, and the availability of pharmaceuticals were important considerations in this shift to preventive health care, as was the emphasis on simple observational methods of diagnosis. The goal was to eventually phase out curative elements and to close PLAN clinics.

Foster Parent Dr. John Biddulph, a Public Health Officer and Professor of Child Health at the University of Papua and New Guinea, visited PLAN doctors in 1974 and gave them valuable advice on the use of paraprofessionals for diagnosis, treatment, and referral. Another physician, Dr. Jan E. Rohde, of the Rockefeller Foundation, brought the lessons learned in India working with refugees from Bangladesh.

While serving in India, Dr. Rohde and his colleagues developed a list of 19 basic drugs and a pamphlet tabulating their daily dosage by age and weight groups. The pamphlet, though designed to be a general guide for the health care management of refugees in India, was as applicable in Indonesia. There was, of course, a major difference in the severity of the health problems of the refugees and the people of Indonesia, but the problems were basically of the same type—respiratory diseases, intestinal disorders and diarrheal diseases, typhoid, tuberculosis, and the ever-present malnutrition.

Doctors Biddulph and Rohde were impressed with the young and enthusiastic doctors in PLAN's urban areas and the PLAN nurses and midwives in the rural area, who made regular rounds of their assigned villages on motorcycles and trail bikes. Though their major role was in public health education, the nurses and midwives also diagnosed and treated common ailments.

Dr. Biddulph returned a few months later to conduct a study of the health program with the goal of further developing its preventive aspects. Essentially, this study taught the PLAN medical staff to gauge community health conditions through data gathered by themselves and the social work staff on birth and crude death rates, population growth, and age-specific death rates. The next step had two parts. The first was to begin standard, regular recording of children's weight to detect malnutrition before it became a serious problem. Second came the compilation of the data to accurately determine the extent of malnutrition in PLAN villages. The overall goal was to reduce the birth and infant death rates as well as the incidence of childhood malnutrition. Through Dr. Biddulph, PLAN's health efforts in Indonesia gained both direction and measurable goals.

This emphasis on measurable goals reflected an increasing concern throughout the PLAN world for designing programs which yielded quantifiable results. For nearly 40 years PLAN had worked to provide for the "care, maintenance, education, training, and well-being of children,"[2] but until the mid-1970's there had been few systematic efforts to measure the achievement of these goals. Until this time, programs had been measured largely in terms of money spent, material goods distributed, or simply by the number of children receiving benefits from their Foster Parents. Impressive as these figures were, they said little about basic improvements PLAN may or may not have been bringing to the families and communities of its Foster Children or the possible dependence PLAN may have been unconsciously promoting.

This last issue of dependence was particularly important in Indonesia where the government had made it clear from the beginning that PLAN would be welcome until or unless its programs led to dependency rather than development. Two major steps were taken to assure the relevance and effectiveness of PLAN's efforts. The first had been the establishment of decentralized sub-offices in the communities being served. The second called for the cooperation of third party agencies for program review or collaboration.

[2]Certificate of Incorporation, Article Two, Paragraph A, 13 July 1939.

The first such review was undertaken by Helen Miller, MSW, for the BPPS in 1973. The review, "The Effect of Foster Parents' Assistance in Yogyakarta, Indonesia, to its First 300 Clients After Approximately Three Years Service," was positive:

> The Indonesian culture of living each day with little planning for the future is reinforced in the low income levels by the necessities of existence living. To change the attitudes of the clients requires much individual attention in the form of counseling, concrete demonstration and time (staff time, and also overall chronological length of assistance to provide repeated experience of the value of planning). The policy of the Yogyakarta office of FPP has been to keep caseloads of workers low in order to provide sufficient services and opportunities to effect such changes. The results of this policy come through "loud and clear."

The BPPS research and statements from PLAN social workers indicated that frequent and large gifts from Foster Parents had a negative impact on PLAN families, that the recipients of such gifts sometimes tended to depend upon them to reduce their own efforts to help themselves.[3] If a becak (pedicab) driver was given the funds to buy his own becak, he could earn more than twice as much money or simply work less and maintain his accustomed standard of living. The dangers of giving without counseling were obvious. The potential benefits of providing guidance to motivated families were equally obvious. The letters from two Foster Families quoted in Nevin Wiley's Quarterly Report (January-March 1972) illustrate the point.

> Since at this time we live much better than before, we have decided to give our right as a Foster Family to Foster Parents again. We will try to stand on our own feet, step by step, and the aid can be given to another family that needs it more.

> PLAN's assistance has been satisfactory for us and the guidance from PLAN's worker was very useful, so for the time being we feel PLAN's assistance can be stopped. Thank you very much to the Director and his staff who always get in touch with us.

The BPPS study revealed that the greatest impact of PLAN enrollment had been in the Foster Families' use and management of money.

---

[3]The "largeness" of a cash gift is a matter of proportion. To a family with an average income of US $3.00 a month, a US $25.00 cash gift is substantial indeed.

Improvement in housing was a close second, but reached a plateau in the second year. Family income and health showed steady improvement throughout their period of enrollment. The majority of the 100 families interviewed said that education, personal welfare, and housing were the areas most positively affected by PLAN aid and they were unanimous in their desire to continue as Foster Families.

The findings of the study were gratifying but hardly surprising. PLAN's program sought to enable families to improve the quality of their lives while stressing the importance of education. To these ends, monthly financial assistance provided for educational expenses while cash gifts and Special Services Funds were used to support economic development and home improvement. The social work staff provided the counseling necessary for the families and communities to make the best use of PLAN resources. The report concluded:

> It would appear that these counseling services are one factor in the families' improvement in handling money, as the focus of counseling is to help the families change their pattern of living for today into a pattern of planning for the needs of the future also. FPP is concerned that the financial improvement be reinforced by improvement in family welfare and community well-being. Toward this goal, medical care and after school programs have been established for FPP clients, and the community development program is designed to help all persons in the area, clients, and non-clients alike. Thus, the overall program seems to be effective in using the financial investment by the Foster Parent as a human investment in Yogyakarta's citizens.

Perhaps the most important function of a third party agency was to act as a monitor, insuring the appropriateness of the program to the local value systems. The value systems of Indonesia, like those of many cultures, tend to be conservative and may inhibit or thwart development. Such systems as fatalism, paternalism, and traditionalism, do not necessarily encourage social or economic change. However, the existing social strengths of the community may be called upon if the program is carefully and sensitively planned. A program which, through ignorance or arrogance, ignores these local values may be in direct conflict with the local culture and will certainly fail. Cooperation with such outside agencies as the BPPS and the Institute of Rural and Regional Studies of Gadjah Mada University helped to insure that PLAN was neither the perpetrator nor the victim of inappropriate and futile programming.

The nature of this collaboration has taken many forms. PLAN's programs are seldom formally integrated with other agencies, rather they are mutually supportive. PLAN staff meet whenever possible with local level officials to better support and complement their plans. Interaction with non-government organizations involves the Yayasan Indonesia Sejahtera, a community and social development organization; Liane Desa, an appropriate technology group; CUCO, a national credit union counselling office; UNICEF, in Jakarta; the Rockefeller Foundation, on occasion; and the Management Centre of the Economics Faculty of Gadjah Mada University.

The greatest collaboration is at the local neighborhood and community level, the level at which PLAN works. PLAN's program is one of participatory, grass roots development, that is, PLAN staff will work with but not for the families of a community. If local groups and individuals do not actively participate in the planning, implementation, and evaluation of a particular project, the project is dropped as irrelevant.

This participatory process, while probably the only effective way to introduce a fundamental change in the attitudes and actions of PLAN families and their neighbors, can be a slow process. John Langford, Director of PLAN/Bali in 1974, wrote of this problem in an October report to Gloria Matthews:

> What with myriad village ceremonies, heavy flooding, difficulty in obtaining materials on time . . . several projects have been slowed down . . . However, from the Balinese point of view, this is not important—"time" in Bali is referred to as "rubber time." Whilst all of our projects have originated from the expressed wish of village people they are, nonetheless, of secondary importance in village priorities. PLAN works with the people at their pace, though in a subtle way, I hope, we try to hasten things along by encouraging greater participation of village leaders . . . regrettably, it appears that many village officials are anxious to start things but lose their enthusiasm as soon as real problems are encountered. Hence, we are working in trying to maintain and develop [their] enthusiasm, but this is a drawn out task which requires much patience on the part of PLAN staff.

Patience paid off. Between January and March 1976, 29 community projects were completed, 47 were initiated, and 21 continued. The projects involved a total of over 12,000 people in building and improvement of schools, houses, roads, reservoirs, community centers, bathhouses, water tanks, wells, and athletic fields. Economic development efforts included agricultural, cattle, and fishery projects.

In the same period enrollment increased by nearly a thousand children; 654 progress reports were written to Foster Parents; 14,000 people received medical services; PLAN social workers were trained in family planning education; and a new program area was opened in East Bali.

This was not an unusually busy quarter for the two PLAN programs in Indonesia. Since 30 June 1975, when the combined enrollments of PLAN/Bali and PLAN/Yogyakarta reached nearly 10,000 Foster Children, Indonesia had been the largest and fastest growing of PLAN's programs. The next year, 1976, there were 15,000 Indonesian Foster Children. Five years later there were over 35,000.

The reasons for this growth are many and varied. The termination of the programs in the former Republic of Vietnam and in Ethiopa in 1975 and 1977 left nearly 8,000 Foster Parents suddenly without Foster Children. Many of these sponsors may have transferred their sponsorship to Indonesian children. Foster Parents Plan of Canada succeeded in attracting nearly 30,000 new sponsors between 1975 and 1983. But most important were the thousands of Indonesian children sponsored by Foster Parents living in the Netherlands. The number of Dutch sponsors grew from 641 in Fiscal Year 1977 to over 100,000 in 1983. Because of the historical ties between the Netherlands and Indonesia, many thousands of these new sponsors chose Indonesian Foster Children.

For whatever reason, or combinations of reasons, Indonesia has been very good for PLAN growth and PLAN growth has been very good for the needy families of Indonesia. It is ironic, in retrospect, that there were fears a program for the children and families in Bali would fail to attract sponsors. After all, it was argued, why would anyone sponsor a child living in a tropical paradise? Some of the more timorous staff members even suggested calling the program "PLAN/Denpasar" to disguise the fact that it was in Bali. However, it was pointed out that, though the program might begin in Denpasar, it would spread to rural villages in what could only be called Bali.

In 1978 a third Indonesian program was established by Frank Ryan in the southern part of the island of Sulawesi (formerly called Celebes). In the first year more than 300 children in villages outside of Ujung Pandang were enrolled. Five years later, enrollment in Sulawesi had reached nearly 10,000 Foster Children and their families.

At the end of Fiscal Year 1983, under the direction of Frank W.

Ryan in Bali, James T. Alger in South Sulawesi, and Gus C. E. Hall in Yogyakarta, PLAN's Indonesian development programs were providing nearly 40,000 PLAN families and their neighbors with the skills and resources to improve their own lives, their children's prospects for the future, and the life and future of their community.

Nepal: 1978-83

The PLAN program in Nepal was established with the 1 May 1978 signing of an agreement between Nepalese authorities and PLAN representative, Dr. William J. Kieffer. Under the terms of the agreement with the Social Services National Coordination Council, chaired by Her Majesty Queen Aishwanya, PLAN would work in conjunction with the Nepal Children's Organization to bring its development program to the children and families of Kathmandu Valley.

Although the program area is within 10 kilometers of the capital city it is a rural area with few signs of the twentieth century. The people live in clusters of rude houses on the sides and tops of hills overlooking rice paddies and the flat bottomlands below. Over the centuries these farmers have built an elaborate system of terraces to make use of every drop of rain and every square meter of arable land. Houses are tucked away on otherwise useless land.

The best land, the fertile, easily accessible bottomland, is generally held by the large landowners, but most of the families own a few scattered parcels on the terraced hills where they grow corn and lentils. Those who own no land rent fields from larger landlords or work as tenant farmers, sharecroppers, or laborers.

Traditional agricultural methods have not been able to keep pace with the demands of a growing population and many of the people are faced with seasonal food shortages and the need for supplemental income. People with marketable skills can sometimes find steady work in Kathmandu City. Others, without such skills, work as day laborers or may migrate to India.

The estimated 25,000 people of the PLAN program area suffer from parasites, respiratory diseases, malnutrition, and the general poor health of people in marginal communities all over the world. As elsewhere in the PLAN world, these conditions are the result not only of poor living conditions, inadequate food supplies, poor housing, and the lack of sanitary facilities, but also result from simple ignorance of the causes and prevention of disease.

One of the preliminary steps in alleviating these conditions is to conduct a systematic survey to determine the extent of the problems and to establish appropriate priorities to remedy them. Therefore, one of PLAN's first efforts in Nepal was to lay the groundwork for the collection of data by assisting local government efforts to number houses. This simple project provided the basis for the accurate collection of the information necessary to design effective health, education, and community development programs.

The next step was to organize Ward Development Committees in the subdivisions of each local administrative district. Today these committees provide the channel for direct local participation in the selection, planning, and implementation of PLAN projects and will serve as the basis for continued community improvement and cooperation long after PLAN leaves Kathmandu Valley.

One of PLAN's first cooperative projects with these committees was to assess the need for a vaccination campaign against smallpox and tuberculosis by means of a house-to-house survey. The survey was conducted by a PLAN nurse and a committee member who kept a tally, by house member, of the children who needed vaccination.

Once the survey was completed, PLAN took the data to the Nepal Children's Organization and received quick approval for the vaccination campaign. The nurse then returned to the homes to give the inoculations while committee members handled the record keeping. The same procedure was followed in a subsequent campaign against roundworms.

PLAN achieved three important goals in these community-wide health projects. First, and most important, was the promotion of better community health. Second, was that the participation of the local community, through its ward committees, provided clear evidence of the benefits of community organization. Third, everyone in the program area saw the advantages of having some PLAN families in the neighborhood. The other side of this third point is that it is through such projects as these that PLAN wins the trust, respect, and cooperation of the people in the community.

Other similarly organized health related projects included rat control, measles treatment, and water projects. The people and their local committees worked together with PLAN staff to schedule doctors' visits, distribute rat traps, and lay water pipe.

PLAN clinics brought curative health care to areas with no other health facilities, but the major focus of the health program was, and remains, disease prevention and community health education. These educational programs are conducted in clinics, in group sessions at the PLAN office, and in schools.

When PLAN arrived in Kathmandu Valley the schools were poorly attended, under-equipped, and inadequately staffed. PLAN's insistence that Foster Children and as many of their brothers and sisters as possible attend school increased pressure on the already strained educational system. In response to this, a school construction and renovation project was initiated. The training of locally recruited teacher's aides helped to reduce the staffing problem.

Whether or not a primary school education will make a substantial difference in the potential earning power of Nepalese children is a matter of some debate. Even if there are no more opportunities for literate than for illiterate young people, there is an enduring faith in the beneficial effects of education. The World Bank's *Investment In Education* makes the point that the change in attitude that goes along with more education may be the most important result of these programs. It is this point and the ability to incorporate this changed attitude into other PLAN and community projects which may finally be of most benefit to people in PLAN communities.

India: 1978-83

Bombay

After Nepal came the first of PLAN's unique cooperative ventures in India. Norman D. Sanders, Jr., arrived in India in the autumn of 1978 to investigate the feasibility of establishing a PLAN program there. It quickly became apparent that there were two avenues available for PLAN's establishment—the direct approach and the indirect approach.

India's long reputation as one of the world's most populous and neediest of countries and her long experiences with charitable organizations of varying degrees of competence and honesty had made the government understandably cautious of foreigners with benevolent intentions. Further obstacles to the establishment of a PLAN program were the government's emphasis on advanced technological development and its preference for native directors for organizations such as PLAN. In addition to these potentially delaying factors, there was a de facto moratorium on the registration of foreign voluntary agencies under the Societies Registration Act, a necessity for PLAN's official establishment.

An indirect approach to establishment in India would avoid these obstacles. Once a voluntary agency has been registered with the Government of India, it may freely collaborate with foreign agencies and sources of funds. This meant that PLAN could collaborate with any willing agency in India and begin programming at once. When PLAN's credibility was established by the joint program, PLAN could either seek official recognition from the Government of India or continue its collaborative programs.

The decision was made to adopt this indirect approach by establishing an urban program in collaboration with the Community Aid and Sponsorship Program (CASP), a highly respected Indian agency led by Mr. S.D. Gokhale. This was done, and in 1980 the first Foster Children were enrolled in the CASP/PLAN project in the slums of Bombay. The program was administered by Vijaya Chauhan, Project Administrator and Mr. Sanders. The CASP/PLAN project is currently led by PLAN Representative Vijay K. Sardana, who replaced Mr. Sanders in July 1983, and Project Administrator Mr. M.G. Gore.

The PLAN families of Bombay live in makeshift houses on open municipally owned or private land. Most of the families have come to Bombay from rural areas and many of them still return every year to help with the harvest. The city government, the Municipal Corporation of Greater Bombay, has provided some limited basic public services through its Slum Improvement Program but much remains to be done.[4]

CASP/PLAN's strategy of grass roots programming gives it a flexibility lacking in governmental agencies which must function within a tightly structured hierarchical framework. While the government's Slum Improvement Program focuses on providing physical assets to the community and has adopted a service oriented approach, CASP/PLAN's efforts are geared more to human development. Thus, programs like health and nutrition education, the provision of school supplies, vocational training, and the process of developing strong community groups and community resources have been given first priority.

A water project in Shivaji Nagar, a slum district of about 450 households, illustrates the process. The families of the district have organized a number of local groups to find solutions to their common problems. One of these groups, Rahivashi Mandal (Residents Associa-

[4]The government's not yet completed program calls for the provision of one well or tap for every 20 households and one water-sealed latrine block for every ten households. CASP/PLAN's water and sanitation projects are augmenting this program.

tion) decided to do something to improve the community's water supply. The scarcity of water was not only affecting the health of the community, but its social life as well. The municipal water tap had to serve a great many more people than it was designed for and, to maintain order, water was available to the people of Shivaji Nagar only during assigned three-hour periods. The orderly life of the community was regularly interrupted as the women accommodated themselves to the inconvenient schedule.

The community group approached a CASP/PLAN social worker with the problem. Since the group could do nothing to improve the supply of tap water, the decision was made to repair one of two dilapidated wells and insure the purity of its water. Once this decision was made, the social worker offered CASP/PLAN's aid for the project if the group could not marshall sufficient community and municipal resources.

Rahivashi Mandal arranged for the municipal testing of the water, met with the families who would use the well, and found out how much money could be raised for the project. Most importantly, they organized a Construction Committee to execute the project.

The Construction Committee did all of the necessary groundwork for the project. They arranged for the water to be regularly tested, motivated the people who would use the well to donate a day's labor and what money they could, and submitted a detailed proposal to CASP/PLAN. CASP/PLAN matched their work and enthusiasm with Rs. 9,000 (US $900). The succesful completion of the project resulted not only in the immediate benefit of an improved water supply for the 2,800 people of the community but also provided a structure for further community improvement projects. Similar cooperative projects have included electrification, home repair, community center construction, and the training of local community groups.

An adult education and literacy program will function at a similar local level. With a 1981 literacy rate of only 36 percent, there is a clear need for such a program. Philip Abraham, a CASP/PLAN Program Coordinator, described it in a September 1983 Informal Report to Foster Parents of Children in India.

> In order to start the Adult Education Programme, the teachers must first be trained. If the teachers are from the community itself they will be able to explain matters, taking day-to-day examples of domestic life. These teachers are also involved in other areas of community development programming. Our

objective is not just literacy but non-formal social education wherein people are not only taught to read and write but are made aware of the various socio-economic factors affecting their daily lives.

Children's programs are similarly contingent upon the active participation of the community. A 1980 community health campaign provides an example. The project was organized to assess and improve the health of the community's children. The campaign provided complete health check-ups, any necessary treatment, and immunizations for more than 5,000 children. The successful project was organized with the help and active participation of the local people. A number of young professionals, including pediatricians, were involved in the project which continued every Sunday until all of the children in the area had been examined. This local participation was a major factor in overcoming the fears many of the parents had of vaccinating their children.

In the educational sector the distribution of children's school uniforms and supplies provided not only otherwise unavailable materials but also a market for the products of local chalk-making and sewing groups organized by CASP/PLAN.

In Fiscal Year 1983, CASP/PLAN continued its emphasis on the development of local groups. The most important of these groups, the Inter-Community Coordination Committee (Sanyojan Samittee), was organized as a local representative body composed of two members from each of the local groups. The committee meets regularly to discuss community needs and to plan ways to meet them. Specialized sub-committees have been formed to address such specific areas as education, health, and housing. The committee has come to be a representative forum for the 70,000 people of the area and has implemented a number of community programs.

The organization and growing effectiveness of these neighborhood and community groups lends hope that CASP/PLAN's two main principles will result in self-sustaining child, family, and community development. These principles are that:

1. CASP/PLAN's programs should lead to long-term achievements by increasing the problem-solving capacity of the people in its program areas.

2. CASP/PLAN assistance should be extended only as a short-term measure and be contingent upon continuing community participation.

Thus, the major goal of the program is organizational and educational development rather than the simple provision of services. CASP/PLAN works to show people how they can work together to provide a better life for themselves, their neighbors, and their children.

H.D. Kote

In January 1982 a similar cooperative arrangement was established by Mr. Sanders with Myrada, a Bangalore-based rural development organization led by William Davinson. MYRADA/PLAN, under Project Officer Mohan Thazhathu and PLAN Representative in India, Vijay K. Sardana, focuses on children and their families in the rural villages of Heggadadevanakote, also called (for obvious reasons) H.D. Kote, in the state of Karnataka in southwestern India. The MYRADA/PLAN program has a dual focus, combining assistance for the most disadvantaged families through Family Development Plans (FDP) with group and community projects. This duality recognizes that, although all families in the area are in need, some are more severely disadvantaged than others. Foster Children are enrolled from these neediest of families who, for the most part, are landless agricultural workers.

These families most often use the funds they receive through their FDPs to meet their basic educational and medical needs. Through these plans, structured financial aid and counseling were made available to nearly 1,000 families in Fiscal Year 1983, and will, according to enrollment projections, provide aid to over 2,000 families in 1984.

Whether the program benefits children directly through their sponsorship by a Foster Parent, or indirectly through a group or community project, the child remains the focal point because, in India, as in the other developing nations of the world, it is the child who is most vulnerable to the effects of poverty. The MYRADA/PLAN staff hopes to show the people of H.D. Kote how they can reduce poverty's effects by working together to establish primary health care programs, train and equip local health workers, implement water projects, and support education through school construction, renovation, and furnishing projects.

Nalluru is fairly typical of the MYRADA/PLAN villages in H.D. Kote. The 40 families of the village came from the state of Tamil Nadu about 30 years ago to work in nearby quarries. When MYRADA/PLAN came to Narullu there was no electricity, no source of unpolluted drinking water, no health care, and only four children in the local school. The first task of the social worker was to get more children in school. The enrollment soon rose to 24. Frequent meetings with the teachers and visits to the children's homes helped to assure that the children would stay in school.

The staff then addressed the health and income of the families. A series of health education classes alerted parents to the occupational health hazards of quarry work and led to physical examinations and treatment. Vaccination campaigns immunized their children against polio and diphtheria.

Even though most of the fathers of the Foster Children worked regularly in the quarries, many were in debt. With wages insufficient to meet even their most basic needs, they were forced to borrow from quarry contractors and obliged to work off the loan. As a result, they were nearly always in debt. After a series of meetings with village elders, quarry workers, and MYRADA/PLAN staff, the families agreed to pool their meager savings to start a credit cooperative. A welfare fund was also established with the ultimate goals of building a community center and assisting tubercular quarry workers. The village committee also took up the cause of raising the wages of quarry workers. As a result of their negotiations, quarry contractors agreed to raise their workers' wages.

Change is gradually coming to the lives and attitudes of the people of Nalluru. With each change they become more confident that they, themselves, can be the agents of change and not its victims.

In other villages of H.D. Kote, where the people rely on agriculture or crafts rather than wages, MYRADA/PLAN has a proposed resources and skills development training program. Such programs are in harmony with the government's stated goal of evolving an integrated strategy to increase agricultural productivity and to develop the resources and incomes of the most vulnerable sections of the population.

These and other projects will be planned, implemented, and managed by local cooperatives, village development associations, young farmers' associations, youth groups, and clubs. Activities will include erosion control and reforestation, the establishment of a stockman's center, two model farms, handicrafts, irrigation and drinking water, model gardens, and agricultural training. Beyond the immediate goals of these projects is the hope that through them the people, and particularly the children, of H.D. Kote will learn that they can have more control over their lives, that the future can be more promising than the present.

Sri Lanka: 1981-83

PLAN's program in Sri Lanka was established by Anthony English in 1981. James Alexander took charge of the program in 1982 when Mr. English was transferred to the Philippines. The first program sites were in the villages around Gampola, in the hill country of central Sri Lanka. The villagers are a heterogeneous mix of Singhalese Buddists; Indian and Sri Lankan Tamils, who are usually Hindu; Muslims of Sri Lankan, Indian, and Malay origin; Christians of various ethnic backgrounds; members of four Hindu and at least 25 Singhalese castes; and supporters of various political parties.

The villages are tightly structured and hierarchical. Decisions are usually made by a small minority representing the highest social and economic classes. Villagers usually accept these decisions with few questions or arguments. Factionalism, mutual distrust, and intermittent eruptions of violence have become characteristic of Sri Lankan village life.

It soon became apparent to Mr. English that aid to individual families in such an environment would not only create further factionalism and distrust, but would also make it extremely difficult to mobilize people to work on projects of benefit to the entire community. After discussions with individuals and groups at all levels of society, he arrived at a strategy which he hoped would serve as a cohesive force in the community, would be conducive both to group and family projects, and would, at the same time, minimize long-standing divisiveness. The cultural climate called for the establishment of heterodox, informal community groups of about 50 families. These groups would examine the problems they shared and make decisions about family projects. The groups would work under the advisement of committees composed of customary leaders, village officials, and PLAN staff. These community groups would work directly to motivate families and have at least one member to represent them on the committees. Through this group approach, the PLAN/Sri Lanka staff hoped to foster a spirit of community cohesiveness which would unite the village without either undermining the existing village authorities or adding to their already overbearing character.

A 1982 project in the village of Rathmalkaduwa proved this process worked. A PLAN family group asked for assistance with the purchase of wooden handcarts for ten of its members who work as porters in Gampola. The men earn the equivalent of US $0.25 a day carrying lumber, cement, grain, flour, and other merchandise for local businessmen. A Rathmalkaduwa village leader told Mr. English that a full day's work for a man on his own might consist of moving five bags of flour, one by one, from one side of town to the other. With a pushcart, the same man could make the same five trips but could carry five times as much flour and greatly reduce his risk of injury. PLAN agreed to help finance the project.

The ten laborers who would receive the handcarts formed a committee to supervise the project and, because of the length of time required to build the handcarts, assigned delivery by lot. PLAN agreed to provide about US $21 towards the cost of each cart. As the carts were delivered the recipients signed an agreement to pay US $8 over the course of a year into a special savings account to finance group and community projects. The agreement was witnessed by a PLAN staff member, a village leader, and a group member. To insure his continuing interest, the group witness was to be one of the last to receive a cart. It was understood that the carts would not be sold without group approval for two years and that they would be used to improve the recipient family's income and not simply to shorten the man's workday.

This project illustrates the responsibility PLAN's staff encourages among Foster Families and communities. PLAN aid is used to augment local family and community efforts. The handcart project was proposed by a villager at a PLAN family group meeting. The recipients of the handcarts are responsible for coordinating the project and understand that PLAN's uninterrupted assistance to the group depends upon the willingness of each group member to meet his agreed upon obligations to the group.

PLAN has similar projects in villages in Mali and Upper Volta which have had similar results: through simple, rudimentary projects, an individual's daily productive capacity can be dramatically increased. A handcart or donkey cart, simple as it may be, can represent a major capital investment and can result in a significant improvement in family income. Because of their impact on village and family life, such programs need to be carefully planned to minimize their potentially disruptive effects. The higher level of community cohesiveness and mutual trust in Mali and Upper Volta simplifies the process of implementation. In the socially fragmented villages of Sri Lanka such projects require all of the careful negotiations and mutual assurances typical of commerce in a much more highly developed country.

Ideally, the successful completion of these and similar group projects will provide concrete proof that the diverse elements in the community can work together to improve their standards of living and the prospects of their children.

The health program in Sri Lanka is primarily preventive and focuses on personal hygiene, community sanitation, diet, and potable water projects implemented largely by PLAN trained local health promoters. Until the program can be fully implemented, PLAN is providing feeding and nutritional education programs for schools, preschools, and when necessary, for individual families with young children. Children needing medical attention are referred to western or traditionally trained medical personnel.

The PLAN staff in Sri Lanka hopes to promote a sense of personal and group responsibility through a comprehensive program whose success depends upon the cooperative efforts of the people in the villages. A report by Pamela Pieris, a PLAN/Sri Lanka Project Supervisor, indicates that this is an effective strategy:

> Naranwita Wasama, near Kandy, is a small administrative unit in which PLAN has enrolled nearly 300 families. The community was responsible for turning a dilapidated government-owned building into a multi-purpose community centre. In spite of heavy political pressure from traditional decision-makers to involve some people but not others, a counter presentation was made by PLAN families and other villagers who insisted that the leadership respect PLAN's impartiality and leave party politics aside. The factions amicably worked out a proposal and implemented the project with a heavy self-help component.
>
> Kahatapitiya and Don Simon villages are two other sites that have begun self-help water supply projects with representatives from all factions in the community. PLAN projects are proposed, discussed, planned and implemented by all villagers with the encouragement of our staff. We are gradually creating conditions under which everyone participates meaningfully, but the process will take many years and will be continually opposed by those who now gain most from the docility of the common villager.
>
> PLAN's approach to total human development is unique in Sri Lanka. In my opinion, this is the first time a local or foreign organization has shown strong signs of eliminating dependant attitudes through actual rather than nominal involvement of poor men and women in decision making.

Thailand: 1981-83

PLAN's program in Thailand was established by James Gershin, a former U.S. Peace Corps Volunteer who had served PLAN as an Assistant Director in the Philippines and as Director in Sierra Leone. The program is based on agreements contained in two documents signed by Mr. Gershin and representatives of the Government of the Kingdom of Thailand. The documents, "A Framework for Cooperation Between the Department of Public Welfare, Ministry of the Interior, and Foster Parents Plan International, Inc." dated 30 June 1981, and "Memorandum of Understanding Between the Government of the Kingdom of Thailand and Foster Parents Plan International, Inc.," dated 2 July 1981, outline the mutual expectations and obligations for the coordination of PLAN's activities and those of the government.

A key phrase in the "Memorandum of Understanding" summarizes a major goal of all PLAN programs:

> . . . to give the host country a legacy, consisting of the Agency's systems and methods developed over years of experience, as well as a cadre of trained, indigenous personnel, so that the developing society may gain from the Agency's experience as its government and private sector is able to accept increasing responsibility for its own people.

Enrollment began in September 1981, when six social workers went to the village of Bankok Sung in the rural northeastern province of Khon Kaen. They spent nearly two weeks explaining the PLAN program to the villagers and interviewing families. The process was soon repeated in three other villages and, by the end of the year, 600 children and their families had been enrolled.

Despite the support and cooperation of Thai authorities the social workers had to explain again and again that PLAN was not a political organization, would not try to change anyone's religion, and was not an adoption agency looking for children to export. Again and again PLAN's goals and purposes were explained in village meetings and in talks with individual families. This initial reaction of distrust is neither uncommon nor unexpected in a new program area, but it usually disappears as Foster Children begin to receive letters and photographs from their Foster Parents and the child's family begins to see tangible evidence of PLAN's determination to listen to the people and respond to their needs.

The first programming efforts in Khon Kaen involved primary health care and community health projects. These projects have a number of attributes which make them an attractive means of initiating a new program: they are inexpensive, quickly and easily implemented by local villagers with a few week's training, and result in visible improvements in the lives and health of the people involved. Through such projects, PLAN can establish the base of confidence and trust necessary to achieve other less obvious long-range goals.

The greatest health problem facing the people of Khon Kaen remains the shortage of potable water and the lack of sanitary facilities. PLAN's water and community sanitation projects provided not the finished products to solve these problems, but rather, the knowledge, skills, and material assistance which the people could use to implement the projects for themselves.

The program began with the selection of 55 people from 24 Khon Kaen villages to receive training as health promoters. Once trained they went home to teach their neighbors the relationship between the foul water they drank and their poor health. They also taught them what they could do about it. The villagers learned to build cisterns, rainwater storage jars, and how to dig and maintain sanitary wells.

With the technical help of their PLAN-trained neighbors and some material help from PLAN, ten people could build a cistern in a week and a half; two people could build a water storage jar in a day; and six people could dig a new well or rehabilitate an old one in a week. PLAN provided cement and toilet bowls, the people in the villages provided the walls, doors, roofs, and labor.

Between June 1982 and July 1983, people in PLAN villages built 1,430 toilets, 76 cisterns with a capacity of 113 cubic meters each, 800 water storage jars with a capacity of two cubic meters each, and dug 40 artesian wells, 25 shallow wells, and three ponds.

Simple as these projects are, they can have a variety of primary, secondary, and long-term effects enhancing all aspects of village life. That they reduce the daily drudgery of long walks back and forth to polluted wells is only the most obvious and immediate benefit. Secondary results are as much economic as health related. These may include less time lost to illness, higher farm output, higher income, and increased employment. Long-term, cumulative impacts will improve the villages' health, social life, environment, and economy.

Water projects alone will not solve all the problems of Khon Kaen or any depressed area but they do help. They also prove that coordinated group and community effort does make a difference.

The water and sanitation projects are only two facets of PLAN's five-part primary health care program. The other three components are health education, maternal and child health, and child immunization.

Though the health program is predominantly geared to health maintenance, there remains a need for some limited curative services for Foster Children and their families. PLAN helps meet these needs through the establishment of medicine banks to assure the availability of the most commonly prescribed medications, dental examinations and treatment, and referral to hospitals of seriously ill patients.

The successful implementation of these programs will depend upon introducing development in a way that is compatible with the cultural values of the area. In Khon Kaen, as in most rural areas, family and village cultural traditions are very highly valued. In communities where PLAN works these traditions may be the only legacy one generation can pass on to the next. Introducing change in such a milieu is therefore either a carefully planned process, involving considerable sensitivity and mutual respect, or a failure.

The concept of planning for long-range development is neither native to the marginal villagers of Thailand nor to popular Buddhism, which holds the belief that suffering is inherent in life and that one's conduct in a previous life has a direct relationship to one's circumstances in this one. The notion that the benefits of meritorious action in this life will only bear fruit in the next encourages an attitude which, while not necessarily fatalistic, is neither naturally conducive to five-year development plans.

It is the intention of PLAN/Thailand to adopt family and group development plans geared to the meeting of annual individual or group goals as determined in consultation with PLAN social workers. The plan calls for family enrollment for a five or six year period during which the families will establish and achieve incremental development objectives. The first months of enrollment are, therefore, more appropriately and realistically devoted to an introduction to PLAN's approach and the establishment of mutual respect and trust. In such new program areas as Khon Kaen, this is the critical time for PLAN to establish its credibility by undertaking community projects.

PLAN's basic approach has been to organize the families into groups under elected group leaders and to teach these groups how to work together to define and achieve individual and collective goals. The hope is that these group processes and projects will have a ripple effect which will eventually involve the entire community.

To insure that the family and group projects are both relevant to and compatible with local and national development priorities, PLAN works with the close support, cooperation, and advice of Thai leaders and authorities. On the local level this support and advice comes from village authorities and respected members of the community. On the provincial and national level PLAN has the cooperation of the Departments of Public Health and Education, Khon Kaen University staff and other appropriate public and private organizations.

Frank Campbell, who succeeded Mr. Gershin as Director in Thailand in February 1982, described the cooperation between PLAN and the local public health authorities in a June 1982 report. He wrote that the Provincial Director of Public Health looked upon PLAN as a partner. It is through this partnership that PLAN will be able to develop the skills and confidence of its staff and families necessary to ensure the program's enduring effects after PLAN phaseout.

13

Latin American: 1962-83

Keith R. Turner established the first Latin American PLAN program in Bogota, Colombia, in 1962. Under the terms of an agreement with the Government of Colombia, signed 27 June 1962, PLAN began its programs and services for desperately needy families in the slums of Bogota.

By 1971 PLAN/Colombia had grown to include the cities of Buenaventura and Tumaco on the Pacific coast. Though the programs in each of the three cities functioned independently, the overall administration of PLAN's Colombian operations remained in Bogota. This was partially a case of making a virtue of a necessity since Bogota then had far more people qualified for administrative and translation work than either Buenaventura or Tumaco. During the period from 1971-1977, the Field Director in Bogota was responsible not only for the administration and supervision of all three programs, but also for the training of Assistant Directors for Buenaventura and Tumaco, and the orientation of prospective Directors for programs in other South American countries.

In September 1977, more centrally located Cali became the administrative and translation office for Buenaventura and Tumaco. The Director was situated in Cali and supervised the three Colombian locations— Bogota, Buenaventura and Tumaco—each now headed by an Assistant Director. Of the three, only Bogota retained its own partial administrative and full translation capacity.

In 1978, upon the recommendation of Frank Campbell, then Director of PLAN/Colombia, the International Board promoted Assistant Directors Martin Fanghaenel, Edward Schiffer, and Ronald Seligman, to full Field Directors, thereby making each of their sub-posts full Field Offices. Cali continued to handle translations for Buenaventura and Tumaco and, in 1980, it, too, was made a full Field Office with its own service program, enrollment quota, and Field Director, Don D. Roose.

Bogota

When PLAN came to Bogota the city was plagued by thousands of child beggars and street children. Most of these children were from destitute families who simply could not afford to feed them, so they had abandoned their families (or had been abandoned) to live by their wits in the streets. When they reached the age of 14 and could get working papers and a job, many returned to contribute to the family income.

The Instituto Colombiano de Bienestar Familiar, the Colombian family welfare agency, spent between 1,400 and 1,600 pesos (US $65-$75) per child per month on institutional care for as many of these children as it could. The children, naturally, did everything they could to stay out of the institutions. PLAN, in contrast, spent 320 pesos (US $16) per month per child to help keep families together.

Bogota was PLAN's first Latin American program area. Keith R. Turner, a long-time Resettlement and Repatriation Officer with the International Relief Organization in West Germany, was named first Director for Colombia in 1961 by PLAN's Board of Directors and arrived in Bogota in February 1962. In June, after nearly four months of discussions, the agreement between PLAN and the Government of Colombia was signed and enrollment began.

The first child enrolled in Colombia was the daughter of a watchman working across the street from Mr. Turner's home. She was assigned to the prominent American journalist Edward R. Morrow. U.S. Senator Paul Douglas of Illinois, whose wife had sponsored a Spanish Foster Child in 1938, became the sponsor of the first Colombian boy enrolled and, shortly thereafter, visited him in Colombia. These sponsorships generated a great deal of publicity and soon there was a substantial Colombian enrollment.

PLAN quickly outgrew its original quarters and moved into a large, Georgian style brick house. Part of the courtyard was roofed over to serve as a waiting room for PLAN families. A visitor to PLAN in 1972 described the office as spartan and unattractive but said "it hums with cheerful activity and a spirit of mutual respect between the staff and the mothers of the families."

The cheerful activity and mutual respect were in considerable contrast to PLAN's original reception. When PLAN staff first started their enrollment interviews, mothers hid their children, set their dogs on the social workers, and threw stones at them. A rumor had spread that

PLAN had come to Bogota to kidnap their children. The problem was resolved after Mr. Turner convinced the local Cardinal that PLAN was not in the business of stealing children. After Mr. Turner had assured him that PLAN had worked for many years in Italy and had excellent relations with the Vatican, the Cardinal became a PLAN supporter and wrote to the parish priests asking them to cooperate with PLAN as much as they could. Armed with copies of this letter, PLAN social workers were able to allay the fears of suspicious families and enrollment soon grew.

The original plan called for the enrollment of destitute families of rural migrants to the city but, in the face of the great need and number of Bogota's poor, this criterion was soon dropped and enrollment was opened to all needy families. The first Foster Children received monthly cash grants of US $8 and parcels of clothing and household supplies either sent from PLAN's New York Headquarters or purchased locally. In addition to the purchase program were the frequent gifts of cash, toys, clothing, and books from individual Foster Parents. The distribution of PLAN-purchased gift parcels continued until 1970 when the decision was made to use the funds instead to expand PLAN's programs and services.

In the early years in Bogota, the program focused primarily on education and health care. Though Colombian law provided for compulsory, tuition-free, primary education and free medical care, the poor received little of either. There were simply not enough schools and teachers. Even if there had been, the cost of the required shoes, uniforms, and school supplies would have been prohibitive for PLAN's families. Medical facilities and staff were equally inadequate. PLAN's clinic and pharmacy provided enrolled families with otherwise unavailable medical care. The pharmacy was stocked with the most frequently used drugs and medicines, either purchased by PLAN or donated by large pharmaceutical houses. The clinic was staffed by six Colombian doctors and five nurses who provided basic medical services to Foster Children and their families. In 1966 a dental clinic and x-ray laboratory were added to the medical facilities. The need for the clinics was obvious by the use made of them. PLAN family members visited them 5,475 times in June 1972 alone. The average cost per visit was US $1.50.

By 1972 PLAN/Colombia offered a wide range of educational, medical, vocational, and social services most easily described by the example of the composite but not atypical Ternera family.

Remedios Ternera was the mother of six children. Her husband was once a mason but, as a result of a back injury, worked as a night watchman earning about US $30 a month. Remedios worked when she could as a laundress earning one dollar a day but, because three of her children were very young and needed supervision, she could not work every day. Her fourth child, Auraliano, was six years old and cared for the two younger children while his mother worked. He and his mother wanted him to go to school, but he was needed at home. Even if he had had the time for school, his family could not have afforded the uniform, shoes, and school supplies he would need.

Remedios may have heard of PLAN through a neighbor with an enrolled child, the local parish priest, or may have been referred to PLAN by a social service agency. However she heard of PLAN, her decision to apply for its aid required that she must spend the carfare to get to the office with Auraliano and leave her family unattended for most of a day.

After waiting in line or on benches with other mothers and children, they are called into the cubicle of one of the social workers to fill out an application form. The form calls for information about the family, their income, way of life, and aspirations.

Since PLAN is committed to the idea that children may best be served in their families, the first enrollment criterion is a stable family unit. The family unit could be a single parent family, grandparents and grandchildren, or a home with both parents. If the family unit is stable the criterion is met. The second criterion was that the Foster Child and as many of his or her brothers and sisters as possible attend school. Finally the family income had to be between US $6 and US $11 dollars per month per family member. PLAN's limited financial resources precluded total support for a family, but could make a decided difference to a family already helping itself.

Once the basic form was filled out, the social worker scheduled a home visit to substantiate the information and get additional data. The substantiated application was given to a selection committee consisting of the original caseworker, her supervisor, the sub-Director, and the Field Director. Once the family was accepted, the social worker wrote Auraliano's case history and arranged for a photograph to be taken. The case history was then translated and sent to PLAN Headquarters to await sponsorship by a Foster Parent.

In her first visit as a PLAN affiliate, Remedios and her social worker made an appointment for all of her family members to receive medical examinations and discuss the ways PLAN's programs and services might best serve them. In particular they discuss the "Capacitacion" program.

"Capacitacion" was based on the idea contained in a saying framed and hanging on the wall of the PLAN Director's office:

To give a man a fish is to give him food for a day,
But to teach a man to fish is to give him food for life.

Begun in 1970 by E. Glenn Rogers who was named PLAN/Colombia Director in 1968, "Capacitacion" was designed to provide training or access to training for PLAN family members to use according to their interest and ability. It was financed by debiting the cash grant one dollar per child. Any surplus funds were distributed to PLAN families in the final two months of the year. Unemployed, underemployed, or interested family members were placed in training courses offered by PLAN, various local institutions, and SENA, Colombia's government sponsored national training program. Courses offered and conducted by PLAN included dressmaking, tailoring, cosmetology, shoemaking, nurses' aide training, cooking, bookkeeping, crafts, machine knitting, domestic service, and basic literacy. Most of the courses lasted from eight to ten months. In mid-1972 nearly 1,200 students were enrolled.

Remedios was also told about the parent education program, in which groups of families, usually 50 at a time, were invited to a series of evening lectures. The talks were often illustrated with slides and addressed the problems and interests of PLAN families. Subjects ranged from nutrition to sex education.

These talks were indicative of the new emphasis being placed on education. Almost everything PLAN did had an educational element. The nutrition program for pregnant women and mothers of young children was another example of this educational function. Mothers and children suffering from malnutrition were identified during enrollment physical examinations and given food supplements of powdered milk, flour, and oil. The children were seen regularly by PLAN's medical staff and their mothers attended nutrition classes to learn about food values and how best to use the food supplements. The point was not simply to remedy malnutrition, but, through education, to remedy the ignorance which so often caused it.

As Remedios learned of these programs and of the other benefits and responsibilities of affiliation with PLAN, she and Auraliano also wrote the first of their monthly letters to his Foster Parent. The letters were translated in Bogota and then sent to PLAN Headquarters. The child wrote for himself if he could, but if he could not, the letters were written by an older family member or the social worker. Foster Parents received 12 communications (letters, cards, or drawings) a year from their Foster Children and an annual progress report from the social worker.

For their part, Foster Parents could also send letters, cards, and photographs to their Foster Children, as well as cash gifts. Usually the money was for the family to use as they saw fit. Social workers were available to suggest effective uses for the money, but, since the money belonged to the families they could spend it as they chose. Occasionally a Foster Parent would insist that a cash gift be used for a specific, and sometimes inappropriate, purpose. A gift of a new red tricycle is thoughtful and generous but not very useful in the muddy alleys of mountainside barrios. Fortunately, such misplaced generosity was rare.

For Remedios and Auraliano such personal contact was still in the future. At this first meeting they decided that the best solution for the problems of the family would be for Remedios to stay home and look after the younger children so Auraliano could go to school. Since she could do this only if she had a way to earn money at home, she decided to take a PLAN-sponsored macrame course. After she completed the course PLAN might lend her money for materials and sell her work through its sales contacts.

Auraliano's oldest sister, 16 year-old Pilar, dropped out of school in the fourth grade when her father hurt his back. PLAN aid would enable her to finish her primary education and she would be encouraged to join social groups and take vocational training.

Auraliano's 14 year-old brother, working as a mason's helper, also dropped out of primary school and would attend PLAN's evening basic education classes. An eight year-old sister, Amarantha, had to drop out of school because the family could not buy her uniforms and school supplies. PLAN aid would now enable Amarantha and Auraliano to attend school.

The first meeting Remedios had with her social worker ended with an appointment to come with Auraliano the following week to see the social worker again and to receive her first US $6 cash grant. In the course of a year she would learn, among other things, how to manage her household budget. In the first annual progress report to Auraliano's Foster Parent the social worker was able to include the following monthly figures: US $8 for rent, US $26 for food, US $5 for school expenses, US $4 for soap and fuel, and US $3 for miscellaneous expenses. These expenses are met by US $30 from the husband's job,

US $6 from PLAN and US $10 from the mother's homecraft earnings.

The 7,400 families enrolled in 1972 came from urban Bogota and the surrounding semi-urban areas of Suba, to the northwest; Bosa, to the southwest; and Los Cerros, in the hills east of Bogota. With the exception of the Director, the Assistant Directors and occasional Canadian University Services Overseas (CUSO) or Peace Corps volunteers who were North Americans, these families were served entirely by Colombian staff members. This policy of keeping expatriate staff to an absolute minimum assured that local values and beliefs would be considered in program-related matters.

The translation section was staffed by two Peace Corps Volunteers and 19 Colombian graduates of bilingual schools. Each translator handled about 400 letters a week. Since translating so many short and repetitious letters quickly became tedious, staff turnover was high, but new translation staff was readily available.

Recruiting new social workers was not so easy, but, happily, turnover was low. For the social work staff, continuity of service—one social worker counseling one family for a number of years—was extremely important. Since graduate social workers were nearly impossible to recruit given their small number and PLAN's salary-scale, PLAN initiated the first in-service training program for social work paraprofessionals in Colombia. Local professionals initially greeted the program with skepticism and some hostility, but the program's success eventually won their admiration.

In 1972 the social work department consisted of 25 women of diverse educational backgrounds working under the supervision of two graduate social workers. As part of their continuing in-service training, a psychiatrist, one of only three in the country and the only one in Bogota, came in twice a month to counsel the social workers. The discussions were based on specific family problems encountered by the social work staff. Other special issues, such as parental responsibility, fulfillment of basic needs, reward and punishment, the psychology of youth, alcoholism, family planning, and sex education were examined in regular staff conferences.

There were also accounting and clerical services to deal with the considerable task of implementing controls and procedures for the payment of monthly financial assistance and thousands of cash gifts. Disbursements were in cash until a 1971 robbery, after which the families received checks. The checks not only provided added security for PLAN and its families but, like everything PLAN did, also had an educational function. Most PLAN families had never used checks before and the experience introduced them to the use of money in modern society—the world of banks, checks, bankbooks, credit, and budgeting.

After 1975 the evolving Bogota program philosophy produced a more participatory development program, with the emphasis on family and community involvement. Direct monthly cash grants to families were reduced from US $8 in 1962, to US $6 in 1972, and to US $3.51 in 1982, with the difference directed to programs and services designed to meet needs identified by the families themselves. The families were expected to take part in the identification of problem areas and contribute as much of their time, labor, and money as they could toward the implementation of projects to meet them. PLAN family groups, together with community groups, built schools, clinics, and community centers with materials and technical assistance provided by PLAN and Colombian agencies.

A family credit union was established in 1975 with seed money from PLAN to provide low interest loans for small business ventures, home improvements, or education. Where PLAN once provided gifts from Special Services Funds for these projects, affiliates now borrowed from and repaid their credit unions. The credit unions not only provided a self-renewing source of loans and interest-bearing savings accounts but, most importantly, they substantially reduced family dependency upon PLAN.

As part of its new approach, PLAN/Bogota promoted greater cooperation with Colombian health, social service, and training agencies. The idea was that PLAN should not be doing anything that existing Colombian agencies, institutions, or groups would or could do for themselves. Family and community independence was the key element in PLAN's new approach.

To promote this independence PLAN emphasized improving the income-producing capability of every member of its Foster Families. Programs were developed in the areas of vocational education, small businesses, animal husbandry, and cooperative ventures. Educational services included support for regular and special education, textbook and local library projects, and adult education classes.

In 1978 PLAN divided Bogota into zones and assigned individual social workers to groups of families in each zone. This enabled social workers to work more closely with clearly defined groups of families who shared common needs and also promoted cooperative self-help ventures among the families themselves.

In 1979 PLAN/Bogota was concentrating its enrollment in three semi-urban zones of Bogota—Suba, Bosa, and Los Cerros. Suba was selected as a target community for the establishment of a low-cost primary health care program planned in cooperation with local public health authorities. The program's three objectives were to assure the active participation of the people in the community, to encourage collaboration with existing government health system, and to reduce dependency on the local PLAN clinic.

At that time PLAN had been working in Suba for more than ten years. An American visitor, Anna M. Pluhar, described Suba as she saw it in late 1972:

> I accompanied one of the PLAN social workers on a series of home visits. Their driver . . . took us out to a suburb of Bogota, Suba, where we drove into a poor village of small houses. Each house was built of red brick and contiguous to each other. This village climbs a small hill and, because the brick is badly laid . . . from a distance I was reminded a bit of a Navaho pueblo. The jeep stopped half-way up the hill by an eight foot square cement platform with a pipe faucet standing about three feet up in its center. This was the only water for this village of 60 houses.
>
> We walked up the rutted dirt lane to the house of the family we were visiting. The door was barely six feet high and led into a two foot wide, seven foot long hall. Inside the house was an open court about ten feet square, which included a cement three foot high drysink for washing clothes. Our guide, Isabel, a 14 year-old girl, then pointed to her home. Their room at the back of the house was about nine feet square with a low ceiling and no window. There was a small wooden cupboard to the left of the door. Against the far wall was a single bed covered with an old green cotton bedspread. A thin blanket was folded at the foot of the bed. To our right as we entered was a nest of three wooden packing boxes on which rested three or four old and dented pots and pans. Next to this kitchen was a small green metal ironing board, which doubled as a table. Another cardboard box with a few clothes on it barely fit between the end of the bed and wall.
>
> The walls were cracked and bare of pictures. The floor was wood that had never been painted or sealed in any way. A great effort had evidently been made to keep this room tidy and reasonably clean. In it lived a mother and five children. The oldest is Isabel who attends a district high school. The mother does day work as a cleaning lady for between a dollar

and a dollar and a half a day. She is a good mother and an ambitious woman who takes full advantage of Foster Parent's Plan. She is studying the fifth grade of elementary school, and taking a course at PLAN to learn to use a knitting machine. Her children are bright-eyed, clean and cheerful. The Foster Child, a boy of nine, had run to wash his face before he greeted us. He asked the social worker if he could possibly get a chess set.

This family is one of six which live in the same house. They pay six dollars a month rent. How do they sleep? Does the mother share the bed, cot-size with the youngest child, while the other four children huddle on the floor? The children are all small for their years. I had thought Isabel to be a ten-year-old. Had they been able to eat properly there would now be no room for them to lie down in their home. I did not see any electric or other lamp. How do the school children study? The high school program here is modeled on the European and requires a lot of work. Where and how does Isabel manage to do it?

This is a successful family. The mother is a good woman who must practice courage, and the active virtues of faith and hope, each day, on a scale which makes me humble.

By 1980 families like Isabel's in Suba and Bogota were working cooperatively with their neighbors, their local agencies, and with PLAN to identify and alleviate their common problems. Projects became community projects rather than PLAN projects and community residents learned that they could, through their own efforts, work together to make meaningful changes in the circumstances of their lives.

In 1983 the decision was made to begin a two-year phaseout of Bogota which was to be completed by 30 June 1985. In his 5 April 1983 memo to National Directors, George Ross gave the rationale behind the decision:

> . . . [because of] improved economic conditions of this capital city, plus the fact that Colombian government facilities and Colombian voluntary agency facilities now exist in health, social welfare, education and skills training areas in Bogota . . . PLAN believes its limited funds should be utilized where there is greater need.

What had begun as a program of relief for the disenfranchised developed over the years into a model of the PLAN philosophy of helping people to help themselves. It is the positive effects of that new direction—the sense of worth and awareness of their own abilities—

that will allow the residents of PLAN communities to continue their own development for many years to come.

Buenaventura

Buenaventura is a city of 96,708 people in the rain forest on the Pacific coast of Colombia. It is the country's principal port for the export of coffee and timber and the only major city on the coast.

PLAN came to Buenaventura in 1965. Keith R. Turner, who established the program, described his first visit in a 1980 memoir:

> In 1965, Gloria Matthews wrote to me from Headquarters in New York to ask me to make an exploratory visit to the port city of Buenaventura for the purpose of studying the feasibility of establishing a sub-office and PLAN program in that city. My first investigation was to determine the best method of getting from Bogota to Buenaventura. Inquiries revealed that while it was possible to travel by road by far the quicker and safer way was by air. While a political solution or compromise had been reached to end the civil war which had taken hundreds of thousands of lives, what the Colombians called "La Violencia" continued and many parts of the country were quite unsafe for travel by road. Moreover, the road between Cali and Buenaventura was mountainous, in very poor condition, and often closed by landslides. So it was considered best to take the regular Avianca airliner from Bogota to Cali and from there a single engine, seven seat plane for about a half-hour flight to Buenaventura. I shall never forget the first time I made that journey. Bogota is located in a high plateau and the weather is eternal spring or eternal autumn depending upon one's choice, but it is always quite cool. The airport in Buenaventura was a swath cut out of the jungle and after landing one stepped out of the plane into the steaming tropics. Buenaventura is said to have one of the largest average rainfalls of any spot on earth. The ride into town from the airport was in itself an unforgettable experience in a rickety, beaten-up, old taxi whose driver seemed bent upon assuring the death of any unwary pedestrian. The population of Bogota is by far a majority of mestizos or a mixed race of the Spanish with Indians. The people of Buenaventura are almost all black and their social and cultural customs are obviously quite different from those of the Bogotanos. The citizens of the capital city are said to be conditioned and affected by the high altitude and cool weather, making them less friendly and helpful to one another. For whatever reason, the people of Buenaventura certainly

seemed to be more spontaneously joyful and to make the most of the sorry conditions of life surrounding them.

My preliminary investigation before leaving Bogota had indicated that the man to see in Buenaventura was Monsignor Valencia. He headed a group of priests who carried out most of the medical and social welfare programs at that time operating in Buenaventura and its surroundings. Monsignor Valencia carried enormous political power and was revered by the poor. Fortunately for PLAN and me he immediately grasped the significance of my proposed PLAN program for Buenaventura's poor. The church owned considerable property in the city of Buenaventura and Monsignor Valencia offered me space in one of the buildings to establish a small PLAN office. He even offered to lend to PLAN some of his own personnel, including administrative and social work staff. These generous offers were readily accepted, and so it was that PLAN's new program quickly got underway.

To my knowledge this was the first area in the world in which PLAN enrolled black children. At that time, in the minds of some, there was doubt that Foster Parents could be found for many black children. The response to PLAN's pleas for assistance has subsequently proved the contrary, as is witnessed by the growth of enrollment in Buenaventura and the establishment of new and successful PLAN programs in Haiti and in Africa. Nevertheless, the number of children enrolled in Buenaventura during the first two years of operation was small.

Some supervision could be done by telephone from Bogota, but frequent trips were also required by the Director. A bit earlier I said that it was considered safer to travel by plane. However, I have another strong and unforgettable memory of one of those trips. Monsignor Valencia took great pleasure in escorting me personally around the city to the various installations he had helped in the past, and which PLAN was beginning to help. On this particular occasion, having completed a days work, Monsignor Valencia insisted on taking me to the airport to catch the plane back to Cali. As usual he hoisted his episcopal skirts, climbed behind the steering wheel of his jeep and started off at breakneck speed. A typical Buenaventura downpour of rain did not slow his progress. When we reached the airport and said goodbye, Monsignor Valencia whirled his jeep around in a sea of mud and vanished into the rain and approaching darkness. I was the only passenger on that flight and sat up next to the pilot in the single engine plane. We could scarcely see the end of the airstrip because of the dense rain but took off nevertheless. We had climbed only a few thousand feet when the motor began to cough and sputter. The pilot worked the hand throttle frantically and furiously, and, just before the plane stalled, managed to get the sputtering engine started again. We continued to climb and finally came out above the clouds of the rain storm. I asked the pilot what the problem had been. He said water in the gasoline. The supply for the plane was kept in a drum at the side of the airstrip and in heavy rains water often leaked in to mix with the gasoline. Normally, the flight time from Buenaventura to Cali was about half an hour, and the pilots flew by dead reckoning. Having lost his bearings while playing with the engine, the pilot now circled around a bit until he delightedly exclaimed to my astonishment that he could see the direction toward Cali. We were forty-five minutes in that trip. On landing in Cali the pilot drew up next to the Avianca airliner so that I could step directly from his plane into the other. On parting we looked at each other as comrades in a near escape from death and shook hands warmly. It was not an uncommon occurrence for a small plane to disappear into the Colombian jungles. Indeed I was saddened to learn several years later after I had left Colombia that Monsignor Valencia perished in a plane crash in another part of the country.

By January 1966, the first 52 Foster Children from Buenaventura had been enrolled. The embrionic program was conducted through the voluntary services of several lay missionary women who did PLAN's work in addition to their own. Travel and communication between Buenaventura and Bogota were difficult and unreliable enough to preclude a large program, but the great need more than justified the difficulty and expense of the small program. A sub-office, staffed by an administrator and two social workers, was opened in July 1966 in space made available by Monsignor Valencia. For the next three years Buenaventura remained a small sub-office with less than 1,000 Foster Children.

Construction of the PLAN offices in Buenaventura began in 1969 and work was completed in time for the Assistant Director to spend Christmas there. The offices consisted of one building with ten offices for social workers, a building with two classrooms and an apartment for the Assistant Director and his wife.

Bob Settle, who would direct the program under the supervision of the Director in Bogota, came to PLAN through Canadian University Services Overseas (CUSO) on a two-year contract. CUSO, operating much like the Peace Corps of the United States, selected qualified volunteers, paid their air fare back and forth to Canada, and provided them with language instruction. PLAN paid CUSO volunteers a salary equivalent to that of the Colombian staff. Mr. Settle's background in child welfare and his wife Win's training as a registered nurse made them an ideal choice to direct the program.

The University of Valle, in Cali, Colombia, had made a study of life in Buenaventura in 1969 as a follow-up to a 1964 study. Its findings graphically showed the need for the type of programs and services PLAN could provide. The population was growing at the rate of 5.06 percent a year. In 1964, 42.9 percent of the population was under 16 years of age, by 1969 this figure had grown to 46 percent. Some progress was revealed in education and literacy: in 1964 only 14.1 percent of children between the ages of five and nine had had one year of primary school; in 1969 this was 31.9 percent. The highest illiteracy rates were for women over 30.

Economic and housing figures were just as bad. Only 35.8 percent of people between the ages of 15 and 64 were working. Over half of the families had a per capita income of less than US $16 a month. The study showed that 69.2 percent of the housing was substandard or inadequate. (In 1968 the mayor of Buenaventura stated that only 5.6 percent of the houses contained adequate sanitary facilities.) Families averaged 5.4 people with free unions and single mothers outnumbering marriages.

The leading causes of death, according to the study, were tuberculosis and malnutrition followed closely by pneumonia, malaria, intestinal disorders, and venereal disease. The climate contributed to the population's ill health with an average rainfall of 350 inches a year, an average temperature of 80°, and an average relative humidity of 88 percent.

The poor general health of Foster Children confirmed the conclusions of the study. Initial diagnoses of 139 children from one to four years of age produced the following unhappy figures:

Malnutrition	28.1%
Umbilical hernia	27.3%
Respiratory diseases	18.7%
Infectious skin disease	10.8%

Only 10.1% of these children were diagnosed as healthy. Children aged five to 12 were no better off. The diagnoses of 161 of these children showed:

Intestinal parasites	31.1%
Malnutrition	24.2%
Hernia	20.5%
Infectious skin disease	4.3%

Ninety-two (92) percent of all the children and 95 percent of the adults had some sort of parasites.

The PLAN clinic provided vaccinations, limited curative services, and referrals to the overcrowded, underequipped, and understaffed hospital. Win Settle worked in the PLAN clinic, gave talks on public health measures, and visited the homes of PLAN families to show them ways to prevent disease. With housing and sanitary conditions so abominable, only minimal improvement could be expected. Useful and valuable as the vaccinations were, they could not eliminate the malnutrition, parasites, pneumonia, and malaria endemic to the slums of Buenaventura.

The Social Work Supervisor quit shortly before the Settle's arrived in Buenaventura so Mr. Settle inherited that task in addition to the job of directing the program. He wrote in an April 1972 report that, although supervising the social work staff prevented him from developing the program as much as he would have liked, it gave him the opportunity to hold group sessions with the social workers to discuss the purposes of their work and the personal resources the staff could develop to increase their effectiveness. Mr. Settle said that these group sessions were successful in helping to improve the relationships between the social workers and the children and families they served.

In 1971 the Instituto Colombiano de Bienestar Familiar approved PLAN's request for a training course for the social work staff and provided teachers, classroom space, and educational materials for the three-month course. The course was part of a continuing emphasis on in-service staff training.

That fall, Foster Children and their families were organized by the districts where they lived and reassigned so that each social worker would have concentrations of cases in specific districts. The social workers then developed contracts with local community action committees, public officials, and other interested parties with the goal of organizing and participating in community development projects.

The first of these projects were modest experiments. The initiation of PLAN/Buenaventura into organized community work came in October 1971 when PLAN helped a family whose house was collapsing.

Using a US $100 gift from the Foster Parent and contributions from the community to buy materials, volunteers took apart the old house and rebuilt it.

In the next few months PLAN participated in projects to build small bridges, repair and electrify community centers, and improve the homes of Foster Families. Home improvements were particularly important because of the close relationship between health and substandard housing.

> You treat, you prescribe and behold the mother takes the child home and puts the child to bed, which just happens to be damp, rotted wooden floor boards. Yes, the child gets pneumonia and dies and you sit down with your staff again and again to talk about how the PLAN program can be better related to the dire needs of poor families.
>
> Housing, in particular, worries me. In some shacks where our families exist in Buenaventura, you go in and want to strike a match and burn the place down, pick up the family, transplant them and start all over. We cannot get our families into so-called low cost government housing (1) because of the initial down payment which is way beyond the means of our families and (2) because you have to have a pretty steady wage earner to meet the monthly payments and most of our families appear to be in and out of jobs—anything but steady. One enterprising family asked me to advance their cash grant for a year for the down payment and I thought, why not? Give them a Special Services loan and apply the cash grant every month to the Special Services loan. But then I found myself being just like the Government and it is useless to call it a loan when there is no chance of the family meeting monthly payments.
>
> This problem I am talking about is not new. In any social service program I have ever had anything to do with, one had to figure out what you could do best with what you had, knowing that you cannot be all things to all people. But that little bit of rationalization never should excuse one from study and relating whatever you've got to whatever you are trying to do. It means upsetting some patterns of service and out of the window they must go if they are not truly related to everchanging needs.[1]

Whether the changes in the program in the next few years were a result of discarding old methods or of adapting them to fit the changing philosophy of development is a moot point. The result was a

[1] E. Glenn Rogers, Quarterly Report (Colombia, April-June 1970).

very different approach which used a wide range of methods in pursuit of a comprehensive and integrated program to meet the child, family, and community development needs in Buenaventura.

One practical and innovative expression of this change came in 1972 when PLAN participated in the Matia Malumba Institute's three-day cooperative information sharing program involving doctors, nurses, midwives, and traditional medical practitioners. The program involved the participants in discussions and demonstrations of the role of modern medicine in traditional rural society and the efficacy of traditional healing methods.

The program was one expression of a broader concern for the preservation of rural Colombian culture. The burgeoning population of Buenaventura was largely made up of people who had come from rural areas in the hope of finding a better life in the city. When the economy could not absorb them, either because they lacked the skills necessary for success in an urban society, or because the economy was in such disarray that it could barely support the present population, the migrants settled into the wretched hovels of the barrios.

In Colombia, as in much of the rest of the developing world in the early 1970s, the government was discovering that the emphasis on urban industrialization at the expense of rural agricultural development had the unhappy corollary of massive migration to the city. Concerned public and private agencies and individuals began agricultural, cooperative, educational, social welfare, and health projects to counter this movement.

Since the PLAN/Buenaventura staff was particularly interested and active in health projects, PLAN was naturally interested in the Matia Malumba Institute. The Directors of the Institute sensibly believed that traditional medical practitioners, midwives and doctors shared common concerns and could not only learn from one another but could also work together. Even if they did not believe this, they knew that the shortage of medical staff was severe enough to insure that people would continue to use traditional medicine out of necessity, custom, and habit.

Dr. Curtis Swezy of the National Council for International Health, in Washington, D.C., speaking on a related subject, said:

> The west has become more aware of what goes on in traditional societies and has come to realize that there may be something significant to be learned from them and also, probably, there is the growing recognition of the economic

realities of providing medical care to much of the world. By and large, western style medical care simply does not adapt readily to the magnitude or the kind of medical problems that exist in developing countries . . . Increasingly we have come to realize that all our medical systems may have something to offer and that they all deserve serious attention.[2]

Other changes included, but were not restricted to, the implementation of projects designed to meet development goals defined by individual families, groups of families working together, and communities. The enumeration of these goals was worked out in consultation with the social workers whose counseling was often needed to insure that the goals were attainable and appropriate.

A family might decide that its educational goals in a five-year period would be for two younger children to finish school and an older brother, sister, or parent taking a basic literacy or vocational training course. Economic goals might include the establishment of a small business, perhaps in concert with other heads of PLAN households. Housing and health related goals could include home repair, the provision of a well, or a community water project. A group of families might decide to work together to electrify their homes, build a school or community center, or form a credit or agricultural cooperative. PLAN and volunteers from PLAN families might work with other agencies and individuals on a community-wide vaccination project.

A rural sub-office of PLAN/Buenaventura was opened in Tulua in 1982. Since then, PLAN and its families in Buenaventura and Tulua have participated in numerous group projects including the construction of community centers, school repairs, vocational education courses, home improvements, income-producing projects, and a primary health care program.

The program which began in 1965 with less than 60 Foster Children and a volunteer staff of three was, by June 1983, providing services to nearly 8,000 Foster Children.

Tumaco

The third major expansion of PLAN's Colombian program came in April 1971 when Director E. Glenn Rogers, Assistant Director Leo Desrochers and his wife, Cathy, arrived in Tumaco, a small seaport on

---

[2]Curtis Swezy, *"Traditional" and "Modern" Healing,* World Development Forum, 30 April 1983, pp. 1-2.

the southwestern tip of Colombia's Pacific coast. When they arrived there was neither office space nor living space for PLAN or its staff. On previous visits Mr. Rogers had determined that the Barrio Panama district would be the best place to begin enrollment. Meetings were held with community leaders and interested neighbors to determine whether or not PLAN would be welcomed by the community and to identify the most urgent needs of the community.

There was general agreement that health service was one of the greatest needs of Barrio Panama. The barrio had no electricity, running water, or sanitary facilities. Over 90 percent of the population (estimated at between 70,000 and 90,000) was multiparasitic; infant mortality rates and the death rates of children under the age of five were equally disturbing.

A clinic was established and Cathy Desrochers, a registered nurse, was soon at work in the clinic and making home visits throughout the barrio. About 80 percent of the people she met had never been to a doctor.

For the first few weeks PLAN social workers used the living room of a member of "Junta de Accion Communal," a local neighborhood group, as a temporary office. On an earlier visit Mr. Rogers had found an old factory building for sale in the heart of the barrio that would be an ideal home for PLAN. Thanks to funds from a Miles for Millions walk in Waterloo, Ontario, PLAN was able to purchase the two-story building and begin the necessary renovations.

Construction lasted from July until December with a work force composed largely of PLAN fathers. In spite of the ongoing construction, the office began functioning in the middle of August. On 12 November PLAN/Tumaco officially inaugurated its almost completed center. PLAN families spent three days preparing for the festivities, cleaning the yard, decorating the building, and rehearsing presentations. All of the PLAN families, local dignitaries, and representatives of PLAN/Bogota and Buenaventura came to the opening. Foster Children put on skits, sang, and played music. Ribbon-cutting honors were shared by the first Tumaqueno Foster Child, Gloria Maria Villota, and Mrs. E. Glenn Rogers.

Once the building was finished, more energy could be put into developing plans for community projects. Suggested projects included community washrooms, recreational facilities, and a community center. The hope was that the fathers of Foster Children would take an active part in any such project.

One of the reasons for having the office in the barrio was to increase the participation of fathers in the program. Fathers were already using the clinic, had worked on the office renovation, and were more acquainted with PLAN and its work than the other men in many of PLAN's urban programs. There had been a feeling in PLAN for some time that the programs would be more effective if the fathers were more directly involved; that PLAN had historically been more mother/child-oriented than family oriented and that it was time for a change. The stratagem worked and the fathers did participate.

Though the program in Tumaco was to focus on community projects, until the specific projects were decided upon and implemented, the medical program and particularly birth control and family planning, would receive greater attention. PLAN had been involved in family planning and birth control in association with the International Planned Parenthood Federation and the Association Pro Bienestar Familia Colombiana in Bogota since 1969. The need for family planning was clear. The population of Colombia was expected to double in 22 years. Even to maintain the very low 1972 standard of living, Colombia would have to double its number of schools, hospitals, water systems and houses. It would also have to train enough doctors, nurses, teachers, social workers, and other professionals so that in 22 years their numbers, too, would double. Such a task, impossible even for a highly industrialized society, was unthinkable for an underdeveloped one. It was unlikely that Colombia could even maintain what Mr. Rogers called its "present level of misery."

According to Dr. Summer M. Kalman of Stanford University, the average Colombian mother went through a progression of attempts to limit the size of her family, starting with ineffective traditional forms of contraception and progressing to primitively performed or self-induced abortions, infanticide, frigidity and, occasionally, suicide. The average family, after the birth of its last child could expect to spend 80 percent of its US $237 yearly income on food.

The medical services in Tumaco, whether curative or preventive in nature, were forms of death control. Without medical care, a family knew that as many as half of its children would die. With the advent of medical programs, PLAN's among them, the children were not dying.

It is ironic that the provision of much needed assistance in one area can, through a ripple effect, create overwhelming problems in another. Mr. Rogers described one such situation in a July 1972 report. Four families with more children than they could feed sought to solve their problem by selling their children—two Foster Children and two sisters of Foster Children.

We were appalled, but we have to try to understand what is operating and what motivates these people to do something of which we do not approve. Obviously, we do not offer medical services so that the numbers of our PLAN families will increase, but that is going to be one of the results. Birth control is one answer, but alone it is not an adequate answer against the cultural factors with which we deal. It also takes a mountain of education repeated and repeated to intervene in the kind of thinking which motivated some of our families to sell their children. The matter becomes further complicated by feelings people have about accepting help. On discussion with these four families, their interpretation of what we said and their cultural reaction, if you will, went something like this: "Well, we never knew that PLAN was going to dictate to us what we could do with our kids and if we had known it we never would have joined up in the first place." Well, yes, we advise and, yes, we offer simple courses about child-rearing, but more important, yes, PLAN offers services to families who are committed to rearing their own children in their own homes. The population explosion may be a best seller and favorite topic of conversation among the intellects, but down here it is not theory—it is a most difficult everyday social problem with which our families and our social workers deal daily. In the four cases cited above, our position was that the families did have a choice, (1) sell their children and be cancelled from PLAN or (2) raise their children at home with the help of PLAN. Perhaps, just perhaps, it could be argued that we could use this experience to further educate our families and we are wrong to cancel—how would you handle it? Bear in mind that the burden of referring the matter to the "Defensa de Menores" falls to us and this is very frightening because the way things get twisted, I was sure it would hit the papers, probably saying that PLAN was involved in this business of baby-selling. So far, nothing, but the feeling that you are sitting on a powder keg is uncomfortable.

In spite of these consequences, the medical program continued and grew. Other PLAN programs enabled families to better support themselves. Cash grants improved family incomes, as did new skills learned in vocational education programs, cooperative ventures and income-producing projects. Finally, with the benefits of primary and secondary education, children would be able to look forward to a better life than their parents had known. But, for any of this to work, children had to survive childhood. By 1975, according to a government survey, PLAN provided services to more outpatients in an average month than three government programs combined.

PLAN social work aides, under the supervision of a public health nurse, regularly surveyed their assigned neighborhoods actively promoting PLAN's health program, checking vaccination cards and providing information on disease prevention. Other PLAN health programs focused on providing pregnant women and mothers of malnourished children with nutrition education, supplemental food, and vocational training.

PLAN's medical programs were not intended to duplicate or replace Colombian programs, and as government health care and facilities developed, they assumed more responsibility for work once done by PLAN. In 1975 PLAN transferred its Tumaco family planning, tuberculosis control, and vaccination programs to the government public health service. Fears that the attrition rate would rise in the moderately successful family planning program when it was transferred to the government proved groundless. Relatively few PLAN mothers even began the family planning program, and more than half of those few who did eventually dropped out. Many of the women who stayed in the program got pregnant anyway. PLAN doctors reported that birth control pills were not the solution to the family planning problems of Tumaco as the women stopped taking them for the slightest problem or discomfort. Tubal ligation was the most effective method of birth control, but no agency, public or private, was willing to do them on a large scale because of the sensitive nature of the issue in Roman Catholic Colombia. The same was true of vasectomies. Thus, the women of Tumaco were usually left to the traditional population control methods of developing countries—high infant mortality and abortion.

The Barrio Panama community center was a much more successful project. Work began on the center in 1973 with funds provided by PLAN, the Canadian Government, and a Miles for Millions fund-raising walk in Kingston, Ontario. SENA, the government's vocational training agency, provided technical assistance and supervision.

The project was based on the premise that the key to barrio solidarity in Tumaco lay in sports programs. The community center was planned around basketball and volleyball courts and playing fields. The number of people who volunteered their time and labor to the construction of the center proved that the idea was a good one. Volunteers first did much of the work on the playing fields and courts, then their enthusiasm carried over to the construction of bleachers, washrooms, and the community meeting hall. The center soon became a focal point for athletic events, public meetings, and community educational, recreational, and social events.

In 1975 PLAN hired a recreation and physical education director for the center. Assistant Director Asbjorn Osland, then in charge of the Tumaco operation, wrote that the high level of motivation among the children of Tumaco was one of the most encouraging aspects of the program. The children, mostly under the age of ten, spent as much time as they could at the center and regularly cleaned up the playing fields and helped in the construction of the playground. They performed skits, played games, and presented folklore festivals. Mr. Osland wrote in 1975 that the children's programs at the center sometimes seemed to grow by themselves and that Foster Children "had made the most vigorous input into programming shown by affiliates in the past year."

He further wrote:

Often in our daily decision-making we're confronted with a multitude of problems such as malnutrition, serious and chronic unemployment, and comparable difficulties. One may question what role our recreation program plays in our programming. When faced with seriously malnourished children can one really justify authorizing funds, even though very limited, for a teeter-totter? Our experience with the recreation program has shown us how valuable and useful a tool recreation can be and how it is a justifiable program:

1. It provides a service to a high number of affiliates, mainly children, at a very low per unit cost.
2. It is something in which affiliates as consumers have expressed a high level of interest.
3. Participation in recreation programs develops basic group skills and discipline in children in an environment such as Tumaco which hasn't proven to be particularly conducive toward the development of these skills. These skills should help in future programming.
4. It's fun and fills a gap in an environment generally lacking in stimulation.

The quarter ended with the graduation ceremony and exhibition of the handicraft and embroidery classes. A quick word picture of this event follows: a schoolroom festooned with embroidered pillows, tablecloths, purses and paper flowers, a tableful of witch-like dolls; 30 middle-aged women in their

Sunday best, singing local songs, changing to native costumes to do folk dances; a sprightly 60 year-old woman recites a poem to a marigold, the neighborhood presses in to watch; a stray dog curls up at the director's feet, people are shouting with laughter and clapping with the music, speeches of appreciation, diplomas, wine and cake, everyone dancing to blaring rhythmic music and the director slipping out to finish his quarterly report.

PLAN/Tumaco was, at the time, providing aid and services directly to 1,500 Foster Children and their families in addition to the programs and activities available to all at the community center. From April to June 1975, these services included a health program which provided injections, lab tests, hospitalizations, home visits, tuberculosis control, and vaccinations to a total of 10,640 people.

Community projects included not only the community center, but also classroom construction which affected 2,217 people. Educational projects, vocational training, scholarships, and adult education programs involved 435 people. PLAN's Special Services Funds enabled the fishermen's cooperative to establish a revolving loan fund to help members buy outboard motors and nets.

By 1977 Tumaco enrollment had more than doubled and the program had added a rural project in the isolated community of Robles, an hour and a half by boat from Tumaco. The 500 families of Robles lived without doctors, nurses, police, electricity, running water, restaurants, or sewage systems. The schools, offering only elementary education, lacked basic teaching materials and too often teachers, as well, whenever funds for their services ran dry. The children of Robles who survived childhood grew up to be ignorant, superstitious, illiterate, and unhealthy. Education, housing, health, and community development projects were soon begun.

An increasing emphasis on group income-producing projects in Tumaco led to a variety of vocational training programs whose graduates worked together in small agricultural, handicraft, or manufacturing cooperatives. A group of 20 PLAN mothers who had taken a sewing course joined forces and established a dressmaking cooperative. They worked only half a day so they could have time to be with their children. This particular cooperative was significant because it provided some income and a measure of independence to a hitherto overlooked group of single mothers.

The nutrition education program, which combined treatment and education for the prevention and cure of malnutrition, was expanded from one barrio to four to meet the increasing community need. The program was designed to distribute food donated by the government to the mothers of 400 malnourished children. The mothers attended classes to learn the causes, symptoms, cures, and prevention of malnutrition with special emphasis on hygiene, food preparation, nutrition, parasite control, and the importance of boiling water.

One of the major drawbacks of the nutrition program was the extreme poverty of some of the participants. "Graduates" of the program often returned a few months later, again suffering from malnutrition. The problem was not that the mothers failed to learn anything in the program, but, rather, that they were simply too poor to buy sufficient food. To remedy this, the nutrition program was supplemented in 1978 with a gardening program which provided education, tools, materials, and seeds which the families would use to grow additional food.

One of the most encouraging events in Tumaco came in 1978 when members of the fishermen's cooperative volunteered to work on Sundays and donate their catch to the nutrition program. Five hundred (500) children benefited from the generosity and community spirit of the fishermen and the project began its transition from a PLAN project to a community project.

After the long delayed completion of the public hospital in Tumaco, PLAN's medical program became increasingly focused on the prevention rather than the cure of disease. Medical services included an outpatient clinic, pharmacy, laboratory, vaccination programs, prenatal and infant care, nutrition programs, tuberculosis and malaria control, and midwife and health promoter training. Related activities, such as home repair and water projects, helped to create an environment more conducive to health.

These were integrated, cooperative projects, dependent for success upon the active participation of national and local agencies and volunteers from the community. The Ministry of Health cooperated in the training courses for midwives and health promoters. Volunteers first taught in the nutrition program and eventually took on most of the responsibility for it. Vaccination programs, too, were cooperative ventures with active and equal participation by the Ministry of Health, PLAN, and volunteers. In the last quarter of 1978, the cooperative vaccination project inoculated 10,000 people.

This cooperation carries over into all aspects of the program. PLAN/Tumaco works with local and governmental agencies, community groups, and volunteers to offer programs to all members of the Foster Families in almost all aspects of their lives. The objectives are to meet needs identified by the participants, needs that the participants are willing to donate their time, labor, and money to meet. There are vocational training and adult literacy classes, income-producing and family and community development projects.

PLAN continues to provide social services to the nearly 6,000 Foster Families in Tumaco and to work with the families and the community at large to implement health, education, and community development projects.

Cali

PLAN/Cali was established in 1977 as the administrative center for the programs in Colombia and made a full Field Office in 1980. The groundwork for the new program—the recruitment and organization of the social work staff and the surveys of potential program areas, was laid by Don D. Roose and followed up by Han F. Dijsselbloem. Mr. Roose had previously served as PLAN's Director in Bolivia (1969-75), Port-au-Prince, Haiti (1975-77), and as an Assistant Program Director at PLAN's International Headquarters. Mr. Dijsselbloem, an engineer with experience in municipal sanitation in the Netherlands and educational work at the Instituto Tecnologico in Cochabamba, Bolivia, had served PLAN in Sucre, Bolivia (1979-80).

One of Mr. Dijsselbloem's first objectives was to introduce PLAN families to the idea of planning to meet specific goals. This was done through the direct deposit of cash grants into savings accounts established for each Foster Family. The savings were used for such short-term goals as school uniforms, kitchen supplies, and minor home repairs.

By September 1981 the Foster Families had been surveyed to determine their greatest needs. The survey revealed that the most strongly felt needs were in the areas of health and education and the program was structured accordingly.

This combined emphasis on health and education continued in 1982 when PLAN began to enroll children in Jamundi, a small town 10 miles south of Cali. As in Cali, the majority of the parents viewed their own poor education as a primary cause of their current poverty and hoped that their children could have the opportunity to go to school.

PLAN's aim, both in Cali and Jamundi, was to make primary education available to as many children as possible by equipping and enlarging the local schools.

Health care for children was an obvious corollary to this emphasis on education. Clearly, children will be more alert and able to learn if they are healthy and properly nourished. Through the enthusiasm and dedication of the PLAN staff, PLAN had successfully coordinated its health program with the efforts of the local Ministry of Health by mid-1982. The PLAN auxiliary nurse, for example, vaccinated more children in the month of April 1982 than her Ministry of Health counterpart had been able to vaccinate in the previous five months. Local officials soon asked PLAN to provide technical support for vaccination campaigns in all areas of Cali.

This cooperation and support soon included school and community health education. The cooperative health education program consisted of formal and informal sessions with children and their families using teaching materials developed jointly by PLAN and Ministry of Health personnel. The primary goal was to reduce the effects of diarrheal diseases and malnutrition by treating their causes—unsanitary conditions, poor diets, and ignorance.

Perhaps the most dramatic of these joint ventures came on 23 April 1983 when PLAN sponsored its first health fair in the town square of Jamundi. Since many of the people were reluctant to go to the hospital, PLAN/Cali Director Emmanuel Edouard decided to bring the hospital to them.

By noon on the twenty-third the ordinarily peaceful town square had the noisy atmosphere of a carnival. Members of the local hospital's staff—three doctors, seven nurses, and four health promoters—were mobilized to check blood pressures, measure children's growth and weight, offer advice on nutrition, child care, and health maintenance and if necessary, refer people to specialists.

Several other organizations also participated in the fair. The Instituto Colombiano de Bienestar Familiar shared the message of birth control and family planning, and volunteers from the Universidad de Valle entertained the children while their parents spoke to the doctors.

Other equally important collaborative health projects have been less dramatic. Surveys showed that poor families often spent up to three quarters of their income on food. Their meager diets of rice, beans, and bananas were only occasionally relieved by fish, eggs, milk, or meat. Although very few cases of severe malnutrition were found among PLAN families, nearly 20 percent of the children under the age of seven were underweight.

Arrangements were made by PLAN social worker Manuel Viadero to collaborate with Bienestar Familiar on a garden project aimed at enabling the families of these undernourished children to improve their diets. The project started with a model garden in the Barrio Polvorines involving ten mothers of Foster Children and PLAN social workers from other barrios who hoped to initiate similar projects.

The harvest of lettuce, tomatoes, radishes, cucumbers, cabbage, spinach, and beets not only improved the diets of the participating families but inspired other families to plant gardens of their own.

At the end of Fiscal Year 1983 Benjamin Ricker in Bogota, L. Roger Braden and Assistant Director Monique van 't Hek in Buenaventura, Emmanuel Edouard in Cali, and Jerry Vink and Assistant Director Leticia Garcia in Tumaco were helping nearly 22,000 Foster Children, their families and their communities discover new possibilities for the future.

Growth In Latin America: 1962-83

Life in many of the countries of Latin America and the Caribbean has been and continues to be marked by social and economic instability. Military juntas replace and are replaced by civilian regimes, either liberal or conservative, well meaning or venal, in noisy or quiet changes of power. In spite of the promises of successive governments, living conditions of the poor change little and slowly. The urban poor continue their meager lives in spreading shanty towns, and their rural counterparts continue their migration to join them in the false hopes of the city.

While the political realities of the region cannot be ignored, there is little that non-governmental agencies can or should do about them. Although PLAN's programs, particularly in Central America, are unavoidably affected by the atmosphere of violence and uncertainty, the nonpolitical, humanitarian nature of these programs has generally won the respect and confidence of people on both sides of the conflict and those, like PLAN families, caught squarely between.

From its American beginnings in Colombia, in 1962, PLAN has expanded to Haiti and eight other countries in Central and South America. Programs have been established in Ecuador (1963), Peru (1965), Brazil (1967), Bolivia (1969), Haiti (1973), El Salvador (1976), Honduras (1977), Nicaragua (1977) and Guatemala (1978). The programs in these countries are similar in many ways to those in Colombia and follow similar patterns of urban and rural development. The objectives of improving the health conditions, educational opportunities, homes and communities of Foster Children, and their families have remained the same.

The programs were usually established in a city, often the capital, with a population larger, poorer and faster-growing than could be served by the under-staffed and under-funded national social welfare agencies. In Peru there was a far greater need for PLAN's services in the city of Chimbote than in Lima. The program was therefore established in Chimbote and served Peruvian children, their families and the marginal community there until 1982. In Bolivia, PLAN was established first in the capital city of La Paz in 1969 and later expanded to Tambillo (1978) and Sucre (1979).

By the mid-1970s PLAN's programs were focusing on rural agricultural areas as well as urban areas. A major factor in this change was the growing belief that PLAN's limited resources could have a greater overall impact in a rural community than in a city. A marginally successful farmer in Tambillo, for example, might not join the unemployed masses in La Paz if he could learn more productive agricultural techniques at PLAN's model farm. In rural areas of Chalatenango, El Salvador, or Croix-des-Bouquets, Haiti, PLAN could bring drinking water to a village that had none by providing materials and technical aid to augment existing skills and resources in the village. With PLAN's help Foster Families and their neighbors could work together on water projects to benefit the entire community and greatly improve the children's chances of survival.

Projects in both urban and rural areas are often initiated by members of the community who approach PLAN with the idea of building a school, digging a well, or implementing some other community project. These projects are joint ventures involving PLAN, the members of the community, and, whenever possible, local and national agencies. The current feeling is that if the families participate directly in the process of identifying their development needs and volunteer their time, effort, and money to meet them, the identified needs will be more than a "shopping list" to be filled by benevolent foreigners.

With the institution of small scale, cooperative family and community projects, families could gain the experience of working together to meet their common needs. PLAN helped the families of La Paz, Bolivia, build stone retaining walls, stairs, and drains to control the erosion, landslides, and floods that threatened them every year. In Guayaquil, Ecuador, groups of families planted trees and repaired their homes and schools. In El Progreso, Guatemala, cooperatives were organized and a community center was built. These are all participative self-help projects. PLAN aid makes them possible, but they depend upon the initiative and continuing motivation of the community for their completion.

When PLAN was first established in Latin America in 1962, the focus of its program was on the intellectual, physical, and emotional development of the child, but clearly included the family. Reference to the community was generally limited to PLAN families within a community.

By 1973, Richard Cabrera, then Director of PLAN's program in Ecuador, was able to write:

> PLAN program priorities are as follows: (1) Programs which will strengthen family life, (2) programs which will improve housing and environment, (3) adult training programs designed to give parents skills leading to increased income and earlier independence, (4) health programs with emphasis on prevention, (5) recreation programs, (6) program of general education in responsible citizenship, and, finally (7) community betterment programs.

Five years later the emphasis had shifted once more. PLAN still worked with Foster Children, their families, and their communities, but now the people involved in the program had a much greater role in the decision making process. George W. Ross, PLAN International Executive Director, wrote from Rhode Island in 1978:

> The object of PLAN is to help children in poor families. Based on PLAN experience, the best way to do this is to assist the total family unit and the community in which that family lives. PLAN is opposed to paternalism whether it is by the host government or by PLAN or by any other agent. PLAN encourages independence, self-sufficiency, and the widest range of human development. In order to do so, it would be wrong for PLAN to make all the decisions for the children and families PLAN is trying to help. So we sit down with them, and help identify goals. We set these goals in a time frame, and we know the number of years we will be assisting the particular family or group of families.

Health

All of PLAN's Latin American and Caribbean programs have provided curative medical services, but by the early 1970s it was increasingly evident that disease prevention and health maintenance were more effective and lasting solutions to the poor health of PLAN families and their neighbors.

The low life-expectancy in PLAN's program areas is allied to high infant mortality rates and the widespread prevalence of chronic and acute debilitating diseases, primarily those associated with insufficient and contaminated water supplies and inadequate waste disposal, and exacerbated by over-crowding.

Such living conditions have a variety of results. Diarrheal diseases are the first or second leading cause of death and the leading cause of morbidity in children under five in all of PLAN's program countries. In marginal communities children with parasites often outnumber those without them. Malnutrition, especially among children, reduces resistance to disease.

Curative programs for these preventable conditions require hospitals, clinics, equipment, and a well-developed infrastructure to facilitate transportation. These services also require expensive and often unavailable personnel—doctors, nurses, dentists, administrators, and the whole roster of skilled technicians necessary to make a medical program work.

The staffing problems of PLAN's La Paz, Bolivia medical program in the early 1970s, while extreme, were not atypical of the difficulty of providing adequate curative care. Skilled medical staff could not earn enough money in Bolivia to make them stay in the country. Bolivia's tremendous underdevelopment led to the bizarre situation of 200 unemployed dcotors forming a union. Director Don Roose wrote in 1972 that PLAN could not afford to pay wages that would induce doctors to stay in the country and the doctors could not resist the lucrative opportunities in Spain, the United States, Venezuela, or Brazil where they would also have access to modern equipment, instruments, and facilities. This experience in Bolivia and similar experiences elsewhere helped persuade PLAN to intensify its preventive activities and to lessen its curative focus wherever and whenever possible.

Programs to maintain health rather than cure disease are much less expensive than curative programs, and can be very effective with minimal numbers of professional personnel. To be successful, however, they require clean water, adequate food and a strong educational component.

In 1979 PLAN submitted a Health Matching Grant Project (HMGP) proposal to the United States Agency for International Development (USAID) to undertake a pilot project to train community health workers in five field locations. The objective was to use these projects as models for the development of similar ones in other PLAN program areas. The proposal was accepted in 1980 and funded for three years with a total of $1,678,000 from USAID and a matching amount from PLAN. The funds were used to fulfill the specific objectives of the proposal but the larger goal was to move from curative programs to health maintenance programs.

Five of the six HMGP locations were in Latin America: Guayaquil and Guaranda Province, Ecuador; Bogota and Tumaco, Colombia; and Jacmel, Haiti.

The proposal to USAID gave as the primary objective of the progam the improvement of the health and nutritional status of PLAN families with a focus on children under six and mothers by incorporating primary health care into PLAN's family and community development programs in each of the project areas.

Specific objectives were:

1. That children or their mothers not die or suffer from illness caused by a disease which could have been prevented by vaccination.
2. That each family reach an adequate level of basic sanitation.
3. That all children achieve an adequate nutrition level (as monitored by weight for age) with special attention to children under six years of age.
4. That mothers receive adequate nutrition and health care during pregnancy and lactation so that they give birth to healthy children and are able to care for them adequately.
5. That all families have information concerning the prevention and treatment of the more common causes of illness, death and injury.
6. That all families have knowledge of and access to effective methods of family planning with due respect to local values and government policies.

The methods used to accomplish these were:

1. The training of health promoters, nurse auxiliaries, and midwives.
2. The construction of community health/nutrition facilities or potable water systems.
3. The integration of health promotion with housing, sanitation, potable water, and other services.
4. The institution of a system of routine collection of baseline health and nutrition data as part of the intake procedure for Foster Children and the collection of basic health data on

housing, breast-feeding, incidence and duration of diarrhea, and the practice of family planning.

5. The yearly monitoring of health indicators for assessing program effects.

6. The development of committees to assist the program staff in identifying health and nutritional priorities within the community and meet regularly with Health Matching Grant Project staff to evaluate and direct the program.

PLAN/Tumaco had always enjoyed a close working relationship with the Ministry of Health and with the funding of the HMGP this relationship grew even closer. The Government of Colombia already had a health promotion project and had established guidelines for training health promoters but a lack of funds and trained personnel severely limited their efforts. The Government was, therefore, enthusiastic about the project and agreed to take over the program at the end of the HMGP funding period.

This close cooperation insured that the project would be relevant to the needs of the community and would continue as an ongoing Colombian project when the three-year PLAN/USAID involvement ended. The use of people from the local community as health promoters further insured the success of the program. Their acceptability to the community was vital since one of their most important functions was to promote change in people's attitudes about their health. For the program to be effective this change had to be presented in a way that would be acceptable to the people and conform to patterns of the local culture.

The HMGP projects encountered problems in its family planning sector. Shirley Buzzard, Ph.D., Project Evaluator, described these difficulties in her July 1982 study, *The PLAN Primary Health Care Project, Tumaco, Colombia: A Case Study*, upon which the following pages are based.

Dr. Buzzard wrote that a man's prestige with other men is based on his ability to attract and hold women and beget children. While some of these liaisons are more enduring than others, one which lasts longer than five years is uncommon. Thus the social organization is centered not on the family unit, per se, but on the man/woman relationship and the mother/child relationship. Both men and women have an interest in having children but their reasons and responsibilities differ.

Some women have their first children as early as 13 or 14, though more wait until they are 16 or 17.

> Maria was 15 years old when she first became pregnant. She is now 25. Of the seven children she has delivered in the past ten years, three died in their first year.

> Teresa, now 33 years old, had her first child at 17 and in the next 16 years had 11 children, five died.

Although there are no accurate statistics, it would appear that about one third of the children die before they reach their fifth birthday.

Children are important to a woman as a demonstration of her fertility and because they provide a measure of security for her as she gets older. Older children care for younger ones and contribute to the family income by shining shoes or selling fruit. The society as yet has few social services and the individuals are dependent upon their children in the event of injury or illness, and in their old age.

The mother and children are the central unit of the household. The woman usually conceives her first child while she is living at home. If the father recognizes the child as his he may help her set up a household. Since both men and women welcome children, little, if any, effort is made to prevent conception. Once children are born the mother assumes the primary responsibility for their care. The fathers are expected to contribute to their care but the extent to which they do varies.

A household, through time, may have several men in residence as the head of the household, and siblings frequently have different fathers. The man is the head of the household as long as he is there and as such assumes authority, if not responsibility, for the children.

Under these conditions the idea of family planning and contraception is quite foreign. Medical personnel who conduct educational talks with the men of the community report that the male ego is strong enough to override the clearly understood economic disadvantages of having large numbers of children. Contraception, like the care of children, is viewed as a woman's responsibility. With these attitudes it is not surprising that male sterilization plays an insignificant role in family planning. When Dr. Buzzard wrote her study, there had been only six vasectomies performed in Tumaco.

Surveys show that there is little awareness of the variety of methods of contraception. Because of an aggressive and widely publicized government program which resulted in 1,000 tubal ligations between 1980 and 1982, many people believe that sterilization is the only way to prevent contraception.

There is more interest in family planning among women than men and there are increasing numbers of women using the pill and IUDs, but misunderstanding continues. Young women often do not realize that birth control pills and IUDs are temporary and, thinking that they are permanent, avoid them. Men may object to "their" women using contraceptives because they, like many of their neighbors to the north, equate contraception with promiscuity. Women, too, are sometimes victims of this prejudice, and may associate contraception with prostitution. These problems are compounded by the ban on family planning education in the schools and the pregnancies that often end a young woman's schooling.

In 1981 the hospital in Tumaco treated over 100 women for the aftereffects of self-induced abortion. About half of these women were young girls pregnant for the first time. The high cost of clinical abortions insure the continuation of these self-induced abortions and the infections and deaths to which they often lead.

Since the early 1970s PLAN's health programs have increasingly focused on maternal and child health and stressed pre and postnatal care for mothers and health maintenance programs for children under the age of five.

Between 1972 and 1974 public health, vaccination, nutrition, and pre and postnatal care programs were well established in all of PLAN's Latin American programs and were implemented in PLAN clinics, schools, community centers, and homes by PLAN medical staff, social workers, community groups, mothers' clubs, teachers, and PLAN trained health promoters. Families with malnourished children received supplemental food, vitamins, and education in nutrition, food preparation, hygiene, communicable disease control, and sanitation. These health projects were closely integrated with, and complementary to, the family and community development projects focusing on water, waste disposal, home improvement, gardening, and agriculture.

The simplest and most important part of PLAN's health maintenance program is the monthly weighing of children. Weight charts with printed graphs are kept for each child and the child's weight is recorded each month. The child's development is immediately apparent by comparing the current month's weight with the previous month's and with the ideal growth rate printed on the chart. If the chart shows that the child's weight has not increased for two months, has fallen, or is below the line of healthy growth, the mother and the community health worker can act quickly to remedy the situation. With a common produce scale, a little training, and a supply of blank weight charts, the people of a community can accurately measure the development of their children and identify malnourished children before their health is seriously threatened.

Once identified, the children can be referred to PLAN nutrition projects where mothers receive supplemental food and vitamins for the children and where they learn how to prevent recurring bouts of malnutrition.

It is hoped that the need for such supplementary feeding programs will decrease as PLAN's income-producing, animal raising, gardening, and agricultural projects raise the families' standard of living and as water, home improvement, and sanitation projects raise the environmental health level of their communities.

Education

PLAN's educational programs include the provision of school fees, uniforms, books, supplies and equipment, school construction and repair, adult literacy classes, special and remedial education projects, day care, support to libraries, recreational and camp programs, and cultural activities.

Although the constitutions of most PLAN program countries mandate free education for all children, a variety of economic and social factors limit the educational opportunities available to children in the marginal communities PLAN serves. Public education for those children is usually limited to a few years of primary school.

The low attendance and high dropout rate in primary and secondary schools result from a variety of factors:

There are not enough schools and children must often travel considerable distances to attend them.

In rural areas often barely qualified teachers in dilapidated buildings must use outdated and scarce teaching materials.

The effects of chronic illness, malnutrition, and parasites can have an adverse effect on a child's ability and interest in study.

The expense of school fees, uniforms, books, and supplies are often prohibitive.

Children often have to work to supplement the family income or remain at home to baby-sit so the mother or an older sibling can work.

Parents, often illiterate themselves, are not always able to see the long-term benefits of sending a child to school, especially in the face of the immediate financial sacrifice it will impose.

Families, including school-aged children, often engage in migrant agricultural work for months at a time.

Teachers' strikes and political instability often disrupt a country's educational system.

One of PLAN's most consistent criterion for Foster Children has been that they attend school. With basic literacy skills children have the basis for further formal or vocational education and can develop the skills, self-confidence, and awareness they need to have some control over their own lives in an environment that is not otherwise going to provide adequately for them.

PLAN's role in formal education has been and continues to be primarily to support and upgrade local educational systems and curricula and to encourage Foster Families to send as many of their children to school as possible.

If there are no schools available, if they are ill equipped, too small or structurally unsafe, PLAN works with communities and local officials to build new schools, repair existing ones, and to provide them with equipment and supplies. Host governments usually agree to staff the new or renovated schools.

Ancillary support includes the establishment of after-school study centers in PLAN buildings and community centers to provide a quiet place for children to study. In some cases, older Foster Children or university students staff these centers as volunteer tutors.

A few promising students have received scholarships to attend universities but the main effort has been on primary and secondary education. Thousands of elementary school students have received special remedial courses to meet secondary school entrance requirements.

Educational social workers in Bolivia and Brazil identified children with mental or psychological problems which interfered with their studies and then worked with the children, their families and their teachers to alleviate them. In Brazil in 1969 and 1970, PLAN studies of poor students suggested that their high failure rate may have resulted from organic damage caused by a lifetime of ill health. The general cultural vacuum of the area only added to their poor academic performance. As a result of these studies children were enrolled as Foster Children at a younger age. The idea was to enroll children between the ages of three and five, detect and remedy their health problems, see that they received adequate nutrition, and provide them with the intellectual and cultural stimulation of kindergarten and preschool programs. These programs also served the purpose of providing day care for children, thereby permitting their mothers to work or to participate in PLAN vocational training and cooperative income-producing programs.

Using the knowledge gained in Brazil, other PLAN Directors soon established nursery schools, kindergartens, day care centers, and after-school study centers. In Ecuador PLAN established libraries to provide books and a quiet place to study in the evenings and on weekends. Summer school programs provided an extra opportunity for secondary school preparation for marginal students.

PLAN's educational programs for adults provide basic literacy and vocational training for the parents and older brothers and sisters of Foster Children. Adult literacy programs provide the means for illiterate adults and older school dropouts to develop their capacity to read, write, and do basic arithmetic to a level that will help them improve their economic condition, productivity, and cultural integration.

Resources and Skills Development

Families living in the marginal communities of Latin America and the Caribbean have traditionally faced high rates of unemployment and underemployment. Employment opportunities are often limited to low-paying, low-status, or service-sector occupations. Domestic servants, laundresses, newspaper vendors, artisans, tenant farmers, sharecroppers, and cane-cutters have highly unstable or seasonal incomes which barely meet their basic needs. Most families lack the opportunity to upgrade their skills and many who have skills, or have the chance to acquire them, do not have the opportunity to make use of them. The problem worsens as unskilled rural families with no source of income and no marketable skills migrate to urban areas.

PLAN's resource and skills development programs teach people how to do things and often provide the means to do them through animal raising, technical training, agricultural projects, market gardens, small businesses, crafts, land purchases, credit unions, and cooperatives. Deteriorating local economies, low wages, limited demand for skilled labor, lack of available land, poor markets for products, and the scarcity or high cost of raw materials can influence the success of these projects.

In urban areas groups are formed and trained in vocational and job-finding skills for work in local industry and in the development of small individual or group cottage industries. In rural areas PLAN enables farmers and fishermen to boost their incomes through programs combining work and education in such areas as technical development, reforestation and erosion control, livestock inoculation, and market development. Small animal raising projects are equally useful in both rural and urban areas.

In Tambillo, Bolivia, resource and skills development combines self-help and education to benefit the entire community. Projects conducted in cooperation with the Ministry of Agriculture and local volunteers have included model farms, animal husbandry, soil fertilization, food storage and marketing, animal dipping tanks, greenhouse construction, training, and agricultural credit.

In rural Daule, Ecuador, one of PLAN's newer program areas, the resources and skills development program has three basic objectives:

To promote the growing of a variety of grains and vegetables to improve the diet of the community.

To improve the rural technology so that Foster Families will be able to earn more money and thereby be able to stay in Daule rather than migrating to the marginal areas around Guayaquil.

To promote small-scale agriculture related businesses as an alternative to farming for families whose farms are too small to provide adequate support.

In Chalatenango, El Salvador, the PLAN Director estimated PLAN family unemployment to be 75 percent. The area has no industrial development, agricultural income is unsteady, and commerce is disrupted as a result of political contention. The majority of the population earn their livelihood as petty vendors and hawkers or as farmers. In 1983 PLAN developed new sources of income by providing material and technical aid for group projects in fisheries, livestock raising, grain processing, and dressmaking.

The success of a 1981 model garden project in Guatemala proved to be a powerful incentive for local farming families to try simple but innovative agricultural methods that have dramatically increased their crop yields. Their children and their neighbor's children are now learning these methods in school garden projects.

Community Development

The first regional conference of PLAN's Latin American Field Directors was held in February 1971. This was only the second such conference in PLAN's history, the first having taken place in Munich in 1957 for the Directors of PLAN's European programs. Directors from Bolivia, Brazil, Colombia, Ecuador and Peru met in Guayaquil, Ecuador, to discuss occurring or imminent changes in PLAN's philosophy and services.

PLAN, said Gloria Matthews in her opening remarks, was created to help children left homeless by war . . .

> From this situation in Spain 34 years ago, and through the World War II years in France and then Britain, a similar situation existed, and PLAN cared for these children in large homes, or, as we called them, "colonies." Whatever they were called, they provided care to large groups of children in institutions.

> When we returned to the continent in the late '40's follow-ing World War II, PLAN for the first time faced up to the needs of a child in a family setting. For the next 15 years, PLAN emphasized aid to one child in a family, hoping that some benefit would accrue to the entire family at least in the long-term effect of having achieved some education for that one child. It is true, however, that assistance to the rest of the families in those days, was a side benefit, and often solely the result of extra cash gifts or gift parcels from the concerned Foster Parents.

> Then in the 1960's PLAN began to consider a new concept and this was a giant step in the organization's history. First, it gave increasing attention to the family. Second, it changed its role from that of a channel for handing out cash and supplies into that of a guide for helping a child *AND* his family to make use of their own full potential. The changes were gradual and even now the various field programs are in different stages of that change, reflecting the dates of their establishment as well as the ideas of the specific Field Directors and the needs and resources of the particular societies.

> Now in the 1970's, PLAN is accepting the community-wide concept, and experimenting with it. And we shall learn, by doing, just what is desirable and what is feasible in commu-nity terms while always maintaining the child emphasis that is our basic raison d'être.

Miss Matthews' remarks led to discussions of enrollment policies, education, and community development as they related to PLAN's overall goals of child development. Don Roose, then PLAN/Bolivia Director, who led the discussion on community development, said that the objectives of his community development program were to meet specific material needs of the community, to establish community responsibility and community decision making, and to develop local leadership.

PLAN/Bolivia's Community Development Department, PLAN's first in Latin America, worked with PLAN families and their neighbors in the Villa Fatima district of La Paz on health, education, and recreation projects. The program was established in September 1969, with two community development workers.

The conferees were impressed with this program and saw it as a way to involve more people in PLAN's work and, at the same time, to complement and support existing or planned programs addressing the specific needs of Foster Children and their families.

In the area of health, for example, many of the children's immediate problems could be alleviated through community water and sanitation projects. An underlying cause of these problems, parental ignorance, could be remedied through group and community education projects or counseling by PLAN social work and medical staff.

Children who went to school out of doors, if they went to school at all, might be more motivated to stay in school if they had a school building and sat at desks instead of on stones. If the parents of the children wanted a school badly enough to build one, they would certainly encourage their children to attend classes.

In La Paz, it clearly made more sense for PLAN to work with the community on flood and erosion control projects than to wait for the flood and then rebuild each damaged home. Between 1971 and 1977 hundreds of community projects were completed by PLAN families working with their neighbors, PLAN staff, volunteers, local and national agencies, and neighborhood associations.

During the mid-1970s, the community development focus expanded to include economic projects and, since 1977, these cooperative income-producing activities have played a steadily increasing role in PLAN's development strategy.

Construction projects continue to provide such needed services as home repairs, water and sanitation projects, feeder roads, community centers, and school rooms, but they have been augmented by cooperative loans, agricultural, fishing, and small business projects.

In Honduras, where farmers have traditionally worked alone on their little plots of land, a cooperative farming project encouraged groups of farmers to work together. The farmers pooled their resources and, with PLAN support, purchased seeds, insecticides, fertilizers, tools, oxen, and plows. A PLAN agronomist provided technical advice and supervision for projects which resulted in larger, more varied crops that, in turn, improved both the income and diet of the participants.

In Bolivar, Ecuador, technical assistance and income-generating projects based on promoting the cooperation of small farmers have led to the establishment of grain mills, pork industries, and a marmelade industry.

The Agricultural Training Center in Tambillo, Bolivia, established in 1977, serves the farmers and herdsmen in the surrounding communities of the Altiplano. The center has an irrigation system, greenhouse, chicken coops, rabbit hutches, a piggery and support facilities. Over 3,000 PLAN and non-PLAN families participate in the center's activities and in the preparation, maintenance, and harvesting of two hectares of potatoes. Using techniques that they later applied to their own fields, the families harvested 54,000 kilos of potatoes from each hectare. Traditional methods used on similar land yielded about 28,000 kilos per hectare.

President Samora Machel of Mozambique might have been speaking for PLAN when he told members of the Fourth Frelimo Party Congress in May 1983 that "small scale projects are a method of making full use of locally available resources, and of taking full advantage of existing productive capacities. Their achievement develops people's confidence, and frees the imagination and creative initiative."

The dependency, initiative, and capacity for growth referred to by President Machel are issues with which PLAN has grappled since its beginnings in war torn Spain. PLAN has always sought to enable people to better their lives, to foster growth and development of children, first by providing assistance directly to the child and, later, by providing the much more important indirect assistance which strengthens the child's family and community. Trial, error, and modification have resulted in a program approach incorporating three elements:

1. The balance of development goals with the meeting of basic needs.
2. The enhancement of people's potential for self-determination and self-help.

3. The participation of the people, themselves, in all aspects of our human resource development programs.[3]

Much of the experience which led to this approach was in Latin America.

---

[3]*The Golbal SAGE (Situation Assessment and Goal Establishment) Report.* (unpublished PLAN document, 1983) p. 9.

14

Africa: 1974-83

PLAN's work in Africa started in Ethiopia in 1974. Two years later programs were established in Mali, Sudan, and Upper Volta. Since then, PLAN has spread to Sierra Leone (1977), Kenya (1981), Egypt (1981), Liberia (1982), and Senegal (1982).

PLAN's program in Ethiopia was delayed, frustrated, and finally terminated as a result of the social and political upheaval of the September 1975 revolution which ended the reign of Emperor Haile Salassie.

The program in Ethiopia was established by Lloyd Feinberg in the rocky hills surrounding the ancient city of Lalibela. After three months, civil unrest made the situation untenable and, on 15 March 1975, PLAN's staff and their families were evacuated to Addis Ababa. In 1976 PLAN moved to Arba Minch, the capital of the southern province of Gemu Gofa.

The traditional domination of the Gemu Gofans by the northern Amharas and Eritrians created immediate and continuing difficulties for PLAN. As a result of centuries of cultural neglect and economic exploitation, there were simply not enough educated and qualified Gemu Gofans available to staff the PLAN program. Social workers, therefore, had to be recruited from the traditional ruling classes. The social workers, some of whom had worked for PLAN in Lalibela, were harassed and threatened by the people of the community and regularly held for questioning by the local police. They were frequently afraid to leave their homes to go to the office. If they did get to the office, they were often afraid to go into the community.

Global politics created further difficulties. PLAN was identified as an American rather than an international agency and was regularly condemned in the popular press as an agent of American imperialism. Even the official support of PLAN by the revolutionary government could do little to dispel this misconception.

These difficulties eventually culminated in the arrest and six-week detention of Leslie Fox, PLAN/Ethiopia's second and final Director.

PLAN's program was terminated in 1977, after Mr. Fox had been released and was safely out of the country. The fact that the program survived for as long as it did was largely the result of the determination of Mr. Fox and the strong support of the government's Drought Relief and Rehabilitation Committee and its Chief Commissioner, Ato Shemelis Adugna.

In spite of the brevity and overall disappointment of PLAN's ill-fated program, the Ethiopian experience provided a valuable introduction to programming in traditional African societies.

The financial assistance program was one of the first areas to be affected. Throughout the PLAN world there had been a growing feeling among PLAN staff that direct financial assistance to individual families was not always the most effective way to use PLAN's limited funds. The People's Revolutionary Government of Ethiopia agreed and said in no uncertain terms that cash grants to particular members of a community would perpetuate an economic class structure that they believed had no place in the new Ethiopian society.

Though PLAN staff did not perceive the problem in such dialectical terms, they did see the disruptive and dependency-producing potential of direct injections of cash into what were essentially non-cash village economies. PLAN funds were better used for such community projects as wells, schools, health, and agriculture benefiting Foster Children and also all members of the community.

In the spring of 1977, Foster Parents Plan of Canada described community projects and the differences and similarities in the PLAN programs of Ethiopia, Mali, and Upper Volta in *PLAN Canada News* (Vol. 4, No. 1), its newsletter to Canadian Foster Parents.

> Foster Parents Plan has been working in Africa for three years. During that time we have been able to collect a respectable amount of information on the areas in which we work. In order that Foster Parents of African children might become more familiar with PLAN's program in Africa, PLAN Canada News has put together this information introducing our field directors and new programs, as well as offering an insight into the African way of life.
>
> PLAN now has operative programs in three countries on the African continent. Soon, case histories will be available from two more, namely Sudan and Sierra Leone. For the present, however, PLAN's work in Africa is centered in Ethiopia, Upper

Volta, and Mali.

The differences between the three countries are marked, yet some similarities do exist. For instance, our whole system of money or "cash" is totally foreign to the tribes of all three countries. Their economy is not based on money, but rather on a barter system.

Since PLAN has no wish to disrupt the fragile social and economic structures of village life, but rather wishes to work in harmony with the customs of the societies, cash gifts and grants are not given to the African families.

Instead of giving a family a gift of ten dollars, for instance, PLAN has found it to be more beneficial to the family if the gift is used for village improvements. An African Foster Child is best helped, at this stage, by improvements to his community, and in fact will benefit directly from the provision of such necessities as uncontaminated water and mass inoculations.

Many Canadian customs and activities are equally unknown to African Foster Families. They have no conception, for example, of what a "letter" is. In fact, they often have no written language at all, and must turn to official "Letter Writers" in order to communicate with their sponsoring Foster Parent.

Following this introduction, the three African Field Directors described their program countries. Leslie Fox wrote of Ethiopia:

Ethiopia is a land of contrasts. Its destitute villages and malnourished people exist in an environment of great natural beauty. Abundant wildlife, with exotic coloring and plumage roams the mountains and plains of Gemu Gofa province. Lions, zebra, giraffes, elephants, cheetahs, leopards, crocodiles and gazelles share the resources of game preserves. Fast-flowing rivers feed cascading waterfalls and unspoiled lakes dot the countryside.

One must look deeply to see the true Ethiopia, the Ethiopia of our Foster Families. Behind that mask of beauty lies a harsh reality: painful poverty, drought-stricken land and widespread famine and starvation. The 25-27 million inhabitants of Ethiopia are considered to be among the most impoverished peoples of the world.

From the time PLAN first established its Ethiopian program in 1974, to this date, medical and educational services have remained for the most part unknown outside of PLAN-assisted communities. Drinking water, housing, sanitation, and nutrition are all sub-standard, and add up to something less than even a minimum standard of living.

Ethiopian families share their traditional round homes (called "Tukuls") with all of their livestock. Ironically, the animals inside might one day be part of the building itself, since the hut's walls are often made of animal skins.

Malnutrition is a way of life, and the infant mortality rate is correspondingly high. Many children die before even reaching the age of eight. Natural disasters, such as drought and soil depletion, couple with economic disasters, such as inflation, in making food scarce.

It is in this atmosphere of frustration and destitution that the hardworking Ethiopians struggle to live out their tribal existence, untouched by the advances of modern life.

Ethiopia has an official language (Amharic); an official currency (the Ethiopian dollar, equal to about 37 Canadian cents); and two predominant religions (Coptic Orthodox Christianity and Islam). Yet its people's acceptance of these institutions is as varied as are their dialects, tribes and religious beliefs. Above all, Ethiopia is a land of diversity.

The prevalent diversity in Ethiopia is due at least in part to the inaccessibility of one village to another, since the majority of Ethiopians live in these small villages (comprised of anywhere from five to five hundred families). Even if two villages are no more than two miles apart, the lack of roads and the abundance of dense jungle vegetation and mountainous terrain will make communication impossible, and keep each village in complete isolation. This isolation is one of the major reasons for Ethiopia's economic problems, as well as for its diversity. The diversity too, is fostered by the fact that few Ethiopians receive a complete education, which would do much to establish country-wide norms. Education is free in Ethiopia, but books, notebooks, pencils and clothing are not. Few families can afford these necessities, and many others need their school age children to tend the herds of sheep, goats, and cattle.

Norman D. Sanders, Jr., Director, PLAN/Mali, and Asbjorn Osland, Director, PLAN/Upper Volta, wrote of their programs in the arid reaches of the Sahel. Here, at least, there was no visible contrast between the poverty of the people and the poverty of the land.

There is little evidence of the twentieth century in rural PLAN villages of these two countries. The villagers live much as their parents and grandparents lived. In many ways, this is to their advantage. The rich cultural heritage provides strong, closely knit family and village ties which help to assure their survival in the harsh and inhospitable land. As expected, with the traditional culture come traditional problems:

unsanitary living conditions, poor health, totally inadequate medical care, backbreaking and inefficient agricultural techniques, malnutrition, superstition, isolation, and ignorance.

Though French is the official language of Mali and Upper Volta, few rural people speak it and fewer still can write in any language. The people in rural villages speak tribal languages and follow traditional tribal customs. PLAN enrolled its families from the Bambara tribe in Mali and the Mossi tribe in Upper Volta. Both tribes are polygynous. The large families live together with their livestock in family compounds; villages are composed of several such compounds.

PLAN's task was, and continues to be, to implement programs of child, family, and community development which are in harmony with the existing patterns of belief and behavior. This effort is founded upon the direct participation of the villagers themselves who work with PLAN through village committees to select, plan, implement, and manage group and community projects to meet their common needs.

Although the statistics relevant to Africa's development needs are not always reliable and may vary considerably depending upon who is doing the counting, there is consistency enough in the figures to speak in general terms of the development needs of the continent. With the exception of the anomalous South Africa, all African nations suffer from slow economic growth, inadequate food production, unemployment and underemployment, low per capita income, a low level of technology, illiteracy, and inadequate health care.

Slow Economic Growth

Statistics from the United Nations' Economic Commission for Africa, collected between 1960 and 1975, reveal that only nine African states achieved the acceptable rate of economic growth of between 5.8 and 6.9 percent a year. These were not the countries in which PLAN was to establish programs. The 22 countries with an average annual per capita income between US $100 and US $300 achieved only a 1.4 percent annual growth rate.

Inadequate Food Production

According to a joint United Nations/Institut African Développement Economique Planification report, no African nation gave priority to agricultural development between 1960 and 1970. By the end of that period Africa was producing only 85 percent of its required food, and cereal imports alone had increased by nearly 40 percent. In roughly the same period, 1961-74, per capita food production dropped by four percent.

Unemployment and Underemployment

International Labor Organization (ILO) studies show that 45 percent of the economically active population of Africa suffers unemployment or underemployment. People living in rural areas account for 84 percent of this total.

Low Per Capita Income

The low per capita income follows naturally from the slow economic growth and the high unemployment and underemployment. In 1973, 83.5 percent of the African population earned less than US $300. According to ILO criteria, 69 percent of the people in Africa were living in extreme poverty in 1973.

Industrialization

According to the United Nations' Industrial Development Organization (UNIDO), a country is industrialized when 30 percent of its GDP is in the industrial sector. It is semi-industrialized when that figure is between 20 and 30 percent. Between 10 and 20 percent, it is in the process of industrialization, and below 10 percent, it is not industrialized at all. Taken as a whole, the countries of Africa were not industrialized in 1960. In 1970, the continent was just on the threshhold of industrialization with manufacturing representing just 11.5 percent of the GDP.

Illiteracy

Based on census figures, sample surveys, and special reports, UNESCO estimated that more than 80 percent of Africa's 273 million people were illiterate in 1960. Ten years later, with the population numbering 352 million, 74 percent were illiterate. In spite of the proportional improvement, the actual number of illiterates had increased by over 40 million. In Mali, in 1970, 87 percent of the adult men and over 99.5 percent of the adult women were illiterate. Ten years later, the figures were 81 and 98 percent. In Upper Volta, in 1970, 91 percent of the men and over 99.5 percent of the women were illiterate. Ten years later, the figures were the same. This massive illiteracy is clearly an obstacle to the acquisition of the technical skills necessary for development.

Inadequate Health Care

The countries of Africa in which PLAN works face a variety of health and health care problems. There were, for example, 31,295 people for every one doctor in 1960. By 1977, that figure had improved somewhat but, at 17,430, was still too high. The availability of nursing care showed similar improvement. In 1960, there were 2,931 people for every nurse; in 1977, 1,753. Though the numbers of professionally trained health personnel have increased, the availability of health care is still inadequate. The unhealthy environment adds to the problem —in 1975 only 31 percent of the people in PLAN program countries had access to safe water. In 1982, the average life expectancy in these countries was 47 years.

These problems are closely related and, taken together, reflect the need for a comprehensive program of development. Since the rural population accounts for 80 percent of the total population, African development must mean the development of rural areas. To be of lasting benefit the development efforts must be comprehensive and integrated, uniting health, education, human development, and resource and skills development projects into a coherent whole. New schools, roads, hospitals, and technologies, by themselves, will solve few problems.

The example of malnutrition and general poor health, common problems in the developing nations of Africa, illustrate this inter-relatedness. One obvious cause of these problems is low food production. Yet this low food production can sometimes be attributed to a labor force weakened by poor health. Similarly, the lack of adequate water retards efforts to promote agricultural development and contributes to ill health. Finally, illiteracy contributes to the low level of organization and management which, in turn, can affect the ability of people to effectively develop their agriculture or deal with their basic health problems.

Throughout the sub-Saharan region of Africa, stretching from the Atlantic to the upper Nile basin and including those of Lake Chad and the Niger, desertification is a major problem. Drought, intermittent heavy rain, and deforestation have resulted in widespread erosion and the loss of cropland and pasturage. The vicious circle continues as reduced vegetation leads to over-grazing, which leads to greater surface water run off, erosion and creeping barrenness, which leads to greater surface water run off . . .

Recognition of this cycle has resulted in multi-agency reforestation, well drilling, fertilization, and irrigation projects. The success of these projects has been impaired by the high cost and poor success rate of drilled wells, the lack of sufficient water for irrigation, voracious wood consumption, and general poor management.

To be successful, these projects must depend upon the mobilization and direct involvement of the people in the communities. This mobilization will assure broad participation in development projects and will help to ensure the continuation of the development process after the specific projects have been completed.

The abstract qualities of these development generalities quickly disappear in the dusty reality of a remote Sahelian village in Mali or Upper Volta. James Emerson, Assistant Director in Upper Volta, described one such village in the newsletter for Foster Parents in the United Kingdom, *PLAN Times* (No. 4, Spring 1983).

> The first thing to strike you about Mossi villages is their remoteness. After leaving the main road (a dirt track) it can take anything from 30 to 90 minutes on a motorcycle to reach a village. The drive will take you through hot dusty arid scrubland in which everything is brown, even the sky has sometimes a brownish tinge due to the dust in the air. Suddenly, literally in the middle of nowhere, one comes upon a small cluster of mud houses and thatched granaries, a few chickens peck at the dust and goats wander round eating whatever they can. Women, dressed only in a wrap-around cloth from the waist down, will be seen pounding their millet or carrying wood or water on their heads. The old men are probably sitting under the shade of a tree exchanging greetings and stories.
>
> Every time I visit a village I'm surprised at the fact that such a sizeable group of people can live in such a barren isolated place. It is, in fact, a difficult task; water is problem number one, and sometimes can only be found at a distance of seven miles or more. When you consider that the only means of covering those miles is by foot, and that all the water has to be carried on your head under a hot sun, you only begin to realize the severity of the problem. On top of all that the water is usually surface water: dirty and full of parasites.
>
> Problem number two is food. The arid countryside is not very favorable to agriculture and all the food has to be grown during the wet months of July to September. A bad rainy season means severe shortages and famine. Those three months are the busiest time of year. Everyone (men, women, and children) are out working in the fields from dawn till

dusk. It's very hard work, and often also it's a time of shortages of food since the harvest of the previous year is now almost finished. The staple diet here consists of a thick porridge-like "stodge" made from millet which is eaten with a sauce of leaves gathered from trees and shrubs; meat is a rare treat. Cooking food presents yet another major problem—firewood. This is also collected by the women and once again requires walking long distances. Each year the task gets harder as tree cover in the area is on the decrease—wood is burned everyday but trees are not being replaced.

Even in these remote areas the modern world has managed to penetrate and introduce its new problems. One of the greatest being exploitation by rich grain merchants. As the rainy season (the growing season) approaches the supplies of millet are running low, villagers are often forced to buy more millet. Since they usually cannot pay for it, they are obliged to sell their harvest (that which they are about to plant) in advance. The price of the millet just before the planting season is very high but afterwards it drops considerably and so for one sack of millet received in June a villager may have to repay 1½ to 2 sacks from his harvest in September—almost a guarantee that next year he will run short and will have to depend on the merchants again. It becomes a vicious circle from which there seems no hope of escape.

The individuals and groups in this village and hundreds of others like it are the foundation of PLAN's rural African programs. The conditions under which Foster Children and their families live are such that virtually none of the amenities identified with even a minimum standard of living are present. The villages are inaccessible, medical and educational facilities are minimal or nonexistent, and housing and sanitary facilities are, at best, substandard. The list of needs is long, but the spirit of mutual assistance and collaboration is as much a part of traditional village life as poverty. PLAN builds its programs on the cooperation and active involvement of the villagers from the initial phases of project planning through final implementation.

Foster Families, their neighbors, local leaders, and PLAN staff work together directly or through elected village councils to determine the community's needs and priorities. Based on these needs and priorities, a comprehensive program is organized through which the families and communities work to improve their health standards, education, community, and income.

Health

Health care projects have the goals of both curing and preventing disease. They include the training of health promoters and midwives, vaccination programs, malaria control, health related home repair, the building, renovation and equipping of hospitals, clinics, pharmacies, health posts, and, perhaps most important, the provision of adequate sources of potable water.

The major health problems are similar in all of PLAN's African program countries. They are the lack of sufficient sources of potable water, the scarcity of medicine, ignorance of basic preventive health care and sanitary procedures, the inadequacy of traditional medicine, the lack of properly trained midwives and village health workers, low earning power, inadequate food production, and unsanitary living conditions.

The scarcity of pure water and the lack of education, by themselves, are enough to insure that most of the population will suffer chronically or intermittently from borderline protein-calorie malnutrition, harbor parasites, and suffer the affects of poor sanitation. PLAN is working with governments and communities to address these problems through a broad range of curative and preventive health programs and related community-level agricultural and income-producing projects.

The Government of Mali, for example, subscribes to the United Nations' goal of health care for all by the year 2000. The idea of primary health care, village health workers, and village pharmacies is discussed at great length, but, with a largely illiterate population and a national treasury near insolvency, the immediate prospects of success are not great.

In Banamba Circle, Mali, where PLAN works in over 230 villages, there were, in March 1983, two doctors and two registered nurses to serve the health care needs of more than 90,000 people. PLAN has established a literacy center to teach prospective village health workers to read and write in the Bambara language. Once they have basic literacy skills, they are trained and equipped to diagnose and treat common diseases. These health workers are recruited on the recommendation of their neighbors in the villages where they will serve. When they return they have the skills to provide community health care through health and nutrition education, diagnosis, treatment, and environmental sanitation education.

The situation is similar in Upper Volta, where PLAN staff works in close cooperation with the various ministries responsible for implementing the overall national development program. PLAN's health program is directly related to the health goals and priorities of the Ministry of Public Health and the Ministry of Social Development and Women's Affairs. The primary objective of the program has been to promote the health care of pregnant women, mothers, and young children. This is done through the construction, renovation, and equipment of hospitals and dispensaries, the support of mobile clinics, the training of midwives and village health workers, child weighing programs, oral rehydration therapy for malnutrition, and educational programs in nutrition, sanitation, and child care.

PLAN's emphasis has been on integrated community health care. The interrelated nature of these programs is exemplified in Asbjorn Osland's 23 February 1983 *Situation Assessment and Goal Establishment Report* for PLAN in Senegal.

The nascent program in Senegal was established by Mr. Osland in 1982 and operates in the areas of Rao and St. Louis in the Fleuve region of northern Senegal near the Mauritanian border.

Since curative medical services are already available in the program areas, PLAN/Senegal can concentrate on disease prevention through a comprehensive community health program.

Obstacles to better community health are varied and considerable. They include:

Limited government and community resources.

Inadequate, salty, or contaminated water supplies.

Poor personal and community hygiene.

Low rainfall, soil erosion, and poor soil.

High population growth.

Poor prospects for agricultural subsistence and economic development.

Unhealthy beliefs and customs.

Mr. Osland hopes to alleviate these conditions through a health program based on the expressed needs of the communities. Working with the people, PLAN will augment the government vaccination program, improve access to potable water, support the planting and consumption of vegetables, train and equip midwives and health promoters, provide education in personal and community hygiene, and improve housing.

Education

Mass illiteracy, combined with the lack of opportunities for vocational and technical training, aggravates the development problems of people living in isolated, tradition-bound rural communities. This ignorance is often an effective obstacle to the understanding of, adaptation to, or participation in the inescapable changes that are affecting not only their daily lives, but also the social and economic conditions of the continent. When the illiterate and untrained rural people move to the cities their poverty only worsens.

These conditions are not dissimilar to those faced by former colonies in other parts of the world. Formal education systems established by colonial powers in their respective colonies followed the Western model in structure, intent, and curriculum. These patterns of formal education, imported from industrializing societies, offered, at best, only a limited response to the very different educational needs of an agricultural economy.

The concurrent introduction of more advanced and mechanized Western technologies engendered a gap between what was introduced and what may have been needed, similar to that in the realm of formal education. Advanced technologies in the colonial period tended to be understood, managed and controlled by a small segment of society, and also to supplant traditional technologies and the labor force which implemented them. Therefore, practitioners of traditional vocations suffered both from exclusion from all but manual participation in new technological developments, and from erosion in the demand of their products.

These problems have been inherited by the people who PLAN now serves through its educational programs. Basic literacy training and vocational education for adults are combined with curriculum development and support for preschool, primary, and secondary education.

In the Banamba Circle of Mali, where 95 percent of the people in PLAN villages are illiterate, the government does not have the resources to support an adequate system of public education. In response to this clearly perceived and expressed need, PLAN and the people of the villages have provided support for existing schools and have built and equipped additional primary schools and learning centers. Nearly all PLAN programs emphasize primary education with primary school construction and renovation as standard aspects of the program. The usual arrangement calls for the government to provide staff for the schools PLAN builds or improves. Canteens have been established in conjunction with the schools to guarantee that children have at least one nutritious meal a day. Educational programs and basic literacy classes have also been organized for adults and older children at these learning centers.

Similar programs have been established in Senegal and Upper Volta. This support for primary school education, adult education, and vocational training is based on three specific assumptions:

That there is a willingness among significant numbers of parents to participate in these programs.

That functional literacy will lead to an ability to participate in the social and economic changes taking place in Africa.

That literacy and technical knowledge will be a basis for continuing development.

The emphasis is on practical skills as well as on basic literacy. For young children, the focus is on primary education, but nonformal education will be required for the vast majority of older children and adults. These programs include training in basic literacy and such skills as village level project management, health maintenance, community organization, agricultural development, and marketing and are closely integrated with health and economic development projects.

Foster Children in urban program areas of Cairo and Freetown have quite different educational needs. The programs for these children are the exceptions to the usual PLAN emphasis on primary education.

In Cairo, where the government provides for primary and secondary education, PLAN's emphasis is on providing the preschool age child with a sound preparation for primary school. This is being accomplished through the construction of preschools and by training preschool teachers.

In Freetown, the capital of Sierra Leone, the completion of secondary school is considered a prerequisite to success and parents therefore make every sacrifice to keep their children in school. Annual school costs average US $216 for tuition, books, fees, and supplies. This figure exceeds the average annual per capita income by about US $30.

Schools are overcrowded, underequipped, and understaffed. The curriculum, modeled on the traditional English system, emphasizes a general Liberal Arts education and results in graduates untrained and unsuited for either agricultural or technical work and ill-equipped for self-employment.

Thus there is an obvious disparity between what the people want and the needs of the government, the country, and the economy. To resolve this conflict PLAN had adopted a program to enable Foster Children to attend secondary school and, at the same time, to upgrade the vocational and technical training available in those schools. The Scholarship Program for Foster Children began in 1981 and, by 1983, was enabling nearly 1,200 needy students to attend secondary school by providing the payment of all tuition fees and about half of all required textbooks. Nearly a third of PLAN/Freetown's Material Aids and Services budget is spent on improving the curriculum through the provision of teaching equipment and materials for vocational and technical education.

Community Development

The emphasis in most of the PLAN programs in Africa is on planned group and community development. The reasons for this emphasis have been discussed earlier and need be only mentioned here:

> The rural communities are often barely affected by a cash economy and operate on a barter system which would be disrupted by injections of cash to some members of the community.

> Large, polygamous families would certainly be disrupted by payments to only certain family members.

> Direct financial assistance can lead to dependency and therefore be counter-productive.

> The final and most conclusive reason for group and community programming is that it strengthens the already highly developed sense of family and community interdependence.

From 1975 until 1981, the community development sector included a wide variety of collective efforts relating to the improvement of the health, education, housing, and income-producing potential of the families in PLAN program areas. After 1981 there were sharper lines of demarcation between program sectors and an increased emphasis on the training of the participants. Thus, potable water projects were now classified as health rather than community development projects. PLAN's efforts to raise the community income level through cooperative gardens or animal raising, for example, were redefined as "Resource and Skills Development" activities. Community development was now limited almost exclusively to projects which would enhance the physical or commercial qualities of the community with the goals of improving community infrastructure and consolidating cooperative relationships among the villagers. These projects include the construction of feeder roads and bridges to improve village contacts with the outside world, village electrification, community center construction, reforestation, and such non-physical projects as leadership training, the organization of credit unions, and the training of village animators.

The building of community centers is among the most significant of these projects. These centers have been built in nearly all of PLAN's African program countries and have become focal points of village life. They function as schools, meeting houses, and training centers for village committees.

One of the most innovative community development projects will take place in Mali. The plan calls for the organization of a traveling theater group. The group will perform plays on developmental themes in Banamba villages in the evenings. The hope is that eventually members of the troupe will disperse and form their own local groups throughout the arrondissements of Banamba.

Resource and Skills Development

Low income, a prime cause and effect of most of the social and health problems of Africa, is the major target of PLAN's resource and skills development programs. Their goal is to increase the income of the participants by dealing with the interrelated problems of under-employment, unemployment, and the inadequate production, storage, and distribution of food.

These problems are the major causes of the large scale migration to urban areas. People in remote and backward villages may be illiterate, ill fed, ill housed and ill equipped for urban life, but they are not fools. If they cannot make a living where they are, they will go somewhere else, usually to an urban area, in hopes of finding a better life or simply to survive. Unfortunately the people who leave may often be the young, bright and ambitious people whose presence will be the most sorely missed.

This process is not necessary, new, or unique to developing countries today. The results now are similar to the results in Europe and America—the cities become overwhelmed by untrained and destitute migrants and the Dickensian slums of nineteenth century London, New York, and Boston have been replaced by the sprawling shanty towns of twentieth century Port-au-Prince and Cairo. One of PLAN's goals, therefore, is to improve the economic quality of rural life enough to help slow this migration to the city.

Community economic projects and cooperatives have been a part of PLAN's program since its establishment in Africa. In 1976, the short-lived program in Ethiopia organized agricultural extension services and demonstration plots to provide instruction to individuals and groups who had received seeds, tools, and oxen from PLAN. Similar projects were begun in Mali the next year and, on the advice of the village committees, reforestation and agricultural credit programs were added to the list of PLAN projects. The village committees, composed of PLAN family members, villagers, and a government representative, worked with PLAN staff to establish program priorities and specific projects.

By the end of Fiscal Year 1978, PLAN had enrolled nearly 3,000 African children in Mali, Sierra Leone, Sudan, and Upper Volta. All of these areas suffered the effects of inadequate food production and insufficient income. PLAN worked with local officials, village committees and groups of PLAN families and their neighbors to design and carry out resource and skills development projects which included the support of agricultural cooperatives, veterinary services, vaccination programs for cattle, oxen and camels, reforestation projects, the training of community development workers, technical and financial assistance, water projects, and cereal banks. Diverse as these projects are, they share the goal of enhancing the economic life of their participants.

The system of agricultural credit described by James Emerson in Upper Volta is typical of the credit systems in underdeveloped rural areas which contribute to urban migration. To alleviate this problem, PLAN has helped community groups establish cereal banks. These "banks" provide loans of grain to get families through seasonal periods of food shortage. Cereal banks are only one approach to the problem of seasonal shortages and, like curative medical programs, are more the treatment of an effect than the prevention of the cause. Like curative medical programs, they, too, are a first step in a comprehensive process and, like them, will become a last resort as preventive efforts come to fruition.

The cereal banks project was initiated in 1977 by Asbjorn Osland, then Director in Upper Volta. Within a year cereal banks had been built and managed by the people in 15 villages. PLAN supplied the building materials and an initial 140 tons of millet to stock them. Within five years most of the other PLAN programs in Africa had instituted similar agricultural credit projects, cereal banks, and grain storage facilities.

The cereal banks and grain storage facilities have a secondary role as important as their primary one. In addition to serving as reserves, they provide secure storage, safe from spoilage and vermin which account for major crop losses every year. In 1976, for example, Mali lost 25 percent of its crop to birds, rodents, and insects. Improved methods of storage significantly reduce that figure.

In Mali and Upper Volta PLAN has developed agricultural extension projects to introduce and popularize more productive agricultural methods and implements. These projects are carried out at the local level by village committees. The projects depend upon small scale technologies appropriate to the skills, finances, and needs of marginal farmers in isolated rural villages. These do not call for tractors, but for plows and carts, with donkeys and bullocks to pull them.

Joy Greenidge, then Director in Mali, described the use of these carts in her September 1982 Informal Report to Foster Parents of Foster Children in Mali:

> One trip with the cart can take all the manure, collected during the year, out to the fields. The average harvest can be brought home in three days, using the cart. People who have no donkey carts carry all of these items on their heads. Daily, one sees mothers coming down the road followed by six children, sized like stair steps, each one carrying a load of wood appropriate to his strength, on his head. To bring in the harvest everyone in the family carries a basket filled with heads of millet, like giant cattails, from the fields to the house. It takes weeks. Imagine the relief of not having to carry bundles of manure on your head from home to field with flies buzzing around, going in and out of ears, eyes and nose.
>
> Of course, two donkey carts per village are not enough. In November, when they vote upon a village project, the village may decide to purchase more carts, or plows, or to buy fertilizer for their fields. In some big villages, they have bought a certain number of carts each year. They hope to place one cart in each household permanently.
>
> The money collected so far from rental of the carts is used in many different ways by different villages. Santiguilla is constructing a mosque. Tenimbala bought a donkey to replace one that had died. Samakele bought some iron rod for a well. Kiban repaired the maternity unit, dug two wells, and makes loans to village members. Tiontala constructed a community granary. Madinani paid a fine, levied by the forestry service, because the village caused a bush fire. Falembougou paid the taxes of a family that was away, and bought cement to install

the pump on the community well. Galo-Bambara bought two tons of millet, to distribute to all families who needed it during the planting season. Diatroubougou helped a family in distress. Kassela is saving money to establish a cooperative. In Touba, where there are two competing religious sects, money was spent to feed policemen, who came at the request of the village to maintain the peace on a religious holiday.

In the rural areas around the PLAN office in Boulsa, Upper Volta, few farming families are aware of the advances made in agricultural methods in the last century. Like their parents and grandparents, they turn the soil with the traditional short handled hoe, the "daba," and broadcast their seed by the handful.

Abdournahamane Sawadogo, PLAN/Boulsa Community Development Head, described PLAN's agricultural credit project in a May 1982 report.

> In order to introduce and popularize newer, more methodical agricultural innovations, and to enable farmers to possess more efficient equipment, PLAN has developed an agricultural credit and extension scheme which functions with the direct participation of the village committees.
>
> Repayment is in annual installments over a five-year period (with one year of grace) at an annual compound interest of 5.5 percent. It is important to note that repayment is not made to PLAN but rather to each village committee. In this way, the committee can build a fund which, in the future, will enable it to continue the credit system on an independent basis.
>
> PLAN's agricultural credit scheme has been in operation for three years and results so far have been very encouraging. Each planting season, participants have received instruction in animal traction and care of animals. Repayment has been, for the most part, up-to-date, beneficiaries have been quick to adopt the new methods, and the list of those requesting credit has grown each year.

The objective of these projects is to improve not only the incomes of the participants but also to improve their planning and management skills to the point where PLAN aid is no longer necessary. The following story, told by Joy Greenidge, illustrates this point:

Not long ago, a young man from Fofanala, a large neighborhood in Banamba, came to the PLAN office to ask for cement to repair the bridge linking Fofanala to the rest of the town. Mr. Diaby, the chief of the Community Development Center turned him down, saying "Fofanala has donkey carts, donkeys, plows and cows, and if they had been properly used, by now your neighborhood council would easily be able to repair the bridge." The astonished young man asked how and, when he found out, went home and organized a meeting. As a result of the meeting, a new neighborhood committee was elected. Within a few months Fofanala had more than enough money in its common fund to repair the bridge and to finance other projects of benefit to the community.

JOHN LANGDON-DAVIES, moved by the plight of homeless and orphaned children during the Spanish Civil War, conceived the idea of Foster Parents Plan.

ERIC MUGGERIDGE drove a supply truck for the Duchess of Atholl's National Joint Committee when he met Langdon-Davies. During the next 6 years he was to function as PLAN's program director.

ESME ODGERS distributed supplies as part of the National Joint Committee's children's relief activities before she joined PLAN as Administrator of children's shelter colonies.

ESME ODGERS with two Foster Children in England, 1940.

ERIC MUGGERIDGE and JUDY MASON in Plan's Woodberry Down Colony in 1941.

JUDY MASON succeeded Muggeridge as Organizing Director in Great Britain in 1944 when he was mobilized by the British Army.

THE LEA in Denham, established in 1945 and maintained until 1956, was to be the last of PLAN's English "colonies." Its large vegetable garden was tended by resident Foster Children.

THE HEADQUARTERS STAFF in 1942 at 55 West 42nd Street, New York City. From left to right: Gloria Matthews, Fleurette Ullman, Helen Seligman, Edna Blue, Robert Yaller and Lili Wohlgemuth. Name of woman at far right is unknown.

EDNA BLUE, PLAN's first Executive Director, visits a PLAN-assisted family in Poland in 1945.

ANNE LANDRESS RABKIN was one of the original U.S. organizers in 1938 and continued to serve on the Board until 1978.

LENORE SORIN directed PLAN's marketing and fund-raising activities from 1945 until her retirement in 1970.

JOSEPHINE BREWSTER purchased food, clothing and other supplies for shipment overseas and was in charge of personnel at New York headquarters. She retired in 1970 after 18 years of service.

ELMA BACCANELLI LAURENZI was PLAN's Director in Italy for 22 years. She died four months after the termination of PLAN's Italian program.

EDNA BLUE with two Italian Foster Children in 1947.

FREDERICK MASON, PLAN's European Business Director, boarding plane for England with George Georgias, a Greek Foster Child who was fitted with artificial legs in an American hospital and returned to Europe dressed as an American cowboy.

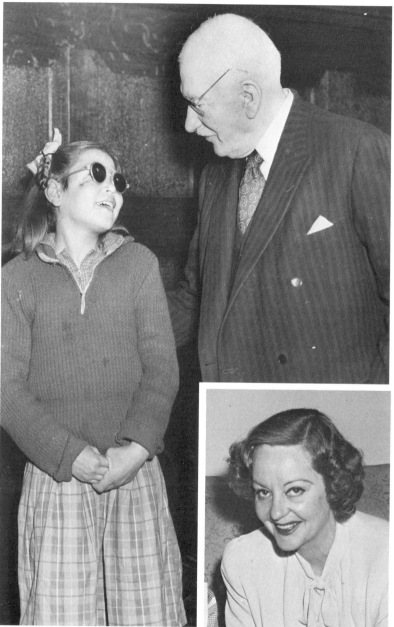

FIRST GREEK FOSTER CHILD, Barbara Nikoli, met then Premier Themistocles Sophoulis and was sponsored by American actress Tallulah Bankhead.

A CAVE ON THE OUTSKIRTS OF NAPLES in 1953 was home for 64 families.

A PLAN SOCIAL WORKER interviews a family on the outskirts of Seoul in 1956.

FIRST HONG KONG FOSTER CHILD, Lin Suk Fong, and her younger brother in 1959.

JULIAN I. BERGOFFEN, shown here with a Foster Child in Italy in 1960, drafted the original by-laws of Foster Parents Plan, Inc. and served on the U.S., Canadian and International Boards during his 40 years with PLAN.

VIETNAMESE FOSTER CHILD, Duyen, and friend lived in the relative safety of their village, fortified with gun towers and barbed wire fences during the Strategic Hamlet Program.

INADEQUATE HOUSING, sanitation and health care remain PLAN's greatest challenges in its rural and urban Latin American programs.

ROBERT SAGE served as Director in Korea, Vietnam and the Philippines during his 24 years with PLAN. He retired in 1976.

FRANK W. RYAN spent 12 of his 23 years with PLAN in Indonesia and also served in Korea, Hong Kong and Vietnam.

SELF-HELP, Skills Training and Income-generating activities marked the evolution of PLAN's development approach in the Philippines.

PRIMARY EDUCATION in PLAN's West African program countries is a critical factor in human and national development.

WATER often must be carried long distances in the hot sun. PLAN attempts to alleviate the chronic water shortage in its African posts with machine- and hand-dug wells.

GLORIA MATTHEWS KANE. During her tenure as International Executive Director (1951-75), the number of Foster Children grew by more than 50,000.

GEORGE W. ROSS became International Executive Director in January 1976.

E. GLENN ROGERS was named International Director of Field Services in 1972. That title was later changed to International Program Director.

A. ELIZABETH BROWN, former Director in Vietnam and a major force in the establishment of the Australian National Company, receives an orchid from Jaap van Arkel, then Chairman of the International Board, in The Hague, June 1979.

ROBERT C. SORENSEN, first International Board Chairman, 1973-76.

SIDNEY LAUNITZ-SCHURER, second International Board Chairman, 1976-78.

JAAP VAN ARKEL, third International Board Chairman, 1978-81.

FREDERIC W. THOMAS, fourth International Board Chairman, 1981-   .

15

Program Development: 1937-83

Since its origin in Spain nearly 50 years ago, PLAN's goals have remained constant. Then, as now, PLAN worked to provide adequate health care, housing, and nutrition to assure the physical development of needy children and to provide the education or vocational training necessary for their social and economic development.

The evolution of development approaches has brought great change to PLAN's activities. The greatest of these changes has been in the scope of the programs. In the 1930s PLAN enabled a concerned sponsor to touch the life of an individual child through financial and material aid and an exchange of photographs, gifts, and correspondence. The aid, in the words of the July 1939 Certificate of Incorporation, provided "for the care, maintenance, education, training, and well-being of Spanish children orphaned and/or distressed as a result of the Civil War in Spain."

Today Foster Parents are still touching the lives of children, but the children are no longer alone, and they are no longer necessarily the victims of war. The children are now members of families and those families are members of neighborhoods and communities. By touching the life of a child, today's Foster Parent also touches the family of the child and the community in which they live.

In spite of these changes, the goals of the organization have changed little. The 24 May 1982 revision of the By-laws of Foster Parents Plan International, Inc., (Article II, Section 1) now states that PLAN's primary purpose is "to provide social services, financial and material assistance to children and their needy families in countries that are unable to provide these forms of assistance themselves."

In the late 1930s voluntary humanitarian aid was thought of in terms of charities, missionaries, and the socially redeeming work of club women and society matrons. There was little talk in those earlier days of "integrated rural development strategies," "human resource units," NGOs (nongovernment organizations), VOLAGS (voluntary agencies), and the host of other initialisms, acronyms, and neologisms which have crept into the development lexicon in the years since World War II.

People then spoke in simpler terms of hunger, sickness, and death. Few had then heard of kwashiorkor or schistosomiasis. Instead, they spoke of a stray child named Jose from an embattled harbor town, a little girl who walked from Poland to France, or a boy who wanted to be a pilot when he grew up. These were the familiar children of Europe, sharing the common cultural background of their sponsoring Foster Parents.

Today most of PLAN's children are uncompromisingly foreign to their Foster Parents. They come from cities and villages with names like Ouagadougou, Tegucigalpa, Kathmandu, and Iloilo, and are as likely to be named Prungchit, or Jiranon as Jose, Maria, or Juan. No longer are they the institutionalized, orphaned, or distressed victims of war, but the Foster Children of today share the same needs as their European predecessors. Food, clothing, safe shelter, health care, and education are basic needs which do not change: the requirements for survival are constant. However, the methods used to meet those needs and to build a foundation upon which PLAN families and communities can base their further development did change. As knowledge grows through experience and innovation, programs change to reflect that knowledge.

Forty years ago PLAN provided assistance to children in the hope that they would, with PLAN's help, overcome the exigencies of war and poverty and be able to provide adequate lives for themselves in the future. Today PLAN works to introduce children, families, and communities to the idea and process of planning for their future. PLAN no longer deals exclusively with the *effects* of war, dislocation, and poverty. Now the programs are more often aimed at the elimination or alleviation of the *causes* of dislocation and poverty. The focus on improving the lives of children has not changed.

This transition from child welfare to child, family, and community development has not always been a smooth and orderly process. In the early 1960s a PLAN Field Director in Asia wrote of what he hoped to accomplish through group counseling for Foster Families. The report, couched in the abstract language of sociology and psychology, was read by a long-term and now long retired member of the Board of Directors. The dismayed Board Member sent the report back to Executive Director Gloria Matthews with a note asking: "What, if anything, is

[he] talking about? I thought we were in the business of feeding and clothing destitute children."

The apparent conflict is more easily explained than resolved. The Board Member thought PLAN should be directly treating the effects of poverty by providing food, clothing, and financial relief to ragged and hungry children. The Field Director saw that changing the attitudes of the parents of Foster Children through education, counseling, and motivation could be as important in alleviating the *causes* of poverty as financial and material aid was in relieving its *effects*.

The parallels with health programs are apparent. Curative and preventive medical programs share the common goal of improving the health of a community. The success of one depends largely upon treating the consequences of an unhealthy environment; the other, upon reducing the causes of that unhealthy environment. Both serve. Curative programs can accumulate impressive statistics of patients treated and visits to clinics, but can also create a dependency upon the continued presence of those clinics.

When a person goes to a doctor to be cured, that person is in effect stating that he or she is no longer capable of dealing with his or her health. The person thereby cedes that responsibility to a medical professional upon whose privileged knowledge and expertise the person, now transformed into a "patient," must depend. The doctor makes a diagnosis and prescribes a cure. The patient passively takes his medicine and hopes to be cured. The environment which may have caused the illness in the first place, and may well cause it again, remains the same.

A similar process can occur with social welfare agencies, particularly those centralized agencies operating at the national or international level. An expert making policy decisions in a national or provincial capital can be extremely remote from the people who will be affected by those policies. The expert is dependent for information on field reports, other experts, and government officials. Occasional fact-finding tours of proposed target areas provide the opportunity to meet the local dignitaries and exchange a few words with a docile victim or two of the current societal ill. After a short visit and, perhaps, a ceremonial lunch, the expert packs up and returns to the city to plan a program.

The pitfalls of such programs are apparent. Private voluntary agencies, by virtue of their limited size and still more limited funds, are more flexible than government agencies, but have occasionally been prone to similar processes. Experts talk to authorities who talk to officials. Programs are then planned to meet the needs which the professional problem solvers have decided must be met.

Social workers then prescribe cures for their clients social ills as doctors prescribe cures for their bodily ills. Rather than developing their own personal and community resources, the clients, like the patients, all too often come to depend upon the professional to dispense the services which may meet an immediate need but will not necessarily prevent its recurrence. Thus, the clients and the patients may become shackled by the programs meant to free them, their problems perpetuated by the very services intended to eliminate them.

One of the most fundamental ways to avoid this trap is to balance the curative—the meeting of basic needs, with the preventive—the development of skills and resources. This dual focus has been a basic tenet of the PLAN philosophy since it was organized in Spain in 1937.

In Spain, as in the developing nations of the world today, there was a clear understanding that the results of war, poverty, or dislocation were only the most immediate problems faced by the children. The remedy called for not only relief but also social and economic development. The "colonies" which PLAN supported for children evacuated from the war zones were not simply boarding schools, but part of a larger development plan.

Dorothy Parker, one of PLAN's first American supporters, described what she saw of this program in "The Siege of Madrid" (23 November 1937):

> Six years ago almost half the population of this country was illiterate. The first thing that the republican government did was to recognize this hunger, the starvation of the people for education. Now there are schools even in the tiniest, poorest villages; more schools in a year than ever were in all the years of reigning kings. And still more are being established every day. I have seen a city bombed by night, and the next morning the people rose and went on with the completion of their schools. Here in Madrid, as well as in Valencia, a workers' institute is open . . . It is a college where workers, forced to start as children in fields and factories, may study to be teachers or doctors or lawyers or scientists, according to their gifts. Their intensive university course takes two years. And while they are studying, the government pays their families the money they would have been earning.
>
> The government takes care, too, of the unfortunates of war. There are a million refugee children in Spain. A million is an

easy number to say. But how can you grasp what it means? Three hundred thousand of them are in the homes of families and seven hundred thousand are in children's colonies. When it can, the government wants to have all in colonies. I hope that will happen, because I have seen some of the colonies. There is no dreadful orphan-asylum quality about them. I never saw finer children—free and growing and happy. One colony was in a seaside resort, near Valencia. There were sixty children, from four to fourteen, who had been going to school in Madrid. And the fascist planes had bombed the school.[1]

After the evacuation of PLAN from Spain, this emphasis on preparing the children for the future continued. Esme Odgers, Administrator of PLAN's colonies for Spanish refugee children in France, emphasized this in a letter to PLAN's New York Headquarters in May 1939:

I do want you to see that we are doing a work not of giving a little food and some beds to children living in wretched barns, prisons, and stables, but taking them into healthy surroundings, educating them, giving them a chance to face life with courage and understanding.

The courage and understanding she wrote of was reinforced by a heavy concentration on practical skills and vocational training which the children would need to earn a living.

During and after the Second World War, PLAN sponsorship provided aid for children in institutions and children living with their families. The program was primarily focused on education and rehabilitation for the children, and the distribution of financial and material aid was a major part of it. The need for PLAN's programs and services in Europe steadily declined as the European economies recovered from the disruptions of the war. As the old programs in Europe were phased out, new programs were established in Asia.

It was in Asia in the 1960s that the focus on development rather than relief and rehabilitation resurfaced. The needs of the children and their families in Asia went far beyond the simpler temporary needs of postwar Europe. The families of Asian Foster Children had, for the most part, been forced by poverty to migrate from rural to urban areas. Once there, they found themselves totally lacking in the skills demanded by

[1]Dorothy Parker, "The Siege of Madrid," in *The Portable Dorothy Parker,* by Dorothy Parker (New York: Penguin, 1976) pp 592-93. Used by permission of the National Association for the Advancement of Colored People.

their new environment. The simple distribution of food, clothing, and money to Foster Children and their families could be no more than a stopgap measure to ease the immediate effects of poverty, ignorance, and ill health. Relief programs could alleviate these effects but could do little to reduce their causes. This is not to deny the efficacy of temporary financial and material assistance to needy families. In a developing economy it is natural to think that temporary measures will suffice, that eventually there will be an improvement in the overall standard of living—a rising tide carries all ships. If, however, the economy is not developing, common decency demands the continuation of financial and material assistance, but common sense demands that it be supplemented with development programs.

PLAN staff began to consider a new concept. First, they gave increasing attention to the family, then they began to change their role from that of a channel for handing out cash and supplies into that of a guide helping the child and family make use of all available resources to reach their full potential. This change was gradual and reflected the needs and resources of particular communities, the individual PLAN Field Directors, and the talents and sensitivity of local PLAN staff members.

By the end of the decade, PLAN was providing a wide range of services addressing both the causes and effects of poverty. Educational support helped Foster Children prepare themselves for the future while adult literacy programs, vocational training, and job placement services increased the incomes of their parents and older brothers and sisters. Vocational training courses were chosen on the basis of family interests, the needs of local industries, and the availability of training staff. Regular PLAN aid supplemented the incomes of the families until they could meet their own needs. Grants or loans from Special Services Funds were available for emergency needs, hospital expenses, or material for home repairs.

As PLAN spread from Asia to Central and South America and Haiti in the 1960s and 1970s, the focus on family development expanded to include groups of families working together to implement group and community projects. There had been occasional group and community projects in the 1960s, but it was not until the successful PLAN projects in Bolivia and the Republic of Korea in the mid-1970s that broadly based group and community projects became a generally accepted element of the PLAN philosophy.

As these community projects spread to other PLAN program countries, they were adapted to suit local conditions and needs in both urban and rural areas. The direction for these changes came, as it should have, from the Field and not from International Headquarters. The Field staff were in direct daily contact with Foster Families, their community leaders, and the local, provincial, and national social service personnel and were, therefore, in the best position to accurately determine local needs and resources. Once the needs were defined, the Field staff and International Headquarters' staff would discuss the various ways to meet the needs. The comprehensive programs which resulted from these deliberations were then submitted to the International Board of Directors for approval.

Thus the programs were worked out from the bottom up, rather than from the top down. This is still PLAN's method. The programs begin with a PLAN staff member talking with an individual family or a group of families about their needs, hopes, and expectations. This direct dialogue helps to insure the relevance, and effectiveness of the program.

With the introduction of the Family Development Plan in the mid-1970s, planned development geared to the achievement of short and long-term objectives became a basic component of PLAN aid. Rather than providing regular monthly allotments of cash until the Foster Child's eighteenth birthday, the Family Development Plan established a structure whereby the family drew upon all available resources, including PLAN, to reach its predetermined goals.

By the 1980s, PLAN staff, families, groups of families, and whole communities were designing, implementing, and evaluating coordinated programs of development. Aside from the achievement of specific goals, typically relating broadly to health, education, housing, and employment, these activities provide an introduction to the idea of planning for future change and prove that individual families working in concert with their neighbors can create a better environment for themselves and their children. Without this direct involvement, this dependence as much upon community participation as upon PLAN's expertise, PLAN would have no program. Because of it, PLAN furthers the very essence of development.

This process of involving people in their own development is an essential aspect of PLAN's work and what differentiates it from simple relief. As a human development agency, PLAN's success or failure depends largely upon people's faith in themselves, on their conviction that they have the power to improve their lives. People who for generations have been unable to provide adequately for themselves and their children are often lacking in this faith.

The challenge for PLAN is to develop that faith, to build a base of confidence, group spirit, and leadership while maintaining the precarious balance between meeting basic needs, on the one hand, and promoting long-term human development on the other. As Foster Children, their families, and their communities acquire the knowledge and skills to reach and sustain adequate levels of nutrition, housing, and health, and learn to organize and finance other improvements in their lives, they are also realizing their individual and collective potential. It is at this point that PLAN can move on to other areas of untapped human potential.

It is ironic that PLAN grows less visible as it grows more effective. In the shambles of postwar Europe the Foster Child was immediately identifiable by his new coat or sturdy shoes. Old advertisements show dark eyes in gaunt faces, or dramatic before and after photographs. The little Greek boy, once legless and sullen on a Piraeus dock, scoots around with new legs on a shiny bicycle in an appeal from the 1950s. A similar appeal now might show the "before" child standing in a dusty lane in front of a dilapidated little house. The "after" photographs might look much the same. Looking more closely, one might see a cement well in the background which was not there before, or, perhaps, a few ducks or chickens. The little house might now have a new roof—not intrinsically dramatic.

What would not show in the "after" photograph is the fact that the child does not have intestinal parasites, or pneumonia, that a community garden provides the vegetables to prevent anemia, that the child now has access to a safer water supply.

These accomplishments are not the result of a simple transfer of funds. They are the result of a development process which depends upon the direct participation of PLAN families and their neighbors. PLAN is increasingly becoming an enabler rather than a provider. PLAN families all over the developing world are learning through formal and informal education and training that they can, through their own efforts, work together to make significant and lasting improvements in their lives.

It is through this educational process that family groups and village committees acquire not only the technical skills to implement development projects, but also the managerial, organizational, and administrative skills to plan and evaluate them. With these skills, and with the growing self-confidence that accompanies them, PLAN families and communities will be able to further their own development long after PLAN aid has ended.

"The time has come to measure progress, not by growth rates, but by the quality of life of the people," said a speaker at the 1983 Non-Aligned Summit Meeting in New Delhi, "four million people—half of them children, die every year from hunger and malnutrition. If we were to decide to observe a minute of silence for every person who died in 1982 owing to hunger-related causes, we would not be able to celebrate the advent of the twenty-first century . . . "

The speaker was, in a sense, misleading his audience. The four million did not die simply of hunger and malnutrition, they also died of poverty, ignorance, and neglect. These factors combine to trap the poor in a downward spiral in which poor parents produce children who, if they survive, will grow up to be poor parents.

In the PLAN world today, 230,000 Foster Parents are helping children, families, and communities break this downward spiral and gain the skills and the confidence to reverse it. Because of their combined efforts, fewer children will die needlessly in the years to come.

16

International Growth: 1949-83

Foster Parents Plan, Inc.

From 1937 until 1973, the history of PLAN is largely the history of the operations and functions of Foster Parents Plan, Inc. Until the establishment of the Australian and Canadian offices, PLAN's New York City headquarters was responsible for the direction of all domestic and international PLAN activities. Edna Blue, PLAN's Executive Chairman from 1938-46 and International Chairman from 1947 to her death on 24 March 1951, was succeeded by Gloria C. Matthews. Lenore Sorin was on PLAN's staff for 25 years and was in charge of all marketing activities until her retirement in 1970. Josephine Brewster oversaw the purchasing program until it was discontinued and also served as Personnel Director during her 18 years of service to PLAN. She retired in 1970.

From 1971 to 1973 the domestic and international functions were becoming more strictly defined. Gloria C. Matthews, Executive Director, and George W. Ross, Deputy Executive Director, focused more and more on the international aspects of PLAN and delegated a large share of the domestic concerns of advertising, marketing, public relations, and fund-raising to the Department of Information.

This created a functional disparity between the American, Australian, and Canadian organizations. In an attempt to remedy the situation plans were begun in 1971 to separate the national and international functions of the United States company. In the autumn of 1972, Keith R. Turner, then Director of the Greek program, was invited to fill the newly created position of National Director of Foster Parents Plan, Inc. This position would be the administrative equivalent of the National Director positions in Australia and Canada and would establish a temporary *pro forma* parity between Messrs. Ashkanase, Coller, and Turner until the formal establishment of International Headquarters.

With the naming of an American National Director, Miss Matthews and Mr. Ross could devote all of their attention to the organization's international activities.

Mr. Turner arrived in New York and took up his new job in January 1973. His first task was to plan and carry out relocation of PLAN Headquarters from its old offices at 352 Park Avenue South to its new offices on an as yet unnamed road in Warwick, Rhode Island.

When Mr. Turner arrived there was a list of some 40 staff members willing to move with PLAN to Rhode Island. As the months passed the list shrank. By June 1973, when the move took place, only seven people remained—Gloria C. Matthews, George W. Ross, Keith R. Turner, E. Glenn Rogers, Constance Griliopulos, Charles Clemens, and Abe Bernstein. The entire Department of Information had resigned.

The weaknesses resulting from the lack of personnel were compensated for by the acquisition of several capable new staff members— Robert M. Bergeron, Controller; Donald Swartz, Accountant; Frank Charette, Manager of the Controls Department; and Donna-Jean Rainville, Personnel Officer.

Special note should be made of the solution of a second major problem connected with the move. Several years before, PLAN had converted from manual record-keeping to electronic data processing using a magnetic tape system. The inadequacies of the tape resulted, after considerable frustration, in the equally trying adoption of a disc system. Just before the move to Rhode Island, the Childbook, the disc containing the Foster Child master file, was broken. Through the efforts of Robert Bergeron, Frank Charette, and their patient staffs, the file was recreated from the old, dog-eared ledger books which were formerly used.

The dedication of the new PLAN building took place 17 September 1973. Governor Phillip Noel of Rhode Island and Mayor Eugene McCaffrey of Warwick spoke at the ceremony and declared the day Foster Parents Plan Day. Two months later PLAN/International was incorporated and Foster Parents Plan, Inc., became the United States National Office.

Once the move was completed and the Childbook reconstructed, the Department of Information was restaffed and restructured. In April 1974 Channing Hadlock was named Manager of the Office of Information. Until then, PLAN had relied on nationwide newspaper and magazine campaigns and public service announcements on radio and television. Additional funds were sometimes raised, as needed, by appeals to Foster Parents and contributors. Mr. Hadlock changed this style by introducing direct mail campaigns using not only lists of Foster Parents and contributors, but also purchased mailing lists.

Mr. Turner served as National Director until October 1975 when he accepted the invitation from the International Board of Directors to establish a new PLAN program in El Salvador. He was succeeded by Reinhart Gutmann who served until his retirement in 1982 and continues in an advisory capacity. Kenneth H. Phillips was named National Director in 1982. In the first half of fiscal year 1984 (July-December 1983) the total number of American Foster Parents grew to over 44,000.

Since 1974 the Board of Directors of Foster Parents Plan, Inc. has been chaired by Solomon Hoberman (1974-78), Robert C. Sorensen (1979-81) and, since 1982, by Ernest L. Sommer.

Foster Parents Plan of Canada

PLAN grew slowly and steadily throughout the postwar years. Foster Parents were, for the most part, from the United States but there were a growing number of Canadian sponsors and contributors. To better serve these Canadian supporters, and to allow them tax deductions for their contributions, a Canadian address was established in Montreal in 1949.

Though Canadian funds were sent directly from the Bank of Montreal to the program countries, PLAN remained, for all practical organizational purposes, an American agency with neither staff nor offices in Canada. Instead, a Montreal advertising agency forwarded all mail, unopened, to the New York City Headquarters at 55 West 42nd Street. The New York staff would then issue receipts for contributions and deposit the funds in the Canadian account at the Bank of Montreal. The major function of the Canadian branch until 1968 was to produce promotional material for the Canadian media.

By 1959 the number of Canadian Foster Parents had grown to 1,393, and, with an additional 700 contributors to the General Fund, their share of PLAN's total enrollment and income had grown to nearly ten percent. By 1968 nearly one Foster Parent in four was Canadian. The growth in the number of Canadian Foster Parents had come about largely as a by-product of the promotional efforts of PLAN in the United States, but the ever-increasing role of Canadian sponsors helped the New York staff realize that PLAN was already international in support as well as in service. This led to the 1968 establishment of an administrative office at 1500 Stanley Street in Montreal.

Formal recognition of this expanded Canadian role came in February 1969 when Foster Parents Plan (Canada), since 1 January 1967 an unincorporated but registered Canadian charitable organization, was incorporated retroactive to 2 September 1968. The name of the new organization became Foster Parents Plan of Canada—Plan de Parrainage du Canada. Its Board of Directors consisted of both Canadians and Americans. The Canadian members were L. Sidney Launitz-Schurer (Chairman), A. George Temple (Secretary), Paul S.H. Lindsay (Treasurer), and J. Martin Fry. The American members, Julian I. Bergoffen, Maurice Piesen, Robert C. Sorensen, and Robert J. Sullivan, also served on the American Board.

On 20 February 1970, Gloria Matthews wrote to the members of the Canadian Board of Directors:

> All of us have accepted the fact that, sooner or later, Foster Parents Plan of Canada would have its own Canadian Executive Director. I propose that now is the time to begin looking for one.

The ongoing discussions concerning the relocation of the Canadian office from Montreal to Toronto were given further impetus by the plans to expand the administrative role of the PLAN/Canada office. The consensus was that if the move took place before the expansion it could be accomplished with a minimum of disruption. Toronto was chosen for a number of reasons:

> The greatest percentage of Foster Parents were in Ontario.

> Toronto was the center for the major corporations and communication media upon which PLAN would call for services and contributions.

> All but two of PLAN's sister agencies were headquartered in Toronto.

> The labor market was better in Toronto than Montreal and salaries were no higher.

The changes in Foster Parents Plan of Canada were announced in a 7 August 1970 letter from Gloria Matthews to the Canadian Foster Parents:

We are happy to announce that in order to accommodate and better serve our Canadian Foster Parents, we have established a new central office for Canada, and appointed Mr. E. Munro Ashkanase as National Director of Foster Parents Plan of Canada. The new address is

> Foster Parents Plan of Canada
> 153 St. Clair Avenue West
> Toronto 7, Ontario

As of August 10, 1970, we ask you please to forward all your cheques and correspondence to that address. International Headquarters of PLAN will be involved only to the extent of issuing your official receipts. This is necessary because donation information from Canada will be fed to our data processing equipment in New York. However, all other correspondence, inquiries, etc., will be handled for you in the Toronto office.

We feel that this event is a milestone in the history of Foster Parents Plan of Canada and one in which we can all be proud. It would not have been possible without your continuing loyal support and the growth of PLAN in Canada. Mr. Ashkanase and the rest of our Canadian staff look forward to serving you from our new facilities.

Over the next six months, all Canadian operations were shifted from New York to the new Canadian office. Mrs. Paula McTavish joined the PLAN/Canada staff in 1970 and held the positions of Executive Assistant and Deputy National Director before succeeding Mr. Ashkanase, as National Director, upon his retirement in December 1983.

Marketing[1]

Mr. Ashkanase was convinced that the marketing procedures which were successful in business would be equally successful for PLAN. To this end, Minor Halliday was named PLAN/Canada Marketing Consultant in January 1971, and his agency, Minor Halliday and Associates, Ltd., was given the responsibility of helping Mr. Ashkanase publicize PLAN/Canada. The growth in the number of Canadian Foster Parents to over 56,000 in December 1983 shows the wisdom of the combined expertise of Messrs. Ashkanase and Halliday.

---

[1]The remainder of this section is largely derived from the history of Foster Parents Plan of Canada prepared by E. Munro Ashkanase in 1983.

The steady planned growth of PLAN/Canada since 1970 has resulted from a comprehensive program of marketing research to identify potential sponsors and a variety of promotional activities designed to attract their support.

Government Matching Grants

PLAN/Canada received its first matching grant from CIDA (Canadian International Development Agency) in Fiscal Year 1973 for C $47,600. During Fiscal Year 1982 PLAN/Canada received grants from CIDA and the Governments of Alberta, Manitoba and Saskatchewan totalling over C $4,000,000.

Federal or Provincial representatives visit PLAN program countries regularly. Their reaction to what they see has resulted in PLAN/Canada receiving a significant share of the government funds available to non-government agencies for overseas aid.

Foster Parents Plan of Australia

The first suggestion that PLAN invite Australians to become Foster Parents came at a dinner party hosted by Australian Embassy personnel in Saigon (now Ho Chi Minh City) in 1963. At that time PLAN had an enrollment of over 4,000 Foster Children in Vietnam. Mr. Bruce Woodberry, then First Secretary at the Australian Embassy, was impressed by the work PLAN was doing in the sprawling suburbs of Saigon and in the provincial villages and suggested to PLAN/Vietnam Director Elizabeth Brown that Australians be recruited as Foster Parents. This marked the beginning of a process that was to result in the establishment of Foster Parents Plan of Australia in 1970 and the internationalization of PLAN's organizational and administrative structure in 1973. Mr. Woodberry subsequently made inquiries in Canberra and reported that the number of charities already soliciting funds in Australia indicated that there would be support for an appeal for sponsors of Vietnamese children.

Gloria C. Matthews, PLAN Executive Director, arranged a meeting with the Australian Ambassador to the United States, Sir Keith Waller, to discuss the establishment of PLAN in Australia. At the end of the meeting the Ambassador gave the project his cordial blessing.

In February 1970 Elizabeth Brown left PLAN/Vietnam to establish Foster Parents Plan of Australia. There were two ways to go about bringing PLAN to Australia as a legal entity. The first, and most familiar to PLAN, was to establish PLAN/Australia as an ancillary organization, subordinate to the New York headquarters. This would be a straight-forward process of registering PLAN/Australia as a subsidiary branch of a foreign company operating in Australia. A second approach would call for establishing PLAN as an Australian company under the Companies Act of the state in which it chose to operate. Since it seemed obvious to the Board of Directors that Australians would be more likely to support an Australian charity than an American one, the second approach was taken. The organization of an Australian company had the added benefit of having its income exempt from taxes.

Complications arose with the requirements of Australian corporate law. An Australian PLAN would have its own Board of Directors that would hire a Director responsible to them for the operation of the company. Since PLAN Field programs were dependent upon their administrative ties to headquarters in New York, it was evident that the Australian office could be neither meaningful nor effective without being integrated into this administrative structure. This integration required making the organization international in its headquarters structure and in its having a truly international Board of Directors.

With these considerations in mind, plans went forward to establish Foster Parents Plan of Australia. PLAN received two grants totalling US $162,000 from the Edna McConnell Clark Foundation to be allocated over a two-year period to meet administrative costs and promotional expenses for the Australian office. Approval came from the Board in June 1970 and, three months later, the first PLAN office in Australia was opened on the second floor of a shop on Park Street South, Melbourne, with the goal of attracting 500 Australian Foster Parents by June 1971.

Foster Parents Plan of Australia was officially incorporated into the international PLAN organization at a meeting held at 400 Collins Street, Melbourne, on 18 March 1971. At that meeting the first Australian Board of Directors was formed under Chairman Frederic W. Thomas. The other members of the Board were Lady J. Clunies-Ross, David Ferber, Ian Leslie and Robin Prentice.

When the Board of Directors met in October 1971, the original quota of 500 Australian Foster Parents had been exceeded and the first major promotional campaign had begun. By the end of the year, Australian National Director John Coller and his staff of five had made thousands of phone calls and written thousands of letters. They succeeded in attracting Foster Parents from as far away as Alice Springs, Darwin, and Perth.

PLAN continued to grow in Australia and by 1980 there were nearly

10,000 Australian Foster Parents. The original offices were outgrown in 1977 and larger quarters were found in a former church in Kew, a suburb of Melbourne.

On the occasion of the tenth anniversary of Foster Parents Plan of Australia, Mr. Andrew Peacock, Australian Minister of Foreign Affairs, paid tribute to the work PLAN was doing for children, families, and communities in the developing nations of the world.

> . . . PLAN, together with other non-government agencies, is seen as a necessary complement to the Government's bilateral and multi-lateral aid programmes.
>
> The people-to-people touch is one of the major reasons why the Government feels that the efforts of non-government organizations should be supplemented from official development assistance funds.
>
> The Government to date has provided some $313,000 in the form of matching grants for PLAN's development projects.

The number of Australian Foster Parents and contributors has continued to grow and, under the direction of Mr. Colin V. Bragg, who was appointed National Director in 1981, the number of Foster Children receiving benefits from Australian Foster Parents reached over 18,000 in December 1983.

Foster Parents Plan International

As the PLAN organizations were developing in Australia and Canada it became increasingly apparent that there was a logical gap between the functions of the various PLAN entities. Foster Parents Plan of Australia and Canada recruited Foster Parents, raised funds, carried on information programs, and insured the regular communications between Foster Parents and Foster Children. Foster Parents Plan, Inc., in the United States, did all these things, too, but was also responsible for all international aspects of PLAN's activities.

This disparity of corporate functions became a subject of growing concern as the numbers of Australian and Canadian sponsors grew and plans were tentatively made to seek Foster Parents in Western Europe. Foster Parents Plan International, Inc., was therefore established in November 1973 to provide a formal structure for the coordination and cooperation of PLAN's National Companies in Australia, Canada, and the United States, and the Field offices in developing countries—a structure accurately reflecting the international character of the organization. With the establishment of PLAN International, Foster Parents Plan, Inc., became the structural and functional equal of the Australian and Canadian National Companies.

The international functions previously exercised by Foster Parents Plan, Inc. were assigned to Foster Parents Plan International, Inc. and conducted by the International Headquarters' staff under an International Board of Directors composed almost entirely of members of the National Boards.[2] These functions include: the establishment and coordination of National Companies; the establishment of Field Offices; the administration and direction of programs of assistance to needy children, their families, and their communities; and the allocation and distribution of funds received from National Companies.

In 1974 the professional staff at International Headquarters in Warwick, Rhode Island, consisted of four people: Gloria C. Matthews, International Executive Director; George W. Ross, her Deputy; E. Glenn Rogers, International Director of Field Services; and Robert M. Bergeron, International Controller. The first PLAN/International Annual Report, for the year ending 30 June 1974, shows US $10,374,047 in total Field expenses, an average of 54,104 Foster Children receiving benefits, and 14 Internationals (Field Directors and Assistant Directors) posted overseas.

During the next two years 10,000 more Foster Children were added to PLAN rolls; Field expenses grew by US $2 million; Gloria Matthews retired and was succeeded by George W. Ross and PLAN/Netherlands was established. By 1978 the explosive growth of PLAN/Netherlands and the steady growth of PLAN/Canada had attracted almost 25,000 new sponsors to the organization. To cope with this growth, the Field Services Director added Assistant Directors (called "Desk Officers") to the International Headquarters staff to act as liaisons between Field Directors and the Headquarters' executive staff.

In 1980 the Field Services Department became the Program Department and grew to include formal research and evaluation staff. Since then, Mr. Anthony J. DiBella has directed the efforts of social science researchers to objectively gauge the efficacy of PLAN's programs and strategies. That year, PLAN also established its fifth National Company—Foster Parents Plan of the United Kingdom.

By the end of Fiscal Year 1982, there were over 50 Internationals

[2]In 1979, by an amendment to the corporate By-laws, the Board of Directors was given the option to appoint former International Executive Directors to the Board. In FY 1980 that option was exercised and Gloria Matthews Kane became a Member-at-Large.

posted overseas, total Field expenses had increased to US $36,826,823, and an average of 195,411 Foster Children were receiving benefits. A year later there were nearly 220,000 Foster Children. The number of program countries in which PLAN operated had doubled since 1974, PLAN employed 3,600 indigenous staff, and the number of Foster Children and total Field expenditures had nearly quadrupled.

The demand for new Internationals to staff PLAN's expanding Field operations led to the appointment of a Personnel Manager in the summer of 1980. That fall, the position of Finance Director was added to the senior management team, as was the position of Administrative Director in 1981. In 1982, two new coordinating roles were created— one to oversee world-wide donor services and the other to meet the training needs of national and international PLAN staff. In 1983 a Manager of Information Systems was made responsible for the computerization of PLAN's world-wide operations, and the number of National Offices grew to seven as Foster Parents Plans of Belgium and Japan were established.

In the decade since its establishment as a separate entity, PLAN International has made, and continues to make, the sometimes difficult transition from the small, family-style operation of 1973 to the larger and more departmentalized organization necessary to maintain, expand, and improve the programs that have made PLAN a model human development organization.

Foster Parents Plan of The Netherlands

Sixteen years after the 1957 phaseout of PLAN's program of aid to Dutch children, PLAN officials began to consider the possibility of seeking Foster Parents in the Netherlands. George W. Ross visited the few Foster Parents already in the Netherlands, who then, for the most part, worked through PLAN's New York office. Hans Bussink, who was later to become the Chairman of the Dutch Board of Directors, and Oscar van Leer of the Bernard van Leer Foundation, were among the Foster Parents visited by Mr. Ross. Elizabeth Brown, who also made an exploratory visit, wrote that "every person interviewed believed PLAN would be successful in enrolling Foster Parents." Finally, in 1975 Foster Parents Plan of the Netherlands was established.

Hein Kolk, was named National Director of Stichting Foster Parents Plan Nederland effective 1 January 1975. The original Board of Directors consisted of Mr. Hans W. Bussink (Chairman), Gloria C. Matthews (Vice Chairman), and Rudolf Eldering (Treasurer), who directed PLAN's program in the Netherlands from 1946 until 1957.

After the death of Mr. Bussink in October 1976, Mr. Jack Haslinghaus, former President of the Phillips Phonogram Record Company, Prof. Dr. Jan P. Roos of the Free University of Amsterdam and Mrs. Saskia Bussink joined the Board. Prof. Dr. Roos was elected Chairman in January 1977.

From 1975 until 1977 PLAN/Netherlands grew slowly. At the end of June 1976 there were only 36 Dutch Foster Parents. By June 1977 there were 641. Since then, thanks to the unerring instinct of National Director Hein Kolk, the growth has been almost explosive. Foster Children have been sponsored and the agency endorsed by people from all ranks of Dutch society—politicians, government officials, television and radio personalities, athletes, editors, writers, artists, and entertainers. By June 1978 enrollment had grown from 641 to nearly 16,000. The next year enrollment doubled, by 1980 there were 54,000 Dutch sponsors. In December 1983 more than 105,000 children in the developing nations of the world were being sponsored by Foster Parents in the Netherlands and PLAN had become the recipient of nearly 10 percent of all Dutch charitable contributions.

In March 1977, Mr. Jaap van Arkel, a partner in the international accounting firm of Moret & Limperg, was invited to serve on the Board of Foster Parents Plan in the Netherlands. Six months later he was named Treasurer and, in October 1978, he was elected Chairman of the International Board of Directors.

Mr. van Arkel provided the dynamic leadership necessary for PLAN during a period of unprecedented growth. From 1977 until his untimely death in March 1981, the number of children and families sponsored by PLAN worldwide grew from 74,000 to nearly 140,000.

A school in Indonesia bears a plaque which reads, in part: . . . This school, like Jaap van Arkel, is committed to enriching the lives of children and helping to build a better future . . .

In an address at an August 1980 PLAN International Conference in Rhode Island, Mr. van Arkel said:

> Try to listen to other people. Try to understand what he or she is saying and, if you do not agree immediately, try to understand why he or she is saying it.

Mr. Aart D.G. Heering was elected Chairman of the Dutch Board in 1979 and continues to serve in that capacity. In 1983, Mr. Andries van Agt, former Prime Minister of the Netherlands, joined the Dutch Board.

Foster Parents Plan of The United Kingdom

In 1978 Foster Parents Plan returned to the United Kingdom, where it had first been organized 40 years before as Foster Parents Scheme for Children in Spain. Mr. John Cox served as Chairman of the United Kingdom Board of Directors until 1979 when professional obligations required that he establish residence outside of the United Kingdom. Mr. Simon A.A. Block, a London solicitor, succeeded Mr. Cox as Chairman and Mr. John d'A. Maycock served as Honorary Secretary until 1980. With the advice and assistance of Mr. Block, Mrs. Elizabeth Liddell, who was appointed National Director in September 1980, organized the London Offices at 114 New Bond Street and launched PLAN on the British market.

In 1981 the Board of Directors of PLAN/United Kingdom consisted of Mr. Block (Chairman), who registered PLAN as a charity (July 1978), the Baroness Jane Ewart-Biggs, Mr. Hamish Nealon, and Mr. Nicholas Tarsh. They were soon joined by Mr. Norman A. Chalmers.

The first two years of PLAN in the United Kingdom were largely devoted to laying the organizational groundwork upon which to base future growth.

The growth in the enrollment of British Foster Parents, from 170 in June 1982, to over 2,000 in December 1983, suggests that the PLAN/United Kingdom Board of Directors and staff have been successful in their efforts to reestablish PLAN in Great Britain.

Foster Parents Plan of Belgium and Japan

The international growth of Foster Parents Plan continued in 1983 with the establishment of National Offices in Belgium and Japan. Prof. Marcel van Spaandonck was named Chairman of the newly formed Belgian Board of Directors, which appointed Mr. Luk M.G. Martens National Director of Foster Parents Plan of Belgium. In Japan Mr. Takeshi Watanabe, former Director of the Asian Development Bank and now Japanese delegate to the Trilateral Commission, chairs the Japanese Board and Mr. Hiroshi Yamamoto is National Director of Foster Parents Plan of Japan.

Appendix A
INTERNATIONAL AND NATIONAL BOARDS OF DIRECTORS

International Board of Directors, 1973-83

ARKEL, Jaap van (Netherlands) 1978-81, Chairman 1978-81.

BERGOFFEN, Charles (U.S.A.) 1979- .

BERGOFFEN, Julian I. (U.S.A.) 1973-75.

BERTRAM, Cecilia M. (Canada) 1975- , Secretary 1976-79.

BLOCK, Simon A.A. (U.K.) Observer 1980- .

BONNYCASTLE, John C. (Canada) 1981- , Treasurer 1981- .

BROEKHUYSE, Jan Th. (Netherlands) 1980- .

BROWN, A. Elizabeth 1973-79, (U.S.A.) 1973-75, (Canada) 1975-76, (Australia) 1976-79.

BUSSINK, Saskia (Netherlands) 1979-81.

ELDERING, Rudolf (Netherlands) 1979-83.

EVERTS, Daan W. (Netherlands) 1983- .

HASLINGHUIS, Jack (Netherlands) 1980- .

HEEMSKERK, Suzanne Bischoff van (Netherlands) 1983- .

HEERING, Aart D.G. (Netherlands) 1979- , Vice Chairman 1981- .

HOBERMAN, Solomon (U.S.A.) 1973- .

JAFFA, Herbert C. (U.S.A.) 1974-76.

JONES, Harold L. (Canada) 1982- .

KANE, Gloria Matthews 1976- , (Netherlands) Observer 1976-77, (Netherlands) 1977-80, Member-at-Large 1980- .

KNIGHT, Harold (Canada) 1979-82.

LAUNITZ-SCHURER, L. Sidney (Canada) 1973- , Acting Chairman 1973, Treasurer 1975-76, Chairman 1976-78.

LESLIE, Ian (Australia) 1981- .

LOCHEAD, George (Canada) 1973-83.

LOON, F.D. van (Netherlands) 1983- .

MATTHEWS, Gloria (See Kane).

MEEKREN, Jaap van (Netherlands) 1980- .

MIDDLETON, Donald W. (Canada) 1976- , Secretary 1979-81, Acting Chairman June-October 1981.

MULLADY, John F. (U.S.A.) 1973-78, Treasurer 1974-75.

NICHOLSON, John (Australia) 1979-81.

ROOS, Jan Pieter (Netherlands) 1978-79.

RUDING, H. Onno C.R. (Netherlands) 1982.

SOMMER, Ernest L. (U.S.A.) 1977- , Treasurer 1979-81, Secretary 1982- .

SORENSEN, Robert C. (U.S.A.) 1973- , Chairman 1973-76.

SPAANDONCK, Marcel van (Belgium) Observer 1983- .

SULLIVAN, Robert J. (U.S.A.) 1973-74, Treasurer 1973-74.

TEHAN, Marie T. (Australia) 1983- .

THOMAS, Frederic W. (Australia) 1973- , Secretary 1973-76, Treasurer 1976-79, Chairman 1981- .

WATANABE, Takeshi (Japan) Observer 1983- .

WING, Roswell B. (U.S.A.) 1978- .

National Boards of Directors

Members of National Boards who have served or are serving on the International Board are identified with an asterisk (*).

Australia, 1971-83

ARTHUR, Vincent 1979- .

*BROWN, A. Elizabeth 1976-79; Int'l. Brd. (representing Australia) 1976-79

BURGESS, Neale 1973- , Chairman 1975-77.

CHARLESWORTH, Stephanie 1975- .

CLUNIES-ROSS, Jane 1971-74.

FERBER, David 1971-75.

*LESLIE, Ian 1971- , Chairman 1974-75, 1981- , Int'l. Brd. 1981- .

MATHEW, Alison 1972.

*NICHOLSON, John 1977- , Chairman 1978-80; Int'l. Brd. 1979-81.

NICHTERLEIN, James 1975-78.

NICHTERLEIN, Sue 1973-75.

PRENTICE, Robin 1971- .

RALSTON, Hugh 1981- .

STEVENS, David Spencer 1972-77.

*TEHAN, Marie 1975- , Secretary 1979-82; Int'l. Brd. 1983- .

*THOMAS, Frederic W. 1971- , Chairman 1971-73; Int'l. Brd. 1973- , Secretary 1973-76, Treasurer 1976-79, Chairman 1981- .

Belgium, 1983

CROLS, Franz 1983- .

LYSEBETH, Herman van 1983- .

*SPAANDONCK, Marcel van 1983- , Chairman 1983- ; Int'l. Brd. Observer 1983- .

Canada, 1969-83

BERGOFFEN, Julian I. 1969-72.

*BERTRAM, Cecilia M. 1974- , Vice Chairman 1976-79, Chairman 1979-82; Int'l. Brd. 1975- , Secretary 1976-79.

*BONNYCASTLE, John C. 1981- , Treasurer 1981- ; Int'l. Brd. 1981- , Treasurer 1981- .

*BROWN, A. Elizabeth 1975-76, appointed Honorary Life Member 1979; Int'l. Brd. (representing Canada) 1975-76.

DOBBS, Mary 1976- .

ERSKINE, Thomas J. 1974- .

FRY, J. Martin 1969-71, Secretary-Treasurer 1970-71.

HILBORN, James D. 1982- .

*JONES, Harold L. 1976- , Chairman 1982- ; Int'l. Brd. 1982- .

*KNIGHT, Harold 1975- , Secretary-Treasurer 1976-81, Secretary 1982- ; Int'l. Brd. 1979-82.

*LAUNITZ-SCHURER, L. Sidney 1969- , Chairman 1969-70, Vice Chairman 1970-73, appointed Chairman Emeritus 1979; Int'l. Brd. 1973- , Acting Chairman 1973, Treasurer 1975-76, Chairman 1976-78.

LINDSAY, Paul S.H. 1969- , Vice Chairman-Treasurer 1969-70, Chairman 1970-73.

*LOCHEAD, George H. 1971-83, Chairman 1973-76, appointed Honorary Life Member 1983; Int'l. Brd. 1973-83.

MATTHEWS, Roy A. 1977- , Vice Chairman 1979-82.

*MIDDLETON, Donald W. 1971- , Secretary-Treasurer 1971-76, Chairman 1976-79; Int'l. Brd. 1976- , Secretary 1979-81.

PIESEN, Maurice 1969-72.

SCHAFER, D. Paul 1972-76, Vice Chairman 1973-76.

SORENSEN, Robert C. 1969-74.

SULLIVAN, Robert J. 1970-72.

TEMPLE, A. George 1969-70, Secretary 1969-70.

WALLER, Donald H. 1978- , Vice Chairman 1982- .

Japan, 1983

HATTORI, Ichiro 1983-   .

NUITA, Yoko 1983-   .

OKITA, Saburo 1983-   .

SHARP, Robert 1983-   , Treasurer 1983-   .

*WATANABE, Takeshi 1983-   , Chairman 1983-   ; Int'l. Brd. Observer 1983-   .

Netherlands, 1975-83

AGT, Andries A.M. van 1982-   .

*ARKEL, Jaap van 1977-81, Secretary 1977-79, Treasurer 1978-79; Int'l. Brd. 1978-81, Chairman 1979-81.

*BROEKHUYSE, Jan Th. 1980-   ; Int'l. Brd. 1980-   .

BUSSINK, Hans W. 1975-76, Chairman 1975-76.

*BUSSINK, Saskia 1977-81; Int'l. Brd. 1979-81.

*ELDERING, Rudolf 1975-83, Vice Chairman 1978-79, 1982, Treasurer 1975-76; Int'l. Brd. 1979-83.

*EVERTS, Daan W. 1982-   ; Int'l. Brd. 1983-   .

*HASLINGHUIS, Jack 1977-   ; Int'l. Brd. 1980-   .

*HEEMSKERCK, Suzanne B. van 1983-   ; Int'l. Brd. 1983-   .

*HEERING, Aart D.G. 1979-   , Chairman 1979-   ; Int'l. Brd. 1980-   , Vice Chairman 1981-   .

*KANE, Gloria Matthews 1975-79, Vice Chairman 1975-77; Int'l. Brd. (representing the Netherlands) as Observer 1976-77, as Member 1978-80.

*LOON, F.D. van 1983-   ; Int'l. Brd. 1983-   .

LOUW, A.A. van der 1983-   .

*MEEKREN, Jaap van 1980-   ; Int'l. Brd. 1980-   .

*ROOS, Jan Pieter 1977-79, Chairman 1977-79; Int'l. Brd. 1978-79.

*RUDING, H. Onno C.R. 1981-82, Secretary 1982; Int'l. Brd. 1982.

WITMER, Peter F. 1975-77, Secretary 1975, Treasurer 1977.

ZAAL-HAECK, M.G.G. 1983-   .

United Kingdom

British Committee, 1937-42

BARTLETT, Vernon Vice Chairman 1939-41.

BERNSTEIN, Sidney Honorary Treasurer 1939-40, Treasurer 1941-42.

DOBBS, Richard Honorary Treasurer 1938-40.

LANGDON-DAVIES, John Chairman 1937-39.

MORLAND, Dorothy Honorary Secretary 1938-42.

MORRIS, Joan Organizing Secretary 1938.

RUSSELL, Audrey 1939-40.

SPENDER, Steven 1939-41.

PRIESTLY, J.B. Chairman 1939-41.

U.K. Board, 1978-83

*BLOCK, Simon A.A. 1978-   , Chairman 1980-   ; Int'l. Brd. Observer 1980-   .

CHALMERS, Norman A. 1982-   .

COX, John 1978-79, Chairman 1978-79.

EWART-BIGGS, Jane 1982-   .

NEALON, Hamish R. 1981-   .

TARSH, Nicholas 1981-   .

Appendix B
PROGRAM COUNTRIES AND THEIR DIRECTORS

BELGIUM
Madeline Bogaert 1945-61

BOLIVIA
Don D. Roose 1969-75
David Youmans 1975-76
Andrew Krefft 1976-78
Albrecht Hering 1979-80
W. Timothy Farrell 1980-82
Samuel B. Johnson 1983-

BRAZIL
Robert H.K. Walter 1967-73
David Youmans 1973-75
Charles E. Winkler 1975-78
Dorn Leslie Winter 1978-79
Vircher B. Floyd 1979-82

CHINA
Gerald Tannenbaum 1948-50

COLOMBIA, Bogota
Keith R. Turner 1962-67
Dale Barnes 1967-68
E. Glenn Rogers 1968-72
David E. McNeely 1972
David Youmans 1972-73
Leo Desrocher (interim) 1974
Albrecht Hering 1974-75
Vircher B. Floyd 1975-77
Ronald B. Seligman 1977-78
J. Andy Rubi 1978-79
W. Timothy Farrell 1979-80
Timothy R. Allen 1980-81
Mark Walker 1981-83
Benjamin Ricker 1983-

COLOMBIA, Buenaventura
Edward W. Schiffer 1978-79
Timothy R. Allen 1979-80
Edward G. Turcotte 1980-82
L. Roger Braden 1982-

COLOMBIA, Cali
Don D. Roose 1980-81
Han Dijsselbloem 1981-82
Emmanuel Edouard 1983-

COLOMBIA, Tumaco
Martin Fanghaenel 1977-80
Jerry Vink 1980-

CZECHOSLOVAKIA
Lawrence Aplin 1946-49

ECUADOR
Frank Corwin 1963-64
Marie Borgnes 1964-65
Rudolfo Paez 1965-67
O'Dessa Shipley 1967-68
Robert H.K. Walter (interim) 1968
Anthony Matuliewicz 1968-70
Richard Cabrera 1970-75
Renaldo Canizares (interim) 1975
Lloyd J. Feinberg 1975-76
Matthew Michaelson 1976-79
J. Andy Rubi 1979-80
Anibal Oprandi 1980-

EGYPT
Hubert van Bavel 1980-83
W. Timothy Farrell 1983-

EL SALVADOR
Keith R. Turner 1975-79
Samuel B. Johnson 1979-82
Larry S. Wolfe 1982-

ENGLAND
Eric G. Muggeridge 1940-44
Ivy (Judy) Mason 1944-57

ETHIOPIA
Lloyd J. Feinberg 1974-75
Leslie M. Fox 1975-77

FRANCE
Eric G. Muggeridge 1939-40
Esme Odgers 1939-40
Maria Sola de Sellares 1939-40
Bishop Marshall 1944-46
Lucette Fourquard 1946-63

GERMANY (Federal Republic of)
Elizabeth Whitmore 1952-62

APPENDIX B (continued)

GREECE
Katherine Clark 1949-51
Yvonne Peterson 1951-53
Ismene Kalaris 1954-58
Fanny Exarhacos 1958-61
Elizabeth Whitmore 1962-63
Jacob J. Burghardt 1963-67
Keith R. Turner 1967-72
Marietta Vafea 1972-74

GUATEMALA
Asbjorn Osland 1978-80
Samuel B. Johnson 1980-82
Han Dijsselbloem 1983-

HAITI
Louis Philippe Pelletier 1974-75
Don D. Roose 1975-77
Paul Dauphinais 1977-79
Keith R. Turner 1979-81
Meredith Richardson 1982-83
Joy Greenidge 1983-

HONDURAS
Albrecht Hering 1976-78
James Byrne 1979-81
Charles E. Winkler 1982-

HONG KONG
George W. Ross 1959-64
Lucile Chamberlain 1964-66
Frank W. Ryan 1967-72
Frederick Chaffee 1972-73
Henry Tsang 1973

INDIA
Norman D. Sanders, Jr. 1979-83
Vijay Sardana 1983-

INDONESIA, Bali
Frank W. Ryan 1972-73
John Langford 1973-74
Frank W. Ryan 1975
Joseph Siwy 1975-76
Lloyd J. Feinberg 1976-79
Frank W. Ryan 1979-

INDONESIA, South Sulawesi
Frank W. Ryan 1978-79
Donald Martin 1979-81
Maman Ali Usman 1981-83
James Alger 1983-

INDONESIA, Yogyakarta
Nevin Wiley 1969-73
Frank W. Ryan 1973-75
Frank Campbell 1975-77
Robert Gurevich 1977-79
Matthew Michaelson 1979-80
Gus C.E. Hall 1980-

ITALY
H.P. Bleach 1945-47
Elma B. Laurenzi 1947-69

KENYA
Leslie M. Fox 1981-

KOREA (Republic of)
Robert W. Sage 1952-60
Frank W. Ryan 1961-67
James Pullman 1967-70
John G. Anderson 1970-76
Dorn Leslie Winter 1976-77
Kim Kyong Mo 1978-79

LIBERIA
Vircher B. Floyd 1982-

MALI
Norman D. Sanders, Jr. 1976-78
Joy Greenidge 1978-83
Marjorie Smit 1983-

MALTA
H.P. Bleach 1944-47
P. McLoughlin 1947

NEPAL
William J. Kieffer 1978-80
William P. Fallon 1980-81
David Shannon 1981-83
Hubert van Bavel 1983-

NETHERLANDS
Rudolf Eldering 1946-57

NICARAGUA
Vircher B. Floyd 1977-79
Edward W. Schiffer 1979-82
W. Timothy Farrell 1983
Han Dijsselbloem 1983-

APPENDIX B (continued)

PERU
Robert H.K. Walter 1965-67
Bud Weisbart 1967-68
David Elder 1968-70
Gerald Casady 1970-71
Robert Jones 1972-73
David E. McNeely 1973-76
Sean Walsh 1976-78
Asbjorn Osland 1978
Raymond Ocasio 1978-79
G. Alexander Gray 1979-81

PHILIPPINES, Manila
Robert W. Sage 1961-76
John G. Anderson 1976-78
Frank Campbell 1978-79
William J. Kieffer 1980-81

PHILIPPINES, Baguio
William J. Kieffer 1981-83
Anthony English 1983-

PHILLIPINES, Cebu
William P. Fallon 1981-

PHILIPPINES, Iloilo
Charles Gray 1981-

PHILIPPINES, Mindoro
Brenda Cupper 1981-

PHILIPPINES, Naga
Ronald B. Seligman 1980-83
Meredith Richardson 1983-

POLAND
Andrew Zoltowski 1947-49

SENEGAL
Asbjorn Osland 1982-

SIERRA LEONE
Jerry Vink 1977-80
James Gershin 1980
James Alexander 1981-83
Mark Walker 1983-

SPAIN
John Langdon-Davies 1937
Eric G. Muggeridge 1937-38
Esme Odgers 1938-39

SRI LANKA
Anthony English 1981-83
James Alexander 1983-

SUDAN
David E. McNeely 1977
Donald Martin 1977-78
Bruce Kennedy 1979-81
Herman DeKoe 1981-

THAILAND
Frank Campbell 1982-

UPPER VOLTA
Asbjorn Osland 1976-77
Leslie M. Fox 1977-78
Ronald B. Seligman 1978-80
Martin Fanghaenel 1980-

VIETNAM (Republic of)
Harry Edward 1957-58
Robert W. Sage (interim) 1958-59
Jacob J. Burghardt 1959-63
A. Elizabeth Brown 1963-69
Frank W. Ryan (interim) 1969
Marion Guild 1969-72
Anne Davison 1972-74
Frank Campbell 1974-75

Appendix C
INTERNATIONAL STAFF 1937-83

This list is limited to those individuals who were Directors or Assistant Directors in 1983 or who had served in the Field in that capacity for a minimum of five years.

Abbey, Edward
Colombia 1982-83
Sudan 1983-

Albrecht, Wm. Steve
Sierra Leone 1983-

Alexander, James
Sierra Leone 1980-83
Sri Lanka 1983-

Alger, James
Sierra Leone 1979-80
Sudan 1980-83
Indonesia 1983-

Allen, Timothy R.
El Salvador 1978
Colombia 1979-81
International Headquarters 1981-

Ames, Charles F.
Guatemala 1979-80
Indonesia 1980-81
Sierre Leone 1981-82
Haiti 1982-

Anderson, John G.
Korea (Republic of) 1970-76
Philippines 1976-78
International Headquarters 1978-81
PLAN/USA 1981-

Bavel, Hubert van
Upper Volta 1978-80
Egypt 1980-83
Nepal 1983-

Bogaert, Madeline
England 194?-45
Belgium 1945-61

Braden, L. Roger
Colombia 1980-

Brown, A. Elizabeth
Vietnam (Republic of) 1963-69
PLAN/Australia 1970-71

Bullock, Richard W.
Honduras 1981-83
Ecuador 1983-

Burghardt, Jacob J.
Vietnam (Republic of) 1959-63
Greece 1963-67

Byrne, James
Philippines 1977-78
Honduras 1979-81
International Headquarters 1981-

Cabrera, Richard M.
Ecuador 1970-75

Campbell, Frank
Vietnam (Republic of) 1974-75
Indonesia 1975-77
Colombia 1977-78
Philippines 1978-79
International Headquarters 1980-81
Thailand 1982-

Chaffee, Frederick
Vietnam (Republic of) 1966-68
Vietnam (Republic of) 1970-72
Hong Kong 1972-73

Cobb, Laurel
International Headquarters 1980-82
Bolivia 1982-

Cupper, Brenda
Colombia 1980
Philippines 1980-

DeKoe, Herman
Philippines 1979-81
Sudan 1981-

Dijsselbloem, Han
Bolivia 1979-80
Colombia 1981-82
Guatemala 1983-
Nicaragua 1983-

Edouard, Emmanuel
Mali 1980-83
Colombia 1983-

Emerson, James
Upper Volta 1982-

APPENDIX C (continued)

English, Anthony
  Indonesia 1978-79
  Philippines 1979-81
  Sri Lanka 1981-83
  Philippines 1983-

Fallon, William P.
  Philippines 1978-80
  Nepal 1980-81
  Philippines 1981-

Fanghaenel, Martin
  Colombia 1977-80
  Upper Volta 1980-

Farrell, W. Timothy
  Colombia 1979-80
  Bolivia 1980-82
  Nicaragua 1983
  Egypt 1983-

Feinberg, Lloyd J.
  Ethiopia 1974-75
  Ecuador 1975-76
  Indonesia 1976-79

Fiksel, Mary
  Senegal 1983-

Filewod, Ian
  Sudan 1983-

Floyd, Vircher B.
  Colombia 1975-77
  Nicaragua 1977-79
  Brazil 1979-82
  Liberia 1982-

Foster, Frederick J.
  International Headquarters 1979-81
  Ecuador 1981-

Fourquard, Lucette
  France 1946-63

Fox, Leslie M.
  Ethiopia 1975-77
  Upper Volta 1977-78
  Kenya 1981-

Franken, Henk
  Ecuador 1980-

Garcia, Leticia
  Colombia 1982-

Geenen, James
  Honduras 1980-

Gemert, Louise van
  Indonesia 1981-

Glenn, Kim
  Haiti 1981-83
  Indonesia 1983

Gray, Charles A.
  Philippines 1979-

Gray, G. Alexander
  Peru 1979-81
  International Headquarters 1981-

Greenidge, Joy
  Upper Volta 1978
  Mali 1978-83
  Haiti 1983-

Hall, Gus C.E.
  Indonesia 1979-

Hawkins, Peter R.
  Colombia 1981-83
  Philippines 1983-

Hek, Monique van 't
  Colombia 1983-

Heldring, Annuska
  Ecuador 1979-81
  Bolivia 1981-

Hering, Albrecht
  Colombia 1974-75
  Honduras 1976-78
  Bolivia 1979-80

Herrick, Gail
  Mali 1982-83
  Kenya 1983-

Hotta, Yasuo
  Honduras 1983-

Johnson, Samuel B.
  Bolivia 1978-79
  El Salvador 1979-80
  Guatemala 1980-82
  Bolivia 1983-

Kadarusamsi
  Philippines 1982-

Kettenis, Francis
  Upper Volta 1981-

APPENDIX C (continued)

Kieffer, William J.
 Indonesia 1977
 Nepal 1978-80
 Philippines 1980-83
 International Headquarters 1983-

Kim, Kyong Mo
 Korea (Republic of) 1970-79

Laurenzi, Elma B.
 Italy 1947-69

Lendekamp, Wietze J.
 Bolivia 1980-

Maclure, Richard
 Upper Volta 1980-83

Mason, Frederick
 England 1946-57

Mason, Ivy (Judy)
 England 1941-57

McMurtry, Mary
 Haiti 1982-

McNeely, David E.
 Colombia 1972
 Peru 1973-76
 Sudan 1977

Merrill, Jon
 Mali 1983-

Muggeridge, Eric G.
 Spain 1937-38
 France 1939-40
 England 1940-44

Nolan, K. Anthony
 Ecuador 1982-

Odgers, Esme
 Spain 1937-39
 France 1939-40
 England 1940-41

Oprandi, Anibal
 Ecuador 1980-

Osland, Asbjorn
 Colombia 1974-75
 Upper Volta 1976-77
 Peru (interim) 1978
 Guatemala 1978-80
 International Headquarters 1980-81
 Senegal 1982-

Parry, Jennifer
 Sierra Leone 1980-83
 Indonesia 1983-

Richardson, Meredith
 Haiti 1979-83
 Philippines 1983-

Ricker, Benjamin
 Bolivia 1981-83
 Colombia 1983-

Rogers, E. Glenn
 Colombia 1968-72
 International Headquarters 1972-

Roose, Don D.
 Bolivia 1969-75
 Haiti 1975-77
 International Headquarters 1977-80
 Colombia 1980-81

Ross, George W.
 Hong Kong 1959-64
 International Headquarters 1965-

Round, Donald
 Upper Volta 1983-

Rubi, J. Andy
 Colombia 1978-79
 Ecuador 1979-80
 International Headquarters 1980-

Ryan, Frank W.
 Korea (Republic of) 1961-67
 Hong Kong 1967-72
 Vietnam (Republic of) (interim)
  1969
 Indonesia 1972-75
 International Headquarters 1975-78
 Indonesia 1978-

Sage, Robert W.
 Korea (Republic of) 1952-60
 Vietnam (Republic of) (interim)
  1958-59
 Philippines 1961-76

Sanders, Norman D., Jr.
 Haiti 1975-76
 Mali 1976-78
 India 1979-83
 International Headquarters 1983-

APPENDIX C (continued)

Schiffer, Edward W.
  Colombia 1977-79
  Nicaragua 1979-82

Seligman, Ronald B.
  Colombia 1977-78
  Upper Volta 1978-80
  Philippines 1980-83

Setunga, Myrna
  Philippines 1980-83
  Indonesia 1983-

Shannon, David
  Haiti 1979-80
  Nepal 1981-83

Sherman, Rose
  Sierre Leone 1982-

Siwy, Joseph E.
  Vietnam (Republic of) 1972-75
  Indonesia 1975-76

Smit, Marjorie
  Indonesia 1981-83
  Mali 1983-

Tesfamariam, Rezene
  Sudan 1982-

Thwaites, Richard
  Indonesia 1982-

Turcotte, Edward G.
  Mali 1977-79
  Honduras 1980
  Colombia 1980-82
  International Headquarters 1982-

Turner, Keith R.
  Colombia 1962-67
  Greece 1967-72
  PLAN/USA 1973-75
  El Salvador 1975-79
  Haiti 1979-81
  International Headquarters 1982-

Usman, Maman Ali
  Indonesia 1978-83
  Philippines 1983

Vink, Jerry
  Haiti 1976
  Sierra Leone 1977-80
  Colombia 1980-

Walker, Mark
  Guatemala 1980-81
  Colombia 1981-83
  Sierra Leone 1983-

Walter, Robert H.K.
  Peru 1965-67
  Brazil 1967-73

Whiticar, Peter
  Indonesia 1980-

Whitmore, Elizabeth
  Germany (Fed. Republic of) 1952-62
  Greece 1962-63

Winkler, Charles E.
  Colombia 1973-75
  Brazil 1975-78
  International Headquarters 1978-82
  Honduras 1982-

Wolfe, Larry S.
  Bolivia 1979
  Indonesia 1980-82
  El Salvador 1982-

Appendix D

Enrollment by Program Country: 1955-83

A country by country breakdown of the pre-1955 enrollment is not available. See chronological outline for available figures.

	1955	1956	1957	1958	1959	1960	1961	1962	1963	1964
ENGLAND	403	358								
NETHERLANDS	433	361								
BELGIUM	569	526	511	552	750	800				
GERMANY	1,263	1,470	1,702	1,899	2,001	1,677	331			
FRANCE	1,119	1,109	1,098	1,201	1,370	1,452	1,592	1,465		
ITALY	1,784	2,302	2,523	2,593	3,150	3,771	4,488	4,745	5,000	5,220
GREECE	1,840	2,295	2,645	2,699	3,552	4,528	5,200	5,701	6,000	6,350
KOREA	1,847	2,285	2,554	2,702	3,519	4,500	5,310	6,101	7,002	7,300
VIETNAM			36	377	662	1,484	2,742	3,753	4,100	4,592
HONG KONG						513	2,075	3,506	4,619	5,376
PHILIPPINES							527	2,121	3,020	3,700
COLOMBIA									1,000	1,800
ECUADOR										608
TOTAL	9,258	10,706	11,069	12,023	15,004	18,725	22,265	27,392	30,741	34,946

APPENDIX D (continued)

	1965	1966	1967	1968	1969	1970	1971	1972	1973	1974
ITALY	5,220	3,420	1,620	780			4,735	3,536	2,854	1,551
GREECE	6,450	6,550	6,600	6,750	6,750	6,200	7,050	7,191	7,304	7,196
KOREA	7,500	7,600	7,705	7,901	8,200	7,200	5,012	5,078	5,777	6,374
VIETNAM	4,608	5,587	6,182	6,402	5,603	5,300	4,114	1,906	252	
HONG KONG	6,131	7,083	7,150	7,250	7,400	6,012	7,200	7,757	8,118	
PHILIPPINES	4,400	5,380	6,429	7,290	7,700	7,399	7,000	7,396	7,729	8,051
COLOMBIA	3,000	4,100	5,100	6,250	7,000	7,100	5,545	6,170	5,972	7,927
ECUADOR	1,580	2,680	3,680	4,605	5,550	5,500	3,525	4,175	4,424	5,860
PERU		351	1,200	2,075	3,176	3,400	2,550	3,235	4,376	4,711
BRAZIL				760	1,690	2,400	1,100	1,942	3,030	4,982
BOLIVIA						800	749	1,626	3,615	3,928
INDONESIA						300				5,940
TOTAL	38,889	42,751	45,666	50,063	53,069	51,611	48,580	50,012	53,451	56,520

APPENDIX D (continued)

	1975	1976	1977	1978	1979	1980	1981	1982	1983
ETHIOPIA	5	1,352	2,749	3,031	4,195	3,364	1,491		
KOREA	7,408	6,703	5,240						
BRAZIL	5,110	5,554	5,469	4,730	4,654	5,717	3,962		
PERU	4,614	4,672	4,255	4,582					
BOLIVIA	5,374	7,586	8,547	10,455	13,012	13,876	16,396	17,944	17,641
COLOMBIA	8,906	9,755	9,566	11,252	13,415	14,860	18,801	22,458	21,398
ECUADOR	5,855	5,516	4,632	5,717	9,005	10,773	12,806	16,407	17,645
HAITI	949	2,366	4,004	8,356	11,360	12,970	14,889	14,958	14,274
INDONESIA	9,855	14,986	17,544	25,958	30,586	33,694	38,349	40,076	39,075
PHILIPPINES	8,855	10,020	10,898	15,331	16,773	20,003	21,318	25,329	26,560
EL SALVADOR		428	2,315	4,247	6,704	8,846	8,952	9,267	9,727
HONDURAS			1	1,076	3,375	5,000	9,049	10,624	10,205
MALI			387	1,907	2,986	4,083	5,699	7,030	8,560
UPPER VOLTA			959	1,849	3,942	6,839	8,375	10,076	10,045
NICARAGUA				228	1,696	2,728	2,537	2,124	1,729
SIERRA LEONE				2,037	3,377	6,282	7,740	8,326	9,103
SUDAN				873	2,094	3,718	6,302	7,801	9,430
GUATEMALA					346	4,286	6,037	7,514	7,756
NEPAL					314	937	1,394	1,467	2,584
INDIA						798	1,935	2,124	4,245
EGYPT							66	1,023	2,117
KENYA								53	1,994
SRI LANKA								603	1,350
THAILAND								924	2,576
SENEGAL									1,116
TOTAL	56,931	68,938	76,566	101,629	127,834	158,774	186,098	206,128	219,130